C(H)AOS Theory

C(H)AOS Theory

*Reflections of Chief Academic Officers
in Theological Education*

Edited by

Kathleen D. Billman *&* Bruce C. Birch

WILLIAM B. EERDMANS PUBLISHING COMPANY
GRAND RAPIDS, MICHIGAN / CAMBRIDGE, U.K.

Published 2011 by
Wm. B. Eerdmans Publishing Co.
2140 Oak Industrial Drive N.E., Grand Rapids, Michigan 49505 /
P.O. Box 163, Cambridge CB3 9PU U.K.

Printed in the United States of America

17 16 15 14 13 12 11   7 6 5 4 3 2 1

Library of Congress Cataloging-in-Publication Data

C(H)AOS theory: reflections of chief academic officers in theological education /
    edited by Kathleen D. Billman & Bruce C. Birch.
        p.   cm.
    ISBN 978-0-8028-6687-5 (pbk.: alk. paper)
    1. Theological seminaries — United States — Administration.   2. Theological
    seminaries — Evaluation.   3. Educational leadership — United States.
    4. College administrators — United States.   5. Deans (Education)
    I. Billman, Kathleen D. (Kathleen Diane), 1950-   II. Birch, Bruce C.
    III. Title: CHAOS theory.   IV. Title: CAOS theory.

    BV4166.C53   2011
    230.071'173 — dc23
                                                        2011017691

www.eerdmans.com

Contents

DEVELOPING COMPETENCIES

Acknowledgments

It takes a community of colleagues to nurture the ministry of a dean. This book is the work of such a community. We acknowledge with gratitude the resourceful and committed people who staff the Association of Theological Schools of the United States and Canada, who support theological schools in so many ways. We are especially thankful for those who work in the leadership development arm of the Association. We remember Marsha Foster Boyd and William Myers, whose work in leadership development paved the way for the formation of the Chief Academic Officers Society and for this volume, who guided both ventures in their early years, and for Stephen Graham, who has supported this work over the past three years since the first essay was submitted in 2008. We remember with affection Karen Kuder, who keeps such careful records of CAOS proceedings, who does so much to prepare for meetings large and small, and whose welcoming smile is always so appreciated. We are grateful, as always, to Daniel Aleshire, whose never-failing encouragement and inspirational reflections on theological education and the work of its leaders are such a blessing. His words conclude this volume, and we believe that those who read them will return to them again and again as a source of both challenge and grace.

We are deeply grateful to the colleagues who accepted the invitation to reflect on their ministry of theological leadership, and for their patience with the protracted process of bringing such a large project to fulfillment. It has been quipped that nations have risen and fallen since this project began. The institutional positions and even sometimes the institutional affiliations of our contributors have changed over the three-year process of writing and editing this book, and certainly theological education itself has weathered some severe storms since the project began. But this book is not about the "last word" regarding any of the issues explored or relationships probed in its pages. It is rather about a conversation-in-progress among a diversity of peers in a variety of institutional locations — a conversation to be invited into and to contribute to in a spirit of mutual encouragement and challenge to do our best work. It is a snapshot of "a community of practice" at work.

Eliza Smith Brown, Director, External Relations and Communications of ATS, deserves special recognition. A consummate wordsmith and editor, she worked with us every step of the way with good humor and dedication, devoting countless hours to this project as she carried on other substantial duties. We owe her a profound debt of thanks. And to our friends at Eerdmans — Jennifer Hoffman, Associate Managing Editor, and Jon Pott, Vice President and Editor-in-Chief — we extend our sincere gratitude for squiring this volume through to completion.

KATHLEEN D. BILLMAN
BRUCE C. BIRCH
June 2011

INTRODUCTION

Honoring Complexities, Celebrating Colleagueship: What to Expect from This Book

Kathleen D. Billman

The acronym of the Chief Academic Officers Society (CAOS) often evokes a chuckle from those who hear it for the first time. This book came into being because of the humor and collegiality that characterize those who have served as active members of that strangely named society and because of the support and encouragement of the Association of Theological Schools in the United States and Canada, which called the society into being and continues to invite and support its work. Since this book cannot be fully understood or appreciated apart from the formation and development of CAOS, sketching that story is important; from that story come the principles and conventions that informed the creation of the book as well as guidance for what to expect in its pages.

"If you only move the . . ." —
The Formation of CAOS as a Community of Practice[1]

During the 1990s ATS sponsored occasional meetings for academic deans, some focused on particular topics of interest and others on information the Association sought to make available to its member schools. One of these meetings introduced deans to the groundbreaking study of CAOs in theo-

---

1. Thanks to Daniel Aleshire, Marsha Foster Boyd, Karen Kuder, Ronald Mercier, and William Myers for the recollections and records that inform the following paragraphs. Karen Kuder has served as support staff for the organization since its inception, and her careful records have been a blessing.

logical schools undertaken by Jeanne P. McLean.[2] This study, funded by a grant from Lilly Endowment, Inc., was motivated by a sense of both how important the role of CAO had come to be in theological schools and how reluctantly (and, at the time of her study, how relatively briefly) the role was embraced by those elected or appointed to fulfill it. McLean's description of the deanship as "leading from the center" and her careful rendering of the sometimes poignant complexities and powerful opportunities of this position continue to be meaningful to many CAOs of theological schools; almost all the authors in this volume referred to her work either in the chapters they wrote or the bibliographies they submitted.

In the culminating chapter of *Leading from the Center,* McLean identifies six vital challenges for theological communities that understand the importance of the role of the CAO in shaping the academic life of a theological institution and are committed to nurturing capable and committed academic leaders:

1. To become intentional about leadership succession in the CAO position and proactive in efforts to identify and prepare individuals to assume the role

2. To develop within the theological education community, particularly among faculty and students, a more balanced and positive view of academic administration

3. To define the CAO position so the role and responsibilities of the office are realistic, humane, and adequately supported

4. To support the personal and professional development of officeholders

5. To address the problem of job turnover and to strengthen the stability and continuity of academic leadership in theological schools

6. To develop within the theological education community a sense of administration as an academic vocation[3]

McLean's text was published in 1999. In 2000 ATS convened a steering committee that included five CAOs[4] and was led by ATS staff members Mar-

---

2. Jeanne P. McLean, *Leading from the Center: The Emerging Role of the Chief Academic Officer in Theological Schools* (Atlanta: Scholars Press, 1999).

3. McLean, *Leading from the Center,* pp. 248-58.

4. The CAOs were Ronald Mercier (Regis College), Bruce Powers (Campbell University Divinity School), Anabel Proffitt (Lancaster Theological Seminary), J. T. Roberson (Shaw University Divinity School), and Richard Weis (United Theological Seminary of the

sha Foster Boyd and William Myers. At a September 2000 meeting of the steering committee, this group drafted a proposed structure for future steering committees, and on March 29, 2001, a meeting of ATS deans was convened in Pittsburgh for the purpose of approving the proposed structure and launching an organization for CAOs of ATS member schools.[5]

The purpose statement for the new organization embraced some of the challenges McLean identified that needed to be addressed if deans were to thrive in academic administration. The society was to be a *collegial network,* embodying a "community of practice" approach to learning in which the wisdom for an area of work is believed to reside in the persons who do it more than in a body of literature about that work. Guided by the leadership of a steering committee composed of diverse CAOs from many kinds of theological schools, the organization was to offer *educational and professional development* opportunities. Finally, the organization was formed to provide a context for *nurturing the vocation of the CAO and envisioning its future development.*

When the plan for the new organization was presented, the proposed name was "Society of Chief Academic Officers" (SCAO). Craig Nessan (Wartburg Theological Seminary) raised his hand during the discussion of the proposal. When called on, he commented, "If you just move the S to the other side and make it 'Chief Academic Officers Society,' you would have CAOS." The suggestion was met with resounding laughter and the name was promptly changed to "Chief Academic Officers Society" — CAOS!

It is significant that *laughter* accompanied the official formation of the society, for it is the grace of shared laughter that contributes so much to fostering collegiality and serves as an antidote to the creeping sense of isolation that can prey on deans, especially when — in that "center" position — it is hard to find someone in whom to freely confide about the discouragements and delights of the work; to share moments of self-doubt or the sense that one has done a good job with a thorny problem; to seek support for standing up for what one believes is best; or to confess that one is terribly uncertain about what approach to take with a given leadership dilemma. Being able to laugh with colleagues while ruminating on serious challenges is a gift difficult to quantify, but it may be at least partly responsible for assisting many

---

Twin Cities). Ron Mercier served as the first chairperson of what was later named the CAOS steering committee.

5. The steering committee now numbers eight members, each serving a four-year term, in classes of two per year.

deans to gain a sense of balance and perspective, and to recognize that there is indeed a community of practice that helps them remember that the work is significant and honorable, even if not always filled with ease or accolades.

The first CAOS seminar was held in 2002, and since that time there have been annual seminars, with scores of workshops offered to academic deans. Many of these workshops are offered by peers on various aspects of academic leadership. Others have been led by skilled consultants who bring a particular expertise relevant to some aspect of institutional leadership (e.g., attorneys who discuss legal issues facing academic institutions or religion reporters who discuss how to relate to news media in the event of an event or crisis that brings a school into the headlines). Whether looking for the latest thinking on assessing student learning outcomes or trying to find peers with whom to talk about how to maintain a scholarly and/or spiritual life; whether looking for a place to discuss a case study or seeking others' work on certain policy matters, the society has sought to provide ongoing personal and professional support to help sustain the vocational life of CAOs, including a listserv administrated on behalf of the society by Richard Weis, dean of United Theological Seminary of the Twin Cities. This listserv has enabled deans to find timely collegial responses to urgent requests for information and advice on a number of issues.

A particular concern of the society is offering collegiality and mentoring for new deans. Annual CAOS seminars always include an event for new deans, and a special feature of these gatherings is the "ferverino" — a term brought to the society by Ronald Mercier from his Jesuit heritage — an inspirational message about the vocational aspects of the academic deanship. This volume attempts to bring together in one place a body of reflection on practice in a variety of areas that will hopefully be of use even to experienced academic deans, but of particular help to new deans who may find themselves thrust into a complex new role with little preparation for the challenges they will face.

Three or four years ago Marsha Foster Boyd, in conversation with the CAOS steering committee, broached the idea of a handbook for CAOs similar to the one created by and for the CEOs of ATS schools; the idea was supported by William Myers and Daniel Aleshire, and a budget was created to fund the project. Bruce Birch and I, who were both serving on the steering committee at the time, volunteered to co-edit the volume, but from the outset the project involved extensive conversations with the steering committee. The initial outline of the book, along with the basic purposes and principles that guided it, was crafted by members of the CAOS community. While some modifications needed to be made along the way, the book is still quite faithful to the original vision and structure.

It is a mark of such a community that, while so many of us who have been involved in the project have experienced role changes since work on the project began over two years ago, the project has continued with the ongoing encouragement and labor of colleagues who were there at the beginning. Whether the changes have been due to retirements or to other kinds of role changes, the experience of sharing in and supporting the work of "deaning" as a community of practice has created a conversation about theological leadership that continues to matter deeply, whatever role in theological education we may play.

The adage that we "stand on one another's shoulders" is an apt description of this project; this, too, is an aspect of being part of a community of practice. We owe much to those who mentored us, both predecessors and peers. What is offered in the pages of this book is offered with the awareness that, while we want very much to share what we have learned about theological leadership and thus make our own contribution to those who come after us, things continue to change in theological education. The economic downturn that surfaced so dramatically in 2008-09 offers a powerful lesson about how significantly institutional life can alter in a short time span.

What is of greatest value in the pages to follow is not that definitive strategies are provided for every challenge of academic leadership, but that it is possible to find colleagues who have found meaning in the work, who have tried to do it faithfully, and whose reflections may stimulate the reflective process and creativity at play in every academic dean who picks up this book in the hope of finding meaning and joy in the work and who wants to do it well. The title, *C(H)AOS Theory,* is a fitting name for the work contained in these pages because it holds the name of the society from which it was created and hints at both the seriousness of the perplexities leaders face in tumultuous and ever-changing times and the playfulness and partnership that bring some order, some "theory," to bear even on the thorniest problems.

Principles and Conventions — from "Handbook" to "Reflections on Practice"

From the beginning of this project, two hopes guided the creation of this book. First, we hoped the project would bring together in one volume a variety of deans' perspectives on academic leadership. We sought to honor the complexities of exercising leadership as CAOs, complexities that are rendered more visible when "thickly" described within the various contexts in which ATS schools strive to flourish. Second, we hoped that the book would serve as a very concrete resource for those seeking guidance on particular aspects of academic leadership and a stimulus for ongoing conversation, revision, and expansion among those who serve as CAOs.

In order to accomplish these aims, the CAOS steering committee invited colleagues to serve as authors who have distinguished themselves in particular areas of academic leadership and who together portray something of the cultural, institutional, ecclesial, and theological diversity that enriches ATS-accredited schools. Rather than ask these authors to address a variety of contexts, we asked them to speak from their own contexts. For every topic there are two or more authors who exercise leadership in very different kinds of schools. This has resulted in lively portraits of particular leaders in particular places engaging in reflection on practice.

The implications of this choice ultimately led us to drop the term "handbook" from the original subtitle of the book *(C(H)AOS Theory: A Handbook for Chief Academic Officers in Theological Schools)*, which implies "a concise manual or reference book providing specific information or instruction about a subject or place."[6] There is rich, specific, concrete information, as well as bold instruction on a host of academic leadership issues to be found in the pages of this book. Perhaps even more valuable than the "specific information or instruction about a subject," however, are the lively narratives of the ways different colleagues have articulated and addressed the challenges of a given area of academic leadership as they have attempted to engage them on home turf.

Those who read this volume in its entirety may come to the conclusion that there is no *one* way to speak with a "dean's voice." Authors' styles range from the more formal (highly-footnoted presentation that uses third-person pronouns to refer to deans) to the more conversational (fireside chat that uses the second-person plural pronoun to address readers, as well as first-person pronouns). We made no attempt to homogenize these differences in style and voice, hoping to convey that there is a place in effective academic administration for many different styles and different voices — it is a *blessing* that there is no *one* way to speak with a dean's voice.

One of the unanticipated benefits of the choice to seek and celebrate diversity has been the discovery of how various academic deans' back-

6. *The American Heritage College Dictionary,* 4th ed., p. 627.

grounds as scholars and teachers offer unique angles of vision on the ministry of academic leadership. From the first chapter, in which Jana Childers (professor of homiletics) brings insights from the field of homiletics to bear on the task of analyzing institutional context, to the penultimate chapter, in which Bruce Birch (professor of Old Testament) employs a metaphor from the Book of Jeremiah to explore what it means to find wholeness in the work of the dean, it is interesting to glimpse some ways in which deans' differing worlds of scholarly endeavor inform how they exercise academic leadership.

Nevertheless, honoring the complexities inherent in numerous diversities required establishing some editorial conventions. Nowhere was that more evident than in deciding when to use the terms *dean, academic dean, theological school dean,* and *CAO.*

Terminology for positions is related to different patterns of relationships schools have with other institutions of higher learning or ecclesiastical bodies.

> . . . Some theological schools have full authority for all institutional and educational operations. Other schools, related to colleges, universities, or clusters of theological schools, may have limited authority for institutional operations, although they may have full authority over the educational programs. Still other schools are related to ecclesiastical bodies in particular ways, and authority is shared by the institution and the ecclesiastical body. All three kinds of schools have different patterns for the exercise of authority, and in some schools these patterns may be blended (ATS General Institutional Standard 8, section 8.1.2).

The term *dean* rather than *CAO* is the nomenclature of choice for many chief academic officers in freestanding and/or denominational seminaries. Generally speaking, rather than pepper the whole book with the term *CAO,* we used *academic dean* or simply *dean* most frequently as the synonym for the CAO who serves in a freestanding and/or denominational theological school. In the context of a theological school or divinity school situated in a university or in some denominational contexts (e.g., most Episcopal seminaries), the term *dean* most often refers to the head of a particular school within the university, who is also frequently designated as the chief academic officer of the school. In ATS gatherings of academic leaders, deans of university theological/divinity schools meet with the CEOs of freestanding seminaries, and often the university leader who is the designated associate dean for academic affairs meets with CAOs. We noted the frequent use of the term *academic dean* by authors serving in this latter capacity and appropriated their efforts to distinguish the two roles to avoid confusion, using the term *theological school dean* to designate the head of the university theological school and the term *academic dean* to designate the person charged with supervising the academic program of a university theological/divinity school. These distinctions do not cover all the nomenclature complexities, but were conventions we adopted for purposes of role clarification.

These nuances of language about the term *dean* and *CAO* are especially important to note because each topic covered in the volume is addressed by authors both from the freestanding and/or denominational seminary context and from the university school context. We have sought to edit in ways that support and foster clarity to the best of our ability, but we doubt that we have managed to eliminate all the ambiguities related to terminology, and the careful reader may observe times when these distinctions were not uniformly preserved.

Of course, there were technical editorial conventions that needed to be applied across the chapters in order to aid clarity and coherence throughout the book, but we sought to employ these conventions in service to the aims of each author's contribution and in a manner that respected each author's style and voice.

The Organization of the Volume — The Order in "C(H)AOS"

C(H)AOS Theory is organized into three major sections, preceded by this introductory chapter and concluded with a chapter by ATS president Daniel Aleshire, who culls from the book key insights about the vocation of CAOs serving in ATS theological schools. The chapters in each of the three sections contain essays written by a host of colleagues who have served as CAOs in ATS-accredited theological institutions during recent years. In the paragraphs below the authors are identified by the schools they served when the essays were commissioned.

I. Reading Institutional Context

Section I, **Reading Institutional Context**, offers three angles of vision on understanding context. The first has to do with the art of contextual analysis itself. The second has to do with the centrality of how a school understands its mission in the context of its particular institutional character and constituencies. The third has to do with both the institutional and the self-understanding of what it means to serve as a CAO. By striving to think contextually about a school, to think creatively about the mission it serves and the vision that animates it, and to think vocationally about the dean's calling, deans lay the groundwork for engaging vital relationships and developing needed competencies that the other two sections of the book address.

Jana Childers (San Francisco Theological Seminary) and Gail O'Day (Candler School of Theology of Emory University) contribute to Chapter 1, "Academic Leadership and the Varieties of Theological Schools." Childers takes as a point of departure the conflicting forces an academic dean who "leads from the center" often navigates, offers a broad view of resources for contextual analysis, and discusses four tools for exegeting context that have been particularly useful to her. O'Day highlights the academic dean's unique vantage point for observing a wide range of institutional dynamics and, after describing the landscape available for observation, proposes three "dispositions" for transforming leadership that observant deans may contribute to their schools.

In Chapter 2, Jay Wade Marshall (Earlham School of Religion) and Richard Benson (St. John's Seminary, CA) reflect on the topic of "Developing Vision and Serving Mission." Marshall starts with the premise that understanding the contextual factors in a school — its images of what "mission" means and the way its governance policies spell out the various roles of a school's constituents in charting a school's mission, for example — all play a role in articulating and embodying the mission of a school; they are all arenas in which the CAO has a key role to play. Benson makes a case for how the dean's work should be grounded in a clear, visionary mission statement and suggests ways that the academic dean, acting as a "dream catcher" and motivator, may assist the school's constituents to better articulate and advance the school's mission.

Chapter 3 covers the final topic related to institutional context: "The Vocational Call and Multifaceted Role of the CAO." Stephen Graham (North Park Theological Seminary) draws wisdom from both ancient and current sources for plumbing the meaning of the term *vocation,* particularly for those who have responded to a call to administrative leadership. Linda Bryan (Shaw University Divinity School) discusses different ways office-holders have described their service as academic deans and reflects on some of the role's stresses and rewards. These essays each point to many contextual factors (e.g., the theological and ecclesial heritage of a school and of a dean, a dean's prior institutional role, the dynamics occurring within institutions as they seek leadership, and the resources of a dean's own scholarly discipline) that are all "in play" as academic deans both wrestle with and embrace the role of CAO as a means of fulfilling their religious vocations.

II. Nurturing Commitments

Section II, **Nurturing Commitments**, includes fourteen essays organized into six chapters that explore six vital relationships. The length of the section reflects the wide variety of relationships and partnerships that simultaneously require attention in academic deans' daily lives, and the significance of these relationships.

Chapter 4 explores a relationship that, time and again throughout the volume, is described as having a significant role in determining whether academic deans flourish or experience diminishment in their position: "Relating to the CEO." Willie Jennings (Duke University Divinity School) paints a vivid portrait of the hermeneutical challenges of "interpreting the one to the many" and "interpreting the many to the one" that academic deans in a university setting face, then suggests strategies for healthy interdependency in the partnership between the university theological school dean and the academic dean. Randolph MacFarland (Denver Seminary) articulates several of the issues involved in building a positive working relationship between the CEO and CAO of a freestanding seminary, then offers five intentional practices for building a dean-president relationship that will help a school further its mission.

Chapter 5 addresses "The Dean's Role in Governance." Cameron Murchison (Columbia Theological Seminary) contends that of the three domains of governance (fiduciary, strategic, and generative), the place where disagreements are most likely to arise between formal and informal understandings of governance is in strategic governance, where diverse stakeholders negotiate concrete decisions that have to do with how a school can best fulfill its mission. Using faculty searches, recruitment and faculty evaluations, and promotions as concrete examples of this problematic, he hypothesizes that deans can assist faculties with impasses in the strategic domain by paying more attention to generative governance processes that invite reflection on what the institution wants to create and what vision will animate its life. Anne Anderson (University of St. Michael's College) images the CAO's role as a fulcrum from which deans convey the voices of faculty and students to the board through the president, and vice versa. She examines both the tangible and the intangible dimensions of this exercise of leadership, in which deans may exert considerable influence due to their fulcrum position.

Chapter 6 turns attention to the subject of "Faculty Leadership and Development." Anne Yardley (Drew University Theological School) images that work as helping to construct "the scaffolding that supports faculty leadership." She offers examples of how academic deans may aid faculty development and leadership through attending to and strengthening the "visible scaffolding" of formal institutional structures and processes, through recognizing and nurturing both individual faculty members' gifts and shared faculty commitments, and through carefully attending to their own sense of vocation as academic deans. Dale Stoffer (Ashland Theological Seminary) sketches a portrait of faculty leadership and development from the Anabaptist perspective, revealing how much ecclesiastical identity and theological heritage influence how deans envision the twin tasks of cultivating the individual vocations of faculty members and the common vocation of the faculty in a denominational seminary.

Chapter 7 introduces yet another commitment: "The Dean's Relationship with Students." Ruth Meyers (Seabury-Western Theological Seminary) describes the dean's role in a denominational seminary as a key leader in a multifaceted educational system, as an authority figure and communicator, as an advocate and disciplinarian, and as a change agent and guardian of the status quo. Her many examples of the interactions with students that occur as these roles are navigated include stories of how she worked with MDiv students through the challenge of the seminary board's decision that Seabury would no longer offer the MDiv as a freestanding, three-year residential program. Providing the divinity school perspective, Richard Rosengarten (University of Chicago Divinity School) describes arenas in which the dean's "self-conscious and reflective practice as a scholar and a professional" exercise a formative influence on students, both at the "macro" level of public conduct and professionalism and at the "micro" level where the dean relates to student groups and individual students on a variety of matters, seeking to cultivate a *habitus* of attentive listening as well as to embody the school's values and commitment to mutual ongoing learning and accountability.

Chapter 8 explores how academic deans cope with the internal and external expectations they face in "Modeling/Leading in Teaching and Scholarship," especially in the press of administrative leadership. Craig Nessan

(Wartburg Theological Seminary) highlights four distinct areas in which deans may model a life of teaching and scholarship: in their ability to understand and convey insights from scholarship in the field of theological education itself, through the means they use to cultivate the teaching and scholarship of others, through the study and writing that goes into the production of administrative documents, and through scholarship in their own disciplines. In the first of these areas, Nessan offers an overview of recent scholarship on theological education that will be especially helpful for those who enter the deanship unfamiliar with this literature. Barbara Mutch (Carey Theological College) discusses what makes a theological school hospitable to teaching and scholarship and how the dean can nurture a community of teaching and learning amid the competitive and individualistic forces at work in much academic life. Contending that a school that is hospitable to teaching and scholarship is marked by conversation, community, and compassion, she describes several practices that nurture these necessary qualities.

The essays in Chapter 9, "Leading in Diversity: Personal Experiences and Institutional Choices," offer several angles of vision on leading in diversity. Some essays focus on how academic deans assist their institutions both to capitalize on the opportunities diversity brings and to creatively navigate the tensions that can arise in diverse communities. Some reflect on the critical question of how deans' own social locations influence their work as deans. Of course, these topics are never neatly separated, and although the authors of each essay may punctuate the institutional over the personal or vice versa, all authors recognize the interconnectedness of the personal and the political in their exercise of leadership.

Stephen Reid (Bethany Theological Seminary) explores what happens when the academic dean who is called to exercise leadership from the "center" occupies that space as a "stranger." He describes the post-Christendom, post-denominational, and globalizing forces that provide the larger systemic context for denominational seminaries today, affirming how his identity as an African American who exercises leadership in an overwhelmingly white denomination/seminary positions him to challenge the seminary to respond to the earthshaking cultural changes occurring in U.S. society. He weaves together personal stories with an analysis of the powerful forces impacting North American theological education. He makes a case for how adopting a stance of "philosophical cosmopolitanism" can contribute to academic deans' teaching and scholarship, administrative oversight, and the need to develop new coalitions and constituencies in a rapidly changing theological landscape.

Faustino Cruz (Franciscan School of Theology) examines the dynamics of race and ethnicity, social class, language, gender, and liminality, with particular attention to how educators are called to take into respectful consideration the diverse cultural and epistemological contexts from which students come. With illustrations from his own life story and through engagement with theoretical resources, Cruz affirms the capacity of marginal groups to be "in-both" worlds rather than "in-between" worlds, and suggests that even in leading from a center position deans may resist the power of centrality itself by inviting diverse partners into the center of leadership and the spectrum of the theological enterprise.

Sherwood Lingenfelter (Fuller Theological Seminary), with assistance from colleagues Winston Gooden and Linda Wagener, explores how a large multidenominational and multiethnic seminary strives to be a community that "does diversity well." Describing this effort as always in progress and never complete, Lingenfelter examines five specific areas of intentional intervention and accomplishment, shares what has been learned from these initiatives, and concludes with a testimony to how life in a global community, while full of challenges, is greatly worth the effort.

Barbara Brown Zikmund, who in addition to her years of service as a CAO and CEO, recently served as project director for the ATS Women in Leadership Research Project, was asked to contribute some of the wisdom gained from interviewing close to 100 percent of women serving as CAOs during the time of the project about the role of gender in their experience of becoming and serving as academic administrators. Zikmund contributes a perspective that is shaped by two very different sources of wisdom: facts and statistics about women who serve as academic administrators and deeply personal testimonies of individual women about the influence of gender in the experience of academic leadership. She engages both those sources of wisdom to reflect on what women contribute as academic leaders. This contribution to the volume reminds deans that *both* careful research on the facts and statistics of gender (as well as other forms of) diversity *and* intentional, deep listening to the "inside" experiences of those who exercise leadership are critically important in any effort to strengthen or expand the leadership of underrepresented constituencies.

III. Developing Competencies

Developing Competencies, the third section of *C(H)AOS Theory*, contains topics requested time and time again in CAOS annual meetings, where academic deans come together to learn best practices in a variety of areas in which they exercise strategic leadership.

Chapter 10, "Orchestrating People and Processes," includes three essays on the art of administration. Gary Riebe-Estrella (Catholic Theological Union) reflects on how the dean relates to multiple constituencies, to myriad tasks, and to one's own self, offering wisdom laced with humor about how to survive the traffic jams deans are frequently expected to untangle. John Carroll (Union Theological Seminary and Presbyterian School of Christian Education) describes major areas of academic oversight that are central to the administrative work of the dean and concludes with identifying keys to effective leadership. Jack Seymour (Garrett-Evangelical Theological Seminary) notes the multiple occasions when the "center" position deans hold thrusts them into helping faculty, staff, students, and others make the most of the tensions and conflicts that not only are inevitable in a school's life, but often hold opportunities for growth as well. His essay offers deans strategies for both navigating conflict and building consensus, which he defines as "engaging together around a common project or a common mission."

Chapter 11 deals with "Building the Academic Budget." Robin Steinke (Gettysburg Theological Seminary) paints a vivid portrait of the denominational seminary dean who sits at the budget table with key seminary administrators who must together negotiate a budget that will keep a school's mission constantly in focus and work together across departments and particular budgets for the good of the whole. For new deans in particular, Steinke's "crash course" on understanding budget terminology will be very helpful, as well as her analysis of how deans may foster the best strategic thinking of both the faculty and administrative colleagues about the relationship of budget choices to a school's long-term mission objectives. Tite Tiénou (Trinity Evangelical Divinity School) portrays how this work is accomplished in a university setting, where as both theological school dean and CAO, one must understand the larger picture of how the theological school budget fits within the larger university budget and the strategies that help the CAO navigate those waters in ways that advance the mission of the theological school.

Chapter 12, "Balancing Formation, Academic Learning, and Ecclesiastical Goals," addresses a series of "vital balances" that academic deans help to preserve and strengthen from the perspectives of leaders in evangelical, Roman Catholic, and Mennonite institutional contexts. Bruce Powers (Campbell University Divinity School) presents the structure of a "classic" curriculum model and a "formation" curriculum model, contending that schools benefit the most not from choosing one model over another but by exploring the strengths and limitations of each, blending and balancing the content and experiences of each into a unified curriculum that best serves the context of a theological school and its mission. He shares examples from his own school's work in this area. Ronald Mercier (Regis College) takes as a point of departure the reality that theological schools may no longer presuppose that students or faculty members are deeply "formed" by an ecclesial tradition. The challenge schools face is not how to balance a subject matter called "formation" (usually identified with "spiritual" formation) with other subject matters, but rather how to respond to "a decidedly different world." Although Mercier focuses attention primarily on the "spiritual element within the broader program," he advocates a more encompassing vision of theological education that strives to offer "a more integrated and integrative vision of formation." Ervin Stutzman (Eastern Mennonite Seminary) describes theological schools as inhabiting a space of intersection between academic and ecclesial cultures, situated amid North America's changing religious landscape, and impacted by some ecclesial bodies' frustrations with their graduates. He presents five questions for exploring the tensions in balancing the concerns of church and academy, and shares some of the Eastern Mennonite Seminary faculty's learning from their efforts to address the concerns of its ecclesial constituency.

Chapter 13, "Understanding and Using Assessment and Accreditation," has been the subject of many CAOS seminars and the source of many deans' sleepless nights. John VerBerkmoes (Grand Rapids Theological Seminary of Cornerstone University) highlights the crucial task of articulating a sound understanding of what assessment means, looking broadly across the institutional spectrum at what good assessment practices involve for students, faculty, administration, and programs. His focus is on creating an *institutional* culture of assessment. Leland Eliason (Bethel Seminary of Bethel University) focuses more specifically on models of assessment of student learning outcomes. After a brief discussion of how to develop and nurture a culture that values assessment, Eliason discusses both the *domains* of student learning outcomes assessment and the *tools* of such assessment, then concludes with discussing the relationship of learning outcomes assessment to institutional planning.

The culminating chapter of the **Developing Competencies** section was written by the volume's co-editor, Bruce Birch (Wesley Theological Seminary). Drawing on a biblical image from Psalm 137 and wisdom from the Book of Jeremiah, Birch focuses on maintaining personal and vocational wholeness while navigating a sometimes dramatic change of role within a theological school. He shares practices and commitments that have been life-giving for him in his eleven years of serving as academic dean, including some reflections on how to "sing the Lord's song in a strange land" when things go badly.

So Much Learned . . . and Still to Learn

The volume concludes with Daniel Aleshire's reflections on this project and what can be learned from it by new deans and experienced deans. As co-editor of the volume, I can speak of one contribution the volume has already made to my work as a theological educator.

We began this project over three years ago (the first deadline we gave authors was March 15, 2008). At that time I was embarking on the last two years of a decade of service as dean and vice president for academic affairs at the Lutheran School of Theology at Chicago, and Bruce was entering the culminating years of an eleven-year deanship at Wesley Theological Seminary. Like all the authors, we worked on editing manuscripts in the interstices of time carved out from busy schedules and amid the life transitions that continue to be interwoven with professional lives and the challenges that the economic downtown of 2008-09 brought to our schools. We conclude this work post-deanship, during a busy "retirement" for Bruce and a sabbatical year for me before returning to full-time teaching.

It was clear, from the first essay submitted to the last, what a privilege it was to be involved in this project. Through the voices of the colleagues who have contributed to this volume, the "deanship," with all its complex challenges and tremendous rewards, has been lifted up, again and again, as a worthy investment of time, talents, gifts, and service. The chapters of this book are not just narratives of problems and practices, situations and standards; they are narratives of lives and leadership. To borrow a phrase well-known by most Lutherans, "in, with, and under" the lines of the chapters of this book are testimonies to the grace of collegiality, a few traces of tears, the sound of laughter, and the serious strivings of committed leaders to faithfully fulfill the responsibilities entrusted to them.

The world keeps changing. Knowledge keeps expanding. There are many additions and corrections to be written in the months to come, new situations to describe, other stories to tell, new and old practices to refine. As the old hymn says, "new occasions teach new duties."[7] What has been attempted here is not a volume that addresses every situation, but rather a witness to the power of a community of practice at work. For new deans, we hope this volume will provide much helpful information and many resources and will encourage you in your work. For more experienced (even "retired") deans, we hope this volume will serve not only as a place to discover old and new friends but also as a reminder of the value of the service you are offering or have offered for the sake of building strong theological schools that nurture gifted leaders. For those considering the work of academic leadership or trying to better understand the experiences and perspectives of those who are engaged in it, we hope you will find clearer understandings of the work and new ways to be in conversation with academic leaders. If this volume serves these purposes, it will have been well worth the journey.

---

7. "Once to Every Man and Nation," #242 *The Methodist Hymnal* (Nashville: United Methodist Publishing House, 1966): verse 3. The larger sentence in which the phrase is embedded is, "New occasions teach new duties, time makes ancient good uncouth; they must upward still and onward, who would keep abreast of truth."

READING INSTITUTIONAL CONTEXT

1. Academic Leadership and the Varieties of Theological Schools

Fins on the Left, Fins on the Right: Reading Context in Seminaries

Jana Childers

An Indispensable Compass for Surviving and Thriving

There are many reasons for a dean to put time and energy into exegeting context. A number of them have nothing to do with self-defense, but protecting your ability to do your job is an exceedingly common motivator. Far from being merely selfish or Machiavellian, it is a legitimate concern. Nobody is going to achieve your agenda for you. Whether your goal is to help your school live out its mission statement, envision a new future, reduce conflict, improve support for faculty, or strengthen student learning, accomplishing *your* goal depends on you. If you are not there to do it, the job won't get done. Something else will.

Most deans lead "from the center." In seminaries, deans live and move and have their being between two large entities, the president-and-board and the faculty. The interests, values, and work styles of the two groups can be quite different. Conflict, competition, or at least confusion over roles is common. When you see shark fins circling on your right and left, and as the song says, "you're the only bait in town,"[1] survival is key. Certainly the work

1. Jimmy Buffet, Deborah McColl, Barry Chance, "Fins," recorded by Jimmy Buffet on the album *Volcano,* produced by Norbert Putnam, MCA Records, 1979.

of the office requires that the dean navigate among institutional forces. The ability to read cultural context can provide the dean with an indispensable compass. If you can read, you can anticipate. If you can anticipate, you can be ready to respond in constructive, effective ways. If you can respond in constructive, effective ways, you can meet your goals.

A surprising number of academic disciplines offer methodologies for exegeting context. Cultural anthropology, interpersonal communication theory, and various subfields within psychology and sociology are just the beginning of the list. Such diverse fields as engineering, archaeology, ethics, and literary theory also take an interest in this kind of work. Whether the focus of the investigation is on culture, ecology, process, or resources,[2] there are many common tools.

1. Cultural approaches are often concerned with establishing identity. In theological education, a school's theological stripe might be examined in order to illuminate its culture. The tools of story analysis or rhetoric might be used to tease out information.

2. Ecological approaches involve focusing on the larger setting. The denomination's assumptions about the school's mission might be observed, for example, in the bishop's sermon or the Committee on Theological Education's report and used, in turn, to describe something of the school's ecology. The tools of rhetoric or content analysis might be used in such an investigation.

3. Process approaches are concerned with the dynamics of a situation. In a seminary, they might focus on governance style as a way of getting at a school's problems. Again, either story analysis, rhetoric, or content analysis might be among the tools used.

4. Resource approaches are concerned with who has what. In a seminary, noticing what programs are offered and/or what degree of participation is common in various programs might be an important way of teasing out information. The tools used to accomplish this might conceivably include any of the tools mentioned above. In addition, tools such as student surveys or longitudinal studies of data might be used.

Bridging these approaches is a four-step method that provides a basic pattern for exegeting many different kinds of situations. In *Practicing Gospel:*

2. R. Leon Carroll Jr. uses the four categories noted in this essay to organize contextual methods in an unpublished handout, "Generative Teaching Congregations." Columbia Theological Seminary, Fall 2004.

Unconventional Thoughts on the Church's Ministry, Edward Farley describes the phases of such a process:[3]

1. Identify the situation's distinct and constituent features.
2. Uncover the suppressions of the past.
3. See the situation in its larger context.
4. Discern the situation's demand.

In seminaries, this method might be enhanced by consideration of additional factors:

- observations about denominational assumptions
- stories of congregations, denominational groups, and the seminary
- complaints of constituents (donors, board members, faculty, staff, students, etc.)
- the felt needs of various groups, how they dress, what lingo they use, what physical setting/use of space is common for them, how they express themselves in nonverbal interaction
- diverse world views
- various views of authority
- differing communication styles among constituents

Values analysis and/or content analysis are part of many of these approaches. They can be used in conjunction with Farley's method as well as others. Nora Tubbs Tisdale,[4] for example, recommends asking questions of congregations such as:

- What symbols are important to this group?
- What traditions, if taken away, would cause trouble?
- What stories about the group are repeated most often?
- What attracts newcomers to the group?
- What key figures and personalities have shaped the group?

Such questions are obviously useful in seminary contexts as well.

---

3. Edward Farley, *Practicing Gospel: Unconventional Thoughts on Church Ministry* (Louisville: Westminster John Knox, 2003), pp. 38-40.

4. Nora Tubbs Tisdale, *Preaching as Local Theology and Folk Art* (Minneapolis: Fortress Press, 1996).

The classic text on exegeting faith communities is James F. Hopewell's *Congregations: Stories and Structures,* which first appeared in 1987. Tisdale and a number of others working on contextual methods build on Hopewell, and there are many books on management and leadership that offer critical insights related to analyzing context.[5]

Although there are abundant resources for doing contextual analysis in many scholarly disciplines, analyzing context from the vantage point of the dean's office may not be an area of expertise for many people who become deans. Any skills I have that are specific to deaning are skills that were learned on the job. Though I have put some effort into finding helpful literature on the subject, the study of context is something I know much more through field experience than through academic work. Some deans do enjoy doing a formal study of one methodology or another, but such systematic work is not necessary.

Each dean will bring a particular discipline to the task. What I know about exegeting context I understood first as a preacher and homiletician. I have expanded that experience through serving as a dean in a freestanding seminary, related to a mainline denomination and part of a larger consortium of nine schools. With this background and experience, I have found four tools especially useful in helping deans avoid becoming shark bait. They have to do with both the art of communication and the ability to step back and observe.

Contexting: Understanding the Community's Communication Style

The first tool helps you make broad observations about your community's communication styles. It provides tools to describe how your community

5. See Eric H. F. Law, *The Bush Was Blazing But Not Consumed* (St. Louis: Chalice Press, 1996), on building multi-cultural communities; Daniel Goleman, Richard Boyatzis, and Annie McKeem, *Primal Leadership: Realizing the Power of Emotional Intelligence* (Boston: Harvard Business School Press, 2002), on building a leadership style; Ronald A. Heifetz and Marty Linsky, *Leadership on the Line: Staying Alive through the Dangers of Leading* (Boston: Harvard Business School Press, 2002), on avoiding leadership pitfalls; Robert Kegan and Lisa Laskow Lahey, *How We Talk Can Change the Way We Work* (San Francisco: Jossey-Bass, 2001), on a humane approach to organizational change; Deborah Tannen, *Talking from 9 to 5* (New York: William Morrow, 1994), on gender communication; and David Batstone, *Saving the Corporate Soul* (San Francisco: Jossey-Bass, 2003), on building communities with integrity. In addition, such Web sites as Link2lead.com provide useful data on specific contexts.

goes about building a common context (i.e., a structure that supports or undergirds its communication). The tool is called "contexting."

Cultural anthropologist Edward T. Hall introduced the notion thirty years ago. In *The Bush Was Blazing But Was Not Consumed*, Eric H. F. Law developed and applied the concept in a way that has been widely used by faith communities. Law claims that all cultures may be grouped roughly into two groups: "high context" and "low context."[6] High context groups are group oriented, they rely heavily on shared understandings ("very little is in the coded, explicit, transmitted message"),[7] conflict occurs when shared understandings are violated, face saving is important, and these communities tend to focus on relationship. Low context groups are more oriented toward the individual than the group, they use a more explicit communication style, their conflicts have more to do with individuals' expectations than the shared expectations of the group, facts are more important than "face," and they tend to focus on action and solutions more than on relationships. High context communities are considered more stable, and low context communities are considered more flexible. Moving from one to another involves obvious challenges.

When "John" applied for a promotion at his seminary, it was widely assumed that he knew what to expect. Having served on the faculty for a number of years, he was familiar with the group's processes and norms. However, few of his colleagues recognized that there were two different cultures at play in John's review process. The review committee's culture was fairly "low." The majority of the group was comprised of people of European heritage, embedded in the wider culture of academia. Norms about "fairness" and "judging a case on its merits" and "objective evaluation" were highly valued. But John's own culture-of-origin was a "high context" culture. His values in the areas of shared understanding and relationship were strongly held. Only his colleagues who themselves had significant experience in high context communities saw the potential for disaster. In the end it was this small cadre of colleagues from racial/ethnic minority groups who played a key role in reconciling the two communication styles.

John got the promotion, largely due to the good efforts of that small cadre of colleagues who were skilled in "contexting." It would be correct, I suppose, to say that the promotion committee was able to assess John's merits more objectively with the enhanced understanding the smaller group

6. Law, *The Bush Was Blazing*, p. 106.
7. Law, *The Bush Was Blazing*, p. 106.

helped them achieve. But I think of it more as them being helped to see (however partially or temporarily) that their "low contexting" assumptions were biasing their evaluation. When their unconscious expectations were made conscious they were able to see John's positive qualities more clearly.

John's experience is not unusual. It was complicated, perhaps, by the fact that the people of his seminary *thought* of themselves as being fairly "high context." They did not realize that relative to other cultures they could easily be seen as "low." Despite their emphasis on relationships among people, their lip service to valuing the collective, and their respect for tradition, it turns out they really were not a high context culture at all.

Many seminary communities in the United States are low context cultures. Academic contexts often value explicitness. An eloquent senior colleague once expressed his frustration with a meeting moderator who wanted participants to shorten their speeches. "I love to be able to lay everything out," he said, extending his arm in a wide gesture. They also pride themselves on being open ("no second class citizens here") and favor direct confrontation — it took me a long time to understand that our faculty meetings are as long as they are because, at some level, we love nothing better than wrangling with each other! They can be very judgmental about high context cultures.

The confrontational style of many seminaries may seem direct, task-oriented, and quick to people from other cultures. People from high context cultures often respond to conflict by backing off, slowing down, and taking time to figure out where they stand in relation to others. "Then," as Eric Law says, "the judgment comes. 'Why can't they be honest? Why don't they want to find a solution? I can't read their minds! Why are they so passive-aggressive?'"[8]

As theological education continues to diversify, the insights provided by contexting will be increasingly important. The conflicts among world views, communication styles, and values of the constituent groups within seminaries must be parsed. Law and others make a good case for starting with communication styles. Fortunately, most academic communities have the facility and interest to analyze communication strategies. Gathering people to talk about talking may be an important first step on a dean's agenda. At the very least, noticing communication patterns is a good place for a dean to start reading context.

8. Law, *The Bush Was Blazing*, p. 105.

Your Leadership Style: What Kind of Motivator Are You?

Just as a sense of how your community communicates is important, it is helpful to identify your own style. On their first day in office, most deans can say whether they prefer a "command-and-control" approach or a "communicate-and-inspire" style. But you will want to know a bit more about yourself than that. Understanding your style in some detail may take time. The literature can be helpful in narrowing down the field. It can also lead a person into deeper confusion, so be judicious about which theorist or theorists you choose to read.

There are three questions that determine much of a person's leadership style:

1. How do you motivate people?
2. How do you manage yourself?
3. How do you deal with conflict?

Many deans think first about their self-management style: *I'm not going to be as buttoned up as my predecessor, I'm going to let them know how I feel,* or *It's not becoming to a dean to wear her heart on her sleeve.* But it can be helpful to start with the question of how you motivate people. Much of the rest of your leadership style will hinge on how you answer this question. Are you a visionary, someone who holds up a compelling picture of how life can be and invites others into it? Are you a coach, someone who is skillful at showing others how what they want connects with what the school wants? Are you a democratic leader, someone who makes others feel valued? Your choice among these three popular options (or a number of others) will have implications for both self and conflict management.

Answering the motivation question as specifically as you can is important. Too many administrators make the mistake common to beginning preachers — they assume that the power to motivate comes with the trappings of office (pulpit, vestments, and seminary degree for preachers; a big desk, title, and office for deans). But just as good sermons hang on the preacher's ability to get under a congregation's skin using imagery, narrative, or oratorical techniques, so good deaning depends on finding ways to motivate people. A chance to make a contribution will motivate some folks. Others will respond to an opportunity to connect more deeply with others. Some people like to hear shared dreams articulated. Still others want recognition, reassurance, or the chance to rise to a challenge.

Motivation almost always involves identifying a need, showing how the need can be satisfied, and "making the close." Leaders who use motivation effectively, however, often add a magic fourth step. After showing the need and establishing the need-satisfaction and before the close, they get others to *visualize:* "Can't you just see yourself chairing the review committee?" "Can you picture what it would be like if we could finish this project?" "I can see you making a real success of this." Different leadership styles employ various ways of motivating folks. But at some level most depend on the leader finding ways to draw others into the seminary's mission.

One caution from the world of preaching might be appropriate here. It is well known that two of the most powerful motivators — guilt and fear — have equally powerful boomerangs built into them. Guilt breeds avoidance, preachers say, and many of us have reason to know how true that is. Similarly, fear, though very effective in the short-term, has disastrous long-term effects, including paralysis and resentment. The long-term effects of fear are particularly difficult to remedy.

Distance: Getting on the Balcony

I once asked Barbara Brown Taylor, one of the nation's best-known preachers, what fueled her ability to do her work. She said her preaching was fueled by, among other things, the chance to get out of the country every so often. She commented that looking back at the United States from some distance and perhaps through the eyes of another culture had become important to her for the perspective it can provide. The ability to achieve critical distance is no less important for the administrative, political, and creative tasks that fill a dean's desk pad.

Ronald A. Heifetz and Marty Linsky are Harvard Business School professors. It should surprise nobody that they are fairly positively disposed toward capitalism. Even those who take a dimmer view of capitalism's prospects, however, can see the truth in the story Heifetz and Linsky tell about Lee Kuan Yew, the founder of modern Singapore. They claim that Lee was

> intrigued by the perspectives of his anti-colonial comrades, such as India's Jawaharlal Nehru, who viewed Western imperialism and capitalism as part and parcel of each other. Lee left Singapore and traveled extensively to see firsthand how the other founders were making progress — as they guided their new nations. But what he saw disturbed him. By ty-

ing their anti-colonialism to anti-capitalism, some of the founding fathers were impeding economic progress in their countries and failing to achieve a decent standard of living for the people of their country. By stepping back and testing the conventional wisdom of his contemporaries in other emerging nations, Lee gained not only freedom from those views, but also a more accurate and complete picture of reality, which then became the basis for his leadership. Unlike most fighters for independence in his generation, he embraced free markets. Between 1965 and 2000, Singapore went from being a poor and racially divided city to an integrated community with one of the world's strongest economies. None of Lee's contemporaries achieved comparable results.[9]

Lee achieved distance; he "got out on the balcony," as Heifetz and Linsky put it, by leaving town. This critical distance led to better data-gathering, better observations, and ultimately better decisions.

Few deans would gainsay the desirability of stepping away from their own contexts in order to see them more clearly and perhaps even to think more clearly about them. But equally few deans would say they find making the break with campus easy. There is so much to do in preparation and so much email to answer after coming home that it is hardly worth whatever good is gleaned from the change of scene. How can busy deans use "distance" to improve their reading of context — especially when the geographic version is so hard to achieve?

Heifetz and Linsky suggest starting by "distinguishing technical from adaptive challenges."[10] Is your school facing a technical issue, i.e., an issue that is focused on one problem or person, something that would lend itself to a technical fix? Or is the challenge before you adaptive, i.e., part of a larger complex of problems, a systemic issue, one where people's minds and hearts need to be changed? Wrangling over lecture styles or budget crises or complaints against a particular professor or administrator are often adaptive, though it can be tempting to treat them as technical. In fact, Heifetz and Linsky say, "Often organizations will try to treat adaptive issues as technical ones in order to diffuse them."[11]

Another step that can help create critical distance has to do with diagnosing. It is important to learn the language (Lee Kuan Yew reportedly

---

9. Heifetz and Linsky, *Leadership on the Line*, pp. 54-55.
10. Heifetz and Linsky, *Leadership on the Line*, pp. 54-55.
11. Heifetz and Linsky, *Leadership on the Line*, p. 59.

taught himself Mandarin) and listen to the stories of the community. But it is the diagnosing step that provides distance. It is not enough to let stories collect on your mental hard drive. Parsing them, interpreting them, identifying the undercurrents in them is what makes a difference. People tell stories in a way that defends their own values, theorists say. Notice the key words, refrains, and images in the way complaints are voiced or stories are related. Let them help you take a step back and identify the themes and values they represent.

Finally, to achieve distance from a situation or setting, pay particular attention to the behavior of authority figures. This suggestion may be a counterintuitive one. It may seem that the more attention you pay to the school's other leaders, the more psychologically enmeshed in the situation you become. But if you are observing *and* taking the distancing step of diagnosing, the behavior of the community's other leaders (president, board chair, CFO, etc.) can yield valuable information. Authority figures' behavior may in fact be the best indicator of what is going on in a social system. Positioned as they are at the "nodes"[12] of the community, they are first to feel the winds of change. Nowhere else in the system will you get such quick and strong clues about whether tension is building or easing in the school, whether the ecology is healthy or unhappy, whether resources are becoming plentiful or scarce. Authority figures' nonverbal cues, in particular, are rich sources of information. Learning to diagnose based on behavior and nonverbal behavior will give you valuable information on a thousand big and small issues.

Reading Nonverbal Communication

Often described as a "sexy" subject, the study of nonverbal communication is fascinating to so many of us because it is *about* us. The endlessly entertaining thing about "nonverbals" is that they tell the truth — and it is the truth about us. Since Freud, we have understood that people cannot, in one sense, really lie. "If we lie with our lips we will chatter the truth from our fingertips," Freud taught. The truth will out us.

Certainly the juiciest method of contextual study, nonverbal communication theory can also be a powerful tool for a seminary dean. By keeping two rules of thumb in mind, most people can strengthen their ability to read nonverbal communication.

12. Heifetz and Linsky, *Leadership on the Line*, p. 55.

The first rule of thumb is really a rule of foot: Feet are the most honest members of the body. They are more likely than any other body part to tell the truth about how a person feels. Have you ever noticed how the feet of a nervous speaker shift on the floor? Such purposeless, small movements betray the speaker's torn-ness. One part wants to stay and speak, while the other is seriously thinking about beating a path to the door. The rule applies equally whether the speaker is standing on a chancel or sitting at a faculty meeting. After a particularly long meeting several years ago, one of my colleagues whose academic discipline was pastoral psychology remarked to me that, although I looked calm from the rib cage up, I had "walked about a hundred miles" during the meeting. She said my feet were so busy that I reminded her of the young women of Ireland doing the traditional dance where the torso and head are kept ramrod straight while the feet tap, stomp, and fling wildly.

The second rule of thumb is that everybody has a nonverbal "home base." Departing from home base is almost always a sign that something is awry. Every person associated with your school is dominantly one of three things: head-, gut-, or heart-oriented. Any school will attract a good number of head-oriented people, of course. Head-oriented people use their fingertips and eyes a good deal. They steeple or point or touch their faces with their fingers. You can see the thinking in their eyes. They like big and little ax-type gestures because they are always parsing, dividing, or separating ideas in their minds. The gut-oriented people at your school are likely to be fans of sports or perhaps Indiana Jones. They are attracted to the big swash-buckling stories in the Old Testament. They may even have a penchant for AK-47 movies. Gut-oriented people favor their torsos. The back of the arm is particularly active in the gut- or kinesthetically-oriented person. Any theological school will have a share of heart-oriented people, too. You will know them by their palms and cheeks. Their gestures display their palms and their cheeks are always moving — dimpling, grimacing, sinking, rising. Heart-oriented people extend their vowels for emphasis, whereas head-oriented people use little rises in pitch to create emphasis, and gut-oriented people tend to thump the word they want to emphasize.

It does not take long to start making small observations about co-workers and students' nonverbal messages. And it is amazing how quickly they seem to line themselves up into patterns. What can be helpful to the context-reader is noticing the departure from pattern. Though it cannot tell you exactly why individuals are not being themselves, it can call your attention to a strategically important moment in the conversation and alert you to the need for more information.

A Sharp Eye for Fins

There are a number of metaphors that describe how a dean does context analysis. Deans "read the tea leaves" or "ride the currents" or "sniff the winds." In the process they "navigate between Scylla and Charybdis," "dance with dinosaurs," and live "between a rock and a hard place." Exegeting both sides of the institutional forces that flow around a seminary dean is not easy. It involves spiritual, intellectual, and creative resources not discussed here. However, a little common sense and reflection go a long way for a seminary dean. That and a sharp eye for fins make it possible for many deans to not only survive — but also thrive — in the dean's office.

Stop, Look, and Listen:
Observation in Academic Leadership

Gail R. O'Day

"Stop, look, and listen." These words, learned by elementary school children from their school crossing guards, serve as good watchwords for the work of an academic dean. To read institutional context and culture effectively, the academic dean needs first to hone skills of observation. Observation will necessarily be followed by assessment and then by action, but a rush to either assessment or action without having stopped, looked, and listened can make for a long and rocky tenure as academic dean. The leadership of the CAO requires a combination of decisiveness and collaboration, and the proper balance between those two can only be determined on the basis of careful institutional and self-observation. Even though the academic dean's office is a hive of activity and is the place where things are supposed to happen, the most important parts of the job involve the places of preparation before action and the times for reflection afterwards.

A Distinctive Vantage Point for Observation

The academic dean's office offers a distinctive vantage point on the life of the theological school. The first place to employ one's observation skills, then, is on the academic dean's office itself. What is the vantage point of the office, and what does the school look like when viewed from behind the academic dean's desk?

The vantage point of the academic dean is different from that of a faculty member. Even though you share in the same core activities that define the work of a faculty member — teaching, research, service, community life — as CAO you see the world of your institution differently than does your colleague down the hall. Perhaps most importantly, you are now the academic dean of all of the faculty members at your school. For CAOs who come to their position from another institution, this point is easy to grasp. But if you are an internal appointment as CAO, this point can be a tricky one. As a faculty member, you had close friends on the faculty, and you also had colleagues whom you did not "like," whose approach to work annoyed you, with whose theology and/or politics you disagreed, and — let's be frank — colleagues who did not like you. Once you become the CAO, none of that can matter anymore, and one of the first observation responsibilities is to try to discover the contribution each faculty colleague makes to the school. Reading course evaluations, for example, shows you a whole different world of teaching at your institution. The colleague whose teaching you previously disparaged as either too easy or too hard looks different when seen through the lens of the students to whom that faculty member, above all others, has been the decisive factor in their vocational formation, who has listened in ways that no one else listened and answered questions that no one else took seriously.

As CAO of all of your colleagues, you also need to observe the range of personality types and the range of situations in which those personality types will be at their best and at their worst. The vantage point of the academic dean's office facilitates this observation because all aspects of committee work and institutional service come through the office. Your sense of who an individual colleague is — with all that individual's strengths, weaknesses, and idiosyncrasies — needs constantly to be tested and retested by field observation. Nothing about your colleagues and their roles in the work of the institution can be taken for granted. It is as counterproductive to the work and health of the school always to assume that faculty member A will give excellent leadership to every committee as it is to assume that faculty member B will never give excellent leadership. The observation that is possible from the academic dean's office enables you to see faculty members as part of a whole, not simply as individual personalities, and with those observations you can create opportunities for faculty leadership and development that benefit the institution as a whole, the faculty collegium, and individual faculty members.

The academic dean's office also affords a unique vantage point from which to observe the work of the school's staff. The CAO has a set of direct reports (and the composition and number of those direct reports vary from school to school), but CAO/staff interaction extends beyond the formal lines of reporting. Because of the variety of tasks that constitute the daily life of the CAO, you will be in contact with the full range of staff at your school — one day you will need help from the financial aid staff; another you will need to work with custodial staff to solve a problem. The CAO will also often be the bridge person between faculty and staff, adjudicating conflicts between faculty needs and staff perception of faculty demands. Even if the official personnel and human resources dimensions of staff oversight belong to someone else's portfolio, the CAO is in a position to recognize possible institutional pressure points due to the many activities that flow through the CAO office. You can use the distinct vantage point of the office to give voice to staff concerns in forums where staff might otherwise not be present or represented.

Just as your relationship with your faculty colleagues looks different from the academic dean's office, so, too, does your relationship with students. As CAO, most of your student contact is now with the "exceptional" students, those at the extremes of the student spectrum. You will have regular dealings with your school's best students, as they will form the cohort to which you turn for institutional leadership and service. You will know the students who receive your school's awards and honors, but you will spend at least as much time, if not more, with your school's weakest students — students who are in serious academic distress or who violate your school's honor and conduct codes. You will learn details about students' personal and financial situations that are not visible to much of your community. You will also now observe student life and learning more in terms of the collective student body than in terms of a particular group of students such as your advisees or the students in one of your classes. As academic dean, you are positioned to look for the commonalities across a very diverse student body and to find ways to develop academic programs that challenge and nurture the full range of the student body.

In addition to the distinctive vantage point on the three key popula-tions of your school — faculty, staff, and students — as CAO you also are in a position to observe the administrative totality of your school. While the re-sponsibility for the whole institutional picture rests with the CEO (president or dean, depending on whether it is a free-standing or university-related school), the CAO is positioned to observe the big picture and the day-to-day details of institutional life. Much of this big picture has to do with the inter-action of the three key populations, but the big picture extends beyond those populations. The CAO must be well-versed in the intersection of a school's various administrative units — admissions, registrar, student services, li-brary, and development. The dynamics of this interaction are often invisible to faculty and students, but the CAO must observe all dimensions if the aca-demic dean's office is to function effectively. Other dynamics come into play depending on the type of theological school at which you are CAO. At a university-related school of theology, the CAO observes the interaction of the school's priorities, programmatic and fiscal, with the priorities of the university. The CAO of a denominationally related seminary observes the push and pull of denominational expectations on the shape of seminary curriculum and programs.

Finally, the academic dean's office offers a distinctive vantage point on the school's CEO. You observe your CEO in moments of public success and private failures; you see "behind the curtain" (to use a well-known image from *The Wizard of Oz*), but unlike Dorothy, you cannot expose what you see behind that curtain. Your CEO depends on you as on no one else at your school: you are the CEO's support and reliable window into the school's daily life, its needs and its joys. Perhaps nowhere is the double-focused and double-voiced nature of the academic dean's job more apparent than in the CAO's relationship with the CEO: the CAO is the faculty's voice to the ad-ministration, but the CAO is also the administration's voice to the faculty.

The vantage point of the CAO is unique, because the role and place of the CAO in the school is not defined by membership in any single group. In-stead, the role and place of the CAO is defined by the fact that the CAO works at the intersection of every group. As a result, the CAO's perspective is shaped at the point where all the school's different stakeholders interact. As the different stakeholders and constituencies meet and plan together, they will be strong voices for their particular perspectives and advocates for the needs of their programs. As the one who resides at the intersection, the CAO is positioned to challenge the members of the academic community to think beyond their own perspectives and envision goals and initiatives that serve the school as a whole. Your work as the CAO, shaped by your unique access to the many constituencies of your school, is to encourage community members to reach higher and broader in order to identify initiatives that build on distinctive strengths and advance common goals.

Three Dispositions for Transforming Leadership

To know the contours of the CAO's vantage point is a beginning point. But simply knowing that the CAO is located at the intersection of the institution's constituencies is not enough. You need to cultivate leadership dispositions that maximize this pivotal institutional location in order to take full advantage of the untold resources and possibilities that this vantage point provides. To highlight observation as key to understanding institutional context and culture is to identify a range of active dispositions for the CAO that contain the seeds of creative and transforming leadership.

Attend to the Forest and the Trees

It is easy as CAO to become primarily a tree person or a forest person, that is, to direct most of your energy to the daily details or the big picture. We may all be familiar with academic administrators who get hooked by solving a detail-ridden institutional puzzle. Often in these circumstances, much time and talent are spent on a puzzle that could be more quickly and easily solved by the member of the community — staff or faculty — who is charged with that particular responsibility and who has the necessary skill set and data more readily at hand. But perhaps because the puzzle was intriguing or because working at the puzzle was less stressful than solving one of the puzzles that do fall directly in that administrator's portfolio, the trees take over and the forest is lost.

The temptation to become dominated by details to the point that a larger vision is lost also occurs when giving leadership to projects that rightly fall to an academic administrator. Examples include the academic administrator who becomes consumed with figuring out the exact numbers for every line item in a proposed budget instead of allowing the finance officer to work with the budget numbers or who, as advance work for a curriculum revision, spends hours and hours calculating the credit hour workload of the school's faculty over the past decade instead of asking the registrar to help with number crunching. The budget numbers and the credit hour distribution are important pieces of information for the work and planning of the school, but to have the CAO's time be consumed by them is both to do someone else's job (and so deprive that individual of an opportunity to shine) and to displace other work of the school that only the CAO can do.

Yet we also may be familiar with administrators who are eloquent about the big picture in which education occurs — the current climate in theological education, developments in the church, sweeping institutional goals and aspirations. Such talk can be inspiring and is needed to fuel an institution's corporate imagination, but talk of the big picture will remain only talk and quickly lose its capacity to inspire if the administrator never works to anchor these goals in an institutional reality. There can be a pattern of declining inspirational returns when the forest becomes so large that it blocks the trees from view.

The CAO must cultivate the disposition to be a forest *and* a tree person: to balance observation of the daily comings and goings of the institution with observation of the hopes and goals toward which it strives. An analogy from another leadership realm illustrates this disposition. The conductor of a symphony orchestra needs to know something about all of the instruments and the players that constitute the orchestra: how each instrument makes its sound, how players must listen to produce the desired blend, what standards to set for first chair, how the sound changes when instrument sections are positioned on different parts of the stage. But during a concert, the conductor can no more sit in the flute section and tell the flutist what and when to play than sit with the audience to determine whether the sound is right. Instead, the conductor needs to know that, through rehearsals and the weekly disciplines of orchestral life, all orchestra members have been enabled to excel in their own parts and to contribute to the sound of the whole. For the orchestra to perform at its best, the conductor needs to cultivate a disposition that simultaneously integrates the details and the big picture.

Honor the "Earthen Vessels"

The CAO needs to observe the school with the combined skills of a pastoral counselor and a careful administrator. An initiative or new program may look great on paper, but it is going to be enacted in the flesh and blood realities of the people who work and study at the school. A curricular plan based on a residential model will not work at a school with a high percentage of part-time students, nor will a distance-learning program capture the culture of a school that has almost no gap between its head count and its FTE. Intensive student advising programs that work well at a small school with close, daily faculty-student interaction will not transfer seamlessly to a school with a large student body and with multiple institutional demands on faculty time, nor to a school where students and faculty spend hours per day getting to and from campus. While a majority of a faculty may agree that an experientially based curriculum is pedagogically and pastorally appropriate, that curriculum may look different when it comes down to the reality of who has the temperament and expertise to teach it.

As CAO, you are positioned to observe the various interpersonal dynamics that make up your theological school's community and culture. Your responsibility as active observer of these dynamics is to recognize the possibilities inherent in the mix of persons and needs at your school and not to be discouraged by the fact that theological education depends on "earthen vessels." This can be one of the most taxing demands of the work of the CAO — and the least appreciated. There is always the temptation to work to the lowest common denominator — choosing the route to program development that eliminates the possibility of disagreement or conflict, or always turning to the people on whom you know you can count to get the job done. Both of these options, while possibly most efficient, run the risk over the long haul of flattening the variety of perspectives and persons that constitutes your community. Disagreement and conflict are not to be feared, nor to be avoided at any cost; people and institutions grow, and indeed flourish, when they are placed in situations where they have to think outside their first instincts or dominant presuppositions. To always turn to the same people for leadership is to eliminate the possibility of surprise and new direction that comes from taking a chance on someone or something different.

Theological education affirms and is built around the full spectrum of God's created order. The responsibility and privilege of the CAO is to find ways to include the full range of human strengths and weaknesses into the planning, programs, and initiatives of the school. A committee meeting may take longer when all differences of opinion and perspectives are given voice, but such a meeting also has the seeds of genuine communal discovery and freshly shared commitments that would not be possible without the attention to differences. When the CAO honors the limitations and strengths of the earthen vessels that constitute a theological community (the CAO included), something extraordinary can emerge from the ordinary.

Cultivate Trust

To speak of cultivating an administrative disposition that affirms human strengths and limitations is not to romanticize difference or to sentimentalize the administrative process. The distinctive vantage point of the CAO by definition means that you know details about the school and have access to the big picture that others don't have, so you can weigh the data and the institutional options and make some of the hard calls — alone. Not all administrative decisions can be communally made, nor can all programs fully incorporate the dreams and goals of every member of the community to the same degree. Nor will all decisions make everyone happy.

These realities of administrative life point to a final key disposition if the CAO is to flourish in the position and if the school is to flourish under sound leadership. For the decision making and initiative taking of the CAO to be effective, the CAO must develop a disposition that cultivates the trust of the community.

It is easy to underestimate the power and authority that accrue naturally to the office of the CAO, with no particular reference to the specific person who occupies that office. To the CAO, most of what you do is by necessity quite literally mundane; you do the tasks that keep the day-to-day academic operations of the school afloat and running smoothly. When you sit at your desk and work, you are not thinking about power and authority, but about who is available to teach introductory ethics at 2:30 on Tuesday afternoon. But when you send an email (or preferably, pick up the phone) to ask a colleague to teach in that slot, that seemingly simple transaction is overlaid with power dynamics. What might have been a casual inquiry, were you speaking colleague to colleague, now becomes a request by "the dean."

The authority that is inherent to the office of the CAO means that no matter what you think about your own power and authority, your faculty, staff, and administrative colleagues ascribe power to your work and your opinions. There is no such thing as a casual aside when you are CAO; a flippant remark you might have been able to toss off as a faculty member is no longer possible as CAO.

To cultivate trust, the CAO must work transparently, taking the power that accrues to the office seriously, but wearing it lightly. Transparency cannot mean that all pieces of data are made public; for reasons of confidentiality, that is impossible. (Here the disposition of honoring human frailties may bump up against the disposition of cultivating trust.) But transparency does mean that you are open and available to answer all questions right up to the point of confidentiality, so that your administrative style and decision making can be scrutinized by your colleagues.

One of the most immediate ways to develop the administrative disposition that cultivates trust is to move around. Although this essay began by talking about the vantage point from behind the academic dean's desk, key to active observation is getting up from behind your desk and moving around your school. The worst thing that can happen to the CAO is to become isolated in his or her office, seeing colleagues only at formal meetings or at set appointments to deal with specific issues. Email has its place, but it usually takes the same amount of time (or often, less) to wander down the hall to someone's office and conduct the whole transaction face to face. The power balance shifts when the CAO leaves his office and chats with others on their home turf, as the CAO implicitly communicates an awareness of their existence and daily work. Not only is a relationship built or deepened by such interpersonal contact, but a trip down the hall to see one person usually also entails "running into" a staff person, faculty colleague, or student. When you sit alone at your desk, your school increasingly becomes a faceless object. When you move around, your school loses its anonymity and becomes a community of people engaged in shared work.

To work out of a disposition that cultivates trust, it is incumbent that you play to your colleagues' better natures. You may be quite rightly irritated beyond words with one of your colleagues, because he has just ambushed you in the last meeting you had together. As CAO, you have two choices. You can deal with your irritation by pulling rank, using the power of your office to put your colleague in his place, or you can deal with your irritation by imagining your colleague's better nature and use the authority of your office to rise above the sting of your personal wound and imagine a better way. To play to your colleagues' better natures takes discipline. It requires taking a step back, drawing on your knowledge of all the institutional pieces, and then reentering the picture as steward of the institution's resources and practices. When you play to your colleagues' better natures, you demonstrate that you do not judge them but trust them to live out their vocations.

Coda

"Ready, set, go." These childhood words, usually initiating a game of tag or hide-and-seek, provide the coda to the childhood refrain with which this essay opened. They are a reminder that we cultivate dispositions for a purpose:

we learn ways to be so that we can act with a deeper and more reflective intentionality.

Most days, the quotidian details of the work of the CAO fill the minutes and hours; the day moves from one meeting to the next, from email to phone call, to the next crisis, to one more cup of coffee. In this constant flow of activity, the CAO can lose sight that every part of the day creates opportunities for active observation of institutional context and culture. The three dispositions that this essay has highlighted — attend to the forest and the trees, honor the "earthen vessels," and cultivate trust — will support administrative practices that make the complexity of one's institutional setting generative of possibility for the CAO and for the institution.

Active observation will help you get ready. The cultivation of administrative dispositions will ensure that you are set for action when your colleagues or CEO shout, "Go!"

2. Developing Vision and Serving Mission

The Centrality of Institutional Mission as an Anchor of Corporate Vision

Jay Wade Marshall

Mission is an ominous word from which deans can never escape, but whose meaning possesses a chameleon-like quality. Depending on the context, the word can suggest an operation with specific imperatives, such as a military action or an act of religious proselytizing. Either carries a commitment to triumph through some mixture of subjugation and conversion. *Mission* may describe an assigned or accepted calling or vocation, such as when one acknowledges a call to ministry and embraces a vocation representative of this calling. In a less intimidating fashion, *mission* can articulate an agreed-upon purpose, as is common in corporate mission statements where a few carefully crafted phrases document institutional commitments. These words are then prominently displayed in places like letterhead stationery and bronze plaques that hang in prominent hallways, often fading quickly from active memory.

This implicit range of meaning crowds the room where discussions of mission occur. What, exactly, is the mission of a theological school? When a dean works with the faculty, the importance of that question cannot be minimized for several reasons. At a bare minimum, a school's mission is a large, directional signpost that points toward the institution's purpose. A school's denominational affiliation, or lack thereof, has a formational influence on the institution's understanding of and commitment to its missional objective. How does it understand its relation to the church? Is the school in blind service to its denomination or tradition? Does it embrace the role of reformer, or even a prophetic voice? How does the question of mission shape faculty appointments and program development? How does the faculty's implicit agenda complement or detract from the school's mission? Questions such as these are embedded in any full, frank consideration about the dean's work with the faculty to develop and serve the mission of the school. Taken together, they illustrate that questions of institutional authority, process, and purpose are interwoven into considerations of a school's mission.

Institutional Clarity

I write from the perspective of a deanship in a Friends' seminary. In our tradition, hierarchy is suspect, and authority is joyfully disparaged in our monthly meetings (Friends' terminology for the local congregation) in a quest for Spirit-filled worship and egalitarian decision making. It is impossible for an educational institution to operate in the exact same manner as a monthly meeting. Even so, many of these suspicions and operative assumptions about hierarchy and authority accompany faculty, students, and other constituents as they observe or engage in work related to the seminary because we Friends have not developed clear organizational principles or leadership strategies for multilayered organizations, including educational ones. For this reason, a discussion of mission benefits from an initial focus on organizational clarity with regard to governance authority and process. I doubt that Friends are the only group for whom such a starting point would be beneficial.

From a foundational perspective, no document is more important in developing a school's mission than its governance documents. These documents do not typically describe mission, but they do specify areas of authority within the institution. In particular, they point to the governance that is shared by the trustees and the faculty — a fact that can quickly fade in daily operations.

In my opinion, no group is more important in discussions of mission than the board of trustees. They have legal authority over operations, activities, and properties of the school. In Earlham's governance documents, they have the responsibility to set the mission of the school, on recommendation of the faculty and after consultation with appropriate constituents. This highlights the importance of selection and education of board members. In all probability, a dean will have little influence over the selection of trustees, but the task of education is one that should be eagerly embraced. The better board members understand the motives and commitments of theological education within their specific context, the better they can contribute to the development and support of a school's mission in ways the faculty can appreciate as complementary in a shared governance process.

A school's governance documents should also articulate the role of the faculty in the development of mission and programs as well as the process by which these commitments are created. A school's denominational and philosophical commitments will shape the operational processes adopted. Traditions that endorse hierarchy and endow particular positions with elevated authority may require less consultation about decisions related to mission. In contrast, traditions such as my own encourage broad consultation in decision making, and the governance documents reflect those expectations.

Regardless of a school's adopted form of governance, two important guiding questions a dean should ask early and often with regard to mission are: "Whose decision is this to make? And, as a consequence of what process?" In governance documents, the board of trustees typically delegates the design and implementation of programs to the faculty, reserving for itself the right to approve and oversee such programs. The faculty, then, has a tremendous burden of responsibility to understand the school's institutional commitments as it develops programs and to utilize research interests and teaching skills in ways that contribute substantially to the overarching mission of the school as it educates its students. As this process unfolds, some decisions belong to the board, others to the faculty, and still others to the president, dean, or administration. The group responsible for making the decision may or may not delegate some portion of the project to a committee or an external consultant. Some decisions are to be made after broad consultation or on the advice and recommendation of selected parties; other decisions could be made unilaterally. However that process unfolds, the path will be clearer if questions about authority and process are considered at the outset of the process rather than in the midst of disagreement about those very questions.

The development of a school's mission, in any meaningful sense, is a complex process involving various groups. As a dean works with the faculty, clarity of authority and process contributes to the health of discussions and decisions about mission. Attention to this detail helps prepare the group for animated and opinionated conversations that are sure to follow, while minimizing the probability of stalemates and political tug-of-war resulting from organizational conflict and power struggles.

Institutional Commitments

The dean is the school's chief academic officer, but the dean does not decide a school's mission alone. Neither does the president or faculty. For that matter, a board of trustees does not operate in a vacuum. Schools exist to serve a clientele — or a constituent base, as we prefer to call them. Like any other business, theological schools need to understand their market. This understanding identifies various stakeholders and helps a school acknowledge its institutional commitments.

Numerous groups form a theological school's constituent base. As in a blended family, each of these groups has a personal history and unique interest even as it expects similar benefits from being included in the institutional circle of insiders. These numerous stakeholders contribute to the formation of the school's mission.

For a theological school, the church is obviously an important constituent. Some need or vision in a particular wing of Christendom spawns the formation of every theological school. The motives for these new creations vary — a better education, more holistic preparation for ministry, or stronger attention to a particular emphasis in spiritual and theological formation. Any number of just and good causes form the base upon which these schools are founded. Alongside these motivations, dollars and energy are invested into the dream. Whether denominational bodies or individual donors, those who invest in the vision expect a return on their investment! The group that helps establish the institution expects to reap the fruits of leadership and ministry from the school's graduates. They also provide gainful employment to many graduates. Consequently, awareness of the church's needs and expectations is important as a school develops its mission. A school that ignores this relationship may well witness an increasing heap of disastrous encounters, a pool of disillusioned alumni/ae, and a long line of angry constituents who question the legitimacy of the school's programs and the integrity of its mission.

Alumni/ae, too, have a vested interest in their alma mater. They incarnate the most credible witness with regard to a school's mission, regardless of what an institution's glossy brochures say or what its faculty thinks about how it conducts its mission. As they provide living testimony to a school's competency with regard to mission, they also experience firsthand the difficulties of translating educational accomplishments into competent ministry. A dean and faculty can learn much about how well the school is fulfilling its mission by observing and listening to the successes and failures of its graduates. And these alumni/ae can provide valuable feedback to the school with regard to needed adjustments and changes to a curriculum as they experience and adjust to the changing cultural contexts in which ministry occurs.

The voice of current students should contribute to conversations about mission as well. These men and women make numerous sacrifices in order to answer their calls to ministry. Decisions about mission that affect programs and curricula have an immediate impact on their dreams and expectations. However, current students are to a school what water is to a river. They fill a school in a particular moment of time. They depend on the riverbed to help them along the way, and they themselves contribute to the quality of the river in that moment. But like the river, they are always passing through. Though they will be forever affected by the experience, they do not bear long-term or ultimate responsibility for the mission or the programs that develop to support it. For that reason, their voice should be heard, but they are not the only, or primary, contributor to the conversation.

Any list of stakeholders must include the faculty. Individual faculty members have a vested interest in the formulation of mission and a tremendous influence on the design of programs developed to support it. They have the educational pedigree to be leaders in theological education. Teaching in a theological school represents their life's work and quite possibly is their own gift of ministry to God, church, and world. It is a gift that has come with great price. In all probability, their own process of theological education led to some degree of deconstruction of their faith and understanding of the church; hopefully, a subsequent reconstruction occurred as well. It is extremely important that professors in theological schools "make their peace" with the church if they are going to prepare leaders to serve it. Having critiqued the tradition in its many manifestations and judged its sins, faculty members need also to love God and church. The maintenance of personal integrity and the balance of roles as encourager and prophetic voice are delicate matters, but ones that are necessary if a school's mission is to contribute toward a better future.

It is one thing to name these various stakeholders; it is quite another thing to actually engage them in meaningful conversation. How a dean decides to engage these constituents in conversations about mission will vary according to the nuances of denominational affiliation and structure, but the value — even the necessity — of engaging these constituents should not be overlooked. Here are a few of the things we have tried at Earlham School of Religion:

- A national consultation with our constituents, overseen by an external consultant. We asked Friends about their hopes and their fears for the future. We also invited critique of our work as a school that prepares persons for ministry. After the consultation, we returned to every area where a focus group had been held in order to share the results of what we learned and to gather additional feedback.
- A strategic planning process that involved representatives from all groups of the institutional family: faculty, students, alumni/ae, advisors, and trustees. This collaborative process built upon the data gathered in the national consultation. The resulting plan easily gained the approval of faculty, advisors, and trustees. Once approved, it provided clear guidance on the initiatives that would support development and implementation of the mission.
- Regular dinner conversation opportunities around the country with alumni/ae, denominational leaders, and friends of the school. During these events we asked them, and we continue to ask them, to think with us about topics that occupy the minds of our faculty. For instance, we recently asked them to help us think about the church's changing needs in the twenty-first century and how that affects the abilities and skills that seminary graduates need.
- Faculty retreats and working lunches to discuss issues surrounding mission, pedagogy, curriculum revision, and assessment. During these occasions, each faculty member was asked to take responsibility for understanding and sharing with colleagues one academic writing devoted to these topics. This strategy built competency, confidence, and collegiality among our group and generated an enthusiasm for becoming better teachers.
- The creation of a speaker's bureau, which we named *Traveling Ministries,* that provides opportunities for faculty to offer workshops and retreats to our monthly meetings. It is a public relations jewel, in that it demonstrates our investment and care in the life of the local congregation. It has the additional benefits of allowing our faculty to contribute to the formation and life of the congregation outside the classroom, building familiarity between the faculty and our constituents, and allowing our faculty to hear firsthand of the concerns and interests of persons at the grassroots of our constituent base.

Opportunities such as these provide fresh, relevant information for a faculty as it considers missional objectives. At Earlham, it is easy to point to certain historic Friends' testimonies that shape our mission: a reliance upon the Holy Spirit to illumine the meaning of the Bible; the spiritual discernment of leanings toward ministry; development of the interior life as a means of knowing God; a commitment to universal ministry; the prominence of historical positions about peace, simplicity, equality, and integrity as manifestations of faithful living. Our faculty can easily build upon that base with the expertise they bring from their particular disciplines and create a curriculum that makes functional sense. Engagement in meaningful conversation among the various constituent groups, however, allows the faculty to think about mission with an understanding of contemporary relevance. This perspective is a contribution to the process that a faculty, however talented, cannot produce on its own.

These various opinions and visions can contribute toward a stronger school and more effective mission together than would occur separately. It is the dean's task to create avenues of communication that accomplish these things: listens to the concerns of those with a vested interest in the educational program of the school; focuses attention on issues to which the school needs to attend; and engages the faculty's consideration of this feedback so that the mission it formulates reflects the needs and concerns of the constituents the school intends to serve. At stake is a holistic understanding of the school's mission, along with its resources and challenges. This is the seedbed from which good and credible vision grows.

Leadership Strategies

When adequate attention has been given to issues related to clarity of process and engagement with relevant constituents, the dean's ability to lead the faculty moves to the foreground of the process. For this to function well, the dean needs to have earned the trust of the faculty. Particularly given the positions of Friends with respect to leadership, and perhaps in academic settings in general, trust doesn't come easily (an ironic tragedy, really, since trust and ministry preparation are inseparable). Trust is built upon established patterns of genuine interest and professional integrity. It does not occur overnight, but some leadership strategies are conducive to the establishment of trust. Regardless of what authority or power is attached to the office of the dean, achieved influence with the faculty is an effective leadership base for an academic setting.

Current trends in leadership studies recognize the value of thinking about the *context* in which leaders serve, rather than focusing exclusively on the character or traits of the individual leader. This shift acknowledges that effective leaders invest time in creating a culture that permits leadership to occur easily and that encourages authenticity and commitment alongside creativity. This type of leader offers acceptance to those with whom they work, but does so without sacrificing accountability. Applied to the work of a chief academic officer, this implies that the dean has responsibility for creating an environment that encourages active participation by the faculty while holding them accountable to the prerogatives of the institution's mission.

Cultivating positive relationships with and among the members of the faculty is a valuable investment of a dean's time and resources. For Earlham, faculty trips to sites in England associated with Friends' origination, to Honduras for cultural immersion, and to off-campus sites for multi-day retreats were instrumental in developing the trust and collegiality we needed to work well together in all aspects of our work. From London, England, to Copan, Honduras, to French Lick, Indiana, we have dined like royalty, lived with the locals, volunteered in an orphanage, felt like babbling fools while trying to learn a new language, and learned from one another about our passions for teaching and ministry. We now share more than office space and health insurance plans. Creating an environment where knowledge of one another leads to appreciation and respect is time well spent in a dean's work with the faculty.

Another facet of a dean's leadership is that of interpreting the mission to the faculty. It is not that the dean is the only one who understands the mission; it is, however, the dean's responsibility to remember it, even if no one else cares to do so. The development of programs that support the mission is the work of the faculty as a whole. So long as the various components of degree programs support program objectives and those objectives connect clearly with a school's mission, this need not be a difficult task. The challenge can be to motivate individual faculty to see themselves as members of a collaborative team rather than advocates of a particular field of study or methodological approach. As the faculty deliberates about program structure and content, the dean raises the question of relevance to the mission, articulates the broad objectives of programs, and invites faculty members to imagine their contribution to the larger goals. In these discussions, the mission must be cast as primary, for truly it is the institution's *raison d'etre.*

This interpretation is more than just a reminder of the primacy of mission; it is also an interpretation of the relevancy of the mission. Denominational spats and suspicions can leave faculty members feeling distant from or hostile toward certain constituent groups. The frustrations many theological educators have with the church's participation in oppression, its inability to address changing social context, or the marginalization of Christianity in much of Western culture can create significant doubt about the wisdom of embracing ministry as a vocation. The resulting sense of isolation can tempt faculty members to concentrate on the individual formation of students without careful thought about their ability to offer transformative leadership in entrenched religious institutions — an outcome that would likely be evaluated as a failure by some constituent groups. The deep commitment to students is to be admired, but graduates will want a place to serve. For reasons such as these, a dean's work includes helping faculty members process and overcome their suspicions, woundedness, and cynicism so that as a collective whole the faculty can embrace its work as making a valuable contribution to God's work and the church's ministry. Any work worth an investment of a faculty's time and energy needs to be relevant.

Alongside relevance, a dean must make a case for feasibility of the mission, as well as apply that same criterion to the suggestions of others. Not every ambition can be managed, nor should it be. Particularly in theological education, schools can be saddled with a messiah complex when their constituents look to them to solve every challenge the world and the church face. A school's adopted mission should match its resources. This is true in terms of personnel, financial resources, the pool of prospective and current students, and job placement opportunities for graduates. Even while encouraging the faculty to new heights appropriate to its mission, for the sake of all involved, the dean must help the group discern what programming is feasible to implement the mission.

When a faculty accepts the responsibility to develop a relevant program appropriate to its mission, a dean will need to accept the role of the visionary. However, I use that term a bit differently than it is used in some standard understandings of leadership. Rather than the dean being one who creates the vision for adoption by the faculty and trustees, a dean better serves the institution by facilitating conversations that allow the rough ingredients of the vision to emerge. The dean gathers those ingredients and begins to develop them, offering them back to the group for revision and commentary. This collaborative process is time consuming, to be sure; however, it allows for collegial participation appropriate to an academic institution. When conducted successfully, collaborative processes build consensus within the group. Participants invest in the process and subsequently are more likely to commit to its implementation.

Visionary leadership of this nature requires specific commitments on the part of the dean. First, this type of vision casting demands a commitment to the mission and to the collaborative process of shared governance, coupled with a resistance of the temptation to control the precise details of the outcome. A dean invests a huge amount of energy in the development of mission and will no doubt have to contend with a few delicate or belligerent personalities. For that reason, a dean who can remain partially detached from the process so that critiques and revisions to the developing plans do not feel like personal rejection will fare better than one who cannot maintain the required distance.

Second, a dean who will commit to helping the faculty to imagine beyond its current commitments increases the possibility of creating a progressive mission that develops over time. This requires creativity and inspiration, not to mention a willingness to gently push involved parties to step outside their comfort zones. One of the most meaningful compliments I have received as a dean was a third party report about a retired faculty member who indicated that I had helped him believe he could do things he never would have imagined on his own.

Third, this type of visionary leadership requires a commitment to speak candidly, though respectfully, with all parties of the institutional family as this process moves along. This models transparency and integrity to all involved; what one can model, one can also request from other participants in the conversation.

Finally, as a dean leads the faculty's development of mission, it is important to make space for the work to occur. This helps combat at least two natural culprits always at work within the institution. First, as every semester unfolds, teaching requirements, schedule demands, the current research or writing passion, and student controversies, as examples, quickly capture the faculty's attention, as well they should. Matters such as these can carry good, dedicated faculty members down isolated paths where attention to minute details or the demands of the moment can blur the larger picture of mission or distract the faculty from giving it sufficient attention. In addition, faculty members can feel overworked, particularly in the midst of the details. When that is the case, little energy or interest remains for envisioning, assessing, or improving their service of the mission. Given the workweeks and conditions of most of the world's workforce, I confess that I have little patience when a faculty complains of being overworked. We have, in nearly every way imaginable, a protected and comfortable life. On my better days, I hold my tongue and work to create enough sacred space that the needed work can occur. A working lunch here, a retreat there, a course reduction when appropriate — small gestures like these send strong messages of value and support and create space for the continuing work related to the institution's mission.

Mission is more than an ominous word; it is a demanding task that needs to sit at the center of a school's self-understanding, programming, and assessment. The task of overseeing that work falls to the chief academic officer. Good governance, engaged constituents, a committed faculty, and a dean gifted with a capacity to lead, are key in the development and implementation of a mission appropriate to a school. When all are present, a school is well anchored and positioned to thrive.

ADDITIONAL RESOURCES

Northouse, Peter G. *Leadership Theory and Practice.* 4th ed. Thousand Oaks, CA: Sage Publications, 2007.

Palmer, Parker. *Let Your Life Speak: Listening for the Voice of Vocation.* San Francisco: Jossey Bass, 1999.

Palomba, Catherine A., and Trudy Banta, eds. *Assessing Student Competence in Accredited Disciplines.* Sterling, VA: Sylus, 2001.

Thrall, Bill, Bruce McNicol, and Ken McElrath. *The Ascent of a Leader: How Ordinary Relationships Develop Extraordinary Character and Influence.* San Francisco: Jossey-Bass, 1999.

From *Vision* to *Decision*: Identifying the Dean's Essential Role in Facilitating the School's Mission

Richard Benson

Being the dean can be too much headache and heartache when there is no vision. *Is this a job I really want? Didn't I go to school to become a professor?*

When will I get a chance to return to my real vocation as scholar? All this administration is holding me back from my research. Why are some of my colleagues angry with me? Maybe it's time to let someone else do this job. So many tasks occupy the time of the academic dean: faculty development, curriculum revision, faculty recruitment, developing learning outcome and degree assessment protocols, assessing transfer credits, reviewing foreign transcripts, updating the faculty handbook, conflict management, setting academic priorities, course evaluations, annual performance reviews for academic office staff, and the list can go on. Many of these tasks come with the dean's office, and some are unavoidably essential and a necessary part of every day. Others, just as important or even more so, come around every semester or every year and are a natural part of the school's academic rhythm. Still others, like self-studies and accreditation visits, come regularly but only every so many years. Some issues just walk into the dean's office, e.g., a student with a concern or question, a faculty member with a thorny issue, or even a school president with another "great" idea for the dean to develop and implement (prior to the next board meeting). It's not hard for every dean to understand what the poet Andrew Marvell meant when he wrote the famous lines, "Had we but world enough, and time. . . . But at my back I always hear, time's winged chariot hurrying near[!]"[1]

It's fairly easy for any dean, doing a credible job, simply to get caught up in a maelstrom of tasks that are essential but that can drain the energy, and sadly even the life and joy, out of any administrator. I don't believe the best response is to resign and retreat into a life of contemplation, as tempting as that might seem, even if it were possible. The answer, at least partly, is for the dean to fully engage in the process of dreaming and envisioning that provides a focus for the many tasks. And the goal is that the dream does not belong solely to the dean but is the corporate dream of the school. To borrow a Native American image, the dean can be the "dream catcher" of the school.

The dream is so important because without the dream, without the vision, the tasks that take up so much of the dean's time have limited impact precisely because they may seem to be simply beads on a string or autonomous moments linked together to form an impossibly busy day. When tasks are part of a dream, when they play a part in a school's vision, they become threads that make up a tapestry, and the tapestry that the school creates is

1. A. T. Quiller-Couch, ed., *The Oxford Book of English Verse* (Oxford: Clarendon, 1919 [c. 1901]).

the enfleshed mission of the school, the mission that is the very *raison d'etre* of the school's existence.

The Anatomy of a Vision

There are at least two essential aspects to every authentic vision that animates and gives life and direction to a school. First is the work of developing or claiming a corporate vision shared by the faculty, administration, and board, and second is the engagement of the school in that vision. When this process is occurring in a school, the dean's role takes on a new meaning. It certainly doesn't diminish the workload and transform the necessary tasks, but it does give meaning, and when there is genuine meaning, then it is possible for the tasks to generate energy, not simply use it up.

Essential to engagement in the vision is planning. The purpose of the planning is to make the mission even more effective. A vision is only helpful when it is transformed into a matrix, a skeleton that supports the mission and allows it to take on a more vibrant spirit.

The Dean, the Mission, and the Vision

Hopefully every dean is a dean at a theological school because of a deep commitment to the church and the school's participation in a greater mission. This allows the dean to re-vision a job into something more, a vocation. The vocation of dean is one that entails both serving the *communio* of colleagues at the school, participating with them, shoulder to shoulder, and corporately serving the people of God. This vocation demands balance and boundaries. The dean balances life as both an administrator working hand in glove with the CEO and a colleague in the faculty. A healthy balance is made possible to some extent by maintaining healthy boundaries that are both transparent and at times appropriately opaque.

The dream or vision originates in the school's mission. In that sense the school's mission is the alpha and the omega, the beginning and the end, the starting point and the ending point. The school's mission provides the impetus for the vision and serves as the ultimate assessment tool for the whole institution. A good theological school must by its very nature be mission driven. A school that allows itself to be "personality driven," or that lurches from one ad hoc decision to another, is a school that rarely accomplishes its mission.

The Importance of the Mission Statement

One of the most important moments for every good theological school is the end of the year. If it is simply a time for everyone to slump into a chair and celebrate another "end," then it is possible to wonder what the point of the year was. For the school with a vision, the end-of-the-year degree conferral is a moment when the school celebrates its mission, the vision is renewed, and the end ratifies why we began.

If the school has a generally understood and corporately owned mission that is articulated well, then the dean is in a great position to understand the tasks that make up so much of the job. If that is not the case, then a good dean's first task is to develop a strategy to work with the president, executive council, faculty, and board to produce a mission statement that articulates clearly why the school exists. Without such a purpose statement and corporate ownership of it by all the stakeholders in general, the school can hardly be more than a degree factory, if that.

A good mission statement is *the essential starting point* for a dean. A mission statement represents the school's corporate aspirations. It provides the basis for policy decisions, for academic programs, and for assessment. The mission statement is the essence of the school's dream. It also is very practical because it is a compass, and when it is known and shared, the school can measure its progress toward the goals it has set for itself. In short, the mission statement is the most essential navigational tool for the school and consequently for the dean.

The mission statement first and foremost must be a "mission" statement. While that may seem to be a tautological declaration, sometimes a mission statement is significantly less than a mission statement. It may have devolved over time into a "maintenance" statement, wherein the school articulates its primary aim as simply to keep itself from going out of business. While maintenance is important, since the viability of every school is essential to enabling the school's mission to happen, maintenance shouldn't be confused with mission. The mission statement should both encompass and venture well beyond maintenance. Mission even goes beyond articulating what the school wants to "be." A mission statement is what the school covenants to accomplish, what it promises its stakeholders to "do." A mission statement describes the dream about how the school will make a profound difference in the world today.

A good mission statement, like a good dean, is a "dream catcher." By itself it animates the whole community of the school: administration, students, staff, and faculty. Everyone plays a part in a project that is beyond any individual. When the mission is articulated, grasped, and owned, the dean can begin to play a part in making the school's impact felt, in helping the school make a difference in the world.

Developing a Shared Vision

On the other hand, the vision must be both grounded and practical. A school's vision, whether it is articulated formally in a "vision statement" or in other, less formal ways, expresses "how" the mission statement is being implemented in the policies and programs that make up the daily life of the school. Proof that a school operates from a vision that throbs with life is found in the apparently mundane details of institutional reality in the handbooks, policies, and traditions of the school. In other words, where the vision is alive, one can find a consistency between praxis and vocabulary that expresses and enables both the affective and effective aspects of the school's mission. The community can feel the mission through the living vision.

The dean is often a trailblazer of the vision. From this unique position, the dean is able to see much of what needs to be done and marshal the appropriate resources to make the school's mission even more effective. This can happen as a result of a three-step process.

Observe and Listen

A good dean takes the time to pay attention to the needs of the school. A good dean understands that he or she is primarily at the service of the faculty (although there are institutions that define the CAO as a representative of the president and thereby much more closely aligned to that office). The learning community of students and faculty is one of the dean's greatest resources. This group should never represent in the mind of the dean a "problem to be solved" but rather a vast resource of talent to be animated to the service of the school's mission.

1. Engage this community in an energetic discussion about the school's mission. Exegete the mission statement together. Is it clear to everyone? Is it owned by faculty? Do the students see the mission embodied in the courses, the degrees, and the school's climate? Can everyone at

the school — board of directors, students, staff, faculty, and administration — accurately summarize the mission statement and articulate what part they play in making it effective at the school?

2. Ask the faculty what they need to better accomplish their role in mission. Technology, classroom space, office space, development funds, sabbatical policies, work loads, salary, curriculum review, and faculty recruitment may be issues that need to be considered if one or more of these issues is compromising the school's ability to more effectively accomplish its mission. A good dean is willing to enter into this conversation even with the knowledge that resources are limited. A dean does his or her level best to lobby on behalf of the faculty when the mission is the focus. Without a mission focus, the dean can get caught in endless discussions about what amount to "ad hoc" needs that are all too often more "personality driven" than mission driven.

3. Listen to the students, alumni/ae, and other stakeholders of the school. These are a great source of knowledge about the effectiveness of the school. A good dean makes some provision for exit interviews with departing students, both those who are abandoning their programs and those who are completing them, asking about their experiences in light of the school's mission. In larger schools the dean may not be able to do all of these personally. Asking alumni/ae and other stakeholders about how the school prepared graduates for their future positions is also an invaluable source of information. These conversations feed the vision of the dean and provide some clear direction as to what needs to be and can be done more effectively.

4. Participate in meetings and conferences with deans from other schools. Listen and share with other deans about how they have been successful in developing a vision that is practical, life-giving, and supportive of the school's mission. A dean who chooses to be isolated from meetings and conferences may find a short-term solution to time and budget constraints but in the long term will run the risk of sabotaging the possibility of discovering and envisioning with the faculty ways for the school to be more effective. A dean who returns from a conference may be confronted with faculty who fear the introduction of "another idea" that means even more uncompensated work for a faculty that is already tired, but a dean who does not listen to the larger community of similarly committed professionals is missing one of the most important ways to stay engaged in imagining the dream and finding practical solutions to practical problems.

Listening is a posture of learning and respect. Listening tells a healthy faculty that the dean knows that every one of them has a piece of the vision, an insight, a part of the truth that can be of help in making it possible for the school to be even more effective, to make more of a difference. A dean who listens is also giving evidence of being a learner. A dean must be open to learning how to be a better dean.

Discern and Judge

A dean who is a good listener will soon learn what is needed to help the school be more effective in its mission. Almost no one has unlimited resources, however, whether of time, money, or facilities. So a good dean begins to craft a vision that is doable. What kind of technology is needed and affordable? How many working ad hoc committees can the faculty afford to engage in while carrying on their regular work schedules? What will the president and board approve? A good dean should learn how to keep a faculty engaged and on task without becoming taxed and weary.

1. Prioritize. The dean needs to look at the needs of the school and realistically assess what are the most important needs for the mission. This may form the heart of a long-term but viable vision. This vision will effectively allow the dean to make difficult decisions but to explain them in light of the mission.
2. Compartmentalize. This allows the dean to work and be fully engaged in a task without trying to do everything at the same time. Be satisfied with doing well with one thing at a time. Do the ordinary tasks that need to be done, but at the same time never lose sight of those other tasks that engage the imagination of the school. The energy of the imagination is not as limited as the energy of our bodies, but the imagination drives the soul and will help the dean stay engaged in the mission and moving the mission forward.

Act and Decide

Ultimately a capable dean is not afraid of making a decision and acting on it after thoughtful consideration. A vision demands praxis. Every fruitful vision eventually evolves into actions, choices, and decisions that give life to a school's direction. As an administrator, the dean has both the responsibility and the authority to help the faculty and administration shepherd the school's academic vision.

A good dean is ultimately a good steward. After assessing what changes will make the school more effective in its mission, the dean is in a unique position in the school to provide the infrastructure that will help support and even drive the positive changes envisioned. Good stewardship will challenge the dean to use the school's resources that are available to enable and sustain a new matrix designed to move the school's mission. At the same time, the dean's position as an administrator enables lobbying of the president and board to garner additional resources to bring the school's vision alive.

When the vision results in a more effective mission, it is inevitable that the dean has been effective in both helping the school develop a credible dream and bringing that dream to life. Curricular revision, technological infrastructure, distance education initiatives, faculty recruitment, diversity concerns and plans, and degree programs are just some of the load-bearing struts in a school's matrix, but when they are solidly connected to a vision, they become prophetic and not simply bureaucratic.

The good dean goes beyond being a good administrator to being prophetic. The prophetic aspect does not neglect the importance of administrative abilities. By all means, a good dean can multi-task, manage an office and staff, and produce quality reports, while at the same time being able to meet the needs of the students and faculty who make up the learning community. No good theological school can be effective without a competent academic administrator. But beyond administration is the call to be prophetic. A dean is prophetic when he or she envisions where the school can go — and in fact needs to go — in order to be more effective and is able to articulate that vision and challenge the faculty to move there. The call to be a prophet is at the heart of the academic dean in a theological institution. It is too easy to settle for academic "maintenance," i.e., churning out the work that needs to be done in order to keep the ship afloat. The good dean accomplishes well all that is essential to maintaining the academic excellence of the school but then moves to "mission." The mission becomes the goal that attracts the dean to ever new and creative challenges, bringing the school closer and closer to the excellence it desires. A prophet "sees" what needs to be seen and holds that up for others to recognize. The prophet denounces what needs to be denounced (old programs, outdated degrees, underperforming departments) and also points to what is essential to meet the needs of the emerging church (new programs, new technology, new faculty, rich and ongoing assessment, etc.).

Celebrating the Mission

Returning to the moment when the faculty considers the conclusion of another academic year allows us to measure the strength of the vision. When the faculty can rejoice and bask in the glow of a mission well done; when a faculty can sense that students have learned to think critically and theologically, have developed scholarly skills and obtained pastoral competencies; when learning and degree outcomes are evident in a school's graduates; and when the faculty senses that the school is essentially accomplishing its mission, then it is possible to enjoy the weariness of hard work, because in all the tasks a deeper meaning can be found. The dean can take satisfaction in having played an essential part in enabling the school to articulate its vision and then in helping shepherd the vision from dream to reality.

ADDITIONAL RESOURCES

Greenleaf, Robert K. *Servant Leadership: A Journey into the Nature of Legitimate Power and Greatness, 25th Anniversary Edition.* Edited by Larry C. Spears. Mahwah, NJ: Paulist Press, 1977, 2002.

Kantonen, T. A. *Theology for Christian Stewardship.* Philadelphia: Muhlenberg Press, 1956.

Nessan, Craig L. *Beyond Maintenance to Mission: A Theology of the Congregation.* Minneapolis: Fortress Press, 1999.

Rivers, Robert S. *From Maintenance to Mission: Evangelization and the Revitalization of the Parish.* New York: Paulist Press, 2005.

Warford, Malcolm L., ed. *Practical Wisdom on Theological Teaching and Learning.* New York: Peter Lang Publishing, 2004.

3. The Vocational Call and Multifaceted Role of the CAO

The Vocation of the Academic Dean

Stephen R. Graham

Over the years I have become convinced that there is a distinctive calling to the good work of academic administration, in particular, for the purposes of this volume, to the vocation of the academic dean. As William Placher has put it, "To believe a wise and good God is in charge of things implies that there is a fit between things that need doing and the person I am meant to be. Finding such a fit, I find my calling."[1] That fit, for some, for a time at least, is to serve as academic dean in a theological school.

The first vocation of those of us who are believers is the calling to be disciples of Jesus. Any vocation to a particular work, place, or role is based on that foundation of discipleship. As Lovett Weems puts it, "Our calling from God represents the essence of our spiritual identity," and Christian leaders "must see all leadership rooted in what God has called them to be and do. But for Christian leaders, calling has additional dimensions."[2] One of the challenges of the secondary calling of academic administration is that

1. William C. Placher, "Introduction," in *Callings: Twenty Centuries of Christian Wisdom on Vocation*, ed. William C. Placher (Grand Rapids: Eerdmans, 2005), p. 3.
2. Lovett H. Weems, Jr., "Leadership as a Channel of God's Grace," a presentation to the Chief Academic Officers Society of the Association of Theological Schools in the United States and Canada, Vancouver, British Columbia, March 22, 2007, pp. 2-3.

it can place a strain on that primary calling, especially since the work we take up in academic administration has many dimensions, and each may have the lure of a "call" in and of itself. To be a theological educator, for example, involves the complex calling of attending to the demands of our scholarly guild — increasingly difficult to do! — and to attend to the *particular* role of serving the church. The complexity of living out one's Christian vocation in academic administration involves constant reflection and choice-making about how to negotiate these various dimensions of faithfulness in one's occupational call so that the primary calling to be a disciple stays foundational — this is no easy task.

Academic administration adds additional layers of complexity and demand to this vocation. It is something like the calls we hear to revise the curriculum. You are pressed to add and add, but it is almost impossible to drop anything! The academic dean *needs* to continue working as a scholar and teacher *in addition to* the multitude of tasks that come with the deanship. It is work that not many can or should do, but it is marvelous work for those called to it.

The Vocation to and Perils of Leadership

As an academic dean, I found myself drawn to the *Pastoral Rule* of Pope Gregory I (the Great). Gregory reflects with depth and wisdom on the vocation to and perils of leadership, in particular those related to the office of bishop. Without equating the two, I believe these insights apply fittingly to the office of academic dean. For example, Gregory notes that "often the case of government, when undertaken, distracts the heart in divers directions; and one is found unequal to dealing with particular things, while with confused mind divided among many."[3] What an appropriate description of the deanship!

The majority of academic deans in theological schools come from within the ranks of the faculty. About two-thirds of deans come to their positions from faculty roles, almost half from within the same institution. Another 25 percent have previously served in other roles as administrators, 11 percent at the same institution, 7 percent at another theological school.[4]

---

3. Gregory the Great, *Pastoral Rule,* in *A Select Library of Nicene and Post-Nicene Fathers of the Christian Church,* ed. Philip Schaff and Henry Wace, second series, volume XII, *Leo the Great, Gregory the Great* (Grand Rapids: Eerdmans, 1964), part 1, p. 3 (chapter 4).

4. Jeanne P. McLean, *Leading from the Center: The Emerging Role of the Chief Academic Officer in Theological Schools* (Atlanta: Scholars Press, 1999), p. 193. McLean's volume

There are those within the faculty who have the skills and aptitudes (at least in latent form) for academic administration but who are reluctant to take on the role — for legitimate reasons. Gregory speaks to that reluctance to accept the burdens of leadership and the calling that comes to do so as well as the personal and institutional consequences that may follow. "Truly such as these, if when called they refuse to undertake offices of supreme rule, for the most part deprive themselves of the very gifts which they received not for themselves alone, but for others also."[5] He continues:

> And so there are some, as we have said, enriched with great gifts, who, while they are ardent for the studies of contemplation only, shrink from serving to their neighbor's benefit by preaching; they love a secret place of quiet, they long for a retreat for speculation. With respect to which conduct, they are, if strictly judged, undoubtedly guilty in proportion to the greatness of the gifts whereby they might have been publicly useful.[6]

To paraphrase the epistle to Timothy, "a person who desires the office of an academic dean desires a good thing!"

Through the next few chapters of the treatise, Gregory names some of the qualities necessary for leadership of this kind. There is a need for humility. If a person doesn't have it already, it won't be found in the deanship. "For one can by no means learn humility in a high place who has not ceased to be proud while occupying a low one."[7] (For the sake of argument, let's grant that the deanship is a "high place" at least in the sense of including a great deal of responsibility, if not necessarily always prestige or respect!)

Gregory goes on to say that the candidate for leadership must be one "who already lives spiritually, dying to all passions of the flesh; who disregards worldly prosperity; who is afraid of no adversity; who desires only inward wealth."[8] This has to be a person "who out of affection of heart sympathizes with another's infirmity, and so rejoices in the good of his neighbor as though it were his own advantage." The academic deanship exists largely to help others be successful in their vocations. The dean is a leader but is necessarily a servant to others' agendas. As such, the dean's time is not his or her

---

is the most important study of the academic deanship in theological schools and is a very important resource for those considering the deanship or serving in that role.

5. Gregory the Great, *Pastoral Rule*, p. 4 (chapter 5).
6. Gregory the Great, *Pastoral Rule*, p. 5 (chapter 5).
7. Gregory the Great, *Pastoral Rule*, p. 6 (chapter 9).
8. Gregory the Great, *Pastoral Rule*, p. 7 (chapter 10).

own, but is given to the mission of the institution, the vision of the president, the needs of the faculty to help them fulfill their individual and shared vocations, and the needs of students whose learning is (or should be) the primary goal of the theological school.

It should be obvious, but perhaps needs to be stated, that the candidate for dean should be on good terms with most, if not all, institutional colleagues — faculty, staff, and president. If a person has a history of conflict with the people with whom positive relationships are essential for effectiveness in the position, the added stress and authority (whether only perceived or real) of the deanship will only accentuate the characteristics that provoked the conflicts in the first place. Conflict is not necessarily a bad thing, and maybe the school needs to have things shaken up, but it is volatile, and everyone should move into the situation with eyes wide open and understand the stresses the system can or cannot handle.

A final insight from the *Pastoral Rule* is the need for the leader to be willing to speak the truth in love. All of us want to be liked and respected, perhaps especially in the relatively small communities of our theological schools. Deans are placed in the difficult position, however, of having to make and communicate decisions that simply cannot please everyone. Gregory notes that "improvident rulers, fearing to lose human favor, shrink timidly from speaking freely the things that are right; and, according to the voice of the Truth (John 10:12), serve unto the custody of the flock by no means with the zeal of shepherds, but in the way of hirelings; since they fly when the wolf cometh if they hide themselves under silence."[9] He continues, "For the language of reproof is the key of discovery, because by chiding it discloses the fault of which even he who has committed it is often himself unaware."[10]

Yet the dean needs a deft touch and a sense of balance. "For whosoever superintends the healing of wounds must needs administer in wine the smart of pain, and in oil the softness of loving-kindness, to the end that through wine what is festering may be purged, and through oil what is curable may be soothed."[11]

So how does one discern whether those gifts are truly present? Gregory warns that "the mind itself lies to itself about itself."[12] Like any other calling, there need to be tests and collaborations of one's own perceptions.

---

9. Gregory the Great, *Pastoral Rule*, p. 11 (chapter 4).
10. Gregory the Great, *Pastoral Rule*, p. 11 (chapter 4).
11. Gregory the Great, *Pastoral Rule*, p. 16 (chapter 6).
12. Gregory the Great, *Pastoral Rule*, p. 6 (part 1, chapter 9).

Discernment of the Call

Theologian David Ford offers profoundly insightful reflections on the nature of vocation in his book *The Shape of Living: Spiritual Directions for Everyday Life*. He connects our deepest desires with our sense of God's calling. "A helpful exercise is to ask ourselves what our main life-shaping desires are. What do we most want to do and to be? What are the priorities we feel most deeply about?"[13] Our desires offer important insights into our calling, so long as our desires have been "educated" and shaped by our desire for God and God's desire for us. He notes Augustine's principle of "Love God and do what you like," meaning "if we get the desire for God right, everything else follows."[14]

One important question to ask oneself when reflecting on the possibility of accepting a call to become dean is whether there have been steps along your path that point in this general direction. Have particular doors opened while others closed? According to Ford, "Nothing is irrelevant to our vocation. We may have what feel like 'hidden years,' spent on apparently disconnected activities and 'details' without any great sense of integrating purpose, only to find later that the quality of those details has been crucial for fulfilling a life's work."[15] That was certainly the case in my situation and the sequence of events that led me to the deanship.

Like most of those who find themselves in seminary administration, I had no intention of doing so through my doctoral studies and well into my teaching career. I loved my discipline of American Church History, I loved teaching, I loved the life of being a member of the faculty and serving the church by teaching and writing. And I still do. I had been hired by the theological school of my home denomination, serving its only school, and thus occupying its only position in American Church History.

My school, like many others, though, faced some daunting financial issues. Seminary enrollment was not what it needed to be, and the larger institution of which the seminary was a part (then a college and since transitioned to be a university) had accumulated a long list of costly deferred maintenance projects. The president mandated deep budget cuts. As the most recent hire and one of the few non-tenured members of the faculty, I

---

13. David F. Ford, *The Shape of Living: Spiritual Directions for Everyday Life* (Grand Rapids: Baker, 1997), p. 51.

14. Ford, *The Shape of Living*, p. 56.

15. Ford, *The Shape of Living*, p. 59.

was told that my position was to be eliminated. With a wife and two small children to support and a recently signed mortgage to maintain, I was in big trouble.

Through an extraordinary set of circumstances, including advocacy by a denominational conference superintendent and pledges of financial support by the faculty, however, my position was saved. Part of the deal was that I would serve half-time as seminary registrar. This was one of those circumstances that make more sense and look better in hindsight, but I was pretty well organized, good with details, and accurate, and the time as registrar went pretty smoothly. I was able to put some good systems in place and learned to work with my faculty colleagues and the larger institution's administrative structures. There was satisfaction in that job when I could use my skills to make the systems work effectively for faculty and students. As many of those who work in student services can attest, though, being registrar is one of those positions in which you get little notice until something goes wrong. And often the things that went wrong were not due to my mistakes at all — though I made enough mistakes on my own! Part of the discipline of the position was learning to serve by helping correct the mistakes of others. This would be good training for my future as a dean!

Serving as registrar was also, in hindsight at least, good preparation for my later work as dean by providing experience in negotiating within the systems of the larger institution and getting seminary students and faculty the university services they needed, even though the seminary was a relatively small part of the overall institution. I learned a lot through this brief foray into administrative work.

In *The Shape of Living*, Ford names six "guiding sayings" that help discern what he calls "the right shape for life." These are also very helpful for those attempting to discern God's call and the call of the community to the leadership role of the academic deanship.

"First, seek and you will find." Ford explores the depth of this biblical phrase and notes that we have already been found by God and called by God, and we can approach God confidently about God's plan for us. Ford also gives a warning. "But beware: God tends to take us more seriously (and joyfully) than we take ourselves. As we timidly ask the big questions about the meaning and shape of our life, we are likely to find answers beyond anything we imagined."[16]

---

16. Ford, *The Shape of Living*, p. 74.

"Second, remember key events, periods, insights, and turning points of the past."[17] We need to pay attention to the signs, some quite subtle and others very plain, of the path God has designed for us. Who was it that said spiritual growth is largely about simply paying attention?

"Third, be alert for some key passages of the Bible to inhabit in a special way."[18] There may be persons, events, stories in the Bible that especially speak to us and our situations. As we come back to these key passages over the years, new dimensions open themselves to our understanding. During my tenure as dean, for example, I related at various times to the frustration and anger of Moses, feeling persecuted and misunderstood with Job, and pondering and praising with the psalmist.

"Fourth, be alert for role models and testimonies to how other people have found and developed their vocations."[19] Obviously, no two vocations or lives are identical, but there are models that can be particularly illuminating for us. Ford notes that there can be "friendships" spanning the centuries that can be sources of insight and illumination.

"Fifth, be looking for accompaniment in following a vocation."[20] Guides such as pastors, friends, spouses, and spiritual directors can provide important insight and confirmation or challenge. During a particularly difficult time in dealing with a case of serious misconduct by a faculty member, within appropriate boundaries of confidentiality I drew deeply on the guidance of a spiritual director, the experience of a particularly close friend, and the wisdom of a friend and golfing partner who was also a psychologist for my own health and wellbeing. Each in a different way affirmed me in my vocation during that especially challenging time and circumstance.

"Sixth, the theme running through all the above sayings is this: Be alert! That is a constant biblical theme: watchfulness, wakefulness, seeing, hearing. It is above all alertness to a God of surprises who is more fully alive and active than we are."[21] This imperative is particularly important and difficult for so many of us in the midst of the multitude of distractions among which we live.

17. Ford, *The Shape of Living*, p. 74.
18. Ford, *The Shape of Living*, p. 74.
19. Ford, *The Shape of Living*, p. 75.
20. Ford, *The Shape of Living*, p. 75.
21. Ford, *The Shape of Living*, p. 75.

The Worthiness of Academic Administration

One of the purposes of Jeanne McLean's appropriately titled study of the academic deanship in theological schools, *Leading from the Center*, was to "affirm the worthiness of the call to academic administration." She notes that academic deans across the spectrum of theological schools represent "capable, committed people, many of whom never aspired to administration," who "develop the skills and personal resources to serve successfully in the role." McLean honestly faces the difficulties of the role: "Everyone attests to the challenges of the job. Even the most skilled and experienced deans acknowledge their disappointments and failures; and even deans facing intractable personnel issues or daunting institutional problems speak of the job's satisfactions."[22]

McLean notes a number of theological school leaders who argue that there needs to be a new view of the calling to administration as not *contrary* to the vocation of teaching and scholarship but as a different aspect of the same calling. "A call to the academic life may be a call to teaching, scholarship, and/or administration, each of which is embraced by individuals differently according to their aptitudes and interests, and may be the focus at different times in a person's professional life."[23] I would note as well that academic administration requires scholarship and teaching, though that scholarship and teaching will sometimes be in the area of theological education or administration rather than in the specialty discipline in which the person was trained. "Consequently," McLean notes,

> the shift from serving primarily as a teacher to serving primarily as an administrator is not a change *of* vocation, but a change *within* a vocation. The academic vocation is rich in the options it holds. Administration is not a sell-out or a loss of that vocation, but simply another way of responding to the call to the academic life and to service of the theological school community.[24]

22. McLean, *Leading from the Center*, pp. 3-4.
23. McLean, *Leading from the Center*, p. 259.
24. McLean, *Leading from the Center*, pp. 259-60. Indeed, McLean cites the work of Neely McCarter and Raymond Rodriguez, both of whom argue that the role of academic administration requires being a scholar and teacher. Rodriguez, for example, speaks of "the scholarship of administration." See Raymond J. Rodriguez, "Campus Administrators as Practicing Scholars," *The Chronicle of Higher Education* 39, no. 26 (March 3, 1993), B3, and Neely Dixon McCarter, *The President as Educator: A Study of the Seminary Presidency* (Atlanta: Scholars Press, 1996), pp. 43-62.

Those of us in academic administration are called first to be Christian disciples. Growing out of that calling, most of us followed a path of scholarship, earning advanced degrees in a theological discipline and then joining a faculty with the responsibility of preparing leaders for Christian ministry. Faithfulness then led us to accept the vocation of academic administration, a new and creative way to use our gifts of scholarship, teaching, and service for the good of theological schools and the people they serve.

This is a point that needs to be stressed. To serve in the academic deanship is sometimes viewed as being reserved for those who could not make it as scholars or who were most expendable from teaching. This is simply not true. To accept the call to be dean means putting some forms of scholarship "on hold" to be sure, but I have become convinced that the multiple skills and intelligences required of the academic dean *include* those of scholar and teacher as well as a wide range of skills that many people do not have. To be called to this role requires *more* scholarship and teaching, but they take different and, in some cases, more challenging forms.

Right now, theological schools need leaders, not just managers. The church has changed and is changing, the world has changed and will continue to change, and the persons serving in many theological schools actively resist the changes that might be necessary for them to serve faithfully in this new context or, in some cases, even to survive. Theological schools need leaders who are willing to name the changes that have taken place, anticipate the changes to come, and lead their schools into the path that will enable them to be faithful to their heritages and stories and also to engage the new conditions that face them.

Earlier I mentioned my service as seminary registrar. That role turned out to be brief. Within a couple years the financial situation had stabilized, and the university history department needed someone to teach U.S. history and church history. My position changed once again to give the university history department some of my teaching time. My primary location was still the seminary, and I was a member of the seminary faculty. This was not my ideal, but it was an improvement from my earlier service as part-time registrar.

The change out of the registrar's office came about in part because of the arrival at the seminary of a new dean who hired an assistant dean who took on the registrar tasks. Unfortunately, what had appeared to be a longer-term solution began to unravel. Neither the new dean nor the new assistant dean was well suited to the position each held. For a variety of reasons including personality, background, preparation, and aptitude, the seminary experienced an unprecedented administrative breakdown. For many months, the seminary was sustained through extraordinary involvement and investment by members of the faculty. At the same time, I had been experiencing some frustrations with my own work. Teaching wasn't the joy that it once had been. I was *very* frustrated by the administrative ineptitude in the seminary and, along with my faculty and staff colleagues, often embarrassed by those who represented the institution in public.

Eventually the university president acted, and both the dean and assistant dean were removed from their positions. I was named to the search committee for the new seminary dean. The search was an eye-opening experience in many ways, as I noted that the qualifications for the position were similar to my own background, saw the importance of capable leadership in this position, and, to my surprise, began to imagine myself in such a role. What would it be like to serve in that way? This imagining struck me as absurd because there was, at that time, no possibility that I would be considered for the position as it was configured. I shared this surprising development with my spiritual director, who was an invaluable guide through the process over the next few months. I was interested in how things worked within the seminary. I loved the place and wanted it to function effectively. I loved my faculty colleagues and wanted them to be able to use their gifts of teaching, research, and writing to their fullest. I loved the staff and their dedication to our common work and wanted to be able to contribute with them to the smooth functioning of the institution so that, ultimately, the mission of the school could be fulfilled.

After the initial attempts of the search failed and position descriptions were re-configured, I was asked to fill the role of academic dean. The offer was initially presented as a three-year appointment, which helped me to imagine taking on the role of dean. I could test my gifts and the fit of the position and I, or the president, could decide after that time whether it was the right role for me in the institution. That three-year term turned into eleven and a half years. During that period, the role of dean changed significantly as the institution's enrollment grew both in number and diversity, new programs were created, new faculty members were recruited, and new staff positions were developed. During this time of transition, I was blessed by a wonderful opportunity to help lead and shape the institution I believed in, the faculty I respected and whose work I affirmed, and the denomination in which I had been ordained.

One of the great blessings I had in my time as dean was the opportunity to work with a president who was a well-respected friend and who began his position just a few weeks before I began mine. Others in this volume will speak of the importance of the president-dean relationship, but I will affirm here just how crucial it is to have harmony in that relationship. Another very important resource for me was the gathering of other deans through organizations like the Association of Chicago Theological Schools and ATS. It was simply *crucial* for me to be able to share joys, insights, best practices, frustrations, and wounds with fellow deans. It may be that only those who are living the same vocation can understand fully the complexities of serving in this role.

While I knew that becoming dean was a significant change of direction for me, there were elements of the change for which I was not prepared. If one decides to embrace the calling to move from faculty to the deanship, it is important to recognize that by making this shift one becomes "different." I was surprised to discover that even faculty colleagues with whom I had served for a number of years as a member of the faculty, because of the role I had taken on, perceived me to be someone different. Some assumed that I would act differently — in some cases with less integrity — simply because I had become part of the administration. For a long time this was deeply troubling to me, because although my role had changed, I was the same person and had the same values. I was occasionally surprised to discover that even though I did everything I could to support the faculty and usually went out of my way to provide whatever benefit I could for the faculty, any time I couldn't do what they wanted or provide what they needed some assumed that I didn't care about the faculty anymore.

One of the challenges of being the dean is that to enjoy it sometimes creates suspicion among others in the institution, especially the faculty. As one experienced dean put it, "Sometimes certain faculty members discover that they like being dean — and sometimes they are good at it. But there is no permission to celebrate that gift." MacLean notes that aspiring to leadership positions can be construed as self-promotion and careerism.[25] Some imagine it is rooted in a hunger for power.

It is also the case that relationships with colleagues on the faculty inevitably change. Becoming dean, I was responsible to do faculty evaluations, and it became my responsibility to recommend salary increases for promotions. I knew what faculty members were paid. I knew what their student course evaluations said. This was hard for some to accept. The change in relationship is so dramatic that, in some cases, service in the deanship will make a transition back to the faculty very difficult, perhaps even impossible.

25. McLean, *Leading from the Center,* p. 236.

Another source of altered relationships was that as dean I became an agent of change. I often was responsible to interpret for the faculty new policies by the university administration, or new requirements of the accreditation agencies, or new expectations of the sponsoring denomination. Leadership required pushing some colleagues into places they did not want to go.

Needless to say, the role of the academic dean is one of unending and fascinating variety. There are daily challenges that stretch us and demand our best. I spent many days constantly "shifting gears" among a wide range of tasks, from working on a budget, to dealing with a faculty need, to filling in for the president who was on the road, to interacting with a denominational official about a student issue, to speaking with the university registrar about an issue of academic policy, to signing a stack of reimbursement requests, to figuring out what went wrong in one of the previous month's reimbursement requests. Then I would need to rush to a faculty meeting in order to "teach" the faculty about a new policy for ordination within our denomination.

In the deanship there are always things to learn and new ways to use one's intelligence, research skills, communication skills, and people skills. I think there is a parallel to Craig Dykstra's notion of pastoral imagination — the variety of skills and intelligences required of pastors — and a dean's imagination.[26] The role involves a frustrating complexity with a vast amount of information that needs to be handled quickly and accurately, within the rapidly changing landscapes of church and theological education.

Conclusion

As Lovett Weems notes, "Leadership always remains a gift from God, confirmed by the church, for the service of others and the upbuilding of the body of Christ. Leadership is indeed a channel of God's grace."[27]

The work of the academic dean is important and rewarding work. Schools need good leaders, and those with the skills need to consider serving in this way. As David Ford puts it, "If we really put the desires of God first, everything else falls into place — though maybe in surprising ways."[28] Consider whether your "surprise" is a calling to serve as an academic dean.

26. Craig Dykstra, "The Heart of the Matter," *Sustaining Pastoral Excellence,* Duke Divinity School, http://www.divinity.duke.edu/programs/spe/articles/200506/dykstra-p2.html.
27. Weems, "Leadership as a Channel of God's Grace," p. 7.
28. Ford, *The Shape of Living,* p. 63.

The Vocational Call and Multiple Occupations of a CAO

Linda W. Bryan

A two-year study of chief academic officers in North American theological schools, funded by Lilly Endowment, Inc., was conducted from 1996 to 1998 and resulted in a series of five monographs and ultimately a book describing the multiple and complex roles of the CAO. These monographs addressed such issues as dean-faculty relationships, the role of the chief academic officer, challenges of academic administration, career paths and hiring practices, and professional development.[1] The documented quantitative and qualitative data reported in the study confirm much of what I have experienced with regard to the vocation and role of chief academic dean. Given my personal journey over the years, I am certain this role is indeed a response to the vocational call.

When we accept the call to academic deanship, we accept the call to be agents of God in an academic context. We accept the call to leadership despite that a number of deans enter the vocation with little or no leadership experience. Kelly Gilmer makes this revealing statement in her article on leadership education:

> Before he was elected a United Methodist bishop in the summer of 2004, Will Willimon had decades of experience as minister to Duke University and professor of Christian ministry. He had written dozens of books, served on boards for several colleges and organizations, and lectured around the world. Yet, Willimon felt overwhelmed by the prospect of overseeing 800 pastors, 157,000 United Methodists, and a $12 million budget.[2]

He confessed to Dean Gregory Jones, "I'm not qualified for this job." While he was proficient in many areas, he was concerned that he did not have the

1. Jeanne P. McLean served as project director for the Study of Chief Academic Officers. The five monographs have been captured in her book, *Leading from the Center: The Emerging Role of the Chief Academic Officer in Theological Schools* (Atlanta: Scholars Press, 1999).

2. Kelly Gilmer, "At Every Turn Church Leaders Face Challenging Choices," *Divinity: Duke University* (Duke Divinity School, Spring 2008), p. 20.

necessary training for this new leadership role. Many, like Will Willimon, accept the role of leadership having to learn the job while performing.

The role of the dean is multifaceted and complex, with responsibility for moving the school forward in a challenging and changing social world order. With all its challenges and complexities, the role of dean remains rewarding and distinctive, contributing to the accomplishment of the institution's overall mission.

The Vocational Call

The term *vocation* from the Latin word *vocare* means "to call." Dennis Campbell states in *Who Will Go for Us?* that "the idea of Christian vocation is related to the passion for wholeness."[3] The notion of Christian vocation transfers the emphasis from employment and earning a living to God's call, thereby rooting the response to a vocational call in the passion for wholeness. The assumption is that the one who accepts the role of CAO is responding to a call of God to this work. The work has to be viewed as ministry; otherwise the passion for wholeness is absorbed in the work.

The vocation of CAO might be defined as a compelling force from within to serve as an agent of wholeness in a theological institution. It is a high calling to integrity, responsibility, and relationships. The CAO is in academic administration and therefore is regarded as a leader. Yet the vocation of CAO may not be readily apparent from the onset of one's journey of seeking a career path. The CAO often evolves out of a previous role within the institution. One may have been hired as a full-time faculty member or an administrator with faculty responsibility and over time evolve as a valuable candidate for the position of CAO. While serving in the previous roles, the candidate was learning the workings of the institution, student needs, and other vital information related to leadership in theological education, yet might have been completely unaware at the time of being prepared for a leadership role within the institution.

Alternatively, the response to the vocational call of a CAO could be relocation to another context. The selection process for the dean is driven by contextual need; therefore, those seeking the position of a CAO may not necessarily find a position in their selected preference. Institutions with vacant CAO positions are seeking leaders who are compatible with the context.

---

3. Dennis Campbell, *Who Will Go for Us?* (Nashville: Abingdon Press, 1994), p. 16.

Compatibility and context become important elements when answering the call to the vocation of CAO. In a focus group discussion led by Karen Ristau, a number of participants felt that deans should "fit" the particular contexts in which they are serving.[4] While institutions are searching for compatible deans, likewise, prospective deans should seek institutions where their gifts, leadership style, and personality are complementary to the culture of the context. With an increase in social concerns by the church, there is the need to give attention to the social context and consciousness of the institution. "Tumultuous social change throughout much of the twentieth century — urbanization, war, economic crises, quests for civil rights — intensifies the contextualization of each seminary tradition."[5]

Institutions that value cultural and contextual significance to their communities are seeking chief academic officers who have a sensitivity to the culture of the context. The context may consist of predominantly African American, bi-vocational, commuting students such as most of those enrolled at Shaw University Divinity School, where the majority of classes are on an alternative schedule for evenings and weekends to accommodate this category of students. The needs of these students would be quite different from those of the full-time day student whose classes are daily Monday through Friday. Students in the first scenario are usually older persons who have been out of school for a number of years, ten to twenty-five years or longer. A good number of these students bring to the program multiple responsibilities, such as careers, pastoring and other ministerial responsibilities, personal ministries, families, and caring for parents and sick family members, while still sensing an urgency to respond to the call of God. While academic standards and expectations remain high, the social and programmatic needs in this scenario may differ from those of the traditional day program. Various cultural and contextual differences among theological institutions require a close examination of the type of CAO best suited for a particular institution.

---

4. Karen M. Ristau, "Challenges of Academic Administration: Rewards and Stresses in the Role of the Chief Academic Officer," *Academic Leadership: A Study of Academic Officers in Theological Schools,* Monograph Series, Vol. 2 (Houston: The University of St. Thomas, March 1996), p. 9.

5. Charles R. Foster, Lisa E. Dahill, Lawrence A. Golemon, and Barbara Wang Tolentino, *Educating Clergy: Teaching Practices and Pastoral Imagination* (San Francisco: Jossey-Bass, A Wiley Imprint, 2006), p. 253.

Understanding the Vocation of Academic Administration

It has been noted by the Steering Committee of the Chief Academic Officers Society (CAOS) of ATS that some academic deans understand their position as an interruption; others see their position as if they were the chair of a department; still others view their position as a vocation. A comparison of these various understandings reveals a multidimensional role for the CAO.

Not only can the position of CAO represent a career interruption, but it is also characterized by a constant flow of daily interruptions that the dean is expected to manage. Both types of interruptions can be stressful, but both can also hold value. The office of the CAO is where the smoldering coals are brought, flames flare up, and fires are extinguished; it is the place where issues and problems are presented at the table to be flushed out and brought to resolution when possible. Mediation occurs in the office of the CAO. To occupy such a pivotal place in the functioning of a school can be both meaningful and frustrating; interruptions can offer both a distraction from one's vocational path and new possibilities for living out a calling. Those who are able to embrace both dimensions of the "interruption" of a call to academic leadership and accent the positive side are more likely to thrive in their new role.

Some chief academic officers view their position as the chair of a department. The phrase "chair of a department or department chair" gives the impression of the organizational structure of a liberal arts college or university. This view, however, is more closely related to the actual role of the CAO than the one-dimensional view mentioned above. Both roles, department chair and chief academic officer, are inundated with administrative matters, monitoring and enforcing academic policies, meetings, reports, program staffing, oversight of course offerings each semester, new course development, leading department meetings, promoting faculty development, research and publishing, mediation, and other unmentioned and unwritten responsibilities as they occur. This view is purely academic, giving the impression of a firmness that gives very little attention, if any, to the special needs of the faculty and students. What might be the difference between the department chair and the CAO? The department chair is more interested in building a department, teaching, writing, research and publishing, and preparing students for the workforce with a view towards prosperity and thereby making a meaningful contribution to society. The CAO has the same desires but is theologically driven by the call to responsibility for educating and preparing clergy and laity to be better servants of God.

Still other chief academic officers view their position as a vocational call. This view is perhaps the sum total of what it means to serve in the capacity of CAO — to respond to the call of God. To fill this role is a calling, an assignment, a divine appointment that the CAO may not immediately perceive. The vocational call is sensitivity to self calling self to a place of ministry. Self must agree with God's call before self can call self to ministry. Just as one is called to pastor, called to chaplaincy, or called to teach, one is called to the position of academic leadership. We are called into existence, we are called into the church, we are called to discipleship, and more specifically, we are called to the ministry of service as CAO. Ristau's survey found that "a significant percentage of respondents accepted the position out of a desire to be of greater service to others or as part of their religious vocation."[6] Another study of chief academic officers conducted by Mary Abdul-Rahman found that a good number of deans were encouraged by their colleagues to serve as chief academic officers.[7] These individuals were identified by others as having the gifts and graces to serve in the capacity of dean. In many cases, they had not recognized their own capacities nor thought of themselves as chief academic officers. This same study revealed that the least common reasons persons choose academic administration are career advancement and higher compensation and that persons moving into administrative positions are primarily more concerned about service to others and fulfillment of purpose than they are about personal advances. The beauty of the gift of service is the many unexpected rewards reaped during the processes of giving.

These three understandings of the CAO role — as an interruption, a department chair, and a vocation — are not isolated individualities but rather varying perspectives representing the complexity of the role.

Transitioning into the Role of CAO

Mary Abdul-Rahman's study of career paths of chief academic officers is an extensive research effort revealing not only why deans become deans but also where deans come from. Her study reveals that 66 percent of deans

6. Ristau, "Challenges of Academic Administration," p. 9.

7. Mary Abdul-Rahman, "Career Paths and Hiring Practices of Chief Academic Officers in Theological Schools," *Academic Leadership: A Study of Chief Academic Officers in Theological Schools*, Monograph Series, Vol. 3 (May 1996), p. 4.

emerged from the ranks of faculty status and 21 percent from other administrative positions. The study further reports that 58 percent of deans were appointed from within their own institutions, 20 percent came from faculty or administrative positions in other theological schools, and only 6 percent came from pastoral positions. In addition, this study reveals that 44 percent of those who came into the deanship came with some previous administrative experience in theological or other higher education.[8]

Moreover, Abdul-Rahman's study found that more than half of the deans who accepted the position of academic dean were deficient in experience in academic leadership. They entered the vocation having to learn their roles as they served. This duality of learning and serving can create enough stress for the new dean to question the call. According to other authorities on the subject, W. H. Gmelch and R. Seedorf, deans transitioning from faculty to administrator must make necessary adjustments, "from solitary to social, focused to fragmented, autonomy to accountability, manuscripts to memoranda, private to public, professing to persuading, stability to mobility, and client to custodian."[9] Academic deans are public figures with heightened challenges consuming their time once spent as faculty reading, studying, writing, teaching, and research. This change can be quite challenging for some deans in transition.

Ristau's study of the role of chief academic officers makes reference to several comments made by deans who had transitioned from faculty to the deanship:

- I did not understand how much paper there would be to process daily and how much I would be caught in the double bind of seeing people vs. writing reports.
- It takes much more time and attention to details. There is a greater amount of unexpected tasks on a daily basis.
- It was more difficult dealing with faculty than I though it would be.
- I thought I would have more time for academic research, teaching, and relating to students.[10]

8. Abdul-Rahman, "Career Paths and Hiring Practices of Chief Academic Officers in Theological Schools," pp. 2-3.

9. W. H. Gmelch and R. Seedorf, "Academic Leadership under Siege: The Ambiguity and Imbalance of Department Chairs," *Journal for Higher Education Management* 5, no. 1 (1989): 37-44.

10. Ristau, "Challenges of Academic Administration," p. 3.

The role of the academic dean is indubitably stressful. Many deans enter their administrative roles with preconceived notions that are not entirely accurate. McLean's study of the role of chief academic officers documents responsibilities that are multiple and vary from one institution to another. "Factors such as institutional traditions and practices, style and personality of the president and the dean, faculty culture, student characteristics, denominational requirements, demographic, economic, and political pressures combine to determine the distinctive ethos of theological schools."[11] The ethos determines the indigenous role of the dean. Over time, some roles are more clearly defined as the CAO understands the ethos of the community.

The vocation of dean assumes a number of roles that are common across institutional lines, such as daily administrative matters, monitoring and enforcing academic policies, meetings, reports, program staffing, oversight of course offerings and curriculum development, new course development, leading faculty meetings, promoting faculty development, research and publishing, mediation, building trust and collegiality among faculty, and other unmentioned and unwritten responsibilities as they occur. In addition, some deans are responsible for oversight of accreditation, budgets, faculty evaluation, faculty promotion and tenure, academic advising, faculty hiring, and fundraising. McLean's study reveals that the primary areas of responsibility for most deans are (1) academic priorities and planning, (2) curriculum and academic programs, and (3) academic policy. Faculty salaries and fundraising rank at the bottom of the list of primary responsibilities.[12] In most institutions, these areas of responsibility are within the domain of the CEO or president.

Among the roles of the academic dean is the pastoral dimension, which is often overlooked and outweighed by the complexities of the many layers of responsibilities. The pastoral role is critical to building community, collegiality, and relationships among the faculty and between the faculty and the dean. The faculty needs leaders who not only know how to develop curriculum, plan programs, and conduct meetings, but also have the capacity to care and nurture those whom the dean has been called to serve. Caring does not equate to weakness or loss of power. It speaks instead to the use of deans'

11. Jeanne P. McLean, "Leading from the Center: The Role of Chief Academic Officer," *Academic Leadership: A Study of Academic Officers in Theological Schools,* Monograph Series, Vol. 1 (January 1996), p. 8.

12. McLean, "Leading from the Center," p. 6.

power to build up the body such that the body is enabled and willing to serve. The Apostle Paul reminded the Ephesians that "God gave some to be as apostles, and some as prophets, and some as evangelists, and some as pastors and teachers, for the equipping of the saints for the work of service, to the building up of the body of Christ."[13]

Why is the pastoral role important to the success of the institution? Deans have to remember that they are building a team of players who are willing to serve for the greater good. Deans have the responsibility to be fair and just in the treatment of faculty and in matters relating to faculty requests and faculty decisions. They are in very powerful positions with authority and capacity to build or destroy and to divide or unify. The team spirit is dependent upon the deans' pastoral capacities, which include nurturing, mentoring, supporting, acknowledging accomplishments, rewards, and celebration.

McLean asserts that "the dean's role in fostering faculty growth and renewal may include good stewardship of sabbatical and travel programs, highly personal forms of counsel and encouragement, and development of teamwork and collaboration among faculty. Through efforts such as these, many deans strive to create a positive climate in which faculty scholarship, teaching, service, and leadership can flourish."[14] The study further notes that "setting the environment for faculty success is the dean's job; the dean is an enabler of the faculty."[15] As true as this statement may be, the role of enabler will diminish if there is no relationship between the dean and the faculty, and the faculty must work with the dean for enablement to be effective.

To further explore the influence of the pastoral role upon faculty, McLean identifies five aspects of the dean's role in nurturing the professional development of faculty:

1. Deans have opportunities to know and understand individual faculty and to work with them to address their professional development needs.
2. Deans can be instrumental in fostering teamwork and collaborative projects among faculty. Deans play an important role in helping fac-

13. Eph. 4:11-12.

14. Jeanne P. McLean, "Dean-Faculty Relationships: Meeting the Challenge," *Academic Leadership: A Study of Chief Academic Officers in Theological Schools,* Monograph Series, Vol. 5 (October 1998), p. 9.

15. James Hudnut-Beumler, "A New Dean Meets a New Day in Theological Education," *Theological Education* 33 (Supplement 1996), p. 19.

ulty see their individual work as integral to the shared mission and part of a larger whole.

3. Many academic deans play an important role in securing and administering institutional funds for faculty development, although in some instances, faculty are encouraged to seek outside funding to support their interests.

4. Deans can ensure that other institutional practices are conducted in ways that support faculty growth and renewal.

5. Deans can foster faculty ownership of professional development programs by involving faculty directly in their design and implementation.[16]

The duality that exists in the role of academic dean is that of being both stressful and rewarding. Ristau's study concludes that 84 percent of deans agree that they have found academic administration professionally rewarding. Seventy-three percent agree the job becomes more manageable the longer they serve, and 64 percent find the job very stressful.[17] Deans in the 84 percent category have managed to find balance in their multiple roles such that stress is held at a level that does not rob them of the rewards associated with this vocation. Persons in the 73 percent category are learning to manage their roles and related stress. Deans in the 64 percent category have yet to attend an ATS CAOS conference or other venue where they may find support and mentoring from more experienced peers.

As academic dean, my personal journey has been similar to that of many deans. At this point in my journey, I can resonate with the 84 percent who have found academic administration professionally rewarding, although admittedly I have passed through the 64 percent category and from time to time still dance with stress.

Fulfilling the Call

My journey began when I was hired as the special assistant to the dean with responsibility for oversight of the day-to-day operation, including admissions, registration, and graduation. Initially, there was some ambivalence about this position in light of my desire to serve as a counselor for under-

---

16. Jeanne P. McLean, "Dean-Faculty Relationships: Meeting the Challenge," pp. 9-11.
17. Ristau, "Challenges of Academic Administration," p. 2.

grad students. It was this strong sense of call to the vocation of counselor/ mentor stirring inside me that I felt I should have been pursuing, but instead I found myself confronted with an offer to fill a newly created position in the office of the dean. Thus, I carried a certain bias that could have potentially blinded me to the privilege presented to fulfill my desired call. To my surprise, this position provided a frame and a context for me to utilize my acquired skill set in administration, coupled with satisfying my sense of call to work with students.

During the completion of my doctoral work, the dean became extremely ill to the point of taking an extended leave of absence for a liver transplant. My scope of responsibility was immediately and significantly increased to include the full range of academic responsibility, including reporting to the board, leading faculty meetings, and serving on the steering committee for accreditation. This was a challenging time in the life of the divinity school and in my personal journey. As with most institutions, our school faced budgetary constraints, and we therefore operated with a limited staff of three full-time persons and now were without a dean.

I found myself occupying dual roles which conjured up inner conflicting emotions. Institutionally, I was committed to filling the gap and seeing the school through until the return of the dean, while at the same time emotionally struggling with the tension created by the dual roles and trying to decipher my identity. With a supportive faculty, staff, and board, we successfully worked together to accomplish the wide range of tasks before us. Following a period of recuperation, the dean was able to return to work.

While faculty members, students, colleagues, and pastors were encouraging me in this intermediate role, it never occurred to me to seek a dean's position. As a matter of fact, in my mind I was not ready for such a demanding leadership role, although I had experienced the diversity, complexities, interruptions, stress and rewards characteristic of the role of academic dean. God often uses others to point out our own gifts and graces for particular roles. One such incident happened when I was called into a meeting with the president who acknowledged that he recognized my work as that of a dean and offered me the position of assistant dean. A few years later, the dean and the president named me chief academic officer.

Career paths for the majority of deans are migrations from faculty status to academic administration. For me, the path took an unusual turn through a less conventional approach. I was not faculty but rather one of Mary Abdul-Rahman's 21 percent from other academic administrative positions who happened to be in the right place in an unfortunate situation.[18] Given the designation of chief academic officer, the question for me was, *Is this a vocational call, a position with additional and multiple roles, a happenstance or God's call to God's chosen vocation for me?* Reflecting theologically on the extraordinary turn of events leading up to this position, I was convinced that I had been guided by the Spirit to God's vocational call. Steve Harper notes in *The Pastor's Guide to Personal Spiritual Formation* that vocation "means another is speaking and we are listening. Another is in control — leading, guiding, guarding, and blessing."[19]

My appointed time of service as academic dean was indeed extremely rewarding, affording me the opportunity to serve in academic leadership, to build relationships with leaders across the spectrum, and to be in colleagueship with other theologians. I am eternally grateful for the support of ATS, particularly gatherings for CAOS and Women in Leadership. These resources were invaluable to me as I meandered through the maze of academic leadership. I encourage you to connect with as many support venues as possible to maintain a sense of balance and to reap the benefit of the wisdom of more experienced deans.

Currently I am fulfilling the call to a new dimension of my vocation — to serve as associate professor of mission and ministry and to create and direct a mission and ministry program. Some deans return to the classroom at the end of their tenure, but for me it was going into the classroom as a full-time professor for the first time.

---

18. Abdul-Rahman, "Career Paths and Hiring Practices of Chief Academic Officers in Theological Schools," p. 2.

19. William Willimon, M. Robert Mulholland, Jr., Steve Harper, et al., *The Pastor's Guide to Personal Spiritual Formation* (Beacon Hill Press of Kansas City, 2005), p. 9.

Nurturing Commitments

4. Relating to the CEO

Leading from the Middle

Willie James Jennings

Behind every academic dean is a university dean.[1] Therein lies a story whose telling would rival any weekly television drama. Universities are complex places, and one of the most complex positions to hold in a modern university is that of an academic dean in a university divinity school or school of religion. The position places the academic dean at the intersection of several busy streets, and from that risky place you must direct a lot of traffic. In this regard, the academic deanship is an ironically "middle position." Its irony is clear only to those who are deans. As academic dean you are at the center of so much, but you are acutely de-centered. That is, so much of what you are responsible for you do not control. It helps to remember this lack of control, because it can place assessment of your appropriate fit for the position in healthy perspective. Whether you feel at any given moment particularly competent (bordering on brilliant) or particularly inept (bordering on suicidal), it is helpful to recognize that the position has a life and personality independent of you that must be respected.

Central to the position is your relationship with the university dean, who also contends with the complexities of a "middle" position. Theological

1. In this essay, *university dean* or *dean* are used to refer to the dean of the theological school, as distinguished from the *academic dean.*

school deans in universities are like ambassadors in foreign countries. They must constantly translate not only administrative concerns but also the religious world they represent to university officials who often exhibit a wide range of difference in understanding and appreciation for that world. Simultaneously, the university dean is immersed in the issues and concerns of the university, a community that includes the university president, the provost or provost equivalent, the university business manager, senior accountants, and the other deans and vice presidents. It is a community only marginally in the minds of the dean's own faculty and staff. It is in the awareness of the university dean's own complex position that the character of the academic deanship as a middle position begins.

Academic deanships in universities differ in important respects, yet one common aspect is the task of helping convey to the faculty, staff, students, and other various constituencies the challenges and issues facing the dean in university interactions and collaborations. This task is distinct from helping the dean convey university issues, concerns, and challenges for the theological school to those same stakeholders. This latter task is a concert performance where you speak along with the dean and other colleagues to your school's community about its life and responsibilities in the wider university. The former task, however, is a more intimate and complex affair in which you serve as the interpreter of the dean. In my years as an academic dean I never announced to anyone in my community that I was acting as an interpreter for the dean. It would have seemed foolish to some and repulsive to others. "The dean can speak for himself," would have been the reply to such a strange statement of hermeneutical existence. Yet in practice this is precisely one role that is built into the nature of a relationship between the dean and the academic dean.

Based on a review of both sides of this hermeneutical challenge, three strategies emerge for employing the academic dean's middle position to foster helpful communication in a theological school.

Interpreter of the One to the Many

Relationships between deans and academic deans are as varied as academic deanships. Yet in most good relationships, there is a bond of trust that develops between them. Fundamental to that trust is a growing sense of each other's actions and intentions and the connection between them. Trust exists in an environment that constantly muddies the water, making clear vision between action and intention very difficult if not impossible. All deans face work that is unrelenting and unpredictable because that work always involves the constant mixture of people, problems, and processes. Such contexts unleash myriad interpretations for almost every administrative act. One of the most important early lessons that a dean or academic dean should learn is that you cannot control the interpretations of your actions or the actions of your administrative colleague. This lack of control can be maddening because it subjects you to over-interpretation by some and uncharitable interpretation by others. Yet this is unavoidable.

The key to interpretation is learning to swim in its ever-widening, never-calm currents by trying to facilitate richer and deeper conversations in your school. This strategy, however, only heightens the middle position of the academic dean in relation to the dean. The dean has much less opportunity to facilitate communal conversations than does the academic dean. The sheer complexity of the dean's position in the larger university community often leaves the academic dean in a better position to offer commentary on specific actions, policies, and behaviors. But facilitating conversation is an intricate matter. Many things said between a dean and an academic dean cannot be repeated to anyone else or cannot be generally disseminated or cannot be repeated verbatim. A dean should be able to take the academic dean into confidence, asking the academic dean to serve as a sounding board for ideas, responses, and plans as well as frustrations, joys, and sorrows. On the other hand, the academic dean has also been brought into the confidences of faculty, staff, and students. In addition, the academic dean usually knows, as one former academic dean colleague would say, "the mood of the village." This means that the academic dean very often knows too much.

As a wise king once said, "In much wisdom is much grief and with the increase of knowledge is the increase of sorrow."[2] How do you facilitate healthy conversation in your community without betraying trust or raising fears that your silence on private matters has been broken? Very carefully. The most critical point of complication is precisely in the academic dean's relationship with the dean, who stands in a central position in the school's ecology. It is not unusual for a significant portion of institutional conversation to revolve around decisions made by or facilitated by the dean. Everything carries the signature of the dean's involvement, real or perceived: configurations of key committees, appointments, terminations, fundraising, salaries, reorganizations of administrative staff, increasing or decreasing

2. Eccles. 1:18.

staff, eradication of existing programs, and new program initiatives. This can create a burden for the academic dean, who is often in a unique position to offer necessary further elaboration on the rationale of these decisions.

It often falls to the academic dean to help people cope with the effect of changes or to prepare them for the changes. Very often at the center of that therapeutic work is answering questions and concerns about the "dean's plan" for this change, even if the change is the result of a fairly wide consensus of stakeholders. Communal consensus does not necessarily negate interpretations that a particular decision was tied to the "dean's agenda" for the school. The difficulty of interpretation increases if the academic dean is less than enthused about the change or, worse, strongly disagrees with it. The middle position in such cases is a tight one, because you may find yourself interpreting changes you dislike to people who also dislike them. It takes significant verbal and intellectual dexterity and quite a bit of emotional anguish to honor your relationship with the dean, acknowledge the frustration of those affected negatively by change, faithfully interpret the new course of action, and hold your own dislike of the change in check so as to not hinder its implementation or the morale of the community. Success rates in such matters are not always high. Success here is measured not simply in what the change produced or how well the community handled the change but also in how you as academic dean feel about yourself in the midst of this interpretive work.

A number of academic dean colleagues have confided that one of their deepest struggles is living with the perception by some in their community that they lack the courage to "stand up to the dean." They begin to be seen as the mouthpiece for the dean, someone whose thinking is just like that of the dean. It takes maturity to realize that an academic dean is part of an administration and carries a dean's trust. Academic deans tend to voice their disagreements in private, while in public space, they fulfill their responsibility to implement agreed-upon decisions. Yet maturity in interpretation is often at risk when the academic or administrative stakes are high or are complicated by the dean's behavior.

We are all human, frail and fallible. But it is an unfortunate reality of leadership that our humanity in all its majesty and messiness can find no shade to shield it from the sunlight. A word spoken poorly by the dean — in haste, in anger, in retaliation, or in laziness, to the wrong person, at the wrong time, or too often — can lead to a host of problems and become a burden to the academic dean's administrative efforts. As the saying goes, "We all have blind spots." Yet covering each other's blind spots is a difficult endeavor for both a dean and an academic dean, because the sheer amount of work and its fluidity create unanticipated situations that often present difficult choices and responses. In such regular situations, new blind spots appear.

Making the optimal response has a lot to do with living with its consequences. An academic dean lives many days with the consequences of a dean's response. This suggests more than simply a need for deans to be careful and considerate of the results of their words uttered in response to situations. Academic deans, for better or for worse, are implicated in the humanity of their deans in ways that are sometimes strange and at some moments tragic. This is not to say that the humanity of the dean is a stumbling block to effective academic administration. It is just the opposite. A mature, open dean who is candidly aware of personal vulnerabilities can make the work of an academic dean a fairly straightforward affair of trying to build a community that compassionately makes room for common human weaknesses and fragility.

Interpreter of the Many to the One

There is, however, an equally complicated task of interpretation that often falls first to the academic dean — interpreting the community to the dean. Again, this may also seem like a redundant and inappropriate task for an academic dean. Just as the dean can speak as an individual, should not the dean have a clear sense of the community over which he or she has responsibility? The answer to both aspects of that question is yes. However, the waters of knowledge of a theological community are deep, shifting currents which require not simply sight but also entrance. The academic dean lives in the waters of a theological community like no one else. The confidence the dean shares with an academic dean is mirrored in the community by many people: faculty, staff, and students. There is a depth and thickness of texture to the relationships an academic dean has with these different groups of folks that normally cannot be matched by the dean.

The difference is a matter of location, of time, and of accessibility. Caring for the curriculum of a school, its lifeblood, puts you as academic dean at the intersection where faculty, staff, and students intertwine. More importantly, it often puts you in touch with their inner struggles, as well as their hopes, fears, anxieties, joys, and frustrations. This means that when you speak with the dean about them you very often know more than you can say.

Your approach to a faculty member, staff person, or student may sometimes differ significantly from the way a dean wants to respond to them. The torturous task becomes trying to explain to the dean this difference of opinion without betraying trust. Just as members of the community can sometimes fail to see the complexity of the dean's work and the depth of thinking behind administrative decisions, so too can a dean sometimes fail to see the thick texture of a faculty member's concerns, the layers of frustrations of an administrative colleague, or the painful plight of a student.

Squeezed on both sides, the academic dean may find that sometimes words do not come easily. How can you explain in the time constraints of a faculty meeting or phone conversation or in the heat of an impassioned diatribe by the dean or a member of the community the layers of issues attending the matter at hand? You cannot. So the academic dean will often fall silent or speak cryptically in meetings despite having much to say. In truth, the academic dean has too much to say and therefore cannot fully say anything. I have left meetings sick of heart because I could not find the words to say what needed to be said in a way that would make sense without betraying trust, engendering confusion, raising even more questions, and generally being profoundly misunderstood. Yet the end of such situations need not be hopeless despair. I have often found the needed time in more intimate settings to help colleagues understand other sides of issues. Sometimes in such settings I have even received the gracious gift of a colleague's wisdom, encouragement, and sympathy.

There are times when particular colleagues or students become thorns in the flesh of the dean or the academic dean. Few matters test one's Christian discipleship like having to contend with someone whose unrelenting hostility and disrespect toward you shows up in committee meetings, emails, and even the classroom. More often than not, the thorns are not the same for the dean and the academic dean. In such cases, it is not unusual for the academic dean to be caught between the dean and a member of the community, each strongly disliking the other and very clear on the other's problem, and each deeply committed to the rightness of his or her perspective. The standard strategies for addressing such situations are important — gently presenting the other's perspective as worth hearing out, bringing in third parties to quietly speak to either dean or community member or both, or shielding the dean from the thorny person as much as possible in order to avoid further conflict. Yet even with these strategies, the differences between the dean and a member of the community may become irreconcilable. In such cases, you simply must weather the storm. There are no easy answers or always effective tactics in these situations, only the constant remembering that we are all flesh, fallible and in great need of grace and forgiveness.

There is something inherently cruciform about being in leadership in theological institutions. People can criticize you, belittle you, betray you, and unleash their anger and frustration at you, but you cannot respond in kind and remain an effective administrative leader. Others may lavish praise on you or draw near to you in hopes of securing for themselves some advantage, or sometimes you can develop a small cohort of people in the institution who become your support net. But you cannot choose to serve and care for only those for whom you have warm feelings and remain a person to whom the majority of people in the institution feel safe honestly expressing their concerns. No one, however, can live this kind of in-between life — between love and hate, acceptance and rejection, support and abandonment — without the risk of developing a distorted soul.

The dangers of the "in-between life" chief administrators live are myriad, including the danger of beginning to tire of the very communities they have been called to serve. You may find yourself tuning out familiar words spoken by familiar colleagues even when they are saying genuinely helpful and innovative things. You may catch yourself or observe the university dean searching for ways to avoid spending time with members of the seminary community. Aloofness, oversensitivity to criticism, insensitivity to the struggles of opponents, becoming manipulative or vindictive — there are many pitfalls leaders face when they become weary of criticism and coping with the fears and frustrations of the people they serve.

One of the surest ways out of such pitfalls is for the university dean and the academic dean to be able to speak truthfully with one another about their administrative experiences, trusting that self-disclosures will be met with genuine care and dependable honesty. Good administrators carry their communities in their hearts, and this is why they can be hurt in so many ways and by so many different people. Given this reality, both the dean and the academic dean need sophisticated practices of self-examination with and for each other, counting on one another to gently confront the times when perspective is lost, hurt is festering into something potentially tragic, and some matter of concern has become too important, even sometimes more important than God.

A therapist may consider my words thus far as bordering on an incipient codependency. That may be true. Indeed it is possible for some academic deans to operate in great independence of the dean either by functional design or by personal preference. I have found such cases to be rare, however, primarily because the worlds of each intersect in such fundamental ways that their minds must think about the same things often at the same times. More likely, a proper codependency or, better, a healthy interdependency exists in the deanships of theological institutions. The dean's administrative life carries inside it the academic dean and in turn the academic dean cannot perform without the dean. In a sense, they are bound together in ways that are unavoidably complicated. Yet I want to take seriously the danger of a codependency that may become destructive by ending this essay with a few points of advice.

Strategies for Healthy Interdependency

Three strategies help in the quest to resist the dangers of codependency and achieve a healthier interdependency.

First, always invite direct conversations among members of your theological community. Fundamental to your work is keeping people talking to each other. This is especially important when it concerns the dean. Whenever appropriate, invite colleagues to approach the dean directly about matters and notify the dean that you have recommended this course of action. It is also crucial to constantly fill in the story (without betraying confidential information) so that people are humanized in their concerns, hopes, and frustrations. It is important to remind people that there is a real person behind their words, no matter how objectionable, irritating, or outrageous the words. Constantly promoting conversations helps keep people moving in the same direction when the political winds pick up or a season of difficult decisions and unanticipated crises arises.

Second, remind everyone that you are bound by the covenantal trust of both the dean and the people of the community. It helps to remind people who come to you that you will hold their words in confidence but that they should not put you in an untenable position with the dean. I once had a colleague come and disclose to me a matter that should have been immediately disclosed to the dean, but he asked me not to share it with the dean. I was placed in an impossible position. Thankfully another colleague who knew the situation told him that he had placed me in an untenable position and that he should disclose this information directly to the dean. It is crucial to demand of those who speak to you to remember your difficult position and your humanity. You are not simply a functionary. You are a real person who should not be abandoned to positions that would create profound emotional conflict.

Third, learn to live in the endless stream of conversation without drowning. There will come a day when interpretations cease, but not while you are in the academic deanship. It is important to keep the words of the community in proper perspective. They are vital, demanding attention, care, concern, and response, but not obsession. They are not the words of God. Admittedly, this third piece of advice is difficult to carry out. Many a night the words spoken to me by someone in the community replaced my sleep and greeted me in the morning. Only a disciplined reading and meditation on the psalms would drive those words back into their proper place. Yet over the years I learned that faith, hope, and love are not simply theological virtues but the modalities through which one facilitates conversations in a theological community — listen through faith, see with hope, and speak in love. This is not easy, but it is necessary.

Behind every good academic dean in a university theological school is a university dean. In front of that same academic dean is an endless array of tasks, endless negotiation, mediation, facilitation, and endless interpretation. Its constant revolutions are not always taxing. They are very often life-giving. It is life-giving when you help the dean and faculty see each other's concerns and operate on the same page to the benefit of the institution. It is life-giving when you help a faculty member truly understand the concerns of a student and change a pedagogical approach or approach to that student. It is life-giving when vigorous, honest, even contentious debate resolves into an innovative policy, an agreement, or at least a better understanding between faculty, dean, and other members of the community; or when you see colleagues or the dean finally gain a greater appreciation of the struggles of the other and show genuine mercy and compassion for the other where there was little or none before. No reports to accrediting agencies, annual review, or evaluation for your reappointment can capture this crucial work, but you know it is there — invisible yet real, always audibly present but never articulated, ever bound to the material realities of caring for and carrying forward the work of a curriculum, a faculty, students, and a university dean.

ADDITIONAL RESOURCES

Foster, Charles R., and Lisa E. Dahill, Lawrence A. Golemon, and Barbara Wang Tolentino. *Educating Clergy: Teaching Practices and Pastoral Imagination.* San Francisco: Jossey-Bass, 2006.

Ha Jin, *War Trash.* Vintage International, 2005. (A novel that powerfully depicts the life of an interpreter in a profoundly difficult position.)

Building a Relationship That Furthers the Mission

Randolph MacFarland

Writing about the president and dean relationship while continuing to serve as dean is a little like writing about marriage while still being married. One quickly realizes that no matter how long the relationship has lasted and how much genuine learning has occurred, there is still much to learn, and there are still new discoveries to be made. Similar to marriage, how one enters the relationship, what each person brings to the relationship, the intentionality within the relationship, and the weathering of stressors (from external circumstances or self-created) all affect the level of joy found in serving as dean as well as the impact for good on the lives of others.

Deanship as a Calling

Each ATS school has a particular context for selecting a dean that is controlled by a range of policies and processes. In all cases, unless the institution is without a chief executive officer (CEO) or president, that individual will have a voice in the selection. No matter how strong the president's voice is in the process, the vetting of the candidate by faculty and board can only help solidify the future dean's understanding of call. "Even though their interpretation of calling may vary widely, most who feel strongly called to ministry have experienced some sense of providential direction or leading. Central to all of these assessments, however, is the correspondence between internal and external call."[1] The call to deanship that includes self-examination, affirmation by the community, and Divine drawing can serve as a great encouragement during times of disappointment, discouragement, and disillusionment. If the decision to serve is solely viewed as a career move, it can lead to actions while in office that are more related to career advancement than to the needs of the institution. In contrast,

> a leader with a clear sense of call represents a formidable force. The sense of destiny emboldens, energizes and empowers the leader. . . . Leaders

---

1. Thomas C. Oden, *Pastoral Theology: Essentials of Ministry* (San Francisco: Harper & Row, 1983), pp. 24-25.

convinced of their call do not easily succumb to disappointment and discouragements. Nor do they calculate odds in the same way as those who are not operating on a call basis . . . a divine unction fuels their determination.[2]

In certain settings, the deanship is cycled among faculty and may be viewed as something to endure before getting back to the classroom and writing. Rosemary Keller, writing in *Spirituality and Social Responsibility: Vocational Vision of Women in the United Methodist Church*, notes that,

> Deanship is not the first calling for most of us in the job and we feel a loss, a hunger for our scholarship. And it's important to find a way to do some in order to keep from burning out. But the dean's call is to help nurture other faculty, to help them see the wholeness of the institution. That's a vocational shift.[3]

Increasingly, the deanship is becoming a calling to affirm and a vocation to live out. In my particular context, the call solidified through the president's invitation to serve in the position, the vetting of my name for the position before faculty (even though I was already a faculty member carrying administrative responsibilities), and the requirement of a board interview and vote.

Managing Expectations and Finding a Voice

To the degree that the president is able to articulate specific reasons for extending the call, the dean candidate might gain some early understanding of expectations. Our president clearly articulated his desire for an educational leader who could develop an increasingly integrated educational experience. As the relationship progresses, new understandings of expectations will emerge from comments made in both public and private settings, and the dean will find a voice that reflects both personal style and community aspi-

---

2. Reggie McNeal, *A Work of Heart: Understanding How God Shapes Spiritual Leaders* (San Francisco: Jossey-Bass Publishers, 2000), p. 96.

3. Rosemary Skinner Keller, *Spirituality and Social Responsibility: Vocational Vision of Women in the United Methodist Tradition* (Nashville: Abingdon Press, 1993), quoted in Melinda R. Heppe, "The Intentional Dean: Nurturing the Vocation of Academic Administrators," *In Trust* (Summer 1996): 10.

rations. In preparing a presentation for newly appointed seminary presidents, Tom Walters (former academic dean at Saint Meinrad School of Theology) surveyed academic deans and posed four questions:

1. How long have you been a dean?
2. How large is your school?
3. What is the most important thing a new seminary president should know about the position of academic dean?
4. What piece of advice would you as academic dean give to a newly appointed seminary president?

One respondent who had served in the dean's office for more than ten years replied to the third question: "The dean stands precariously between faculty and administration seeking to be loyal to both worlds. The dean needs to have the freedom to *speak* [author's emphasis] into both worlds."[4] It is incumbent upon the dean to find a personal voice of leadership, realizing that growth and development as an educational leader will help support the leadership effectiveness of the president as well as further the mission of the institution.

The ability to find an individual voice while seeking to be loyal to both worlds and speaking into both worlds is enhanced by a growing level of self-awareness, healthy sense of personal identity, and discernment of how the president and dean are both alike and different. The dean needs to reflect on past experiences, gifting, and personality that will work effectively with a particular president in a particular season of the institution's history. Posing the following questions may be helpful: How have past experiences prepared me for this role? How will the position be shaped by my particular gifting? What have I learned from past responsibilities that required loyalty to different constituencies at the same time? In addition, it is important for the president and dean to reflect on how they are alike and how they are different. Where do areas of strength overlap? Do some areas pose shared challenges? Are there any common areas of weakness? Are there individual strengths that should be leveraged? High levels of self-awareness and appropriate levels of self-confidence can encourage the kind of transparency and self-disclosure which can make for exceptional teamwork. The dean also needs to understand faculty expectations surrounding the president/dean relation-

---

4. Tom Walters, Survey of Academic Deans in the Association of Theological Schools, 2 November 2006, p. 8.

ship. Establishing the relationship will be furthered or challenged by the lens through which faculty view the relationship. Faculty perspective is easily impacted by institutional tradition, practices of predecessors in the two roles, or experiences at other institutions (particularly in the case of new faculty).

In a 1999 *Harvard Business Review* article entitled "Managing Oneself," Peter Drucker advises that "only when you operate from a combination of your strengths and self-knowledge can you achieve true — and lasting — excellence."[5] Drucker suggests asking an important question: "To decide how you can best enhance your organization's performance, first ask what the situation requires. Based on your strengths, work style, and values, how might you make the greatest contribution to your organization's efforts?"[6]

Recognizing Limitations

It is equally important to reflect on what might limit the dean's contributions. Mitigating areas of particular vulnerability can help maximize effectiveness. As C. K. Gunsalus advises,

> Another important early step is to think about your personal vulnerabilities, and to act, consciously and purposefully, to keep them from diminishing your effectiveness in your new role. What pushes your buttons? What kinds of interactions cause you to overreact? Some people — and they're the ones who will cause you the most misery and stress — have an instinctive ability to find your weaknesses and exploit them. Letting yourself overreact in work settings, responding emotionally or unprofessionally, will put you in the wrong and can shift the focus of the interaction to your conduct instead of the issues. Neither effect is helpful.[7]

There will be times, both publicly and privately, where unfair criticism will be leveled and the temptation to over- or underreact will be present. "What is the common element in situations where you say or do things you later wish you hadn't? These are situations in which your buttons are being pushed. Common triggers include feeling blamed, insulted, disregarded, or

---

5. Peter F. Drucker, "Managing Oneself," *Harvard Business Review*, Best of HBR 1999, p. 1, originally appeared in *Harvard Business Review*, January 2005.

6. Drucker, "Managing Oneself."

7. C. K. Gunsalus, *The College Administrator's Survival Guide* (Cambridge, MA: Harvard University Press, 2006), p. 14.

put down."[8] The opportunity to process and role play challenging interactions with the president can help the dean respond appropriately to the various challenges that accompany leadership.

Understanding Boundaries

It is important for the dean to have a clear understanding of the president's role and scope of responsibilities, how their roles and responsibilities are different, and the appropriate boundaries that must exist between the two leadership positions. Understanding the president's role, responsibilities, and vision for the school, as well as written and unwritten expectations for the dean, is foundational for beginning the relationship.

Jeanne McLean served as Project Director for the Lilly Endowment–sponsored "Study of Chief Academic Officers in North American Theological Schools." Her research, conducted over a two-year period (1993-1995), included site visits, focus groups, commissioned essays, and a survey instrument that yielded a 75 percent response rate. The results of this study led to the publication of *Leading from the Center: The Emerging Role of the Chief Academic Officer in Theological Schools.*

McLean's study revealed that, "while presidents and deans found it relatively easy to define their respective duties, describing their roles, separately and relative to one another, proved to be a more complex and uncertain task."[9] In addition,

> clarification of presidential expectations concerning the role of the chief academic officer and the dean's acceptance of that role are critical to their working together successfully. Where the role is misunderstood by either party, missteps and confusion can result. Findings of the study suggest there is considerable clarity and agreement between presidents and deans regarding the duties of office, which are commonly specified in writing and discussed, but there are less well-defined and more implicit understandings of their respective administrative roles and areas of formal and informal authority.[10]

8. Gunsalus, *The College Administrator's Survival Guide,* p. 15.

9. Jeanne P. McLean, *Leading from the Center: The Emerging Role of the Chief Academic Officer in Theological Schools* (Atlanta: Scholars Press, 1999), p. 85.

10. McLean, *Leading from the Center,* pp. 86-87.

The president has a stewardship responsibility for the whole institution and is usually the only administrator directly accountable to the board of trustees. The dean has a stewardship responsibility that varies in scope depending upon the size and organizational structure of the institution. The president may spend as much as 50 percent or more of his or her time on board interaction/development and donor cultivation. By contrast, nearly two-thirds of a dean's time is expended doing paperwork, attending meetings, and working with faculty, staff, and students.[11] Since the educational program is at the heart of the school, the dean might expect it to receive the president's greatest attention. The mission of the school is only furthered, however, when the president attends to increasing responsibilities of donor cultivation and monitors the efficiency/effectiveness of each department through the appropriate senior administrator.

In most organizational structures, the president bears final responsibility to the board for institutional leadership and decision making. Recognizing the lines of institutional authority is essential to good deaning. Mike Bonem and Roger Patterson's helpful book, *Leading from the Second Chair: Serving Your Church, Fulfilling Your Role, and Realizing Your Dreams*, while principally focused on the relationship between the lead pastor or senior pastor and the executive pastor in a local church, provides a helpful discussion for anyone serving in a second chair position. One of the issues they discuss is the importance of clarity regarding lines of authority:

> First, recognize that a line exists. It defines responsibilities and authority, and it is much more than what is conveyed in a job description. Second, those who cross the line do so at their own peril. Crossing the line is insubordination, and the relationship between first and second chair cannot survive if insubordination exists.[12]

Understanding the location of the line will impact the scope of decision making and which decisions may or may not be made without consultation with the president.

11. Karen M. Ristau, *Challenges of Academic Administration: Rewards and Stresses in the Role of the Chief Academic Officer* (St. Paul, MN: University of St. Thomas, 1996), quoted in Melinda R. Heppe, "The Intentional Dean: Nurturing the Vocation of Academic Administrators," *In Trust* 7, no. 4 (Summer 1996): 11.

12. Mike Bonem and Roger Patterson, *Leading from the Second Chair: Serving Your Church, Fulfilling Your Role, and Realizing Your Dreams* (San Francisco: Jossey-Bass Publishers, 2005), p. 45.

The line defines your responsibilities — what you are expected to do, what you are authorized to do, and what is out of bounds. Do you have a clear idea of where the line is for you? Can you describe with certainty which decisions you can make without consulting your first chair, which require first chair approval, and which you should not even touch? If you are a second chair leader, this answer may not be found in a job description.[13]

It is also fair to say that a certain amount of trial and error is part of finding the line. It is important for the longevity of the relationship that the reality of the line is clearly understood. "Healthy, long-term relationships require three things: recognition of the existence of the line, flexibility in placement of the line, and caution in crossing the line."[14]

Analyzing Institutional Culture

A good beginning to the president and dean relationship also requires an understanding of the historical position of dean in your school and any anticipated changes to the position. At our school, the creation of an enrollment management department under the leadership of a new vice president was taking place concurrent with my appointment. In addition, another senior leadership position was being eliminated, and the responsibility and role of the dean was shifting from that which was historically understood. A new dean must reflect on additional (and very significant) issues that may arise for the first person of a particular gender or ethnicity to serve in the position of dean at the institution. Freestanding, university-related, and denominationally affiliated seminaries each will nuance the position and authority of the dean and president in different ways.

Every institution has an ethos and tacit curriculum that is important to exegete. Reading historical documents in the archives and interaction with individuals who've had extended involvement with the institution (residential historians) can help the dean better understand the institution. *Being There: Culture and Formation in Two Theological Schools,* authored by Jackson Carroll, Barbara Wheeler, Daniel Aleshire, and Penny Marler, is an excellent example of ethnographic research describing culture and forma-

13. Bonem and Patterson, *Leading from the Second Chair,* pp. 45-46.
14. Bonem and Patterson, *Leading from the Second Chair,* p. 44.

tion in two theological schools.[15] The research suggests some ways to better understand the unwritten curriculum at an institution. Knowing institutional history, being able to articulate institutional values, and understanding institutional centers of power all contribute to effective leadership. Serving in the role of dean is challenging and demands cultural analysis from the outset.

Wilson Yates, who served as faculty member, academic dean, and president at United Theological Seminary of the Twin Cities, in an address to chief academic officers at an ATS conference in October of 1997, reminded his audience that the entire school can be impacted for good or for ill by the president/dean relationship. There couldn't be a clearer call for cultivating, supporting, and protecting the relationship with some very intentional practices.

> The most important two-person relationship in theological education is that of the dean and the president. If it is a politically and morally good relationship, it can become a pivotal model and source of creativity, collegiality, and trust for the whole school; if it is a bad relationship that is politically uneven, if not acrimonious and questionable in its moral trustworthiness and relationality, it can become a devastating model and source of power plays, stalemates, and alienating behavior for the institution.[16]

Intentional Practices for Good Relationships

What are some intentional practices that can contribute to a good relationship?

Trust

First, as with all relationships, is the ingredient of trust. McLean stresses the importance of trust in *Leading from the Center*. In chapter three she dis-

---

15. Jackson Carroll, Barbara Wheeler, Daniel Aleshire, and Penny Marler, *Being There: Culture and Formation in Two Theological Schools* (New York: Oxford University Press, 1997).

16. Wilson Yates, "The Art and Politics of Deaning," *Theological Education* 34, no. 1 (1997): 88.

cusses the dean/president relationship and notes that "the offices of president and dean are historically interdependent,"[17] and "at the heart of the dean/president relationship is their need to trust one another to be true to their word and to act accordingly."[18] "Deans and presidents invariably found trust to be, as one dean put it, 'the coin of the realm.'"[19] Trust takes time to build and can be quickly broken. Airing disagreements publicly, not following through on agreed upon responsibilities, violating confidences, or allowing triangulation to occur with various constituencies can quickly undermine trust. Yates cites the fallout of a lack of trust in his helpful address:

> If they do not trust each other, if they are not good colleagues, if they engage in end runs and power plays, then they undercut their capacity to provide each other critical evaluation, mutual support, and their responsibility to provide the institution a sound sense of its own vision and destiny.[20]

Avoiding Triangulation

Avoiding triangulation is the second practice that requires intentionality. It is not a question of "if" but "when" the opportunities to become triangulated occur with board members, faculty, staff, donors, church leaders, students, and, yes, even parents of graduate students. With the advent of email, the indirect attempts to triangulate are multiplied. Copying one another on responses that involve or impact one another is usually required. Meeting with one another in person when there is a direct attempt on the part of a third party to triangulate is a necessity. All communication of the dean with members of the board of trustees should be shared with the president except in cases of reporting a legal or ethical violation on the part of the president, and this should only occur when the facts are irrefutable and the CEO has rejected the counsel of the dean or when the board of trustees has issued a specific directive.

17. McLean, *Leading from the Center*, p. 81.
18. McLean, *Leading from the Center*, p. 98.
19. McLean, *Leading from the Center*, p. 98.
20. Yates, "The Art and Politics of Deaning," p. 88.

Communication

The third practice essential to relationship health is regular and timely communication. Some presidents and deans have fixed scheduled meetings. For others, open access and many informal meetings throughout the week may work. "When asked to describe the elements of an effective relationship, deans and presidents agreed, 'Communication is the key.' . . . On the survey, theological school deans estimated they spend an average of 2.2 hours per week in substantive conversation with their presidents, which is close to the 2.4 hours they consider optimal."[21] A part of learning to "manage up" and good deaning is learning how the president likes to communicate. Does the president desire a fuller and more narrative kind of communication or a more bulleted style? Does the president acquire information best by reading or hearing? In addition, deans must do all they can to ensure that presidents are not surprised or caught off guard by decisions or events they may be questioned about. Part of good deaning is the ability to weigh what does/doesn't need to be communicated with the president. It is most helpful if presidents are given time to reflect on their responses to difficult issues or confrontations that are pending rather than being placed in situations in which they are forced to react (unfortunately, both leaders are never fully given that luxury). "Presidents and deans also depend on each other to be open with information, forthright in their opinions, and able to keep confidences. When these principles are not followed, the integrity of the communication and ultimately of the relationship is threatened."[22]

It can be helpful for the president and dean to talk about whether each one is a more internal or external processor of information. External processors need to remind internal processors that they are thinking out loud when they comment, or misunderstandings can quickly occur. An external processor needs to carefully respond to any comments made by an internal processor. An annual performance review should include a discussion that extends beyond the accomplishment of yearly goals and includes reflection on whether an appropriate level of communication is taking place. In the event of an institutional crisis, it is essential for the president and dean to quickly access one another and ensure that institutional communication is singular. Rights to privacy, disability laws, and an increasingly litigious society require processing the wording of communication with one another be-

---

21. McLean, *Leading from the Center*, p. 90.
22. McLean, *Leading from the Center*, p. 91.

fore responses are given. In certain situations where litigation is a perceived or real threat, it is important to seek legal counsel first.

Managing Conflict

A fourth practice that requires intentionality is managing conflict that occurs between the president and dean. Effective conflict management requires understanding how each typically responds to conflict. For those who are conflict avoiders, tension and disagreements can surface in unhealthy ways that can negatively impact the institution.

> The ability of deans and presidents to work through their differences — to manage conflict, to resolve disagreements, and, on rare occasions, to agree to disagree — is critical to their relationship and to the effectiveness of both offices. Often deans and presidents use their private meetings to process issues so their public stance, whenever possible, can be unified and mutually supportive.[23]

Agreement on Strategic Issues

A fifth intentional practice is agreement by the president and dean on the most strategic issues that must be accomplished for the sake of institutional health and advancement.

> Consider the experience of a newly appointed hospital administrator. The hospital was big and prestigious, but it had been coasting on its reputation for 30 years. The new administrator decided that his contribution should be to establish a standard of excellence in one important area within two years. He chose to focus on the emergency room, which was big, visible, and sloppy. He decided that every patient who came into the ER had to be seen by a qualified nurse within 60 seconds. Within 12 months, the hospital's emergency room had become a model for all hospitals in the United States, and within another two years, the whole hospital had been transformed.[24]

23. McLean, *Leading from the Center*, p. 97.
24. Drucker, "Managing Oneself," pp. 7-8.

Strategic initiatives that are clear, significant, and manageable provide an opportunity for prioritizing the dean's workload and clarify how pursuit of those initiatives will further the mission and vision of the institution.

Building trust, avoiding triangulation, communicating well, managing conflict, and agreement on strategic initiatives are intentional practices that will serve the president/dean relationship well. Preventive care will strengthen the relationship for pressures brought to bear from outside as well as within the institution. Regular prayer for one another recognizes the dependence on God that is a non-negotiable for serving in either role and serving effectively together. Genuine appreciation for one another and the gifts and strengths that each contributes will create a genuine sharing of the burden as well as the joys of leadership. For anyone who has completed an institutional analysis of strengths, weaknesses, opportunities, and threats (SWOT analysis), the convergence of threats with institutionally identified weaknesses can create the kind of perfect storm that can challenge or strengthen the best of relationships. Building the relationship before the challenges inevitably come will benefit both the president and dean as well as the institution they serve.

In any relationship, common values and commitment to a mission that is more important than one's own agenda can generate a synergy that furthers the work of the kingdom through providing a vibrant and transformative graduate theological education. When the mission is compelling and jointly embraced, there can be a common focus, a filter for decision making, and motivation to persevere in challenging times. The president/dean relationship must be intentionally cultivated and protected for the sake of the seminary and all those connected with the advancement of its mission.

ADDITIONAL RESOURCES

Bonem, Mike, and Roger Patterson. *Leading from the Second Chair: Serving Your Church, Fulfilling Your Role, and Realizing Your Dreams.* San Francisco: Jossey-Bass Publishers, 2005.

Drucker, Peter F. "Managing Oneself." *Harvard Business Review,* Best of HBR 1999, originally appeared in *Harvard Business Review,* January 2005.

Gunsalus, C. K. *The College Administrator's Survival Guide.* Cambridge, MA: Harvard University Press, 2006.

Heppe, Melinda. "The Intentional Dean: Nurturing the Vocation of Academic Administrators," *In Trust* 7, no. 4 (Summer 1996): 8-11.

Keller, Rosemary Skinner. *Spirituality and Social Responsibility: Vocational Vision of Women in the United Methodist Tradition.* Nashville: Abingdon Press, 1993. Quoted in Melinda R. Heppe, "The Intentional Dean: Nurturing the Vocation of Academic Administrators," *In Trust* (Summer 1996): 10.

McLean, Jeanne P. *Leading from the Center: The Emerging Role of the Chief Academic Officer in Theological Schools.* Atlanta: Scholars Press, 1999.

McNeal, Reggie. *A Work of Heart: Understanding How God Shapes Spiritual Leaders.* San Francisco: Jossey-Bass Publishers, 2000.

Oden, Thomas C. *Pastoral Theology: Essentials of Ministry.* San Francisco: Harper & Row, 1983.

Walters, Tom. Survey of Academic Deans in the Association of Theological Schools, 2 November 2006.

Yates, Wilson. "The Art and Politics of Deaning," *Theological Education* 34, no. 1 (1997): 85-96.

5. The Dean's Role in Governance

Governance and Faculty Leadership:
Routine, Complex, Contentious, and Collaborative

D. Cameron Murchison

It seemed like good-humored deference when I first became dean. Even people whom I had known for many years referred to me (in my presence) as "the dean" or, with clearly mock obeisance, even as "your dean-ness." I assumed that this was part of a congratulatory phase in which colleagues were acknowledging a new role I had assumed when, after having been a member of the faculty, I was elected dean of faculty. After several years in the role, however, I have discovered that these ways of identifying me in terms of the office in which I function persist, leading me to the conclusion that, at least in my institutional setting (and I suspect in a number of similar institutional settings), there are implicit (though perhaps inchoate) assumptions about the dean's role in governance. Certainly the vocabulary used with reference to the office presumes a certain authority attached to it as well, although whether that authority is judged to be well-placed or wisely exercised is another matter.

As may be familiar in freestanding seminaries, my specific role is a hybrid one that involves both specifically academic administration and general institutional administration. In the former regard, I am dean of faculty. In the latter, I am also executive vice president. This general administrative role in the institution's life consists of occasionally standing in for the president when she is otherwise occupied and some institutional presence is needed. But more routinely, it consists in functioning as a member of the presidential/vice presidential team in developing institutional plans, assessing institutional effectiveness, and dealing with myriad operational issues that are constantly arising in institutional life.

There is no doubt that my faculty colleagues are aware of my general administrative role in the life of the institution — sometimes applauding it and sometimes questioning it, while always scrutinizing it. But it is telling that they never speak of me as "Mr. Vice President"; instead they most typically speak of me as "the dean." I take this to mean that they regard the most crucial role for one occupying the office to be that of authority and governance in academic matters. The range of such academic authority and governance extends to two core areas of academic life: developing the educational program and nurturing faculty leadership. Both of these areas represent fertile ground for analyzing the problematic proposed for this chapter: how formal governance procedures are sometimes rendered complex — if not contentious — by informal governance understandings. Here I will focus on faculty leadership.

Domains of Governance

To explore this dynamic I will look at two interrelated components of academic administration in relation to developing faculty leadership. On the one hand there are issues surrounding faculty searches and recruitment, while on the other hand there are corollary matters of faculty development and promotion. As a theoretical framework for analyzing the interplay between formal and informal governance understandings in such matters of academic governance, I have found the schema derived from Chait, Ryan, and Taylor and mediated through the faculty vocation and governance workshops sponsored by ATS to be especially illuminating.[1]

This framework provides analysis of institutional governance in terms of three overlapping but distinct domains. Fiduciary governance consists in core managerial governance that is properly concerned with oversight and

---

1. Richard P. Chait, William P. Ryan, and Barbara E. Taylor, *Governance as Leadership: Reframing the Work of Nonprofit Boards* (Hoboken: John Wiley & Sons, Inc., 2005). I am especially indebted to David Tiede's parsing of their schema with respect to faculty governance in the academic domain in his workshop presentation on April 1, 2006.

accountability, with doing what has been agreed upon in an effective and efficient manner. Strategic governance, by contrast, casts its eye to the horizon of the future and asks what steps may help an institution make progress toward a new state of affairs. In turn, generative governance asks the even larger question of what it really is that the institution wants to create, of what vision should and will animate the life of the institution at all levels.

Experience over time has convinced me that in many matters of academic administration, a faculty willingly cedes authority to a dean in most if not all matters of fiduciary governance. When it comes to the arena of strategic governance, however, the dissonance between formal governance assumptions and informal understandings can become quite pronounced, leading to serious contests about what strategic choices should be made. If an institution is to find a way beyond such governance impasses, it is worth pondering how fresh attention to matters of generative governance might create a practice of shared governance that can forge an institutional vision that, in turn, opens a viable way to the future. In what follows, an effort is made to trace these matters concretely with reference to faculty search and recruitment and with reference to faculty development and promotion.

Fiduciary and Strategic Governance in Faculty Search and Recruitment

In many respects, nothing is more important to faculty members than finding and recruiting new faculty members. As just suggested, governance at the fiduciary level may readily be entrusted to the dean when it comes to this work. To begin with, a dean will be expected generally to monitor predictable transitions in faculty composition. The most obvious way this happens is by tracking particular faculty trajectories toward retirement. Fiduciary governance on the part of a dean will involve projecting the timetable for these changes and readying the institutionally approved processes for finding replacements. Occasionally faculty members become aware of such impending changes, but it is obviously part of the dean's responsibility to constantly maintain such awareness and to plan accordingly. A dean who is functioning in this activity of institutional oversight can provide reassurance to faculty members who occasionally (and sometimes suddenly) become concerned about an approaching faculty vacancy.

Once the need for a faculty search is thus identified through the practice of fiduciary governance, a dean continues exercising governance in this domain by coordinating the activities of the search itself. My personal experience in the dean's office demonstrates that faculty chairs of search committees vary significantly in how much fiduciary governance they want to undertake in that role. Some have been very active in coordinating the work of the search committees they chair, while others have actively sought the resources of the dean's office to give oversight and maintain accountability in the committee's work. But whatever the case at the level of committee functioning, certain background work of advertising the position, developing an agreed-upon description for the position, and coordinating the receipt and review of candidates' dossiers inevitably require the active engagement of the dean. The primary point to make about this work of fiduciary governance in faculty search and recruitment is that usually formal organizational arrangements are well established, understood, and accepted by both the faculty and the dean. So at this level of the work, complex and contentious relationships between formal and informal governance understandings do not typically occur.

When the attention of such a search process shifts to the arena of strategic governance, the possibilities for such complexity and contentiousness multiply. In strategic governance the focus is not so much about oversight and accountability in institutional processes as it is about judgments concerning which choices in faculty searches might bring the institution closer to the future it imagines for itself. In my own institution, for several years the strategic plan has projected a balance among new faculty invited to the collegium with respect to more senior appointments of prominence and more junior appointments of promise. To be sure, a fiduciary principle of governance is operative here as well, since budget constraints would never allow all appointments to be from the first of these categories. A second projected strategic balance has to do with at least two forms of diversity, racial/ethnic and theological. But of course such strategic principles come closer to setting an agenda for a particular search committee to consider than offering the committee a conclusion to follow. And here lie the possibilities for complexity and contentiousness.

The dean's role in this domain of strategic governance in search committee work is quite different from the same dean's work in fiduciary governance. There is far less deference to or dependence upon the dean on the part of faculty (and other members of search committees) at this juncture. Clearly the dean has responsibility to identify for the committee's work the strategic balances that have been institutionally identified, such as those indicated above. Moreover, the dean is more likely than most other members of the search committee to have knowledge of how other search committees are proceeding and what choices they are making with respect to these strategic priorities. Thus keeping the larger institutional picture before the work of a particular committee is important work for the dean. Yet having done so, important, contestable decisions remain for the work of the committee.

Even if all committee members are equally committed to the strategic priorities, the fact that the ones named above deal with balance among options means that decisions still have to be made. When we take note of the fact that the balances referred to have extensive subjective elements ("promise," "prominence," "theological diversity"), not to mention the meaning of "balance" itself, the opportunity for significantly contested decision making is obvious. As a consequence, the strategic decision making that goes on in this context is scarcely scripted as it often is at the preceding, fiduciary level. Informal or personal understandings of all these "balance" variables will come into play, and a dean's view of such matters will be just one (and not even first) among equals. Deans in such circumstances will be unwise to expect any undue deference to their opinions about which of those "balance" variables applies to the particular search at hand. While a dean might be able to inform the committee about how the variables have been applied in other recent or concurrent searches, whether the committee will agree on the implications of those decisions for its work is another matter.

Moreover, a further complexity arises when it happens that, notwithstanding official strategic priorities, some members simply have not bought fully into the strategy itself. For example, some members may be functioning with a private commitment not to balance appointments of promise with others of prominence, but rather may be earnestly committed always to finding the most accomplished person available for any position. Alternatively, committee members may have significantly different views about the acceptable range of theological diversity that is healthy and creative for the life of the institution. That a dispute with the official strategic direction of the institution is taking place may not necessarily be consciously acknowledged, because these conversations can easily proceed under the guise of striking the right "balance" among those strategic priorities. Perhaps the best service a dean may provide at this juncture of strategic governance is to lead the conversation back to legitimate choices among strategic priorities, as contrasted with contention over those strategic priorities themselves.

In any case, the dean finds a different situation when the move is made from fiduciary to strategic governance in the matters of faculty searches. A first principle to be observed is that it is unreasonable to expect as much acquiescence to the dean's initiative and perspective in the strategic moment as may be the case in the fiduciary moment. A second principle is that, while it is the dean's responsibility to frame the institution's strategic priorities as they bear on the work of a search committee — especially in relation to the work of other such committees — and to keep them before the committee at moments when it may tend to ignore or otherwise disregard them, real decisions rightly remain for the committee to make. Thus in the actual rendering of the committee decision, the dean has the same governance role as every other member of the committee — contributing to an informed and wise decision by the committee as a whole.

The emerging picture for the dean's role in governance around the case of faculty searches may appear to be one of a well-ordered reliance on the dean's leadership and initiative in the fiduciary area (oversight and accountability) that devolves into a free-for-all among committee members in the strategic area (choices about moving to a desired future) as informal, personal, and even idiosyncratic understandings about strategic balances come into play. While this latter strategic level of decision making is certainly shared governance in the sense that everyone has a vote in deciding, it also is easily burdened with contentious possibilities that may not bode well for long-term institutional effectiveness. The obvious question is whether there are other dimensions of governance that have any promise of informing the work of faculty searches with a collaborative vision that may transcend and transform the informal, personal, and idiosyncratic understandings that otherwise may dominate the selection process.

As suggested earlier, the third, generative level of governance is the most promising place where a larger vision might be cultivated. By nature this type of governance is collaborative, or else it is not truly generative. Moreover, it is an overarching component of governance that cannot be undertaken in the exigencies of immediate decision making. As such, generative governance does not provide a quick remedy for the kind of impasse into which search processes might wander. Instead, it challenges the dean to structure and facilitate occasions in which the collegium might generate a framework for understanding the character of the faculty leadership it most wants to create and maintain in the institution's life.

Since this generative level of governance necessarily operates apart from the specific case of faculty search and recruitment, it is appropriate before turning directly to it to consider another related matter of faculty leadership. By turning our attention briefly to an analysis of fiduciary and strategic governance issues in faculty development and promotion, we will find our way by a parallel road back to the matter of generative governance around faculty leadership as a whole.

Fiduciary and Strategic Governance in Faculty Development and Promotion

Many theological schools devote a fair amount of energy and attention not only to bringing new faculty into their collegium but also in seeking to nurture their development as they move along in their work. My institution is probably similar to many others in its tenure/promotion processes. Through these processes, junior colleagues are counseled about what developments in their teaching, scholarship, and writing and what contributions to institution, church, and community will most fully embody the expectations of their school and lead thereby to success in negotiating the tenure and promotion process. Reflecting on the governance role of the dean in this process reveals a familiar pattern of relative acquiescence to the dean's leadership in the fiduciary dimensions of the process and relative contentiousness among all parties in the strategic dimensions of the process.

In my institution the dean's fiduciary responsibilities for faculty development and promotion are considerable. They begin with budget development and cultivation of financial resources that not only seek to provide fair compensation for faculty but also fund specific opportunities for faculty development through workshops, study grants, and sabbatical leaves. In addition, the dean meets annually with each member of the faculty to discuss relative allocations of time and energy across the range of faculty responsibilities as well as specific goals faculty may have for further development in those various areas. The dean also makes appointments to standing faculty committees in a manner that seeks to honor both the institutional needs and the development needs of particular faculty members. While faculty members are likely to lobby for particular assignments on those committees, all these activities of fiduciary (oversight and accountability) governance are generally received charitably, with not infrequent comments by faculty suggesting they are glad to yield such responsibilities to the office of the dean.

Something similar holds for the fiduciary elements involved in governing the tenure and promotion process. In our case, the most time consuming features have to do with structuring the evaluation committee's work in a particular year, prompting various parties to contribute relevant materials to the evaluation dossier, soliciting external reviews of the candidates, and facilitating input from faculty colleagues and students. With the occasional exception of selecting the external reviewers, faculty committee members have typically been eager for the dean to exercise initiative and judgment in attending to these fiduciary tasks for the evaluation process.

But as in the case of faculty search committee work, evaluation committee work becomes increasingly complex and contentious when it reaches the strategic dimension. Here the focus moves beyond the organizational level of the committee's work to strategic choices about colleagues who will be invited to lead and sustain the educational mission of the institution indefinitely. In the system developed in my institution, the dean has several specific responsibilities toward the work of the committee as it undertakes its strategic decision making. Chief among these is reminding everyone of the policy provisions as they pertain to particular tenure/promotion decisions. Typically this consists in calling attention to the general rubrics for evaluation and noting the counsel that may have been provided candidates at earlier stages of the evaluation process.

Experience with these procedures suggests that, just as in the case of faculty searches, official policy on the grounds for tenure and promotion (viz., the fourfold criteria of teaching, scholarship/research, institutional contribution, and church/community service) still leaves a lot of decision making to be done. The complexity is again related to the inevitable subjective dimension of judgments entailed in all the criteria, as well as to the fact that the policy makes explicit that the weighting of the various criteria may differ from candidate to candidate, depending upon the gifts and capacities of candidates and the needs of the institution. The record of such relative weighting is maintained at each step of the process in order that there may be continuity of judgment by the evaluation committee over the course of a faculty member's progress through the system. It is the particular responsibility of the dean to maintain and make this record available to the evaluation committee as it conducts its evaluation of particular candidates, especially since the composition of the evaluation committee changes over time.

Nonetheless, the informal, personal, and indiosyncratic understandings of the criteria and of the prior counsel of evaluation committees appears to be inevitable and can lead to the same contentiousness earlier observed in relation to faculty searches. Here as there, the dean's role in governance receives little deference. A particular publication record, a particular profile of student course evaluations, a particular record of institutional or church service — whether any of these constitutes the level of excellence expected by the evaluation committee for tenure or promotion is still a decision that is at least complex and in some cases contentious. While the dean does have a special responsibility of strategic governance in keeping the prior work of the evaluation committee with the candidate in view so that it may have its proper weight at the current point of decision, there is no other unique strategic function for the dean's office.

The same question that arose with respect to strategic governance in faculty search processes recurs here: Are there other dimensions of governance that have any promise of informing the work of faculty evaluation for tenure/promotion with a collaborative vision that may transcend and transform the informal, personal, and idiosyncratic understandings that otherwise may dominate the evaluation process? Again, looking at this second area of cultivating faculty leadership in an institution's life has returned us to the domain of generative governance. What is needed is a means of transcending and transforming the personal and informal understandings faculty bring to their work on search committees and on evaluation committees. What is needed is a collaborative vision or framework for understanding the character of the faculty leadership the institution most wants to create and maintain in its life.

Generative Governance and the Cultivation of Faculty Leadership

In two instances of faculty life we have seen tendencies that broadly affirm a dean's specific and generally deferred-to role in matters of formal, fiduciary governance. At the same time, we have seen in these two instances tendencies for informal and personal understandings of governance to dominate in strategic moments of governance, when long-term decisions are being made about who will become or continue as faculty in the life of a given institution. Thus we have been suggesting that a dean's leadership in generative governance might turn out to be the most critical for decisions about faculty leadership. For to move beyond the domination of search and evaluation decisions by informal and personal understandings, something more is needed than strategic priorities for faculty composition or strategic criteria for evaluation and promotion. What is needed is a generative conversation that promotes deeply collaborative exploration of what the character of an institution's faculty should be. Only with clarity about the character of the faculty that the institution wants to create and maintain can there be confidence that decisions (while always complex and always contested to some degree) nonetheless reflect formal governance assumptions, rather than surrendering to the most powerful informal and personal assumptions operative in a particular case.

At this point both the reader and the writer of this essay are destined for some disappointment. The overarching thesis evolved in this project has been based on the limits of fiduciary and strategic forms of governance respecting faculty leadership, and the benefits of generative governance have yet to be tested. Moreover, the generative governance conversation needed is one that should involve not only faculty but also members of the board of trustees.

However, even if we cannot conclude with a report on what a dean might have done in fostering healthy shared governance that overcomes dissonance between formal and informal governance arrangements, we can point to some possibilities with which many of us might experiment. Already we have identified shared governance at the generative level as a promising avenue for such an experiment. One major advantage of this dimension of governance is that it is the most broadly shared in an institution's life, fittingly bringing into common conversation both faculty and board members around the matter of faculty leadership.

The precise venues for developing occasions of such collaborative conversation among faculty and between faculty and board members will doubtless vary from institution to institution, but finding such venues is a worthy venture for a dean who seeks to promote healthy forms of shared governance. Why it is a worthy venture may best be illustrated by imagining a possible outcome of such a collaborative exercise in shared governance. First, we will imagine a possible collaborative vision for the faculty that an institution wants to create and maintain. Then, assuming it has been reached as a broadly affirmed institutional vision, we will suggest how such a collaborative vision might transform the informal and personal contentiousness observed in both faculty searches and faculty promotion/tenure decisions.

The imagined collaborative vision for the faculty of our hypothetical institution is this: Faculty will embody differentiated excellence as scholars and teachers who contribute variously to the preparation/formation of leadership for Christian communities and to creating resources that sustain and encourage the church's mission. Although such a collaborative vision would not determine in the case of a search committee whether it would seek to appoint a colleague of "promise" or of "prominence," it would invite the committee to give some attention to the current composition of its faculty as a way of making an institutionally appropriate judgment concerning which kind of "differentiated excellence" ("promise" or "prominence" in this case) may be most needed at this juncture of the institution's life. Similarly, such a collaborative vision would not dictate to an evaluation committee how it should evaluate a particular candidate for tenure or promotion, but recognizing that faculty "contribute variously" to multiple dimensions of the educational mission of the school may provide reinforcement for paying closer attention to the way a candidate's contributions have been weighted over the course of their work in the institution.

The important point in both cases is that having achieved a collaborative vision does create a framework in which cases of faculty leadership can be considered. Because consistency is provided by agreed-upon utilization of the same framework, it is not a matter of applying all specific criteria in the same way to each case. It is rather a matter of judging each case explicitly and formally in terms of a collaborative, public framework, not implicitly and informally in terms of something more private and unacknowledged. None of us, least of all deans, should expect disagreement and contention to disappear from the horizon of faculty leadership decisions on the basis of such a collaborative vision. However, we should have good hope that the disagreement and contention will be public, appropriate, and healthy as a result.

ADDITIONAL RESOURCES

Chait, Richard P., William P. Ryan, and Barbara E. Taylor. *Governance as Leadership: Reframing the Work of Nonprofit Boards.* Hoboken: John Wiley & Sons, Inc., 2005.

Bennett, John B. *Academic Life: Hospitality, Ethics, and Spirituality.* Bolton, MA: Anker Publishing Company, Inc., 2003.

Boyer, Ernest L. *Scholarship Reconsidered: Priorities of the Professoriate.* Stanford, CA: The Carnegie Foundation for the Advancement of Teaching, 1990.

Martin, James, James E. Samels & Associates. *First Among Equals: The Role of the Chief Academic Officer.* Baltimore: The Johns Hopkins University Press, 1997.

Morrill, Richard L. *Strategic Leadership in Academic Affairs: Clarifying the Board's Responsibilities.* Washington, DC: Association of Governing Boards of Universities and Colleges, 2002.

ANNE T. ANDERSON

Fulcrum Leadership and the Varied Dimensions of Governance

Anne T. Anderson

A Handbook for Seminary Presidents[1] notes that one of the most common designs for institutional governance is a tripartite process that invites board, president, and faculty into a strategic partnership. The president's relationship to the board chair is explored in some depth, as is the role of the faculty. Leadership and management roles are differentiated. The need for presidents to have reliable information and data for the optimal function of their boards is underscored.

One of the pivotal roles in this governance process is that of the dean. The success or failure of the dean in a governance role is, of course, dependent on the dean's relationship with the president. Trust and mutual respect are foundational for a harmonious and productive relationship, as are a clear definition of boundaries and acceptance of the scope and breadth of delegated authority and the concomitant accountability. Both the president and the dean need to exercise due diligence in ensuring that "end runs" around either party are not encouraged or permitted so that the unique roles of both positions may be effectively and collegially fulfilled.

Since seminaries and many colleges/universities are faith-based organizations, one foundational presupposition is that in these interrelationships the *educational mission* of the organization is the defining lens through which the institution plans, organizes, implements, controls, and evaluates. In this complex milieu, the dean's role in governance might aptly be conceived of as a *fulcrum*. The dean ensures that the voices of the faculty and student body are communicated though the president to the governing body. The dean also ensures that communication from the board and president to the faculty and student body is timely, transparent, and authentic. The president, of course, has direct access to the faculty and student body, but more often than not the role and function of the presidency looks outward, while the role and function of the dean has an inward focus. This inward focus gives the dean a particular role in governance, which is in effect a

---

1. G. Douglass Lewis and Lovett H. Weems Jr., eds., *A Handbook for Seminary Presidents* (Grand Rapids: Eerdmans, 2006), pp. 35-57.

ministry to the educational mission of the school. This particular ministry is both tangible and intangible.

Tangible Dimensions of the Dean's "Fulcrum" Leadership in Governance

The Relationship between Educational Mission and Governance

The core mission of a seminary/college/university is education. A focus on excellence is a constant, whether the institution prepares graduates for the practice of ordained ministry or for other forms of ministry including professorial roles in seminaries, colleges, or universities. The educational process itself sets up a web of governance relationships that is vital to the ongoing life of the institution. The dean's role offers many opportunities to exercise leadership of this process.

Continuous Quality Improvement (read assessment) provides the hard data as to how an institution is meeting its educational objectives and is realizing its institutional mission. This data takes on a two-fold function. For the dean and faculty, the data enjoys a key role in the ongoing and strategic planning of educational goals, course cycling, and modes of delivery. It also serves as a harbinger of where courses and programs may need either minor changes or major modifications. Enrollment (part-time or full-time) and the resulting tuition revenue are also essential elements of evaluation. Sound evaluation is the bedrock of successful strategic planning.

The second function of this data is to enable the dean to provide concrete information for the president and board in their exercise of composite governance for the entire institution. This data often has a direct bearing on the amount of endowment funds required as well as the amount of funds that development officers are asked to raise in an annual fund drive to support a particular program that is imperative for the school's mission but unable to sustain itself. Deans must be grounded in and familiar with the overall institutional strategic plan and budgetary processes so that they are able to nuance the data and draw out both benefits and implications for consideration by their presidents and boards.

The more stressed the economic reality faced by a school, the more the president and board need the information/vantage point that the dean may offer to assist them in thinking through the implications for the school's educational mission of the difficult choices they face. For example, in a market downturn, planned revenues may not materialize, thereby limiting the amount of funds available for entrance scholarships. The dean's acumen in assisting the president and chief financial officer to assess the potential impact of cutbacks in entrance scholarships on other vital dimensions of the school's revenue streams and educational programs may help the president and board to consider whether alternatives to radically reducing entrance scholarships should be considered. If the cuts must be made, the dean's input is vital to the examination of what programmatic modifications are necessary to help the school sustain its educational mission over the long haul.

Faculty "buy in" to the evaluation/strategic planning process is essential, since it consumes precious time that could be devoted to research, writing, or a host of other pursuits. However, when the feedback loop is closed and all the data has been mined, reported, discussed, and authenticated, the interaction with president and board often mandates change. Some proposals for change may have originated with faculty, and others may come mandated by the board. In each case, the challenges are unique and often pervasive.

All change, whether major or minor, is disruptive at various levels but particularly at the level of faculty, staff, and students. This is yet another area where the dean's role and leadership in governance is called into play. Donna Markham offers the notion of "spirit linking leadership"[2] as one way of leading a mission-driven group through change. She defines this type of leadership as "the deliberate and untiring act of working through resistance to organizational transformation by building a circle of friends, fostering networks of human compassion and interweaving teams of relationships through which new ideas are born and new ways of responding to the mission take form and find expression."[3]

It is this ability to look creatively and constructively at the common good through a kaleidoscopic approach that strengthens and enhances the role the dean is called to play in both the tangibles and the intangibles of the governance function. Working with and through change is perhaps one of the most significant and essential roles the dean plays in governance. The manner in which the dean understands and manages resistance must ultimately lead toward a communal appreciation for the implications of continued resistance for the mission of the institution as well as its faculty, stu-

---

2. Donna J. Markham, OP, *Spirit Linking Leadership: Working Through Resistance to Organizational Change* (Mahwah, NJ: Paulist Press, 1999).

3. Markham, *Spirit Linking Leadership*, p. 5.

dents, and staff. This process leads those engaged in it to either commit to the change required or be willing to own the consequences.[4]

"Fulcrum" Leadership with Faculty

Good governance demands authentic communication at all levels of the dean's sphere of influence. The consistency of such authentic communication liberates human creativity and fosters cooperation and collaboration, all of which are essential to moving the mission into new and changing contexts without a complete destabilization of the institution.

However, it is the faculty and the development of faculty that is the bedrock of sustaining and delivering the institutional mission. Since faculty members report to the dean, it is the dean's particular responsibility to give systematic and focused attention to them, bearing in mind that with every retirement and/or new hire, the dynamics of the faculty change. It is therefore incumbent upon the dean to resist moving forward without an intentional orientation for newcomers as to where the group has been in discussion as well as to offer an indication of where the group appears to be moving. It is also important for newcomers to know that they have a voice in the group from the outset and are not expected to simply fall into a preset mold. Changing, pressured, and uncertain times often provide the context for the dean's role in faculty development, recruitment, and retention.

So how does the dean go about developing faculty, aside from attending to the requirements of annual evaluation and the preset requirements of the faculty handbook? Early on in my tenure as dean, I raised the issue of faculty development with a friend and mentor who had previously held the office of dean. He spoke at length about private entrepreneurs held together by a common heating system and gave me some other tips with respect to the difficulty of herding cats. Taking the warning seriously yet determined to try, I crafted a plan for developing the corporate leadership of the faculty.

Our comprehensive ATS visit was to occur the following year, so I asked the faculty if they would be willing to come to a three-day, off-campus retreat to look at what the self-study told us in the light of our mission and current context. I will admit that there was not universal enthusiasm, but all agreed that it was worth a try. We have never looked back! Each August for the last several years, our faculty has taken the time for a three-day retreat.

4. Markham, *Spirit Linking Leadership*, p. 44.

We use this precious time to update each other on current research and publications. We evaluate the year that has just passed in the light of our goals and outcomes for the various degree programs. We monitor our progress in the implementation of our strategic plan. We also plan the agendas for our faculty council meetings for the coming year, thus ensuring that we are moving forward carefully and intentionally.

A vital part of this annual retreat is that we take the time to relax together and to "talk theology." Our preparation for the faculty retreat has gone from a one-page "bare bones agenda" to a binder with pre-reading and background material for the various items to be discussed.

Over the first seven years of this practice, we had five new colleagues and an equal number of retiring colleagues. I believe that the retreat process has provided a platform for orientation of new members into the faculty and fostered a sense of integration and belonging. In addition, new faculty members are each assigned a mentor for the first year of employment.

The time invested in the retreat process has given the faculty a reflective and unified voice in their reporting and requests to the president and board through the dean. The board has approved a revised tenure process which includes a formal internal and external review at the end of the initial three-year contract. If this review is positive, a second contract of two years is offered, at the end of which an application for tenure may be presented. During this two-year contract a "junior leave" of six months has been instituted and is offered in order to ensure that there are sufficient publications for the tenure review.

Another benefit of the retreat process is ownership of the decisions that are informed by accurate data and ample discussion and put forth with the assurance that, to the best of the faculty's knowledge, nothing has been overlooked. The voice of a united and reflective faculty is heard with more respect and attention simply because it is clear, eloquent, and measured. This type of communication empowers and enhances the relationships among the board, president, and dean and allows the board to develop a proactive rather than a reactive stance toward the faculty and its concerns and agenda.

The ATS-mandated renewal and redevelopment of our MDiv curriculum has provided yet another opportunity for faculty development and growth. As we worked through curriculum development, design, and assessment issues, long conversations were focused on the development of syllabi. All core MDiv syllabi were presented to the entire faculty by the faculty members responsible for teaching each course. The presentation was followed by a discussion and critique of each syllabus presented. As a framework process for this exercise, we used the "Five Principles for Faculty Development" set out in *Educating Leaders for Ministry: Issues and Responses.*[5] Together we learned what it means to develop an integrated curriculum, and together we planned ways to assess student learning outcomes and integration. We also took comfort in the notion that "integration requires of students a tolerance for complexity."[6]

Sustained attention to faculty development is one of the most essential governance functions delegated to the dean. This task is never quite completed. "Spirit linking leadership" is a management tool that facilitates and enables faculty development through empowering and welcoming each member to contribute from the security of that individual's strengths. Faculty development is always in a state of flux and is an ever-present challenge, one that requires the dean's constant attention.

The printed material and Web sites of our institution keep the school's mission statement front and center, clearly articulated for all to see. We carefully outline and explore in goals and objectives the ways in which this mission shapes and informs all that we do as an institution. But it is in the classroom and in the interactions among faculty, staff, and students where the mission is most alive and active. In their various teaching, mentoring, and advising roles and functions, faculty members exemplify the institutional mission in a manner that is vibrant, relevant, interactive, and bursting with energy and potential. As Ralph Waldo Emerson once remarked, "What you do speaks so loud I cannot hear what you say."[7] Probably more than any other group in an institution, the faculty shapes the living face of the institutional mission and is aided in this critical role by a dean who assists them to present that "face" in a compelling and winsome way.

Closely aligned to faculty development is the concept of quality of work life. It is essential for a dean to recognize that the time individual faculty members spend in the institution is but one portion of the faculty member's life. However, it is a significant portion and as such has the power to affect other aspects of the faculty member's life. The converse is also true.

Deans are well aware that the personal and professional problems with

5. Victor J. Klimoski, Kevin J. O'Neil, and Katarina M. Schuth, *Educating Leaders for Ministry: Issues and Responses* (Collegeville, MN: Liturgical Press, 2005), pp. 57-74.

6. Klimoski, O'Neil, and Schuth, *Educating Leaders for Ministry,* p. 64.

7. Ralph Waldo Emerson, *The Conduct of Life* (New York: Houghton Mifflin reprint of 1860 text, 1982), p. 216.

which individual faculty members contend may at times come to the attention of the president and, in some instances, be subject to board action. An astute dean will endeavor to create an atmosphere within the faculty where there is a respectful, comfortable, and professional relationship with each member of the faculty — a relationship that allows for disclosure of a current or possible difficulty before it becomes an issue with the potential to affect the entire faculty or the school. This does not imply that the dean can single-handedly address, much less resolve, every situation. But open communication can help the dean support a faculty member who faces a painful challenge, e.g., a parent with Alzheimer's, the dissolution of a marriage, a sick child, a spouse with compromised health, repeated rejection by publishers, a serious issue with a student — the list could go on endlessly.

Not one of these issues can be compartmentalized and "put away" when a faculty member comes to work each day. In many instances, issues within the faculty also have the potential to affect the family life of a faculty member. Thus it is incumbent upon the dean to be aware that quality of work life extends far beyond the regular replacement of computers, access to color photocopiers, and the painting of offices. Quality of work life is yet another face of the living mission of the institution.

From time to time an issue arises wherein a complaint (e.g., a boundary violation, harassment, breach of confidentiality regarding a faculty member) requires a hearing and most likely disciplinary action by the board. It falls to the dean to ensure that policies within the faculty handbook are coherent and interface seamlessly with board policy and procedures. This is not a time for oral tradition. Due diligence requires that policies and procedure be scrupulously followed. Original documentation is required and must be signed by the complainant. In this case, the paper trail is absolutely essential. Early in any tenure, a dean is wise to add items of significance, both positive and negative, to faculty files. It is also good practice to make "notes to file" of significant conversations. These "notes to file" are often useful in establishing patterns of behavior. The faculty member should receive a copy of the notes as a part of the conversation process. Respect, transparency, and fair play are foundational to a successful resolution of sensitive issues. If an issue requires public disclosure, there should be a single spokesperson and discreet statement agreed upon by both parties.

Objectivity is an essential trait if the dean's role in governance is to be successful. This is particularly true when the dean has been appointed from within the faculty itself. Overnight the appointee goes from being one of "us" to being one of "them." The old familiar camaraderie shifts, and for a time there is a subliminal wariness until both sides become secure and comfortable in a changed reality. As a dean who was appointed from within faculty ranks, I struggled with the desire to right every real and imagined issue where we as a faculty perceived that we had been short-changed by "them." Externally appointed deans face their own challenges in exercising due diligence. Their quest for greater objectivity may lead them to research issues from both documented origins and their own insightful questions as they seek to avoid falling prey to the agenda of one or another special interest groups. Objectivity in interpersonal relationships, as well as sound analysis and presentation of issues, requests, and/or projects, is one measure of developing and sustaining a dean's credibility not only with the faculty but also with the president and the board.

"Fulcrum" Leadership with Students

At the very heart of the dean's role in governance is the overall responsibility for the quality of student learning, student life, and student experience. Of course, this is a responsibility that is shared with faculty, staff, and other personnel, but it is up to the dean to keep a finger on the pulse of student life. To a certain extent, this is achieved through evaluations of the quality of student learning and good teaching that are becoming increasingly refined through outcomes-based assessment processes.

What other components go into ensuring a quality of student life? Klimoski et al. suggest that "integration is at the heart of education and formation."[8] Creating an ambiance and a safe place for this transformative integration between life experience, curriculum, theory, and praxis to occur is an essential element in formation for ministry, which is the business of theological education, whether the focus is on the ordained, non-ordained, or professorial level. Klimoski et al. also posit that there are signposts that signal that this process is indeed in process. They note that a learner is undergoing the transforming process of integration when "what a learner knows moves from mechanical acquisition to reflexive response and the practices of professional ministry are no longer the application of certain routines or sequences of steps but the fluid artistry of one who understands that beneath this practice runs the electric current of theological wisdom."[9] For each student this inte-

---

8. Klimoski, O'Neil, and Schuth, *Educating Leaders for Ministry,* p. 61.
9. Klimoski, O'Neil, and Schuth, *Educating Leaders for Ministry,* p. 51.

gration is a personal process that cannot be forced but must be supported in the culture of learning that is created in the institution.

To maintain direct contact with the student experience, I have found it helpful to teach one course each semester and to remain part of the assignment roster for advising students. Regular attendance at worship and other student-sponsored events are other helpful ways of staying "au courant," as is ensuring student representation on committees and well-communicated avenues for student response and feedback. At our year-end commissioning service, one male and one female member of the graduating class talk about their experiences of the program. Last year, the male student announced that he was going to give a list of fifteen "wow" moments. Number three on the list was "The dean knows my name." I was truly humbled. It is important to be able to call students by name even when they have not been subject to a disciplinary visit to the dean's office.

It is important for the dean to know firsthand the quality of the student experience. It is also vital for the dean to recognize that in order for the student experience to maintain its integrity and authenticity, what is perceived from within the institution must also be validated by those who entrust the school with the formation of their personnel and with those who employ its graduates. These are two essential constituencies who require ongoing attention and focused attention from the dean.

Last but not least, students go on to become graduates and alums. Alums figure largely in annual fund appeals and in capital campaigns. A few even go on to join the major donor category! All graduates have the potential to become ambassadors who promote the school as a great place to be educated. In time graduates may hold positions where they are able to hire newer graduates or influence a denomination to designate a particular school as the place for formation for ministry. The vitality of the school and its mission tomorrow is directly affected by the experience of today's students.

An Intangible Dimension of Governance: The Art of Soul Tending

One of the great privileges, and perhaps one of the most elusive tasks, of the dean's role in governance is one that might be termed "tending the soul of the faculty." Individual faculty members bring the living face of the institutional mission to the classroom, but it is deans who create and foster a general ambiance for living the mission within the larger faculty through the ways in which they carry out the role and functions of the dean's office. This pastoral presence is pervasive but not intrusive, respects good boundaries, and pays particular attention to the common good while encouraging from all concerned a response and interaction steeped in the values expressed in the institutional mission.

Soul tending also requires that deans hold themselves accountable for how they manifest the living face of the mission to the faculty not only in the culture and ambiance created but also in the very concrete ways in which meetings are chaired, discussions held, decisions rendered, and changes instituted.

To be attentive to this task, deans need to be intentional about developing and sustaining their own interior focus[10] — a contemplative stance, if you will — to engage the issues of the faculty and its members from a position that is non-defensive and does not seek to create control and maintain order but rather seeks to facilitate and liberate by creating a common understanding that gives birth to a mutually acceptable and credible path through uncertainty and chaos.

A contemplative stance, coupled with an ability for honest self-evaluation, ensures that a dean is able and willing to focus and re-focus objectively on larger realities as new data and information emerges. This reflective self-evaluation also supports deans in formulating a realistic perception of where their role fits and/or necessitates leadership initiatives in the overall institutional perspective. The ability to re-focus from a contemplative stance offers a peaceful, non-reactive approach to dealing with issues as they arise, even when deans are surprised and chagrined by unexpected issues that seem to emerge with unfailing regularity.

In the sphere of spiritual leadership Leonard Doohan[11] believes that informed self-evaluation often leads to a process of conversion. This type of conversion not only heightens a new awareness of self but also produces a deeper and more comprehensive appreciation of the gifts that already reside within both the dean and the faculty/institution.

Deeply embedded within all ministry is the potential to change and re-shape the minister if we are open to the experience. The dean's ministry of governance is indeed a ministry to the mission, and in that ministry, the personal integrity and spirituality of the dean are essential supports in the exer-

10. Margaret Wheatley, *Finding Our Way: Leadership for Uncertain Times* (San Francisco: Berrett Koehler Publishers, Inc., 2004), p. 127.

11. Leonard Doohan, *Spiritual Leadership: The Quest for Integrity* (Mahwah, NJ: Paulist Press, 2007), p. 132.

cise of good governance. One of the enduring graces of the office, however, is a sense of gratitude for the steadfast commitment of colleagues and an abiding belief that the intangibles support, facilitate, and sustain the tangible.

ADDITIONAL RESOURCES

Collins, Jim. *Good to Great.* New York: HarperCollins Publishers, Inc., 2001.

Doohan, Leonard. *Spiritual Leadership: The Quest for Integrity.* Mahwah, NJ: Paulist Press, 2007.

Jones, L. Gregory, and Stephanie Paulsell, eds. *The Scope of Our Art: The Vocation of the Theological Educator.* Grand Rapids: Eerdmans, 2002.

Klimoski, Victor J., Kevin J. O'Neil, Katarina M. Schuth. *Educating Leaders for Ministry: Issues and Responses.* Collegeville, MN: Liturgical Press, 2005.

Lewis, G. Douglass, and Lovett H. Weems Jr., eds. *A Handbook for Seminary Presidents.* Grand Rapids: Eerdmans, 2006.

Markham, Donna L., OP. *Spirit Linking Leadership: Working Through Resistance to Organizational Change.* Mahwah, NJ: Paulist Press, 1999.

Wheatley, Margaret. *Finding Our Way: Leadership for Uncertain Times.* San Francisco: Berrett-Koehler Publishers, Inc., 2004.

Whyte, David. *The Heart Aroused: Poetry and the Preservation of the Soul in Corporate America.* New York: Doubleday, 1994.

6. Faculty Leadership and Development

Scaffolding That Supports Faculty Leadership: The Dean's Constructive Role

Anne B. Yardley

"The plumbing doesn't work," commented one seminary dean as he announced his resignation to the faculty. He was referring to the structures of the university in which the seminary was located and expressing his frustration with the ways in which he felt thwarted at every turn by the upper administration. Even the offer of a plunger did nothing to convince him to stay! While faculty leadership and development may often rise and fall on the personal characteristics of the academic dean, in many cases the underlying scaffolding of the institution stymies the best-intentioned efforts of faculty and administration alike.

In many ways, the academic dean's job may be likened to the work of the construction crew who puts up the scaffolding for a project. It is not the most glamorous of jobs, but it is an integral part of the academic exercise. As Gary Gunderson says in his book on leadership, "As an old carpenter, I know that sometimes the hardest part of the job is building the scaffolding that makes it possible to do what most people think of as the 'real work.'"[1] Academic deans must be mindful of the ways in which their vision and leader-

---

1. Gary Gunderson, *Boundary Leaders: Leadership Skills for People of Faith* (Minneapolis: Augsburg Fortress Press, 2004), p. 60.

ship style intersects with the faculty culture. Some changes may just modify a portion of the scaffolding; some may seem to undermine it entirely, placing the whole enterprise in jeopardy. The dean who wants to successfully develop the faculty needs to make structures transparent, seek to support the ideas and creativity of the faculty, and find ways to help the faculty discover a sense of common vocation.

The Context of This Essay: Academic, Ecclesial, Personal

Each seminary has its own particular ethos, just as each academic dean brings a certain set of experiences to the position. A few words here about my own context will provide the context for my remarks. I am in my ninth year as associate academic dean at Drew Theological School in Madison, New Jersey. As a university-related theological school, Drew is led by a dean who serves in the role of CEO and an associate academic dean who is the CAO. Maxine Beach has been the dean at Drew since 2000; I have served as the CAO since July 2001. Drew has about 225 Master of Divinity students, as well as small cohorts in the MTS, STM, and DMin programs. The full-time faculty of approximately twenty-five members also teaches and mentors numerous PhD students in our doctoral program.

Drew is one of the thirteen official seminaries of the United Methodist Church. The faculty has had significant turnover in the last decade due to the retirement of over one-third of its members. The faculty is extremely conscientious in searching for new faculty members, and an unwritten faculty expectation is that each faculty member will make every effort to attend candidate presentations during the selection process.

I hold a PhD in musicology and never went to seminary! I have a lot of experience as a church musician as well as an academic interest in a broad range of sacred music. I taught in the theological school as a contract, non-tenure-track faculty member for several years before becoming dean in 2001. Since that time I have made use of numerous opportunities offered by ATS to increase my understanding of theological education.

The ideas and suggestions in this essay grow out of that experience and especially out of my close association with Maxine Beach. Her transparent leadership style and her success in creating a climate where faculty can flourish have been a major force in my education as an academic dean. I have learned that academic deans can better support faculty members when they experience how important institutional and personal support is for their own leadership and development.

With this context in mind, there are at least three dimensions of exploring and constructing the scaffolding that supports faculty leadership and development. One has to do with the visible, explicit dimensions of scaffolding that already exists in institutions and that must be reckoned with as CAOs seek to support faculty development and leadership. Another has to do with the concern to both recognize and nurture individual faculty gifts and leadership and to facilitate the shared vision and commitments of the faculty as a whole. The third concerns how a CAO's own sense of vocation contributes to nurturing faculty development and leadership.

Attending to Formal Structures and Processes: The Visible Scaffolding

To enter the institution as a dean is to enter into the midst of an active organism that began before we arrive and will be there after we leave. Studying the stated, explicit structures of faculty life is a great starting point for a new dean. Or to put it another way, examining the obvious parts of the scaffolding that are in place can help the new dean understand how things already work. As boring as they may seem at first glance, the rules and regulations of the faculty reveal much about the community. Which committees, if any, are elected by the faculty? Which are appointed by the dean? Do faculty members choose their own leaders within their disciplinary areas? Are there restrictions on which categories of faculty may serve in various capacities (tenured, tenure-track, contract, adjunct)? Where does the dean intersect with the faculty in a consultative way?

These rules and regulations do not give the whole picture, but they do indicate some important dimensions of faculty interaction and the ways in which the faculty itself views its roles and responsibilities. In my experience, faculty members do not cast their votes haphazardly. They will work with colleagues on committees as assigned, but when they have a chance to elect members to a committee that carries some power, they do not want to spend their vote on someone who will miss committee meetings or be unwilling to make difficult decisions.

At my institution the committee on faculty (CoF) handles faculty reviews and promotion and tenure decisions. The dean meets with the committee at the beginning of the year to discuss faculty colleagues who need to be reviewed, but for the most part the committee functions autonomously. Five faculty members are elected to the committee; each year two are elected for two-year terms and one for a one-year term. The members are equally divided between full professors and those below the rank of full professor. At many institutions only tenured faculty may serve on the corresponding committee; at Drew, tenure-track, non-tenured faculty members are eligible for election and are frequently elected.

One of the most vehement discussions I have seen in a faculty meeting occurred when the CoF brought a recommendation to the full faculty to change that provision of our regulations and limit committee service to those already tenured. The change would have avoided the possibility that persons might serve on the CoF in the same year in which their tenure decisions were made. Several faculty members viewed this as a potentially major shift in faculty culture from one in which junior faculty are viewed as full partners in the academic enterprise to one in which their opinions would not be valued. Both tenured and non-tenured faculty spoke passionately on both sides of the proposed change. Ultimately, we left the by-laws alone; the culture change was too great to support.

The composition of this particular committee might seem a small point to a newcomer reading the regulations, but it clearly embodies the faculty's self-understanding in important ways. Someone who studies our regulations would see immediately that the section on the CoF is the longest and most detailed section of the regulation covering tenure and promotion proceedings. That would accurately portray the CoF as the locus of faculty leadership and development. Thus a new dean would be wise to look closely at the CoF as a place for encouraging the development of the faculty. The rules are just the starting place because there are many unwritten rules in any institution, but they are an excellent starting point.

Caveat emptor

Before I became academic dean I was elected to the dean's council. The accreditation visit was looming, and the dean designated the dean's council to meet with the ATS staff person assigned to us. Somehow I ended up in the room alone as he entered. He asked me, "Is being elected to the dean's council an honor for a faculty member?" I hesitated before answering because the answer was a very qualified yes. The dean's council had been added to our regulations several years earlier, but it had never really been embraced by the deans as a council of advice. Thus the faculty, correctly perceiving that the committee exercised very limited power, could elect to the CoF faculty who were not the "A-Team." I did not want to insult the ATS staff person by suggesting that we had lined up the B-Team to talk with him, but my answer may have implied it.

In retrospect I see that we were embarking on a shift in culture. At that time the dean's council looked good in the regulations but had less power in actuality. Maxine Beach takes the dean's council seriously. She shares plans, ideas, and even the budget with faculty on the dean's council, which includes four elected faculty members as well as the dean, the associate academic dean, and the associate dean of contextual learning. After several years, the faculty has finally taken notice. Election to the dean's council is, today, a vote of confidence by the faculty.

These two examples indicate a basic principle for encouraging faculty leadership: Make use of the places where faculty members are supposed to take leadership. Expect them to do so, and welcome their input and leadership.

Recognizing and Nurturing Individual Gifts and Shared Commitments

Faculty leadership is not only, or even primarily, exercised in the formal structures of the institution. It is usually obvious to some degree in faculty meetings. Who speaks up? Whose voice carries the most weight? It is also present in the water-cooler conversations, the email exchanges, and all the other informal settings of the school.

The relationship of the academic dean to these conversations is somewhat ambiguous. It is not the dean's job to monitor or manipulate these conversations beyond encouraging an open environment in which faculty colleagues feel they can express themselves without any punitive reactions. On most faculties the members fall into certain predictable roles. An observant dean can probably identify faculty members who fill these roles. For example, deans are often easily able to answer the following questions: Who in the faculty is most respected as a scholar? Who is most likely to speak out against injustice? Who is most likely to get the conversation started? Who seeks consensus? Who is widely admired as the best teacher? Who is most concerned with due process? All of these people are exercising leadership. Take time to acknowledge this individually in faculty reviews. It is important to take note so that when leaders are needed for particular tasks, colleagues may be selected whom other faculty members acknowledge as those who will exercise the necessary commitments and leadership gifts.

A Common Vocation

Faculty members arrive at the profession of theological education from many different routes. They bring their own sets of expectations and understanding to their roles. Many may not see their work as a vocation. When they arrive, they intersect with the already entrenched understanding of the faculty, the explicit goals of the institution, and the reality of their work in the classroom. The academic dean needs to find ways to encourage a discussion of the "common vocation" while still leaving plenty of room for individual variations and approaches.

Some theological schools have very explicit faith statements that must be signed by both faculty and students. These statements offer one approach to a common vocation. Faculty members in these schools can relate their own individual goals to the faith statement.

I work in a different type of school — one in which the faculty is allergic to the concept of a faith statement. (I hurry to add that they are not at all allergic to faith.) We have to find other ways to articulate our common vision and mission. Catalog statements and other official documents express some aspects of that vocation, but I think that our strongest approach is through the annual (or semi-annual) faculty retreat. I suspect that for many faculties this time of retreat is a time to (re)connect with colleagues and discuss some aspects of the common vocation. In my experience, a "good" faculty retreat does much to solidify communal well-being, and a "bad" faculty retreat can be quite destructive.

New deans can learn a lot by inviting faculty members to share anecdotes about events and experiences that they believe have shaped faculty identity and vocation. It is probably useful to note how and when these occurred. It is, however, not easy to plan for such an event. We can plan the topic and the structure and the location. Sometimes it is best to leave the rest to the Holy Spirit.

I do believe, however, that the dean has a major role to play in raising the questions that may lead a faculty to identify a common vocation. For example, we spent time on one retreat pondering two questions: What is the church for which we are preparing our students? What is the church for which we *want* to prepare our students? The discussion engendered by these questions did not lead to one clear answer. It *did* encourage the faculty to affirm its commitment to prepare pastors who can go into ministry now and yet have a vision and understanding that will allow them to thrive into the future. It also allowed several members of the faculty to prepare materials for the broader church discussion at the next General Conference of the UMC.

The common faculty vocation will vary depending on many factors. Our faculty is always balancing the preparation of PhD students for the vocation of teaching with the preparation of MDiv students. We balance being United Methodist with being ecumenical. It is probably more accurate to think of multiple faculty vocations. The academic dean helps a faculty by being aware of these "calls," which often feel more like being tugged in different directions rather than having one cohesive vocation. By encouraging the faculty to reflect on these issues and giving them permission to shape this call, the dean exercises a vital role.

On a more practical note, the academic dean needs to be aware of opportunities for faculties to be connected to the broader enterprise of theological education. ATS is a magnificent partner in this matter. I strongly encourage colleagues in the academic dean's office to send new faculty members to the ATS-sponsored colloquium for new faculty; encourage women faculty to participate in the Women in Leadership events; take part in the CAOS meetings. All of these help to broaden the faculty's as well as our own deeper understanding of theological education. I have been personally impressed with the ways in which ATS encourages us to find commonality despite widely divergent theological views. I have learned an immense amount by serving on accreditation committees at other institutions. One colleague aptly describes such committee service as the best continuing education available for academic deans.

Another wonderful resource is the Wabash Institute for the Teaching of Religion. Encourage faculty colleagues to participate in their seminars. Invite their resource people to campus for a discussion of pedagogy. That, too, will help to form faculty vocation.

Other essays in this volume will talk more specifically about encouraging faculty scholarship. I would like to suggest here, however, that encouraging faculty participation in such academic guilds as the AAR and SBL is also crucial to faculty vocation. As faculty members understand their own roles as teachers, scholars, and mentors, they can incorporate all of those roles into the common faculty vocation.

Attending to One's Own Vocation as CAO

CAOs come to the ministry of academic leadership in a variety of ways. For some the opportunity to be a dean is experienced as a vocational call; for others it is a position to be filled for a few years. Some deans are called to their roles from within the faculty, and some are brought in from the outside to fill this role. Facilitating the vocational aspirations of others raises questions of the CAO's own sense of vocation. The academic dean needs to be able to both support faculty members and challenge them to grow. This work is undoubtedly the most challenging part of the job. In one sense the CAO is a faculty colleague, especially if we have been called to the position from a position on the faculty we serve. More than any other administrator, the academic dean needs to be able to think like a faculty member, especially when representing faculty concerns to the president, board of trustees, and others. At the same time, the academic dean is also a "boss" responsible for conveying administrative viewpoints to faculty and for making difficult decisions. We soon become the "other." Or as one of my faculty colleagues put it, "You've gone over to the dark side."

Before moving to some specific suggestions for supporting faculty vocations, I want to reflect a bit on this middle ground where the academic dean lives. Inhabiting the dean's office requires a sense of humor, a willingness to apologize for mistakes, and an enjoyment of the details that make communal life work effectively. I think it is almost impossible to be an effective academic dean if there is not a relationship of deep respect with the president and if the job is experienced as a great burden. Martyrdom on the altar of academic deanship is not the way to go!

The next advice I'm going to give might sound as if it comes from a teen dating magazine: building a good relationship with faculty members requires listening to their hopes and dreams for their career/vocation. It requires understanding where they are headed and what motivates them. When deans need to offer criticism of faculty members' work, it helps to have developed a positive relationship. Most theological schools have fairly small full-time faculties, and getting to know the faculty is not difficult.

For most deans, the annual performance review is the place where we officially evaluate faculty members. Being consistent and fair in these evaluations is very important, especially when such reviews are tied to faculty compensation. Inviting faculty members to reflect on the year at the outset can allow us to relate our remarks to issues that they have already raised.

Often the concerns that need to be raised in performance reviews are ongoing issues — failure to turn in grades on time, lack of scholarly output, negative student evaluations, etc. Most people have a tendency to focus on the negative remarks and to shrug off the positive ones as perfunctory. As much as we try to balance things in the actual performance review, the ongoing nature of our interactions may have more to do with success in communication than the specific conversation of the review. Have we read the colleague's recent articles and talked about them? Have we read student reviews and taken the time to highlight some positive remarks at a different time? Have we been able to find institutional resources to support travel to a meeting? These tangible proofs of support can help but sometimes we still just have to "dean" them. And by that I mean that as CAOs we are responsible for conveying real concerns and problems. We are the leaders called to balance the needs of the institution with the needs of individual faculty colleagues. An effective dean must be willing to be disliked sometimes.

With the power of the dean's office comes an awesome level of responsibility. As individual faculty members, we are free to like and dislike our colleagues without those feelings having many repercussions in their lives. As deans we must find ways of treating people as fairly as possible. Some will probably "push our buttons," and we will invest time trying to figure out why and even get some professional advice if necessary. The faculty person we instinctively dislike may be a brilliant teacher, a formidable scholar, and a wonderful colleague to others. When our own responses create obstacles to exercising our best care for a colleague's development, it can take considerable effort to remember that we are not called upon to like each faculty member but to find ways to support and encourage each one's contribution to our common vocation and, as much as possible, to offer appropriate support for each colleague's individual quest.

The concern to be just and fair, whatever our personal feelings may be, at times takes us back to formal structures and processes. One example is a regular examination of the records of faculty salaries, in order to examine whether all faculty members are paid appropriately according to their rank and years of service. I know one faculty member (not at a theological school) who after thirty years of teaching is earning less than some starting assistant professors because the dean and department chair above her do not appreciate her outspoken ways. Students regularly nominate her for teaching awards. Examining the record of faculty salaries may indicate ways in which biases based on personal preferences may have allowed injustice to gain a foothold and may also offer ways to ameliorate these situations.

One spring I reached the end of the academic year feeling angry and attacked and downright cranky. A couple members of the faculty had been really irritating, attempts to make faculty decisions on policy had stalled, and I was feeling burned out. I planned a personal, one-day retreat at home to reflect on my vocation as dean, scholar, and teacher. I prepared a dish with slips of papers with the names of each faculty member, administrator, and staff person. At the beginning of the retreat I spent about an hour listening to shakuhachi music and holding each person in mind. Some brought a small smile to my face, and I moved through them quickly. For some it took a much longer time as I consciously named the things I needed to relinquish. I called to mind Henry Nouwen's book *With Open Hands*[2] and tried to let go. I found the process very freeing, and it allowed me to move into the summer without such a heavy load of grievances. It is life-giving to develop practices that help us to let go of resentments and grievances against faculty members before they poison not only the institutional environment but our own souls.

Concluding Reflections

Observing, utilizing, building, and maintaining the scaffolding that supports faculty development and leadership requires knowledge, patience, and insight. As academic deans we are entrusted with helping our institutions offer the best possible education to prospective clergy. Our leadership practices impact both students and faculty. If we can model real hospitality to faculty dreams and gifts, we will not only create a good environment for our institutions, but we will also help our students learn some skills to take with them into the church. Working in higher education is a great privilege. Working as an academic dean of a theological school is an opportunity to provide the support and structures necessary for a faculty to do the central work of theological education — nurturing and challenging the minds of future religious leaders.

ADDITIONAL RESOURCES

Elkins, Heather Murray. *Holy Stuff of Life*. Cleveland: Pilgrim Press, 2006.
Foster, Charles R., et al. *Educating Clergy: Teaching Preactices and Pastoral Imagination*. San Francisco: Jossey-Bass, 2006.
Nouwen, Henri. *With Open Hands*. Notre Dame: Ave Maria Press, 1972.

2. Henri Nouwen, *With Open Hands* (Notre Dame: Ave Maria Press, 1972). See especially the Introduction.

[Compact Disc] Chanticleer, *And on Earth Peace: A Chanticleer Mass.* This CD is an unusual and magnificent compilation by Chanticleer of commissioned sections of the Mass ordinary by composers from different religious traditions interspersed with motets from the Renaissance. The ending, "Agnus Dei," definitely leaves one with a great sense of peace.

Faculty Leadership and Development: Lessons from the Anabaptist-Pietist Tradition

Dale R. Stoffer

The Brethren tradition, with roots in both Anabaptism and Pietism, often refers to its characteristic leadership style as servant leadership. Modeled after Jesus' own approach to leadership and ministry, this leadership style values relationships above the structures and titles of authority. (See Matt. 20:20-28, especially v. 28; Matt. 23:8-12; and, a foundational passage for the Brethren, John 13:1-17.) Authority derives not so much from one's institutional rank or status but primarily from the respect that comes because the people in a community of faith know that their leader values them and seeks their welfare. Governance tends to be collaborative and shared rather than hierarchical and role-determined. For example, committees and even departments have a mixture of administrators and full-time faculty whose presence on such organizational entities is based on function and expertise rather than solely on title and rank. Ashland has had a long history of a collaborative decision-making process that involves both administrators and faculty working in a collegial manner. (The faculty is defined at Ashland as the president, academic dean, librarians, administrators with teaching responsibilities in their contracts, and full-time teaching faculty.) Ashland has generally been able to avoid the usual "we-they" dichotomy between administrators and faculty throughout its history. There are challenges to living out this pattern of leadership and community interaction, but the benefits in shared vision, collegial rapport, and mutual trust and respect are worth the effort. In this essay I will be considering the issues of faculty leadership and development from this vantage point, being candid about the tensions inherent in this approach as well as the benefits that can be realized. Though many specific elements, especially in relation to faculty development, will be similar across the theological terrain, the difference arises from the "atmosphere" that pervades the educational landscape at Ashland.

The Common and Individual Vocations of Faculty

A tension that is quite pronounced within all of higher education is the inherent friction between a school's need for a common understanding of its mission and the tendency of scholarly training to enhance individualism. Skills that promote independent thinking are honed in graduate studies so that a person's work is valued according to the extent to which it articulates and defends a unique thesis related to a narrow field of study. Distinctiveness, novelty, and creativity are prized. But these very characteristics can work at cross-purposes with the need to arrive at a shared vision and a unified sense of calling. Common and individual vocations can, and often do, collide, but a savvy dean can navigate this inherent tension.

Common Vocation

In theological education, common vocation manifests itself on two different levels: (1) the common calling shared across our theological schools for the training of men and women for various forms of ministry and (2) the common calling specific to each institution, expressed in the mission and identity statements that guide the individual schools.

While it is obvious that all those involved in theological education share a common vocation, there is also a sense in which the vocation of theological education is distinct from training for other professions. Many institutional traditions underscore the conviction that theological education is not merely a job but a calling and that the Lord's calling applies just as much to the professor in the seminary classroom as to the pastor in the local parish. Even the IRS recognizes the uniqueness of seminary teaching, extending the generous "double deduction" of the housing allowance to ordained or licensed faculty members as well as to pastors and priests. Those who have moved from the pastorate to the classroom can also be very sensitive to occasional chiding that they have "left the ministry."

One of the interesting trends observed when comparing data from the 1993 and 2003 studies conducted by the Auburn Center for the Study of Theological Education is that the percentage of ordained faculty in theological schools has been dropping. Various factors account for this trend, as suggested in the study, but one of the possible explanations is that increasing numbers of people are going into theological education because of academic interest in their field of study in contrast to a sense of calling in service to the church. Note also the observation that 10 percent more doctoral students in the 2003 study "say their field is 'religion' rather than 'theology.'"[1] Theological educators today have a dual allegiance to the academy and to the church. Of course the inherent tension in this twofold allegiance is at least as old as the late second and early third centuries when Tertullian posed his questions, "What has Athens to do with Jerusalem or the Academy with the Church?" Certainly Clement of Alexandria and Origen would have disputed Tertullian's either/or thinking.

The tension that at times arises from this dual allegiance is one that can impact the work of the academic dean in faculty development. It is evident, for example, in consideration of the primary purpose of the study leave. Is it to produce publishable works that can advance the reputation of the faculty and the school within the academy, or should it also provide opportunities to remain on the cutting edge of practical ministry and to teach in international theological schools, thereby advancing the work of the church? The dean must strive for a balance on this twofold sense of calling, noting that the seminary needs to have one foot in the academy and one foot in the church.

The second sense of common vocation is specific to each school. The welfare of any organization depends upon its ability to develop a common sense of mission and vision. Without this unified direction, people tend to focus on their own interests or those of a subgroup; in either case the organization can suffer from internal friction and even fracture.

Identity statements like mission, purpose, and vision statements are significant priorities in the life of any institution. No doubt deans are often called upon to play key roles in guiding the processes that formulate these

---

1. Barbara G. Wheeler, Sharon L. Miller, and Katarina Schuth, "Signs of the Times: Present and Future Theological Faculty," *Auburn Studies* 10 (February 2005): 15-19. Commenting on this point, the article notes: "Leaders of Protestant denominational schools, which still have high percentages of ordained faculty, view the development as an alarming signal that seminaries' ties to the religious communities they serve may be on the wane."

statements. But deans play equally important roles in keeping the institution true to its agreed-upon identity. Deans should query candidates for faculty positions regarding their ability to support these statements. Deans as well as presidents ought to refresh the mind of the community about its identity when decisions are being made that could divert or subvert the institution's calling. In these cases deans serve as guardians of the community's identity.

Individual Vocations

The heirs of the Enlightenment's stress on reason and the Renaissance/Reformation/Enlightenment's stress on the individual accept the advancement of individual vocation as almost an inalienable right. Certainly Americans have elevated individualism beyond even their European counterparts. This is especially true of those in academia, who have been schooled well in the art of advancing their careers. The independence of faculty is the reason why the adage of "herding cats" brings a wry smile to the countenance of any dean.

Deans of theological institutions, however, have a significant role to play in supporting each faculty member in the area of career advancement. One important way they do this is through the awarding of various faculty development grants (more will be said about this below). The amount of personal support required by individual faculty is often in an inverse relationship to the number of years that a faculty member has been employed in the seminary. Newer faculty members need far more encouragement and support in their sense of calling than do established faculty. There are numerous reasons for this: the unfamiliarity of a career for which most new faculty have little training; being thrust into new relationships, especially with colleagues who have formed settled patterns of interaction already; the concern about whether one's scholarship will be sufficiently valued when issues of advancement in rank and of tenure are being considered; and finding a realistic balance in life among teaching, research and writing, community service, and family. A gratifying personal gift to faculty, especially newer faculty, can be the gift of "opening doors," that is, introducing them to people and organizations that can encourage them in their vocation, develop their teaching and research skills, and provide insight in navigating the new terrain of theological education. The grants, conferences, and workshops offered by such organizations as the Wabash Center and ATS are wonderful resources for junior (and senior) faculty. Of special note are ATS's Roundtable Seminar for Newly Appointed Faculty and the Wabash Center's Workshop for Pre-Tenure Theological School Faculty.

The Tension between Common Vocation and Individual Vocations

There are within any educational institution both centripetal and centrifugal forces at work that inevitably create dissonance within the life of the academic community. The dean occupies a critical position relative to both forces. Strategic planning processes and the institution's identity statements (mission, purpose, vision, and core value statements) are centripetal forces that provide a centering focus for the institution. The commitment in higher education to academic freedom, the historic isolation of departments from one another (the "silo" effect), and the tendency for administration and faculty to have an adversarial relationship are centrifugal forces that can draw faculty away from a common vocation. Because deans must "lead from the center,"[2] the need to live with these competing forces can pose one of the most difficult challenges to their leadership.

The resourcing of individual vocations is a much easier task for deans, but several strategies will help in addressing the more challenging responsibility of working with faculty to foster a greater sense of common vocation. There may be no more important expression of common vocation for an institution than its identity statements. Yet the time and energy that need to be invested in developing these statements are significant, and a school must carefully weigh the pros and cons of engaging in this process. Schools may find it advantageous to reconsider their identity statements in several contexts. The first context is when a school is considering initiating a strategic planning process. The discipline of bringing a faculty to consensus about its core identity is foundational to a successful strategic planning process. The hard work of forging a common vocation as expressed in mission, purpose, and vision statements lays a solid foundation upon which to build a planning process. A second context that may call for a reconsideration of a school's identity statements is when a large number of new employees has been added to a theological school. In order to bring them into a conscious

2. For the development of this concept of "leading from the center," see the monograph by Jeanne P. McLean, *Leading from the Center: The Emerging Role of the Chief Academic Officer in Theological Schools* (Atlanta: Scholars Press, 1999).

commitment to its identity, a school may find it beneficial to take a fresh look at such statements. In either of these scenarios a dean, one of the chief figures charged with maintaining the identity of a school, should play a key role.

A trait that theological schools generally have in common with other institutions of higher learning is the tendency to wall off distinct disciplines from one another, thus creating the silo effect so common today in Western universities. One facet of working toward a greater sense of common vocation is to develop strategies for increasing conversation across disciplinary boundaries and for creative forms of teaching and learning that highlight integration. A commitment to engage in more integrative, cross-disciplinary teaching and discourse can help to deconstruct the disciplinary silos. Support for cross-disciplinary team teaching might be demonstrated, for example, by giving each faculty member of a team full course credit. Curriculum review is typically not without its tensions, but one of the positive outcomes of the process can be a desire to engage in interdepartmental conversations, which can prove quite fruitful in promoting greater understanding and appreciation of the work of the various departments. Another useful strategy to break down the walls between departments is conversation about what scholarship looks like in different disciplines. When faculty in practical theology and counseling departments come up for advancement and tenure, for example, they should be evaluated by standards of scholarship more appropriate to their disciplines rather than the classical disciplines. Likewise, faculty colloquia, at which faculty members who have delivered papers at professional societies share them with the faculty and administration, can also help faculty to appreciate the type of research and writing found in other disciplines.

It may seem trivial, but one of the best strategies to maintain common vocation is to share fellowship together as a community. A wide variety of activities can gather the entire body together, including groundskeepers and housekeeping personnel. Such gatherings as monthly or semi-monthly birthday celebrations, summer cookouts, meals prior to faculty meetings, euchre parties, and chapel services provide opportunities to share time together as a family of faith. The Anabaptist and Pietist heritage, in particular, encourages fellowship among all sisters and brothers in faith, including groundskeepers, staff, faculty, administrators, spouses, and other family members. Such forging of community can be difficult in a community composed of multiple denominations, but it is nonetheless fruitful.

The Role of the Dean in Cultivating Faculty Leadership

Cultivation of faculty leadership is essential if an educational institution is to fulfill its common vocation. This observation is no less true for schools in the Anabaptist tradition. Because of the emphasis on community in this tradition, all members of the institution, including faculty, must have a common commitment to those qualities that make community possible: the valuing of relationships, the fostering of mutual trust and respect, and, at times, the elevating of the good of the whole above personal preferences and even individual vocation. The model of leadership most conducive to the creation and sustenance of such community is servant leadership; it must become the normative *modus operandi* for all in leadership positions, whether in the administration or in the faculty.

Servant leadership does not mean an abdication of the role of leader, but rather a willingness to lay aside the prerogatives of title and rank in order to lead people, through highly relational means, to goals that advance the welfare of each individual and ultimately of the community. (The apostle Paul's seminal teaching on this truth is found in Philippians 2:1-11.) Such an approach to leadership runs counter to many of our cherished American ideals, even in higher education: glamorizing rugged individualism, valuing people based on their title and rank (or degree), fostering a competitive spirit, organizing social relationships through formal structures (institutionalism). The countercultural community that can result when servant leadership is lived out is able to enrich the lives of every member of that community — from the maintenance worker to the president. An example of this truth occurred several years ago at Ashland Seminary in connection with the Senior Banquet. Each spring the senior class nominates the person to speak at the banquet who has most impacted their lives while at the seminary. The class that year selected one of the housekeepers, who was known for taking time to pray for and with anyone in the community who needed the Lord's touch, whether staff or student, faculty or administrator. This "servant" within the community demonstrated profound spiritual leadership within the seminary that was honored by the graduating class.

A community that seeks to live out true servant leadership faces a variety of challenges: (1) Such leadership can grow only in ground seeded liberally with trust and respect. Because trust and respect are fragile fruit, there is always a danger that serious erosion of trust can occur for any number of reasons. Trust takes time to sprout again once it has been uprooted. (2) The erosion of trust is especially serious when senior members of the community conduct themselves counter to the values they espouse. (3) Significant growth inevitably introduces people into the community who are unfamiliar with the concept and practice of servant leadership. Tensions and misunderstandings can arise when members of the community, often unintentionally, operate out of models at odds with this concept. (4) The downside of highly relational structures is that they often have porous boundaries. But significant growth brings with it the inevitable need to define more precisely the lines of authority and responsibility, even in communities built upon a consensus and servant leadership model. Any group facing the challenges of growth must balance this need for structural definition with an intentional commitment not to forsake the interpersonal dynamics that had drawn people to the community in the first place. When the life of a community becomes predominantly defined by its formal structures and rigid lines of responsibility and authority, there is a very real danger that the relational bonds of nurturing, of supportive interaction, and of the valuing of every member of the community will be severed.

One other challenge of this model of leadership is inherent in trying to mix a relational model of leadership with a structure, like a seminary, that invariably has lines and positions of authority. A former dean at Ashland once described the type of governance most befitting educational institutions as a circular organizational design where there was neither top nor bottom. Though this may be the ideal, there are power dynamics that inevitably enter into the arena of education: faculty rank and tenure, the perceived or real power of the president, and institutional prerogatives that belong ultimately to the faculty, the president, or the board. If the ideal governance model is circular, a realistic version of such a model might be on a sloped plane with some constituencies of the institution having more authority in certain areas. This reality does not preclude a servant leadership model, however; it merely recognizes that those of us committed to such a model need to be very discerning about how authority can be misused and manipulated within this model, whether by faculty, administrators, or the board.

The dean has a significant role in cultivating the type of faculty leadership that enables a community committed to consensus to develop and flourish. Several elements are crucial to this process. First, faculty who have the gift of dialoguing, collaborating, and negotiating with people on different sides of an issue and drawing them to a common understanding need to be encouraged to take leadership. This gift is rare and should be recognized and fostered by the dean. Another important leadership gift that strengthens a consensus-based community is the ability, after ample discussion by people on all sides of an issue, to develop a proposal or motion that attends to the major concerns of the various constituencies in the discussion. When someone exercises this gift, especially after intense debate, groups can experience a collective sense of wonder that a wise solution has been found that satisfies seemingly contradictory perspectives.

The dean should also encourage senior faculty to share their views about important discussions within the community. Sometimes they feel reluctant to speak, feeling that, as their time of involvement is drawing to a close, they need to let younger faculty shape the course of the school. Yet these senior members have a collective remembrance of the history and calling of the institution — what has made it distinctive, what has drawn faculty and students to the school, and the rationale for why things are done as they are. These are necessary ingredients of community discussions that ought to be voiced in the deliberations.

The dean has another important role in fostering faculty leadership: promoting a method of selection of department chairs that serves the best interests of the department and the faculty as a whole. One useful method rotates department chair positions among faculty with associate and full professor rank. This method can yield a realization that not everyone has the administrative and leadership gifts necessary for the position, which is a crucial one for a consensus-based community because the chair needs to be able to work collaboratively with other department chairs to come to decisions that are in the best interests of the community as well as their respective departments. A department chair who creates polarizing situations with other departments by looking out for the interests of only one department can undermine the good-faith interaction that is fundamental to the welfare of the school.

The Role of the Dean in Faculty Development

Faculty development traditionally has been one of the main areas of responsibility in the dean's job description. Nothing communicates more powerfully to faculty that they are valued than a full-orbed faculty development plan. But providing adequate funding to underwrite regular conference attendance and study leaves is not in and of itself sufficient for creating a culture that fosters faculty development. The dean must take the lead in this area through the attitude modeled to the faculty. Beyond serving as an advocate at the time of the development of the budget to be sure adequate funding is available, the dean must also keep an "open hand," within budget constraints, regarding legitimate faculty requests; recognize and correct situations of inequity that inevitably arise; and make faculty aware of opportunities for training workshops related to teaching, for research grants, and for study leaves.

Deans have a number of opportunities to promote faculty development in the three areas in which faculty are usually evaluated: scholarship, teaching, and service. Deans are generally the recipients of information from various agencies that offer grants for study leaves and other research opportunities. Each year ATS sends out information to deans about the Henry Luce III Fellows in Theology and Lilly Theological Research Grants. The Wabash Center also makes grants of varying size available to faculty.

Deans should look for every opportunity to recognize faculty who have published books and research articles through such vehicles as notices in seminary-wide emails, announcements at faculty meetings, public book signings, exhibition of faculty publications in a display case, and presentation of autographed copies of faculty works to board members.

Faculty representation at their appropriate guilds not only advances their recognition in the academy but also builds the reputation of their schools. Ashland has made several significant increases in the amount of funds budgeted for conferences so that I am able to fully fund one professional conference for each faculty member. Funds are also available for a second conference if the faculty member is presenting a paper, serving as an officer, or playing some other significant role in the conference.

Ashland offers all tenure-track faculty a study leave of one quarter plus an associated summer every three-and-a-half years. There are also arrangements for a full-year study leave. Special opportunities made available to our faculty include study at Tyndale House, a center for biblical research in Cambridge, England, and participation in the Tel Gezer Excavation and Study Program in Israel.

Deans should be aware of the rich resources for faculty training related to teaching through the Wabash Center. In recent years Ashland has hosted Wabash Center resource people who have led workshops on various issues of teaching and learning, including interdisciplinary team teaching. Being connected to a university with an outstanding School of Education also affords Ashland exceptional resources for enhancing the craft of teaching. The seminary has used personnel from the School of Education not only to provide specialized workshops but also to observe new faculty in a classroom setting to aid them in the development of their teaching skills.

Though deans probably play a lesser role in fostering faculty involvement in service to the church and wider community, they ought to lead by example in such service. They should exemplify commitment to a local congregation and, if possible, be involved in some form of congregational service. Because the Brethren Church is a small denomination, Brethren members of the faculty and administration, especially deans, have been acutely aware of their responsibility to serve in district and national leadership roles and to share the unique resources of the seminary with the denomination.

Anyone who has served in the dean's role knows that it is located at one of the most complex junctions of an educational institution: at the intersection of faculty, administration, students, staff, and board. This role can be very complex, but it can also be extremely rewarding when a dean sees faculty developing their gifts and abilities in the classroom, academy, and church. However, it is especially rewarding to a dean when faculty work together collegially for the good of the entire educational community and when, because they know they are valued, they serve as sources of encouragement and support for one another and the school at large. For this to happen, the dean must be a role model for faculty both in servant leadership and in an ongoing commitment to scholarship, teaching, and service.

7. The Dean's Relationship with Students

The Dean and Students:
A Denominational Seminary Perspective

Ruth A. Meyers

In February 2008 the board of trustees of Seabury-Western Theological Seminary decided that the school would no longer offer the MDiv as a free-standing, three-year, residential program. Since its founding in the nine-teenth century, residential theological education in preparation for ordained ministry in the Episcopal Church has been Seabury's core mission. Without the MDiv, what would be our identity and our ministry?

The board's decision had not been widely anticipated before its meeting and so came as a significant shock to the entire seminary system. The president[1] called a meeting of the community — students, faculty, adminis-trators, support staff, and family members — to announce the decision. (The faculty received the news at a meeting with the president a few hours before the community meeting.) After that meeting, it was my responsibility as academic dean to develop plans for our current students to complete their programs.

---

1. At Seabury, the president's official title is "dean and president." As at other Episcopal seminaries, that individual is commonly referred to as the "dean," an ecclesiastical title signi-fying pastoral and spiritual authority. In this essay, I use "president" when speaking of the dean and president, and "dean" or "academic dean" to speak of the chief academic officer.

In my work with students in the weeks and months that followed, I drew upon everything I had learned in my preceding four-and-a-half years as academic dean. The crisis presented by the ending of the residential MDiv program serves as a window into understanding both the student realities and the multiple roles the dean exercises with students; these understandings guided me as everyone at Seabury experienced profound disruption.

Student Realities

Not surprisingly, the president's announcement that Seabury was closing its residential MDiv program generated enormous anxiety among students. Nearly every student who comes to us is in the midst of a significant life transition. Some have just completed their undergraduate education; many have had successful careers in teaching, law, business, health care, social services, and other fields. They come to seminary because they have felt the stirring of God in their soul, calling them to something new. For many, that "something" is ordained ministry, and in the Episcopal Church that means a lengthy process of discernment and a series of perceived "hoops," getting approval in both their home congregation and their diocese. They are still under scrutiny from their diocese throughout seminary, and consequently most students carry a certain amount of anxiety. That anxiety often colors my interaction with students, and while I am not always conscious of it, it was unmistakable in the aftermath of the board's decision to discontinue the MDiv program. Where would they complete their education? How would their bishops respond?

While the stress of the ordination process is one key dynamic affecting the dean's relationship with students, this reality is situated in the context of the adult learning experience.[2] Adult learners bring a wide range of life ex-

2. The characteristics that follow are taken from Stephen Lieb, "Principles of Adult Learning," http://honolulu.hawaii.edu/intranet/committees/FacDevCom/guidebk/teachtip/adults-2.htm and "Assumptions about the Adult Learner," http://literacy.kent.edu/-nebraska/curric/ttimI/aaal.html. The literature on adult learning is significant. See, for example, Malcolm Knowles, *The Modern Practice of Adult Education: Andragogy versus Pedagogy* (New York: Association, 1970); Malcolm S. Knowles, Elwood F. Horton III, and Richard A. Swanson, *The Adult Learner: The Definitive Classic in Adult Education and Human Resource Development,* 5th ed. (Houston: Gulf Publishing Company, 1998); and Carol Hoare, ed., *Handbook of Adult Development and Learning* (New York: Oxford University Press, 2006).

perience and knowledge to seminary, and they engage the learning and formation processes of seminary with varying levels of ability and self-confidence. Students coming to seminary have often left a work environment where they felt competent and were well respected and rewarded, and the experience of returning to a classroom, sometimes after many years, can be intimidating. Their professional goals are an important motivator for the overall experience of seminary, but they may be distracted by other responsibilities such as families or jobs, and their responses to particular academic or formation requirements may not always be positive, especially if they do not see the value or relevance of a requirement. Adults are autonomous and self-directed, often eager to participate actively in the learning process, and most prefer to have some control over their learning.

Because students are highly motivated, goal-oriented, and self-directed, I can count on them to help me understand their needs. Thus, when I was making provisions for students to complete their programs as Seabury ended its residential MDiv program, I sent a brief email to the students, identifying the issues I already knew to be significant and inviting them to tell me their concerns. Several responded. Some of the issues related to a student's specific situation, and a few were of minor concern. Other matters, though, were significant for many in the student body, and in response I was able to modify my planning. It was a collaborative effort, drawing upon the students' experience and wisdom as well as my wider institutional and inter-institutional perspective as academic dean. Inviting responses from students also helped to address their anxiety by giving them some agency at a time of great uncertainty about their future.

The Dean's Balancing Act: Tending to Many Roles with Students

Understanding student dynamics is a key component of working effectively with students. Equally essential is recognizing that the various responsibilities of the academic dean sometimes result in creative tension in relationships with students.

The Dean as Key Leader in the Educational System

One dimension of my relationship with students is systemic. At Seabury, my formal responsibilities center on leadership of the faculty; fostering communication and understanding among the faculty, president, and board; and external relations with other seminaries and our accrediting bodies. Recognizing my leadership and administrative roles in the institution, students seek my assistance in navigating the seminary system or effecting change. Even if students do not engage me directly, I try to be mindful of the impact of my decisions on them.

Individual relationships with students have multiple dimensions. Direct responsibility for students is not included in the academic dean's job description at my institution. As a member of the faculty, however, I teach both required and elective courses and serve as advisor to some students, a role that involves not only advising students about their academic program but also supporting them in their formation. As academic dean, I oversee academic programs and policies, which requires me to develop a detailed understanding of them. Students (including prospective students) often call on me to interpret those programs and policies, and in some instances I have a formal role in implementing policy, for example, approving a late registration or recommending discipline in a case of plagiarism. Because I oversee the faculty, students on occasion call upon me to adjudicate their complaints about faculty. On an interpersonal level, because I am a priest in the Episcopal Church, not only do student expectations about clergy help shape their perceptions of me, but also some students, particularly women, look to me as a mentor and role model as they prepare for their own ordination.

The Dean as Authority Figure and Communicator

The position of academic dean increases the already existing power differential between faculty and student. In the classroom, a professor is in a place of relative power as the one who designs the learning environment, decides the content of the course, makes assignments, and determines grades. At Seabury, our denominational polity also requires the faculty to make recommendations about a student's suitability and readiness for ordination, and students are acutely conscious of this particular power. The academic dean has additional power, perceived as well as actual, including the power of a senior administrator in the institution, the ability to influence the faculty (here students may perceive more power than an academic dean is actually able to exercise), knowledge of the institution and its programs and policies, and authority to implement academic policies. How might an academic dean exercise this power judiciously and responsibly?

First, it is important to acknowledge this power and the unequal relationship it creates with students. Regardless of a student's status outside the seminary, I cannot develop a truly mutual relationship with a student. Because the seminary is a community of formation as well as academic learning, it is important to come to know my students outside of the classroom and the academic dean's office. Self-disclosure is part of that relationship building, yet as the person with greater power, I have particular responsibility to maintain appropriate limits. I cannot seek my primary emotional or spiritual support in relationship with students, though friendship may develop. At the same time, because I have evaluative and disciplinary authority, I cannot be the primary pastoral support or spiritual director for any student, although my training and experience as a priest help shape my responses to students.

Building trust is essential to a wise and just use of the power inherent in the role of academic dean. Can students trust that I will use my power to serve them? Seabury is a small school, and I use a variety of formal and informal interactions, including conversations after worship or at lunch (or in the hallways), email, and meetings in my office (both informal drop-bys and scheduled appointments) to learn about my students and their concerns. On some occasions it takes me a long time to walk from point "A" to point "B" in the seminary because I'm stopped so frequently. A willingness to listen and a prompt response to email and telephone calls helps cultivate trust, and I make it a priority at least to acknowledge inquiries from students even if I don't have time immediately to give a full response. Sometimes I am unable to make a decision right away because I need to consult with others or look more closely at student records or school policy. In such circumstances, informing the student of the process and moving expeditiously to a decision helps maintain trust.

To foster trust, clear communication is important. About a week after the president's announcement that Seabury was discontinuing its residential MDiv program, I had negotiated enough of a teach-out plan that I was ready to announce it to students. I prepared a written letter to students, detailing the plan, and announced a meeting at a time when no classes were scheduled. No information about the plan was released to students prior to the meeting. Faculty maintained this confidentiality after they had received and approved the plan, and staff who prepared materials for distribution to off-campus students likewise did not divulge any information. The meeting enabled the majority of the student body to hear the same message at the same time, seek clarification, and identify concerns that had not yet been addressed. The written document, distributed during the meeting, helped prevent later misinformation and misunderstanding.[3]

The enormity of the change at Seabury called for extraordinary care in communication, but the underlying principles of good communication have wider application. Being clear about what is to be conveyed, who needs the information, and how and when the message will be transmitted is essential. Choosing not to communicate until I am fully prepared, although at times frustrating for students who want information immediately, facilitates greater clarity and prevents some incomplete or misleading communication. Listening carefully to determine whether my message has been received accurately is equally necessary. In my small academic community, rumors are sometimes rampant, and correcting misunderstandings is crucial.

In short, care in communication builds confidence among students that I will be responsive to their needs and concerns. As the one with greater power, it is particularly incumbent upon me to manage the flow and content of information. Although my ideal is clear, consistent communication, the reality often falls short. When that happens — when I realize that I have not communicated accurately, or in a timely fashion, or to everyone who needs the information — acknowledging and correcting these lapses helps maintain or restore trust.

The Dean as Advocate and Disciplinarian

As academic dean, with primary oversight of the academic life of the institution, my interactions with individual students range from advocate to disciplinarian. The disciplinary role is usually formally prescribed in our institutional policies, while advocacy more often results from students seeking my assistance.

These two modes of operation are the ends of the spectrum of the academic dean's work with and on behalf of individual students. As the dean I am thoroughly familiar with the seminary's academic programs, processes, and policies, and I also take care to understand individual student needs and concerns. My knowledge then enables me to help students navigate the aca-

---

3. Immediately after the board made its decision, Seabury hired Michael Barwell, a professional communications consultant, to assist us in presenting the message to our constituencies: students, faculty, staff, alumni/ae, and wider publics in the church. His assistance was invaluable as I developed a communication plan.

demic system and processes and to use my power in the system to address concerns.

Attention to individual students became particularly important when Seabury made a transition from academic quarters to semesters. Academic dean colleagues in other schools recommended that I develop contracts with all continuing students detailing their program requirements, that is, requirements already satisfied under the quarter system and the credit hours and courses that would be required to complete their program in the semester system. With the registrar, I prepared a written contract for each student, and the registrar and I met individually with students to present the contract and answer questions. Each student left the meeting with a contract signed by the academic dean, the registrar, and the student, and we distributed a copy to the student's advisor as well as placing one in the official file. Students expressed great appreciation for the care taken in this process; the reduction in their anxiety was palpable.

The need for one-on-one meetings with students was evident at a time of institutional change. More often, I rely on students to come to me when they have questions or concerns. I expect that as adult learners, they are primarily responsible for their educational program and will turn first to their advisor for assistance in making decisions about their course of study. I am also aware that faculty advisors differ in their level of understanding of the seminary's academic programs and policies as well as in their ability to help students solve problems. Moreover, sometimes as academic dean I have information about future course offerings or other academic matters that hasn't yet been published. When a student comes to me for assistance, I often follow up my conversation with an email to the student and the advisor. Not only does this confirm what I have told the student, preventing later misunderstanding, but it also brings the advisor into the conversation, allowing the advisor to follow up with the student. When several students come to me with similar questions, I know that it is time for wider communication.

In spring 2008, two months after I had made the initial announcement of our teach-out plan for continuing students, the faculty had agreed to a course schedule for the upcoming academic year, and the registrar opened registration. I realized that the course schedule was a work in progress, as faculty colleagues made decisions about their immediate futures and I finalized arrangements with adjunct faculty. So I was not altogether surprised when I began to get inquiries from students. Was this faculty member actually returning? Would the course still be offered if he didn't? Another faculty member had offered to teach a new course; when would it be taught? Ten students needed a course that would satisfy an area requirement; some students took initiative to talk with a potential adjunct faculty member who might teach such a course. Observing the pattern of inquiry, that is, the questions that the registrar and I were hearing several times a day, I prepared a written communiqué to be issued in both electronic and hard copy. We addressed all of the questions we had heard repeatedly, and we asked students to register on the basis of an updated course schedule, assuring them that there would be opportunity in late summer for a period of drop and add, once final decisions were made.

In this process, students were active participants both in identifying their needs and in finding solutions to what they perceived as common problems. I strove to respond non-defensively and non-anxiously, choosing to view students as collaborators with the faculty and me. Recognizing that many of the inquiries I was receiving were issues of concern to a number of students, I shifted from responding to individual concerns to addressing the entire student body.

Not only do students seek my assistance in addressing their questions and concerns about program, policies, and processes, but from time to time they also come to me to adjudicate disputes with a member of the faculty, for example, a complaint of unfair treatment in the classroom, an allegation of racism in a comment made to a class, or frustration with a faculty advisor. These interactions challenge me to determine whether and how I can be an advocate for a student.

After hearing the student's complaint, my first response is to determine what steps the student has already taken to address the concern. Has the student talked to the professor? When the student has not done so, I will coach the student, exploring how the student might approach the professor, what might be said, and what solution might be sought. Often I offer to meet with the student and professor together, though most students prefer to start without such assistance. I ask the student to let me know the result, and I continue to work with the student until we attain satisfaction.

If a student has already addressed the concern with the professor and is still disgruntled, my next step is to meet with the professor myself. As is usually true in a conflict, the professor typically has a different perspective on the situation. Together we mull over how to work with the student and respond appropriately. After I meet with professor, I report back to the student and ask the student to let me know if and when the matter is resolved.

Depending on the severity of the matter, I will consult with the president or with other faculty to brainstorm solutions and to find support for my stance with the student and/or member of the faculty. Even when I am fully in support of the student's concern, I am also mindful that faculty must receive due process and that my action in one situation will affect trust levels and working relationships with other students and faculty. Because of my position in the institution, I cannot limit my role solely to that of advocate for a student.

Soon after I became academic dean, two new students came to me to report what they perceived to be racism evident in remarks made by a faculty member during an orientation presentation. The students had already met with their faculty advisor, who supported their complaint. As I addressed the situation with the students, the accused professor, the seminary president, and eventually the entire faculty, it became evident that there were a number of systemic issues affecting the situation. In due course, a faculty committee made a number of recommendations addressing institutional racism, and I worked with faculty to develop evaluation policies for part-time faculty. In hindsight, I recognized that our institution does not have good grievance policies for academic matters and many other areas of seminary life, policies that would adjudicate conflicts and grievances while providing protection for faculty and students. I regret that I did not realize this in time to develop them.

At the other end of the spectrum, opposite the role of advocate, as academic dean I am required to be a disciplinarian from time to time. Having clear policies and following them is essential. In a small institution such as Seabury, where there is a high value on relationship, it is tempting to give significant weight to individual circumstances and needs. When I was appointed academic dean, one of the faculty priorities was to develop clear policies and procedures. I learned very quickly how time-consuming and emotionally tiring it can be to make case-by-case decisions about academic matters for each student. As the academic affairs committee and faculty worked together to develop policies, my work became much easier. Increasingly, I could consult the student handbook to determine the procedure or the consequence for a student. Exceptions to stated policy are rare, since they open the possibility of exceptions in other cases.

More significant disciplinary matters, such as plagiarism, still require an investment of my time and critical thinking skills. In these cases, consultation with other faculty members and with the president is helpful, and sometimes this consultation is required. (Our policy on plagiarism acknowledges its moral dimension, an important matter for students who are preparing for ordination, and our president makes the final decision after consulting with the faculty.) When I am in the role of disciplinarian, I make sure that the student is receiving support from someone else such as the faculty advisor or the seminary chaplain. Following our published policies, including attention to due process for the student, builds trust in the wider community as students experience a process that is fair and compassionate.

The Dean as Change Agent and Guardian of the Status Quo

In addition to addressing the needs and concerns of individual students with regard to academic programs and policies, the academic dean's position in the seminary system opens the possibility of being a change agent or a guardian of the status quo. Like the continuum of advocate-disciplinarian, the dean has a range of possible actions and responses.

Students come to seminary not only with goals for personal development but also with expectations of the institution. Their life experiences and values, including prior educational programs, theological and moral convictions, church life, family background, geographic context, and cultural heritage, interact with an institution with its own history, priorities, values, and patterns of common life. Each new class of students brings fresh perspectives. Sometimes a student will quickly determine that some aspect of seminary life needs improvement. Sometimes informal conversation among students or a class discussion will yield a proposal for institutional change. At Seabury, students designate representatives who attend faculty meetings, and on occasion, a student comment at a meeting results in recognition of a need for change.

My first impulse on hearing a recommendation for change, whether from a student or from anyone else, is to resist the possibility. I have learned to recognize this in myself, and even if my first response is negative, I will continue to ponder what the proposal might mean. Humility is important! Others may have a good idea or a solution to a problem that I haven't seen, and I try to remain open to that.

As I discern how to respond to a particular proposal for change, I weigh the idea in light of my understanding of the institution's history and goals. Do I know why we operate in a particular way? Did we try that solution and learn that it doesn't work? How does the proposal fit with the institution's immediate priorities and longer-term goals? What resources, human, financial, or otherwise, would be required? I may explore the proposal not only with the student(s) who come to me with the idea, but also with faculty colleagues, support staff, or the president or other administrators.

For many years, Seabury has been addressing the issue of racism, and the faculty has articulated explicit goals for this work. A few years ago, the administration decided to use the annual Martin Luther King, Jr., holiday as a day for a seminary-wide educational experience. The event in January 2008 was powerful for many. We began the day by watching the documentary *February One,* which tells the story of the 1960 lunch-counter sit-ins in Greensboro, North Carolina, through historical footage, interviews, and dramatization.[4] After the video, discussion focused on the implications for us today.

The feedback from that day was overwhelmingly positive, and many commented that they did not want to wait until the next year for another event. The planning committee asked me whether and how we could schedule a follow-up workshop during the spring semester. Because this was consistent with the seminary's long-term goals, I brought the idea to both the faculty and the seminary's administrative committee (which comprises all senior administrators). With their support, the planning committee announced a meeting and extended an open invitation for others to join them. That meeting turned out to fall a few days after the board's decision to discontinue the residential MDiv program. I encouraged the committee to meet anyway, and I participated in the meeting. As people considered how to structure the day, there was considerable energy for using this event to address people's feelings about the institutional change. I discouraged this plan, recognizing that it was too soon to know the results of the board's decision and stating that there would be other opportunities to respond to our new situation.

As the planning process continued, the committee organized an event focusing on institutional racism, this time through the lens of artistic depictions. The president decided that attendance would be optional; nonetheless, many students and faculty, and a few staff, participated. Not surprisingly, it did not have the same positive energy of the earlier event. Yet participants reported that the event helped them explore another aspect of racism, and they were appreciative.

In this process, I served initially as agent of change and then as guardian of the status quo. The proposal was consistent with our long-term institutional priorities. While it would require an investment of time by a planning committee and a smaller time commitment from the faculty, staff, and students who participated, I deemed this to be a reasonable amount of time.

---

4. Information about this video can be found at http://www.pbs.org/independentlens/februaryone/.

As we did for the January event, we would use leadership within the community and so would not require a significant financial commitment for a facilitator or trainer.

Having decided to support this change, I brought the proposal to the president. We discussed possibilities for scheduling and for content, and we considered the resources that would be needed. With the president's support, I placed the proposal on the agenda for the next faculty meeting and administrative committee meeting. For the faculty meeting, I asked the faculty member of the original planning committee to present the evaluation results from the January event and the proposal for the follow-up. I then participated actively in the planning process. In all of these ways, I used our institutional processes and my authority as academic dean to foster wider support for the proposal.

I knew that a follow-up event would be successful only if there was willingness to plan and to participate. Having gained the formal institutional support (approval by the faculty and the administrative committee), I left it to students and faculty to form a new planning committee and publicize the event. I stepped back so that there could be broader "ownership" of this new event.

When the planning committee met and tried to redirect the agenda of the event, I shifted from change agent to guardian of the status quo. I understood the high level of anxiety at that moment and the consequent desire to respond to the immediate concerns. But in my position as academic dean, I had more perspective on the institutional planning process that was just beginning. I was confident that the president would lead the community in dealing with the emerging realities, and I knew that things would be very different by the time we got to the event. I attribute my ability to dissuade the planning committee from altering the purpose of the event not just to my personal persuasiveness but also to the authority and respect that I have earned as academic dean.

This event suggests the range of possible responses when students seek the academic dean's support for change. Rarely do I say a simple "no," unless something appears to be detrimental to the institution or its members, or if I am the person with the authority and responsibility to make the decision. Sometimes I help a student understand how to propose a change in the seminary system without taking any action myself. For example, the student could ask a student representative to bring this to a faculty meeting, or the student might approach a professor who has significant interest in the matter. This allows a student to test out a proposal with the wider system, rather than my deciding that something should or should not be done. Sometimes, as I did initially with the proposal for a new event, I take the initiative to bring a proposal to the seminary's leadership, thus using the authority of the academic dean's position to support the idea. Sometimes I give my time to implementing a change, as I did when I joined the planning committee.

Qualities of Relationship

The dean has various roles, both formal and informal, in relation to students. Undergirding all of them is my theological anthropology, my belief that they are beloved daughters and sons of God. At my best, I use the power and authority of my position to serve them by creating an environment that will enable each student to flourish, to profit from the learning and formation at seminary, to attain individual goals, and to contribute to the institution.

The multiple and sometimes competing demands of the academic dean's responsibilities in the entire seminary system have challenged me to develop and hone a broad repertoire of skills as leader, educator, and pastor. When I am able to apply those skills effectively in the service of students and their education and formation, I reap rich rewards. At graduation, students sometimes ask me if it is difficult to say goodbye year after year. My answer is always "no," because my relationships with students rarely end altogether. As they go out into the church and the world, developing their ministries and building on their seminary education, they become my colleagues, and I rejoice as I see them thrive.

ADDITIONAL RESOURCES

Bridges, William. *Managing Transitions: Making the Most of Change.* Second ed. Cambridge, MA: Perseus, 2003.

Csikszentmihalyi, Mihaly. *Good Business: Leadership, Flow, and the Making of Meaning.* New York: Viking, 2003.

Heifetz, Ronald. *Leadership without Easy Answers.* Cambridge, MA: Belknap Press, 1994.

Heifetz, Ronald, and Marty Linsky. *Leadership on the Line: Staying Alive through the Dangers of Leading.* Boston: Harvard Business School Press, 2002.

The Dean and Students: A Divinity School Perspective

Richard A. Rosengarten

Let me risk churlishness and begin with a demurrer from the chapter title: it is of course a matter of relationship*s*, and that is the crux of the matter. The dean is many things to students or, perhaps better, has many roles to play. In this respect the relationship is arguably no different formally from that of the dean with the faculty: by turns but sometimes simultaneously, the dean serves as mentor, friend, disciplinarian, official spokesperson, and — for better and for worse — living and breathing metonymy of the institution. It is crucial to recognize this and to acknowledge — even to make one's peace with — the fact that the dean's relationships with all constituents are to some meaningful degree beyond full control or management.

But if that is a truth not universally acknowledged, it is also and at least equally true that deans control what they do and how they proceed. In the broadest sense, this means that the dean can do the right thing and can do things right. So it is worth the dean's time to consider what would constitute doing the right thing, and similarly what it would mean to do things right, and to follow through on those answers. I am persuaded that this consideration is as important in its application to students as it is to faculty. What, then, can we stipulate about a dean doing the right thing, and doing things right, with respect to students?

Fostering an Academic Relationship

First and foremost, there should be an academic relationship. The dean should interact with students as teacher, as advisor, and ideally as scholar. This matters in several material respects. It is important that the dean not become inured by bureaucracy — excuse me, I mean administration! — from the fundamental activities of the institution that administration exists to serve. If learning really is the chief institutional goal, a dean who does not teach, advise, and research is not really exemplary. From the perspective of the dean, this can be a challenge. Many of the immediate demands of the job are urgent, and always seem — and on occasion are — all-consuming. Time to prepare to teach well, to sit with students and offer them counsel, to read and think and write, are not usually part of either the job description or the reality. But there is no more resonant interaction the dean can have with students than the one that constitutes the institutional heartbeat.

This also has implications for how the dean performs administrative tasks, because in teaching and advising and doing research, the dean will experience firsthand, on an ongoing basis, the challenges and rewards of these core activities of the institution. The composer Andre Previn, in the midst of a successful transition from pianist to conductor, was asked why he continued to work so hard at playing the piano when conducting was manifestly a full-time job. He explained that the two were in fact related: he continued to play the piano because he loved to make music, and his conducting was an extension of that primal love; but he also noted that he continued to play, despite the demands conducting made on his time, because it helped him to keep firmly on his frontal lobe the degree of difficulty of the things that he daily asked his orchestra to do in his role as conductor. Like a good conductor of an orchestra, the dean of a theological school loves to make music and goes on doing so both for the love of it, and for the help it affords in conditioning an appreciation for the work of the school's chief sources of intellectual capital: its faculty and students. A dean who does not recognize the time and energy and patience and *sitzfleisch* that are the hallmarks of learning will ultimately be a poorer administrator and may also relate poorly to students in terms of the fundamental tasks of teaching and learning.

Modeling Professionalism

A second, complementary dimension of the dean's relationships to students concerns professionalism. The dean is often *de facto* a metonymy of the institution for students. The dean's own conduct, both of and within institutional life, is inevitably a model of professionalism for them. My professional sensibility was decisively formed by observing the deans and the dean of students who presided over the University of Chicago Divinity School during my years as a student and later as a member of the administrative staff. My understanding of myriad tasks — of how to speak about religion in public, of how to pray in meetings, of how to write memoranda and to conduct collegial relations, to name just three examples — took their initial, and in many cases decisive, bearings from observing how these three deans did each of those things. I was not unusual in this: students will often regard the dean as an exemplar of public conduct. And they will draw lessons — positive or negative — from what they see.

A paradox of the institutional sense of deans' work is that this exemplary function is rarely noted while they are doing the job. Yet it will prove to be the cardinal facet of the way they will be remembered. As deans everywhere know, what goes unnoted does not at all go unnoticed; and in this case, the widespread recourse to it post-administration suggests its importance in the duration. So this is important to recognize. I would underscore an important nuance of it. There is no such thing as *the* decanal style. But there is such a thing as authenticity and integrity in decanal practice. Students particularly look for and attend to authenticity and integrity (and if they see it and respect it, they will freely lampoon it in annual follies). The dean who prepares for public occasions, whether large or small; who works to represent the institution powerfully and with resonance, yet also with candor; and who neither shrinks from the role nor augments it unnecessarily, goes a long way toward conveying crucial lessons to students about professional conduct. The inverse does not bear rehearsal here, but it is also true.

Managing "Micro" Relationships

These initial notes purposely underscore the general and public dimensions of the dean's relationship with students. I emphasize them in the conviction that the dean who underestimates this aspect of the job is probably going to succeed only partially at one of the most essential aspects of relating to students. We might term these the "macro" dimensions of the dean's relationship with students.

At the same time there are many other kinds of "micro" relationships, local and personal, that the dean has with students. In terms of the elementary forms of institutional life, the dean usually will experience these as either small groups or individuals. The dynamics of these differ significantly. Just as the dean must exemplify scholarship and professionalism on the "macro" level, so the dean must recognize and be responsive to a range of expectations for response on the "micro" level — expectations for a mentor, a minister, an academic, a friend, a disciplinarian, etc. I will comment about the dynamics of group and individual relations, and then about these specific personae that students seek in the dean.

Students who meet the dean in a group usually do so because of some principle of organization, such as a shared degree program or a common interest or concern. It is important for the dean to take care to discern what organizes a group and what attitudes its members have toward that organizing principle. It is also important for the dean to gauge, to whatever degree is possible, the circumstances that have motivated the meeting. (These can be implicit. One not uncommon experience: Are the students there for an audience before a presumed "higher court" of appeal?) Last but not least, it is crucially important for the dean to approach such meetings as wonderful opportunities to get a firsthand sense of how the institution looks and feels and operates for some of its membership. Often such groups are organized around a particular view of the institution's strengths and weaknesses, and their decision to visit the dean, combined with strength in numbers, will afford invaluable instances of candor.

Meetings with groups often result in a call for action of some sort. The dean's relationship with students in this setting can thus assume a "call and response" formula. For reasons that are at least understandable, and often good, the dean may tend reflexively to resist an immediate response. This can be disappointing to students. The dean can and should address this disappointment in two ways. One is in the context of the meeting. There and then the dean can invite the students to think together about the prospect of the requested response. Such conversations can, and in my own experience usually do, yield insights on all sides about "the one," "some," and "the many." They have the added advantage of responding to candor with candor. A second way to address the inadvisability, often the impossibility, of an immediate response is by setting a timeline at the meeting for a response, and honoring it. In doing so, the dean would be wise to remember the experience of Paul with the Christian community at Corinth: appeals to the common good, however powerful, may nonetheless require elaboration and further discussion!

The dynamics of the relationships the dean has with individual students will be as variegated as those students and their respective perceptions of the dean. These individual relationships are also a crucial extension of all the relationships we have discussed — indeed, it would at least arguably be very odd for a dean who took seriously the dual roles of scholar and exemplar not to have such relationships. At the same time, the dynamics are personal and the ensuing considerations significant.

Here, too, the word "relationship" points with special acuity to issues of appropriateness, which merits every dean's consideration and ongoing care. It is not news to anyone in the academy that issues of harassment have in the last two decades become more acknowledged and discussed in institutional life. Whatever one's particular understanding of this development, it is indisputable that teachers have powers of evaluation in relation to their students, that these are appropriate, and yet that they can become inappropriate and/or abusive. Deans, who at least appear to hold institutional power in addition to the evaluative power of a faculty member, need to be especially attentive to appropriate behavior both as a condition of their own interactions with students and as a function of their responsibility for the healthy and free exchange of ideas that is central to learning. Regrettable as faculty misuse is, such misuse by a dean is doubly so.

A second general consideration, one which complicates further the issues of appropriateness, is confidentiality. The dean will almost inevitably have conversations with individual students that are conducted with the understanding that they must be kept between the two of them. The dean will sometimes want to avoid such confidences, but they are inevitable. It is worth noting that a real challenge in such circumstances is to distinguish clearly the fine line between the extension of empathy for the student's situation and the drawing of definitive conclusions about other members of the community or the institution itself. The dean must honor the student's confidence and empathize as appropriate, without endorsing uncritically the institutional worldview the student presents.

Dynamics around issues of harassment and confidentiality may seem in this rehearsal seriously and even decisively to complicate the dean's relationships with individual students. When well-considered, however, attention to these dynamics will engender trust and reflect consideration about the balance of authority and collegiality that must characterize student/faculty interactions on all levels. Indeed, the dean's attention to these matters makes it much easier for both the student and the dean to recognize and address the student's particular needs and expectations.

I was particularly fortunate in my own experience as a student to have as a faculty advisor someone who practiced what I would describe as "partial impartiality" toward me. This is to say that he conveyed both his unambiguous support for my commitment to the education I had undertaken, and his equally unambivalent willingness to convey his candid judgments of my strengths, "growing edges," and — yes — weaknesses as a student and developing professional. What initially seemed to me an almost perverse act of will on his part — faith yoked with criticism — was in fact something that I came to recognize as coming from a common well of commitment to excellence that affirmed at once both my own professional goals and the highest institutional standards for the education that was undertaken in their service. It was not incidental that his approach became for me a metonymy of the institution and promoted a healthy sense of my contribution to that larger endeavor.

I rehearse this because it illustrates an important general point about relationships with students. This is that the dean, like all educators, will need to remember that relationships with individual students inevitably evolve. This will be true from the points of view of both the dean and the students. To speak of evolution in this context is not to speak of intelligent design: such perceptions are not random, but neither are they determined extrinsically to the environment. Given these considerations, a dean might aim, or at least aspire to, something like Mark Twain's description of his relationship to his father. When he reached the age of fourteen, Twain once remarked, he was entirely convinced that his father was an utter fool. When he turned twenty-one, he was astonished to discover how much his father had learned in seven short years.

I have chosen to focus here on the hallmarks of the relationships the dean has with the students, rather than on types of those relations. My purpose in so choosing reflects my own experience, which is that the types in fact interact and shift even in the course of individual conversations. Thus the dean should not make the mistake of categorizing the role(s) to be played in a particular conversation in advance, or even during one or a series of conversations. Far better to heed general principles and let the student categorize, usually retrospectively, the role(s) the dean played.

A final hallmark is to my mind the *sine qua non* of the dean's relationship to students. If the particular *caritas* of the dean is to lead the institution, no virtue is more crucial to that leadership than the capacity to listen. This hackneyed truism bears rehearsal. With all the constraints acutely operative in the dean's work — the demands on time, the deep institutional knowledge in all its gory detail, etc. — the requisite patience to listen can come under duress. It is also the case that deans must at least occasionally listen to what they really would rather not hear. This combination of daily demand and psychic toll can make even a well-disposed dean go through the motions of appearing to hear while not listening very closely.

Like all theological virtues, the dean's capacity to listen can and should be cultivated through *habitus*. Some deans schedule monthly or quarterly meetings with students to discipline their awareness. Others sponsor social occasions or maintain dedicated office hours for walk-in visits. These can be useful, and when well-organized, they send a positive signal to students about the sort of relationship the dean seeks with them. It is also important, as noted above with regard to groups, that the dean follow through with students on specific aspects of conversation. All these formal checks are essential to an ongoing and developing habit of listening to students.

Taken alone, however, such arrangements do not, in my experience, afford sufficient discipline. Really to cultivate good working relations with students, the dean must take seriously the protestant principle of *semper reformanda* and regard the students as one major constituency in the ongoing health of institutional life. As in the wider Christian communion, this particular principle is amenable to both overstatement and understatement and requires care in its articulation. Overstated, it can suggest that the dean's sense of the institution in its present and future incarnations should reflect directly and immediately the judgments of the present student cohort about it. Yet students, as deans who ignore the example of Pilate and stay for an answer soon realize, pass through an institution relatively quickly and really only know it in their particular moment. Theirs is a deeply felt, and at the same time inevitably partial, view. Yet *semper reformanda* can also be understated. It can suggest that students need to be consulted *pro forma* but not, in the end, terribly seriously. Yet students, as deans and anyone who has taught at a theological school realize, are indispensable to the school's culture and climate of learning, and are truly on the proverbial "front lines" of its efforts to produce scholars for the church and the academy.

The bottom line is that the dean can be a wonderful empathic listener but must truly believe that students' opinions matter or theirs is a pseudo-relationship. It is not serious. At the same time, the students can be deeply engaged and committed to the institution, but if they do not recognize that their acquaintance is passing, theirs is a pseudo-perspective. It, too, is not serious. The dean's fundamental responsibility is to take the students very seriously and to invite them into the broader institutional volume of which their tenure is the latest extended chapter. Like all chapters, it is essential to the full story even as it depends on prior events and will take its final cast in part from future, as-yet-untold occurrences. Recognition of this will help to constitute something close to the ideal dynamic for the relationships between the dean and students, because it takes its bearings from complementary recognitions: that the institution is larger than any one moment and that its particular moment is utterly crucial in itself and ultimately in the cumulative venture that is the institution writ large.

In sum, the relationships that the dean has with students are myriad and probably not usefully categorized with reference to the roles played in the job. Instead the dean should cultivate self-conscious and reflective practice as a scholar and professional, recognizing that these "macro" public acts will be viewed by all the school's students and will be formative — and will not incidentally condition corresponding "micro" relationships with students. "Micro" relationships tend to take one of two forms, those with groups and those with individuals. In each form it is crucial that the dean cultivate a *habitus* of attentive listening to engage students, whether in smaller collectives or individually, wherever they report themselves to be in their course of study. At the same time, the dean needs to find ways to connect those experiential reports to larger institutional values, for the sake of transformations than can take place in all parties — the student(s), the institution, and the dean as an individual. In these ways the dean can best begin to embody the fundamental values of scholarship and learning that should be nothing less than the heart and soul of the theological school.

8. Modeling/Leading in Teaching and Scholarship

The Dean as Teacher and Scholar: Four Ways to Lead

Craig L. Nessan

Upon becoming an academic dean, one inevitably hears this kind of comment: "My condolences — so much for your academic career!" So strong is the bias against academic administration in relationship to the activities of teaching and scholarship that the vocation of academic dean can fall victim to self-fulfilling prophecy. The stereotype prevails that the academic dean is so consumed by meetings and administrative responsibilities that little or no creative energy can remain for teaching or original scholarship. Fear about the shift in duties away from teaching and scholarship is likely the central factor that dissuades candidates from considering service as academic dean.

There is a kernel of truth to this impression, of course. Academic deans do have major responsibility for the organization of degree programs, overseeing the academic calendar, responding to student matters, and facilitating faculty work. By accepting the calling to serve as academic dean, one becomes a steward of the well-being of the school as a whole, not just of a particular discipline or area. Increasingly, the office of academic dean is called upon to represent the school not only in its internal affairs but in its external relations as well. Moreover, those called to the vocation of academic dean often have little or no preparation for the rigors of academic administration, having prepared themselves for a career in teaching and scholarship.[1] Therefore, there may be much to learn about the task of administration and the challenges that perplex, leaving teaching and scholarship as low priorities.[2]

In spite of the real issues that confront the academic dean in relationship to conventional classroom teaching and academic scholarship, it is vital that the vocation itself be construed as an exercise in teaching and scholarship with its own scope and parameters. Instead of using the classroom as the primary venue for teaching, the academic dean serves as a teacher to the entire institution, including the student body and faculty as a whole, through the varied occasions where the academic dean exercises leadership: for example, among the student body at convocations, committee meetings, and individual appointments or among the faculty at faculty meetings, in drafting grant proposals, and participating in evaluations. Furthermore, the scholarship of the academic dean encompasses not only the discipline in which one was trained but also the entire scope of theological education.

The modeling and leading of the academic dean for teaching and scholarship involves at least four dimensions: (1) the field of theological education itself, (2) cultivating the teaching and scholarship of others, (3) a "body of work" that includes the composition of administrative documents, and (4) one's own area(s) of academic interest.

Interpreting the Nature and Purpose of Theological Education

In recent decades there has emerged a body of significant scholarship about the enterprise of theological education itself. This literature provides CAOs with insightful and relevant resources to assist colleagues, boards, and students to gain perspective for understanding the competing concerns and agendas that are so often present in discussions about a school's educational mission, for example, in the process of curriculum revision in a rapidly changing educational environment. In considering this topic, a look at the central texts in this literature is instructive. These texts illuminate key issues

---

1. Cf. Deborah L. Rhode, *In Pursuit of Knowledge: Scholars, Status, and Academic Culture* (Palo Alto: Stanford University Press, 2006), for a trenchant analysis of the strengths and weaknesses of academia today.

2. Jeanne P. McLean, *Leading from the Center: The Emerging Role of the Chief Academic Officer in Theological Schools* (Atlanta: Scholars Press, 1999), remains the most comprehensive introduction to the vocation of the academic dean.

CAOs face in their scholarly role as interpreters of the nature and purpose of theological education.

In 1983 Edward Farley launched a vigorous debate among theological educators in North America about the nature and purpose of theological education with the publication of his book, *Theologia: The Fragmentation and Unity of Theological Education.*[3] Since that time numerous authors have made fruitful contributions to address the fundamental *raison d'etre* of theological education, yielding many significant insights.[4] One of the key teaching and scholarly contributions of the academic dean is to articulate the location of one's own school in relationship to this wider conversation. As a central feature, this literature reveals a fundamental tension between two competing directions in theological education — loyalty to the academy on the one side and loyalty to the church on the other. How does one address the fundamental issues of the fragmentation of knowledge in academia and the needs of the church for unity in the formation process — an issue that challenges all of theological education, not just theoretically but in practice, through the curriculum of one's own school and its degree programs?

Farley argues that theological education is fragmented and lacks fundamental cohesiveness due to an unresolved conflict between two incompatible paradigms. First, "the clerical paradigm" emerged as a consequence of understanding theological education as grounded in the research university, whose academic disciplines provide the intellectual foundation for the clergy profession as knowledge is "applied" to ministerial practice. Second, Farley proposes the recovery of an ancient paradigm that he names *theologia,* the formation of a person in sapiential wisdom that habitually interprets the world through theological lenses.

Repeatedly in discussions of curriculum with seminary faculty, I have discovered Farley's fundamental distinction to be incisive regarding conflicts between faculty members about the overall purpose of theological education and also regarding internal tensions within a particular professor about competing educational values. There are many ways in which a conflict between these two paradigms continues to plague theological educators, par-

3. Edward Farley, *Theologia: The Fragmentation and Unity of Theological Education* (Philadelphia: Fortress, 1983).

4. Among the important contributions are Robert Banks, *Reenvisioning Theological Education: Exploring a Missional Alternative to Current Models* (Grand Rapids: Eerdmans, 1999); John Pobee, ed., *Towards Viable Theological Education* (Geneva: WCC, 1997); and Max L. Stackhouse, *Apologia: Contextualization, Globalization, and Mission in Theological Education* (Grand Rapids: Eerdmans, 1988).

ticularly as professors have been trained in particular specialized disciplines, while the task of most theological schools is to graduate practitioners whose theological learning is thoroughly integrated toward the various tasks of ministry.[5]

One of the pivotal contributions to this conversation is that of David Kelsey. Kelsey names the first paradigm the "Berlin" model and the second "Athens."[6] The Berlin model emerged during the rise of the modern university in post-Enlightenment Europe. This paradigm found classical form in Schleiermacher's *Brief Outline on the Study of Theology*, in which he divides theology into three distinct disciplines: historical theology (including exegesis, church history, and dogmatics), philosophical theology (inquiring about the truth of Christianity), and practical theology (articulating the normative rules for the practice of ministry).[7] The Berlin model is distinguished by its commitments to scientific method and the pursuit of research agendas. Within the university, the place of the study of theology is analogous to the study of medicine or law, in order to provide competent practitioners for the church.

Within the Berlin model, however, there exists a major paradox, even contradiction. On the one side, Schleiermacher offers a teleological answer to the question about the purpose of theological education, the aim of practical theology to prepare clergy for service in the church. On the other side, however, theology as a science deals with the truth of Christian revelation, the "distinctive essence" of Christianity.[8] Schleiermacher fails to resolve the tension between these two express purposes: either to prepare clergy for their distinctive profession (practical preparation for pastoral ministry) or to investigate the truth of Christian theological claims (which entails rigorous academic research). Consequently, a fundamental bifurcation has haunted theological education. First, the functionalism of the clerical paradigm made large inroads into much *seminary* education.[9] Second, the

---

5. Joseph C. Hough, Jr., and John B. Cobb, Jr., *Christian Identity and Theological Education* (Chico, CA: Scholars, 1985), pp. 95-129, thereby articulate the goal of theological education as the formation of the "practical theologian."

6. David H. Kelsey, *Between Athens and Berlin: The Theological Education Debate* (Grand Rapids: Eerdmans, 1993).

7. Friedrich Schleiermacher, *Brief Outline on the Study of Theology*, trans. Terrance Tice (Richmond: John Knox Press, 1966).

8. Farley, *Theologia*, pp. 92-94.

9. This tendency was critiqued in the study of theological education by H. Richard Niebuhr et al., *The Purpose of the Church and Its Ministry: Reflections on the Aims of Theological Education* (New York: Harper & Brothers, 1956).

eclipse of Christianity as the favored religion in the university led to the emergence of the new discipline of *religious studies*, replacing theology as that discipline most fitting for the academic study of religion.[10]

One sign of this internal tension is the perennial challenge of resolving the divide between theory and practice. Theological teachers are normally trained in graduate programs within research universities where they become specialists in a particular discipline. Doctoral candidates are prepared as researchers in a particular field, seek to publish their findings, and become expert theoreticians. By contrast, churches are in need of excellent practitioners in the theological arts: those who lead worship, preach, teach, counsel, and administer effectively. This tension deprives theological education of unity of purpose. Those who teach in theological seminaries find themselves caught between loyalties to the academy and commitment to the preparation of clergy who are excellent practitioners. In some schools this contributes to a *de facto* class system between those who teach in the "academic" disciplines (Bible, history, and systematic theology) and those who teach in the "practical" areas.

Farley's proposal for the integration of theological education draws upon the classical concept of *paideia* as represented by the formation model of ancient Athens. In contrast to either the intellectual or practical purposes of theological education in the Berlin model, the Athens model aims at forming a *habitus* of being. Farley names the cultivation of *theologia* as the goal of this formation process. *Theologia* refers to a unified approach to theological understanding based on "a salvifically oriented knowledge of divine being."[11] Theology is a kind of wisdom, a way of seeing the world, a disposition toward interpreting reality. *Theologia* does not preclude critical reflection on the truth of Christian teaching but subsumes such reflection as one moment within the larger horizon of theological understanding. It is a more holistic way of knowing, transcending all division between theory and practice. Recent trends in curriculum revision reveal the influence of this argument as increasingly both theological faculties and accreditation standards have sought to increase the coherence of theological curriculum by giving serious attention to integration and formation.[12]

10. This divide is symbolized by the movement to separate the American Academy of Religion from the Society for Biblical Literature.

11. Farley, *Theologia*, p. 33.

12. Much of the ensuing discussion has involved the retrieval of notions of formation and spiritual discipline in response to Farley's proposal. In one major study, a team of scholars provide a thick description of how such formation takes place in two starkly contrasting

Kelsey affirms the value of the Athens model "to analyze specifically Christian theological education, not in terms of the overarching purpose of conveying information, but in terms of helping [students] to become formed (or in-formed) by certain dispositions to act in certain ways."[13] After analyzing the theological education debate, Kelsey develops his own original proposal, arguing that theological education has one "overarching goal: to understand God more truly."[14] Yet this purpose does not itself provide a unifying vision for a theological school, insofar as one could reflect on the tradition either in the manner of Berlin or Athens. Therefore Kelsey adds another qualifying dimension to his proposal: that theological schools focus on the "Christian thing" as it becomes concrete "in and as various Christian congregations or worshipping communities in all their radical pluralism."[15] The unity of theological education is attained by focusing neither on the skillful application of theory by a practitioner nor on the formation of an individual for the art of ministry, but rather through *understanding God truly for the life of congregations.* Such a purpose accords with the recent holistic understanding of "practices" in the theological education literature.[16] Furthermore, it strengthens the rationale for the recent turn toward "congregational studies" in theological education.[17]

One valuable teaching and scholarly role for the academic dean is to become conversant in the literature about theological education, in order to give leadership in one's own school to the conversation about the nature and purpose of the school's academic programs.[18] I have found this body of lit-

---

theological schools. See Jackson W. Carroll et al., *Being There: Culture and Formation in Two Theological Schools* (New York: Oxford, 1997). Rebecca Chopp, *Saving Work: Feminist Practices of Theological Education* (Louisville: Westminster John Knox, 1995), articulated the particular contributions made to theological education through feminist reflection and practices. In the 1980s and 90s, there emerged a strong focus on formation through the globalization of theological education, an emphasis which came to shape accrediting standards. See Alice Frazer Evans, Robert A. Evans, and David A. Roozen, eds., *The Globalization of Theological Education* (Maryknoll: Orbis, 1993).

13. Kelsey, *Between Athens and Berlin,* p. 48.

14. David H. Kelsey, *To Understand God Truly: What's Theological About a Theological School* (Louisville: Westminster John Knox, 1992).

15. Kelsey, *To Understand God Truly,* p. 110 (italics omitted).

16. Cf. Craig Dykstra, *Growing in the Life of Faith: Education and Christian Practices* (Louisville: Geneva, 1999).

17. Cf. Nancy Ammerman, Jackson Carroll, Carl Dudley, and William McKinney, eds., *Studying Congregations: A New Handbook* (Nashville: Abingdon, 1998).

18. A masterful overview of the purpose and prospect of theological schools is Dan-

erature extremely informative in a number of settings within my own school, for example, in discussions with faculty colleagues about their own careers, in faculty and board reflections about the purpose of seminary education, and in my own involvement in matters of accreditation. Furthermore, familiarity with this literature equips the academic dean to enter into discourse about theological education in the ecumenical arena with other academic administrators. Teaching and scholarship about theological education is an important field of inquiry in its own right to which academic deans need to devote serious attention.

Cultivating the Teaching and Scholarship of Others

While academic deans do not need to be the best teachers, they do need to be able to equip others in the art of teaching and the practice of scholarship.[19] Insofar as theological schools are by definition in the business of teaching and learning, the academic dean bears special responsibility for fostering high quality teaching and excellent scholarship in the school. At one time there was a seeming dearth of resources for this undertaking, but in recent decades the focus on teaching and learning in theological education has been given new life, especially through the programs and resources of the Wabash Center for Teaching and Learning in Theology and Religion.[20]

Academic deans have several ready-made venues for enhancing the teaching of the school. First, as leaders in the process of evaluating faculty members for reappointment, tenure, or promotion, they have the opportunity to encourage others toward professional growth in the art of teaching. Academic deans can recommend literature, arrange for consultation, and suggest workshops to individual professors to promote growth in pedagogical skill. Faculty members often have little training in teaching methods based on their own graduate school education, so there is often a genuine readiness to engage solid literature in the area of education in general[21] and

---

iel O. Aleshire, *Earthen Vessels: Hopeful Reflections on the Work and Future of Theological Schools* (Grand Rapids: Eerdmans, 2008).

19. Cf. Peter C. Hodgson, *God's Wisdom: Toward a Theology of Education* (Louisville: Westminster John Knox, 1999).

20. See www.wabashcenter.wabash.edu.

21. bell hooks, *Teaching to Transgress: Education and the Practice of Freedom* (New York: Routledge, 1994), and Parker Palmer, *The Courage to Teach: Exploring the Inner Landscape of a Teacher's Life* (San Francisco: Jossey-Bass, 1998).

theological education in particular.[22] One new area for teaching competence is online instruction.[23]

Second, theological faculties can establish times for engaging together in the practice of faculty development with the academic dean as a key leader in these activities. Some schools schedule regular weekly or monthly sessions to focus on professional enrichment, including attention to the teaching and learning process. Many schools hold an annual retreat to devote dedicated time to particular themes, such as the vocation of teaching.[24] A few schools may commit time to both regular sessions on teaching practices and annual retreats. Third, the academic dean can be at the forefront in developing grant proposals especially aimed at accessing expertise and resources to enhance the teaching and learning at one's school. The academic dean can encourage not only individual faculty members at different junctures of their teaching careers to pursue grants for developing skills in teaching but also the faculty as a whole to participate in workshops on teaching and learning.

An excellent resource for cultivating the teaching and learning ecology at one's school is the major study, *Educating Clergy: Teaching Practices and Pastoral Imagination,* funded by The Carnegie Foundation.[25] The conceptuality of this project will shape the discussion of teaching and learning for the next generation and serve as a benchmark well beyond that. *Educating Clergy* describes the purpose of theological education as "cultivating the pastoral, priestly, or rabbinic imagination necessary for clergy to embrace this multifaceted and public work."[26] This purpose is fostered by the "pedagogical imagination" of teachers, a way of seeing and interpreting one's contribution to the educational mission of the school through

> decisions about what to teach from all that could be taught; how to engage students; how to assess the extent to which students learn what was

---

22. Mary Elizabeth Mullino Moore, *Teaching from the Heart: Theology and Education Method* (Minneapolis: Fortress, 1991) and Malcolm L. Warford, ed., *Practical Wisdom on Theological Teaching and Learning* (New York: Peter Lang, 2004).

23. Rena M. Palloff and Keith Pratt, *Building Learning Communities in Cyberspace: Effective Strategies for the Online Classroom* (San Francisco: Jossey-Bass, 1999).

24. L. Gregory Jones and Stephanie Paulsell, eds., *The Scope of Our Art: The Vocation of the Theological Teacher* (Grand Rapids: Eerdmans, 2002).

25. Charles R. Foster, Lisa E. Dahill, Lawrence A. Goleman, and Barbara Wang Tolentino, eds., *Educating Clergy: Teaching Practices and Pastoral Imagination* (San Francisco: Jossey-Bass, 2006).

26. Foster, Dahill, Goleman, and Tolentino, *Educating Clergy,* p. 22.

intended; how to negotiate one's sense of obligation to the students' expectations, traditions of knowledge, and the religious communities that will be receiving them as clergy and leaders in ministry; and how to respond and adapt to new situations and challenges while teaching.[27]

A "signature pedagogical framework" involves methods and strategies to engage students in four activities: interpretation, formation, contextualization, and performance.[28] Faculty discussion of these key themes can do much to enhance partnership in the teaching and learning enterprise at a school.

Academic deans are also well situated to promote the scholarship of other faculty members, both formally and informally. Formally, the academic dean can advocate for just sabbatical policies at the school and interpret the necessary place of research to those in authority who sometimes undervalue scholarship. Moreover, the academic dean can give encouragement and direction to faculty scholarship not only through evaluation processes but also in the shaping of sabbatical proposals. The academic dean can provide feedback to sharpen research agendas or broaden horizons. Moreover, the academic dean can see the scope of faculty scholarship as a whole to make constructive recommendations about particular projects and promote collaboration among the scholarly endeavors of different faculty members.[29] Informally, there may also be a significant role for the academic dean in relationship to the scholarship of faculty colleagues. The academic dean may serve as an encourager in the face of obstacles, a sounding board for nascent ideas, a proofreader of early drafts, or a consultant regarding publication strategies. Much depends on the relationship of the academic dean with particular colleagues in fostering scholarship both through formal channels and in informal ways.

The Scholarship of Academic Administration

How should one conceive the scholarship of the academic dean in relation to the many and various kinds of administrative documents produced as part

---

27. Foster, Dahill, Goleman, and Tolentino, *Educating Clergy,* p. 40.

28. Cf. Foster, Dahill, Goleman, and Tolentino, *Educating Clergy,* pp. 32-34.

29. Ann E. Austin and Roger G. Baldwin, *Faculty Collaboration: Enhancing the Quality of Scholarship and Teaching* (Washington, DC: Clearinghouse on Higher Education, 1991), pp. 83-90.

of the job? This is a particularly neuralgic question for those academic deans who may already serve in the office but are still in a position that is yet to be tenured. The work of the academic dean involves the composition and editing of many kinds of documents necessary for the operation, assessment, and improvement of the school.[30] These include evaluation materials, grant proposals, reports to the board of directors, and major responsibility for accreditation self-studies. How should an institution think about these authorial duties of the academic dean? And how should the academic dean construe the laboring to compose these documents in relationship to the work of scholarship?

While such compositions have not usually been considered a part of conventional scholarship, it is important that such an estimation of their status and worth be reconsidered. In many ways, conducting research in the form of gathering assessment, evaluation, grant, and accreditation data is original scholarship on behalf of the living institution. Organizing and writing up such findings constitutes a form of scholarship that contributes to the present and future self-understanding and self-interpretation of a school. Knowledge about both qualitative and quantitative research methods can contribute greatly to the performance of duties by the academic dean. This knowledge is put into the service of the institution through the types of documents produced by the academic dean's office.

Although one would not wish to reduce the understanding of scholarship by the academic dean to such administrative documents, a strong case needs to be made that they be valued as a substantial contribution to the body of scholarly work compiled by an academic dean. In considering the scholarship of the academic dean (particularly when the academic dean undergoes performance, tenure, or promotion evaluations and decisions), it is important for the institution to operate with an expansive notion of scholarly production to encompass these kinds of contributions to the life and functioning of the school. Furthermore, it is to the enhancement of the academic dean's own vocational self-understanding to view and value the research and writing of these administrative documents as part of one's scholarly production. In fact, theological schools function less well and are impoverished by the absence of the academic dean's scholarship in these areas.

---

30. Cf. Elliot W. Eisner, *The Educational Imagination: On the Design and Evaluation of School Programs* (Upper Saddle River, NJ: Prentice Hall, 1994).

Teaching and Scholarship in One's Discipline

For those educated in a discipline other than academic administration (and this would apply to the vast majority of academic deans in theological schools), it is critical to practice one's vocation so as to incorporate ongoing teaching and scholarship in one's discipline as part of the regular work of the dean. This is important for two reasons: first, to sustain and extend the passion and interest that originally motivated one to enter the field of higher education in the first place; and second, to demonstrate one's competence in teaching and scholarship in solidarity with the academic enterprise of the school. While the demands are great, the academic dean wins authority for the role of administrator, both among students and faculty members, through integral participation in the activities of teaching and scholarship.[31] Lest administrators become abstracted from the front lines of the educational process, ongoing involvement in teaching and scholarship is vitally necessary.

How is it possible to sustain such interests in face of the increasing demands placed on the office of the academic dean? First, one must think differently about the scale of one's participation in teaching courses and writing for publication. By virtue of the workload, the academic dean does well to concentrate teaching and scholarly research on fewer areas. By limiting the scope of one's teaching and scholarship and becoming more strategic about one's involvements, one can maintain command of the literature, make a solid contribution to teaching, and continue to publish in one's area of specialization. The academic dean as teacher needs to reflect on such considerations: Are there particular courses where my unique contribution, both as instructor and academic dean, makes strategic sense? Are there particular courses that better further my own scholarly pursuits? Can certain courses be taught more efficiently than others, that is, in a less labor-intensive manner? The academic dean as scholar does well to reflect carefully on such questions as these: How does this scholarly project contribute to my service as academic dean? How does this scholarly project work in symbiosis with my teaching? Are the parameters of this scholarly undertaking vital to my own professional growth? In discerning among the many possible ventures, the academic dean needs to become more selective and strategic when engaging in the activities of teaching and scholarship.

31. Cf. *The Dean as Scholar: Clinical Competence, Teaching, Research and Publication* (Washington, DC: Baker and Taylor, 1981), p. 22.

Second, the academic dean as teacher and scholar needs to look for opportunities to work collaboratively in teaching and publication. Team teaching provides an excellent venue for the academic dean to share scholarly expertise and course administration in partnership with others. Furthermore, mutual accountability and the building of mutual regard can be gifts from a team teaching arrangement. In a parallel way, the academic dean can seek ways to make collaborative contributions as a scholar. More and more scholarly projects have become multi-authorial in recent decades. Serving as the editor of a collaborative book project can offer excellent use of the networking and managerial skills of the academic dean. Or, contributing a single chapter to a book in one's field can be a great way to maintain scholarly competence, while making a substantial contribution in a concentrated way.

Third, the academic dean as teacher and scholar needs to learn to befriend deadlines. This recommendation takes us into the challenging area of time management, probably the most important issue in relationship to the service of the academic dean as teacher and scholar. How does one make productive use of the hours in the working day, while maintaining one's health and sanity? If teaching and scholarship are to remain high priorities, the dean must allot the necessary hours to these tasks. This means budgeting time and scheduling out blocks of time for teaching, reading, research, and writing. In order to accomplish this without slighting other duties, one needs with intentionality to schedule days in accordance with those things that are the most needful. This is not necessarily the same as attending to those things that appear to be the most urgent.

While academic deans do not have the same freedom of calendar belonging to other faculty members, one does retain sufficient freedom to establish appointments with oneself on a regular basis for the purposes of preparation for teaching and scholarship. Also there may be rhythms to the academic year that allow for more attention to scholarly activities during certain seasons. In the end, there is nothing like a deadline to promote discipline in teaching and scholarship. For this reason, it is useful to accept a certain number of invitations for teaching, speaking engagements, and/or writing projects in order to establish external motivators toward these priorities.

The Dean as Steward of Teaching and Learning

The teaching and scholarly vocation of the academic dean encompasses a range of venues and activities. It is crucial that those serving as academic deans recognize and appreciate the diverse opportunities to model and lead in teaching and scholarship that are afforded those occupying the office. To imagine teaching exclusively in the conventional forms of classroom lectures and seminars or to envision scholarship only in terms of publication in one's discipline is myopic. While conventional teaching and scholarship retain great inherent value, the academic dean has the opportunity to be a teacher in profound ways among the whole faculty, student body, staff, board of directors, and external constituencies. The scholarly contributions of the academic dean through solid and reflective administrative work have the potential to enhance the life of the entire institution and even the realm of theological education itself.

One of the most important legacies of any individual is the contribution made to the building up of excellent and functional institutions that fulfill their respective missions.[32] This is especially true for institutions serving theological education. Both the church and society are publics in need of the leadership provided by graduates of theological schools. Faith communities thrive through the leadership of well-prepared ministers who are skilled in the theological arts, and society is in need of public theologians who are able to articulate the religious dimension at the intersection of faith and life. The very existence of theological institutions depends on the service of academic deans who offer their peculiar gifts of teaching and scholarship in the cause of institution building. While particular status accrues in academia to certain forms of teaching and original scholarship (to which an academic dean also aspires), the most lasting — though often invisible — contribution of the academic dean to teaching and scholarship takes place through daily and yearly commitment to the stewardship of the theological school as an institution of teaching and learning.

32. Denise Lardner Carmody, *Organizing a Christian Mind: A Theology of Higher Education* (Valley Forge: Trinity Press International, 1996).

Leading as an Act of Academic Hospitality

Barbara Horkoff Mutch

Centered at the confluence of multiple rivers within the geography of a theological institution, the role of a chief academic officer is complex and challenging. Competency and skill are required in areas as diverse as curriculum development, budgetary administration, and faculty development. Yet beneath the various streams of the dean's work, several salient questions flow as a constant current. What makes a theological school hospitable to teaching and scholarship? What practices nurture the academic life of an institution? How can an academic dean cultivate a community of learning? The academic dean is uniquely placed within the theological institution to nurture the community of learning in its commitment to teaching and scholarship and to cultivate a terrain that is hospitable to academic life and work.

Hospitality can be traced as a significant biblical theme. The reception of a stranger as a guest was a sacred duty and an expression of righteousness throughout the ancient Mediterranean world. The practice of hospitality was woven into the religious culture and kept more heartily and stringently than many written laws.[1] Each stranger was a potential enemy, yet the welcome, provision, and protection regularly extended to the unfamiliar one witnesses to the sacredness of the responsibility. Response to the human "other" demonstrated interior responsiveness to God. As early Christians continued the practice of their ancestors, hospitality brought a bond and connection to the churches scattered throughout Asia Minor. Hospitality is so foundational to a reading of the gospel that it may be identified as residing at the core of Christology. Elizabeth Barnes, in *The Story of Discipleship*, posits that the action of Jesus is to invite us into God's house, opening the doors of hospitality to God's world house *and* otherworld house of salvation, transformation, rest, jubilation, and life. In turn, Barnes suggests that faithful discipleship and ministry do the same thing, as believers join Christ in the hospitable act in faithfulness to God and thanksgiving for God's own gracious acts.[2]

---

1. V. H. Kooy, "Hospitality," *The Interpreter's Dictionary of the Bible*, Volume 2 (Nashville: Abingdon Press, 1962), p. 654.

2. Elizabeth Barnes, *The Story of Discipleship* (Nashville: Abingdon Press, 1995), p. 129.

In addition to being a noteworthy biblical theme and a formative Christian practice, hospitality can also serve as a helpful lens for appreciating and understanding the work of theological education. John B. Bennett, in his fine book, *Academic Life,* claims that hospitality is an essential virtue in academic work and that large values are in the balance when the hospitality and thoughtfulness of a learned profession are absent.[3] Bennett contrasts hospitality with the insistent individualism that is marked by self-promotion and self-protection and their clamouring concerns for self and controlling power.[4] On the contrary, he suggests that hospitality incarnated in the academy means being radically open to others, sharing resources, and receiving with care the new and the strange, while also critically reviewing the familiar.[5] The academic dean's invitation is to join Christ in Christ's hospitable act through actively and intentionally cultivating hospitality for teaching and scholarship.

A theological school that is hospitable toward teaching and scholarship is marked by conversation, community, and compassion. These commitments can be distinguished from one another but are ultimately intricately interwoven.

Conversation

Conversation assumes dialogue. Hospitable schools are talkative places. As Kina Mallard suggests, "professors need a community that encourages the kind of productivity that comes from formal and informal faculty interaction . . . a community where dialogue is prevalent, energizing, and productive."[6]

While in their public roles, faculty members are seen most frequently in speech — instructing, informing, explaining, questioning, probing, and critiquing. Those not involved in theological education "from the inside" may imagine that these same faculty members spend the balance of their working hours similarly occupied, engaged in enriching, stimulating, invigorating dialogue with their academic colleagues. The world of academia, however, is often experienced as individualistic and competitive.

3. John B. Bennett, *Academic Life* (Bolton, MA: Anker Publishing Company, 2003), p. 2.

4. Bennett, *Academic Life,* pp. 6-9.

5. Bennett, *Academic Life,* p. 47.

6. Kina S. Mallard, "The Soul of Scholarship," *New Directions for Teaching and Learning,* no. 90 (Summer 2002): 59-69.

The model of insistent individualism has a long history, but in recent years it has gained vigour and eclipsed the standing and strength of a relational model. Insistent individualism promotes the isolated self — it advances disconnection among faculty and staff as well as between faculty, staff, students, and institutions. It works against internal integration and separates personal from professional lives. It encourages exclusiveness rather than relational knowledge.[7]

There are many incentives for faculty to work in isolation. The pressure to "publish or perish" is real and urgent for faculty at many institutions. Published research functions as the sole or primary currency of promotion and tenure. When combined with personal insecurities, this urgency results for some individuals in a focus on the building of personal careers to the neglect of a shared institutional mission. Other faculty members may retreat into self-imposed scholarship exile, maintaining a facade of connectivity but spurning genuine interest in the common good. Loneliness rattles down the hallways.

The arena of the classroom is not necessarily an improvement, for teaching may actually be the most privatized of all the public professions. Parker Palmer draws attention to the familiar reality that

> though we teach in front of students, we almost always teach solo, out of collegial sight — as contrasted with surgeons or trial lawyers, who work in the presence of others who know their craft well. . . . When we walk into our workplace, the classroom, we close the door on our colleagues. When we emerge, we rarely talk about what happened or what needs to happen next, for we have no shared experience to talk about.[8]

Teaching that advances learning, however, is not an isolated activity. Teaching and scholarship are enriched in contexts in which high levels of dialogue, support, and collaboration are present.[9] Lecturers in a study of rewards for good teaching in Australian higher education hold the view that understanding teaching as a collective obligation as well as an individual one is vital to enhancing its status.[10] The work of a faculty, both individually and

---

7. Bennett, *Academic Life*, p. 22.

8. Parker Palmer, *The Courage to Teach* (San Francisco: Jossey-Bass, 1998), p. 142.

9. Paul Ramsden, *Learning to Lead in Higher Education* (London: Routledge, 1998), p. 158.

10. Ramsden, *Learning to Lead,* p. 176.

collectively, is stimulated by dialogue and consultation. Scholarly activity and output are enlivened when faculty perceive their departments to be places that provide a collaborative environment, clear goals, intellectual challenge, equitable workload distribution, and a large amount of dialogue and consultation.[11]

Conversation, in essence, is all about welcoming the stranger, the one that is other than me. Conversation suggests that people with different intellectual interests and histories have important things to say to each other. The simple back and forth of comment or question, response, rejoinder, and so on brings people into active participation with each other. True conversation is marked by humility, identifying the other as a necessary participant in one's own learning.[12] It is conversation — conducted both within the community and directed outward to other communities — that both creates and expresses the collegium.[13]

But what if something as simple as conversation — meaningful, rich conversation with all the give and take that this implies — is becoming an endangered commodity? A growing body of literature suggests that the ability to concentrate is being affected negatively. Capacity for the sustained mental attention necessary for reflective, integrative thought is being compromised and crippled by the ways our brains are currently reading in this increasingly digital age.[14] We are learning that multitasking lowers our working intelligence and compromises our ability to think deeply. If it is true that deep reading is indistinguishable from deep thinking, may it also be true that both are related to and necessary for deep conversation? The ability to cultivate conversation is crucial not only to our work as faculty but to our identity and life as thoughtful people.

Community

The kind of conversation that is a mark of hospitality emerges out of the experience of a community that enjoys shared work. It may be the kind of community that Wendell Berry refers to as "the membership." Berry's Port

11. Ramsden, *Learning to Lead,* p. 182.
12. Bennett, *Academic Life,* p. 99.
13. Bennett, *Academic Life,* p. 145.
14. See Maryanne Wolf, *Proust and the Squid: The Story and Science of the Reading Brain* (New York: HarperCollins, 2007), and Nicholas Carr, *The Big Switch: Rewiring the World, from Edison to Google* (New York: W. W. Norton, 2008), among others.

William membership is marked by "an economic purpose and an economic result, but the purpose and the result were a lot more than economic."[15] In Berry's membership, a whole company of people might be at work together at some times. At other times, the work is carried alone, but at all times there is an involvement and connection and knowledge of the others within the membership. This interconnectedness looks considerably different than the experience of many faculties of higher education and dramatically different from the insistent individualism described recognizably by Bennett.

Another word for the concept of the membership and the kind of community that embodies hospitality in academic life may simply be friendship. Paul Wadell's book, *Becoming Friends: Worship, Justice, and the Practice of Christian Friendship,* speaks directly to the isolation that often exists in academic life.

> . . . [F]riendships are imperilled by the haughty individualism of our culture. We live in a society that teaches us to put ourselves and our needs before the needs and well-being of others. Even our moral vocabulary reflects this. Gone is the language of the common good. In its place is the language of individual rights, personal choice, and privacy. . . . The very qualities requisite for friendship, qualities such as generosity and thoughtfulness, are hardly nurtured in a society that tells us we must look after ourselves first because nobody else will.[16]

Wadell goes on to say,

> This is not to say that every person in a Christian community [or academic community] must be an intimate friend with every other person, but it does mean our churches [theological schools] should be communities in which people respect one another, support one another, challenge one another, encourage one another, love one another, and share together a gracious and hopeful vision of life.[17]

It is difficult to imagine a community of learning not comprised of persons who, at the least, feel friendly toward one another. It is impossible to imagine

15. Wendell Berry, *Hannah Coulter* (Washington, DC: Shoemaker and Hoard, 2004), p. 93.

16. Paul J. Wadell, *Becoming Friends: Worship, Justice, and the Practice of Christian Friendship* (Grand Rapids: Brazos Press, 2002), p. 44.

17. Wadell, *Becoming Friends,* p. 53.

hospitality that does not contain the offer of friendship through receiving with respect the new, the unfamiliar, and the strange.

Compassion

Community and conversation are embodied in the regular and practical expression of compassion. In his work on a spirituality of teaching, Parker Palmer writes of a knowledge born of compassion in which the act of knowing *is* an act of love. Such love and compassion are lived out in the act of entering and embracing the reality of the other, of allowing the other to enter and embrace our own. In such knowing we know and are known as members of one community, and our knowing becomes a way of reweaving that community's bonds.[18] Palmer adds that our spiritual heritage does not merely claim that knowing *ought* to begin in love, but that the origin of knowledge *is* love. The failure of modern knowledge is the failure . . . to allow love to inform the relations that our knowledge creates — with ourselves, with each other, with the whole animate and inanimate world.[19]

Practices That Nurture Conversation, Community, and Compassion

Conversation, community, and compassion are necessary qualities for a theological school that is hospitable to teaching and scholarship. Each of these qualities has attendant practices that nurture the academic life of an institution. Conversation practices include establishing mentoring relationships between new faculty members and those with more experience. Mentoring is critical for younger faculty members during the early years. The research momentum generated during dissertation work easily dissipates in the pressure of preparing classes, grading papers, serving on committees, and supervising students. Older scholars working alongside of and dialoguing with younger faculty members can create synergy, build meaningful relationships, assist with the challenges of interpreting the culture of a particular institution, and produce valuable scholarship. Academic deans can help nurture mentors and mentorees by providing opportunities for the

18. Parker Palmer, *To Know as We Are Known: A Spirituality of Education* (San Francisco: Harper and Row, 1983), p. 8.
19. Palmer, *To Know as We Are Known*, pp. 8-9.

pairs to share their experiences in public forums. Some scholar mentoring programs result in joint research projects, whereas others help faculty members build fruitful relationships and develop respect for different research tools and research methods.[20] Meeting regularly with a chosen or assigned colleague to think, talk, and reflect together promises rich benefits to faculty members at all stages of their development.

Conversation can also be conducted more broadly across the faculty through regular opportunities for faculty members to report on their projects and ongoing research. Structuring such opportunities into the calendar of the academic year signals clearly that research and scholarly activity are valued and that people with different intellectual interests have important things to say to one another. Researchers gain feedback about their ideas while their colleagues have the opportunity to think outside of the disciplines and territories that are most familiar to them. Faculty seminars or brown bag lunches allow research, on occasion, to be approached collectively. Rather than structuring such opportunities as a simple reporting on research findings, it may be more productive to "share concepts, ideas and problems" as a way of creating knowledge, rather than simply "retailing" it.[21] An entire faculty benefits from an academic dean's determination to create space and structure for conversation throughout the halls, offices, and classrooms of the institution, between colleagues, faculty and administration, and faculty and students.

In addition to conversation about research and scholarship, conversation with colleagues about teaching is critical. Sharing the teaching experiences that bring life and those that diminish it, naming the various hurdles and delights of the classroom, and dialoguing together about the innumerable practical and interior challenges faced by those who teach builds solidarity and nurtures freedom. Faculties commonly read theological books together in order to discuss the way in which the themes intersect with their various disciplines. Participating in a common reading of books that explore the teaching life offers stimulation of a different sort and promotes the possibility of conversation that is vulnerable, honest, and human.[22]

20. Mallard, "The Soul of Scholarship," p. 67.

21. Peter T. Knight and Paul R. Towler, *Departmental Leadership in Higher Education* (Buckingham: The Society for Research into Higher Education and Open University Press, 2001), p. 127.

22. Books such as Palmer's *The Courage to Teach* and *To Know as We Are Known*, Bennett's *Academic Life*, and Wendell Berry's essay "The Way of Ignorance" in *The Way of Ignorance and Other Essays* are valuable resources for common faculty reading assignments.

Community nurturing practices are closely related to those that support conversation. Saint Norbert's College has developed a number of effective practices in support of community, including an event they call "Celebrating Collegiality." Kenneth Zahorski describes this practice as originating out of a simple concept. He says that because faculty members are separated by disciplines and buildings, agenda-free social activities are warmly welcomed to draw colleagues together for interaction that helps nurture collegiality and community. The "Celebrating Collegiality" event is set in a comfortable room, late in the afternoon, and features live piano music and plenty of good food and drink. Mellowed by candlelight and soft background music, faculty members chat and forget, for at least two hours or so, the papers, committee assignments, and lecture notes back on their office desks. This event is both well-attended and highly successful at their college and has been enhanced by a closely related activity called "Celebrating Scholarship." In an adjoining room on tables lining the walls, displays of faculty scholarship, ranging from articles and books to computer software packages and videotape productions, are displayed. Members of the faculty move leisurely from one room to another, sipping refreshment and carrying on conversations while examining the scholarly achievements of their colleagues.[23] Considerable research evidence exists indicating that cooperative educational environments involving a high degree of inter-colleague communication and support appear to nurture better teaching and research.[24] The insistence of isolation and individualism can be transformed only by persistent prioritization of opportunities for persons to talk together and to welcome each other into their thoughts and experience, as well as by a determination to work together toward creating something more enriching and powerful than can be achieved in isolation.

The practice of compassion is essential to both conversation and community. "Faculty who rigorously remind themselves of the importance of hospitable conversations are likely to become successful teacher/scholars. But the most successful are those already disposed toward openness to the other and for whom rules and principles are only guides."[25] Continual reflection on how to teach and research in such a way as to draw others into

23. Kenneth J. Zahorski, "Nurturing Scholarship through Holistic Faculty Development: A Synergistic Approach," *New Directions for Teaching and Learning*, no. 90 (Summer 2002): 36.

24. Ramsden, *Learning to Lead*, p. 162.

25. Bennett, *Academic Life*, p. 125.

the conversation contributes to the formation of a community of learning. This is teaching and researching for the larger community and not just for the insistent individualism of one's own career. This is teaching and scholarship for compassion.

The role of the academic dean in nurturing conversation, community, and compassion and in fostering a hospitable terrain cannot be overstated.

> Our academic leadership task is to enable staff by establishing through example and coaching a team environment where both dialogue and discussion occur. A key skill of academic leadership is to help our colleagues see each other as colleagues — to bring out the positive aspect of the collegial spirit, to help them feel they are in an environment where it is safe to suspend assumptions.[26]

Hospitable deans create opportunities for conversations that help people change and develop. Such deans lead meetings that encourage productive dialogue while producing a sense of direction. They elicit the contributions of others and listen well. Hospitable deans lead faculty teams that learn to work well together in situations of disagreement. They develop a positive emotional climate that lets all members of a faculty know that they matter as fellow learners.

> Being academically hospitable involves treating others . . . as worthy of intellectual attention . . . recognizing that each could supplement or correct the other's work and self-understanding. Hospitality points toward active sharing and willingness to learn from others. Being hospitable is adverbial in character. It refers to *how* one relates to others.[27]

Academic deans who are hospitable know that nurturing a community of learning requires involvement in a shared life — a life full of conversation and honest reflection that embraces one's own contribution as well as academic programs, teaching and scholarship, and the theological institution as a whole. Hospitable deans know that such a life does not come without intention, effort, and perseverance. However, they are convinced of the value of such effort, because they believe that good teaching and good scholarship matter, and they believe that contributing to these goods is in their power.

26. Bennett, *Academic Life,* p. 162.
27. Bennett, *Academic Life,* p. 53.

Academic deans who "join Christ in the hospitable act" do so both in practice and in their personhood. They lead in ways that are open, attentive, and respectful of others. The integrity of their character and their leadership nurtures the building of safe places where change can become possible. Hospitable deans do not have to be the best teachers or the most prolific, awarded scholars on their faculty, but they do need to be willing to lead the way in talking with others about ways to improve their own teaching and in admitting their own teaching disasters. They need to lead the way in offering the fruit of their own scholarship to the faculty as a whole. They need to model the conviction that good teaching matters and that their scholarly lives are an essential part of their leadership and service.

Ultimately, the academic dean assumes the position of host, welcoming all members to the conversation and community of learning. The dean models the reception of the unfamiliar and the strange — both ideas and individuals (!) — as a sacred duty. The dean provides resources for the community of learning to come together in conversation and to celebrate collegiality, teaching, and scholarship. The dean offers the hospitality of protection to the new faculty member by making possible a lighter teaching load in the first year so that skill in teaching can be developed, and connects inexperienced persons with mentors and companions for the journey. Supplying excellent coffee and space for conversation can bring together members of a faculty scattered geographically over a campus as well as by the diverse disciplines and guilds they represent. Welcome, provision, and protection are not just symbolic, but concrete ways in which the academic dean can join Christ in the hospitable act and nurture the community of learning in its commitment to teaching and scholarship.

9. Leading in Diversity: Personal Experiences and Institutional Choices

The Stranger in the Center:
The Academic Dean as Racial Minority

Stephen Breck Reid

We had moved from subsidized housing to a new subdivision in west Dayton, Ohio. I did not realize that our small subdivision was a Negro enclave due to the de facto segregation of Ohio in the mid-twentieth century. We lived in a small bungalow. My parents made sure that my brothers and I walked up the street to the local black Baptist church for Sunday school. Then one Sunday morning after I got back my mother scooped me up, and we went to a church someone told her about. It was a Church of the Brethren congregation. We would learn that the Church of the Brethren is a denomination shaped by the German immigrant experience of the eighteenth and nineteenth centuries. At the time a desegregated church was a rare thing in Dayton, Ohio. We arrived at about 11:30 a.m. with still plenty of time by the liturgical standards my mom knew. However, it was just in time for the end of the sermon, the last hymn, and the benediction. My mother, embarrassed by the mistake, grabbed me and hurried to the car. The pastor rushed out to greet us, eschewing the normal greeting line. My mother was quite impressed, and we have been part of the African American 2 percent of the Church of the Brethren ever since.

When I was called as academic dean at Bethany Theological Seminary, I became the only African American on the faculty. I have worked for four seminaries so far. I began my career at Interdenominational Theological Center, a historically black seminary. However, most of my career has been on European American faculties where there were a few people of color. An irony of black life in the Church of the Brethren parallels the metaphor lifted up by Ralph Ellison of the "invisible man."[1] I am visibly different and simultaneously invisible. The invisibility shows up in the language exchanges where my colleagues and I miss each other's language worlds. The visibly different invisible man registers as a familiar stranger.

Fast-forward a few years. We were talking about what it meant to be a denominational faculty and the role of so-called ecumenical students and faculty and the future of the seminary. Philosophically I argued that a denomination is a cultural linguistic entity.[2] Faculty must have the ability to help students become more facile and adept in negotiating that cultural linguistic enterprise, and membership is not a litmus test for those competencies. In the days following this faculty meeting, the discussion continued in offices. Faculty member 1 confided to faculty member 2, "I am not sure Steve gets what it means to be Brethren." Of course, faculty member 1 shared this with me. Being a racial ethnic minority in the denomination means that at some level I do not get it, if by "it" one means the Eurocentric conventional denominational wisdom.

The social location of academic dean shifts these realities. Jeanne P. McLean observes that academic deans lead from the center of the institution.[3] But what happens when the center is occupied by a stranger, visibly different and socially invisible? Such an arrangement offers some assets for the school, and a careful reader will tease out how differently distinguished academic deans may capitalize on them.

These personal stories illustrate the shape of my professional bias. As an African American male, I see three forces when I survey the horizon of theological education in North America: the end of Christendom, the rise of post-denominationalism, and globalization. These large, systemic forces give a wider context to the particular stories I share. My experience as an African American faculty member in European American seminaries has created in me a bias for philosophical cosmopolitanism even in a small free-

---

1. R. Ellison, *The Invisible Man,* second edition (New York: Vintage, 1995).

2. G. A. Lindbeck, *The Nature of Doctrine: Religion and Theology in a Postliberal Age* (Louisville: Westminster John Knox, 1984).

3. J. P. McLean, *Leading from the Center: The Emerging Role of the Chief Academic Officer in Theological Schools* (Atlanta: Scholars Press, 1999), pp. 4-5.

standing denominational seminary. The bias creates certain advantages in the present contexts of theological education in North America.

On the surface, one might think that cosmopolitanism fits the research university value system, but it threatens the very existence of U.S. denominations. The research university grew up in the context of a type of Constantinian perspective of Christendom where the church was the established authority. The Enlightenment loosened the bounds of Christendom with rational thinking. The shift to a postmodern context marks the death of Christendom in Europe and North America. Even in the waning days of Christendom, however, Christendom thinking still pervades institutional life.[4] Nowhere is this more the case than in seminaries.

End of Christendom: A Post-Christian Postmodern World

At the international meeting of the Society of Biblical Literature in Capetown, South Africa, Helmut Koester of Harvard Divinity School and Vincent Wimbush of New York's Union Seminary each gave a short lecture on the state of New Testament theology. Wimbush posed the challenge that the category "New Testament" itself introduced into the field a category error. That is to say, the name New Testament is a confessional tag, a vestige of Constantinian Christendom. That presentation indicated to me how fundamental was the cultural work of Christendom. The response of the audience pointed to the bifurcation of the field of biblical studies into those who chafe under the confessional privilege in biblical studies and those who consider and perceive the professional and confessional overlap as irrelevant.

When Constantine set up Christendom to provide a political center, he established Christianity as the official religion. In the U.S. context, however, disestablishment of religion is not new. Whenever plurality de-centers a religious community of privilege, disestablishment ensues. Craig Van Gelder argues that there were three moves in this process of disestablishment in the United States. The negotiations reflected in the Constitution and the Bill of Rights put in place the first disestablishment, the separation of church and state. The religious diversity already present in the colonies commended such a strategy. The wave of new immigrant populations from 1890 to 1920

4. C. Van Gelder, "Defining the Center — Finding the Boundaries: The Challenge of Re-Visioning the Church in North America for the Twenty-First Century," in G. R. Hunsberger and C. Van Gelder, eds., *The Church Between Gospel and Culture: Emerging Mission in North America* (Grand Rapids: Eerdmans, 1996), pp. 26ff.

created the second disestablishment by increasing the religious diversity of the country. This period saw a dramatic increase in the number of churches as well as the types of churches. Further, this influx brought increased Jewish and Catholic presence. These communities joined the Protestant community as engines in the nation's cultural factory. The 1960s and 1970s brought the collapse of Christian culture and the third disestablishment.[5]

Liberal Christendom rests on a philosophical foundation of positivism. The early Enlightenment philosopher David Hume's emphasis on facts and values frames the idea of a modern relativism. In the less pluralistic world of the early Enlightenment and modernity, this was a manageable relativism. However, a post-modern context makes positivism untenable. "The deepest problem with positivism, however, is not its conclusions. It is in its starting point."[6] It misconstrues the nature of values. ". . . [Y]ou must see them [values] not as guiding us as individuals on our own but guiding people who are trying to share their lives."[7] To the degree to which positivism has been a foundational philosophical tool for the self-understanding of the vocation of theological education, the academic dean now must facilitate a process of finding philosophical alternatives.

Post-Denominationalism

The religious movements also have a profound impact on the small denominational seminary. The missionary movement gave rise to a proliferation of seminaries.[8] "The ecumenical movement was the emotional bridge that provided the needed impetus for change."[9] The extension of missionary and evangelical zeal gave rise to an ecumenical movement spirit. "After 1890, few, if any, evangelical organizations were denominationally centered. . . ."[10] The rise of ecumenism meant a challenge for denominationalism. "One key to understanding denominations is that a particular denomination tends to

5. C. Van Gelder, "Great New Fact of Our Day: America as a Mission Field," in Hunsberger and Van Gelder, *The Church Between Gospel and Culture*, p. 64.

6. K. A. Appiah, *Cosmopolitanism: Ethics in a World of Strangers* (New York: W. W. Norton, 2006), p. 27.

7. Appiah, *Cosmopolitanism*, p. 27.

8. G. T. Miller, "Historical Influences on Seminary Culture," in M. Warford, ed., *Practical Wisdom on Theological Teaching and Learning* (New York: Peter Lang, 2004), p. 116.

9. Miller, "Historical Influences," p. 117.

10. Miller, "Historical Influences," p. 118.

define itself in terms of differences over against other denominations."[11] However, the rhetoric that accompanies denominationalism is itself breaking down and becoming incoherent.

I grew up in the Church of the Brethren, and many persons have asked me, "Who are the Brethren?" My response now begins, "The Church of the Brethren is a denomination rooted in the Anabaptist/Pietist tradition with approximately 125,000 members." This answer creates more questions. So I try another response: "We are one of the three historic peace churches." This answer also prompts more questions. So finally I resort to a more hackneyed response rooted in the denominational world: "We are like the Mennonites." This answer makes sense in a denominational world. For in a denominational world each Christian denomination can be analogous to or distinguished from other denominations.

The distinguishing elements of denominations have shifted over the course of years. Denominations were for many years a reflection of immigrant patterns: English Baptist, Scotch Irish Presbyterians, African Methodist Episcopalians, etc. Even in postmodernity the cultural linguistic trappings still reflect in some way the immigrant past of these denominations.

"The Positivist holds that with facts, when we disagree, one of us has the truth, one of us is underwritten by the way things are, whereas with values, there is nothing to underwrite our claims. . . . We enter every conversation — whether with neighbors or with strangers — without a promise of final agreement."[12] The positivist philosophical underpinnings of theological education often subvert the ecumenical or interfaith aspirations. "Cosmopolitans suppose that all cultures have enough overlap in their vocabulary of values to begin a conversation. But they don't suppose, like some universalists, that we could all come to agreement if only we had the same vocabulary."[13] The positivist impulse in theological education puts forward a force for compliance and assimilation at some level.

Globalization

The ATS standards challenge member schools to a combination of globalization and contextualization. The counter-intuitive bias of marginal persons

---

11. C. Van Gelder, "Defining the Center," p. 44.

12. Appiah, *Cosmopolitanism*, p. 44.

13. Appiah, *Cosmopolitanism*, p. 57.

serving as academic deans may be timely. Thomas Friedman describes life in the twenty-first century as a flat world. The end of Christendom and the post-denominational situation seem to correlate well with his observations. A small denominational seminary could be tempted to push denominationalism with even more force as a strategy, but that would be a mistake. Friedman suggests "Rule #1: When the world goes flat — and you are feeling flattened — reach for a shovel and dig inside yourself. Don't try to build walls."[14] The student and faculty profiles of small denominational seminaries will need to morph in this new age. Institutions that have made space for me as an African American have shaped me into someone who prizes an institution that makes space for the demographically other.

When you are African American on a European American faculty, you have to collaborate and build bridges. Once again that background works well in the flat world. "Rule #4: The best companies are the best collaborators."[15] The operational default for the old world seminary is Why collaborate when you can buy? That is to say, the temptation for duplications of programs presently outstrips the seminary impulse to collaborate.

The Context of the Freestanding Denominational Seminary and the Philosophical Cosmopolitan Perspective

At the same time, a bias rooted in the cosmopolitan perspective creates its own set of tensions. The small denominational seminary on the one hand looks to the large research university divinity school as a model, but on the other hand the CAO of a small denominational seminary increasingly realizes that they inhabit different worlds. The observations of the Lexington Seminar[16] make this apparent. "[T]he size of the seminary enterprise demands that everyone be 'on board' for every major decision."[17] The research university provides a view of faculty member as a "free agent" in a manner that works substantially less well in a small denominational seminary. While the American university casts a large shadow over the development of the denominational seminary, the religious awakenings also

14. T. L. Friedman, *The World Is Flat: A Brief History of the Twenty-First Century*, updated and expanded (New York: Farrar, Straus and Giroux, 2006), p. 426.

15. Friedman, *The World Is Flat*, p. 439.

16. http://www.lexingtonseminar.org/.

17. Miller, "Historical Influences," pp. 104f.

shape the institution. A shift occurred as the colonial pattern of tutorial theological education gave way to one reminiscent of a German university. "The meaning of an advanced education changed. Whereas learning had previously been measured by the mastery of traditional texts, it was now measured by a professor's research and its place in the complex pedigree of the current 'state of the question.'"[18] A re-adjustment of status took place from the early to the late twentieth century. "Professional status was determined by a professor's standing in the guild and not by ecclesiastical recognition."[19] The shadow of the university is alive and well even in the small denominational seminary. Nonetheless, the university could not provide sufficient nurture. "[T]he university and professional model lacked religious power. At best, professionalism commanded the allegiance of the mind, but never the heart."[20] The recent efforts to recapture pastoral excellence and professionalism[21] attempt to change the situation described by Miller.

"Seminaries are receiving less money from the church."[22] At the same time, the challenges shift in expensive ways. The participants of the Lexington Seminar consistently described diversified student bodies and a growing awareness that one size no longer fits all students.

The denominational seminary in a post-Christendom and post-denominational world must perform a counter-intuitive feat. The new seminary graduate and the faculties that nurture them must develop a context that gives rise to cosmopolitan virtues. This cosmopolitanism is different from a commitment to globalization or multiculturalism. "Cosmopolitanism dates at least to the Cynics of the fourth century BC, who first coined the expression cosmopolitan, 'citizen of the cosmos.'"[23] The Cynics, and later the Stoics in the third century BC, sought to get beyond the limited perspective of a polis of a particular community. This notion found even greater acceptance as one of the hallmarks of the Enlightenment process. However, the confluence of Cynicism, Stoicism, and the Enlightenment project led to a

18. Miller, "Historical Influences," p. 108.

19. Miller, "Historical Influences," p. 113.

20. Miller, "Historical Influences," pp. 116f.

21. J. W. Carroll, *God's Potters: Pastoral Leadership and the Shaping of Congregations* (Grand Rapids: Eerdmans, 2006), and L. G. Jones and K. R. Armstrong, *Resurrecting Excellence: Shaping Faithful Christian Ministry* (Grand Rapids: Eerdmans, 2006).

22. G. E. Ziegenhals, "Faculty Life and Seminary Culture: It's About Time and Money," in Warford ed., *Practical Wisdom on Theological Teaching and Learning*, pp. 26f.

23. Appiah, *Cosmopolitanism*, p. xiv.

preoccupation with the value of a human life in its generic quality, not as a theological and particular entity.[24]

The Role of the Academic Dean and Philosophical Cosmopolitanism

Jeanne P. McLean describes four themes that characterize the task of chief academic officer: complexity, centrality, link to the presidency, and theological context.[25] A chief academic officer with a cosmopolitanism perspective creates a distinct set of tensions in each of these themes. The role of the academic dean derives from the presidency. It began at Harvard in 1870. By the mid-twentieth century the office was widely established in freestanding Protestant seminaries.[26] The academic dean typically fulfills three roles: teacher/scholar, academic administrator, and senior officer of the institution. The first role is often a prerequisite for the position. The second role is "their administrative responsibility for the academic area that constitutes the central work of the office."[27] Finally, the CAO is almost always a member of the president's cabinet.

Teacher/Scholar

When Appiah subtitles the book *Ethics in a World of Strangers,* he makes an almost biblical invitation. One might more effectively reclaim the Gospel story of the Good Samaritan who at the end of the story is still a Samaritan. The academic dean with a commitment to cosmopolitanism facilitates a community that allows the Samaritan to remain a Samaritan. This requires the academic dean to facilitate and nurture critical thought and conversation/discussion.

How does an academic dean do this sort of work? An academic dean begins with a commitment to pedagogy. If there is a commitment to pedagogy, then there are metrics that mark the success or failure of cosmopolitan pedagogy. These metrics will give the students a voice. Only safe strangers can disclose they have encountered the teaching of the seminary. The sociol-

---

24. Appiah, *Cosmopolitanism,* pp. xiv-xv.
25. McLean, *Leading from the Center,* pp. 4-6.
26. McLean, *Leading from the Center,* p. 17.
27. Mclean, *Leading from the Center,* p. 27.

ogy of dominance sabotages the classroom, faculty meeting, and board meeting unless the academic dean nurtures a spirit of critical thinking in every venue.[28] The academic dean can facilitate conversations and should nurture democratic exchange of ideas.

When the academic dean models critical thinking, five characteristics emerge: clarity, consistency, openness, communicativeness, and specificity. Clarity describes behavior that is easily observable. Consistency indicates the use of iteration that moves the observations from the short-term memory to the long-term memory of students, faculty, and board members. Openness respects the integrity of the stranger. Communicativeness indicates a bias for the ability to give voice to rationales for actions in ways that students, faculty, and board members can easily apprehend. Specificity describes behavior that can be imitated by others. These characteristics model critical thinking.[29]

Still there is no fire. Critical thinking is but one element of cosmopolitan pedagogy. The vehicle of critical thinking is conversation, dialogue, and discussion. Susan M. Simonaitis observes what happens when conversation is a learning method. "[O]nce in a while the circle of learning becomes the site of a bonfire. Now and then, fleeting manifestations of the sacred blaze up, and the God who speaks consumes us."[30] That is the fruit of cosmopolitan pedagogy.

Academic Administrator

The academic dean makes the courses run on time while also functioning in a leadership capacity to help the organization change. Jeanne P. McLean sets out the key administrative tasks of an academic dean: setting the academic agenda, directing the decision-making process, exercising influence, empowering others, dealing with conflict and controversy, and securing final approval.[31] The tasks can be informed by cosmopolitanism. The academic dean is a key player in determining the academic agenda. The tendency will include the proclivity to institutional openness.

---

28. Stephen D. Brookfield, *Developing Critical Thinkers: Challenging Adults to Explore Alternative Ways of Thinking and Acting* (San Francisco: Jossey-Bass, 1987), pp. 5-9.

29. Brookfield, *Developing Critical Thinkers*, pp. 86-87.

30. Susan M. Simonaitis, "Teaching as Conversation," in L. Gregory Jones and Stephanie Paulsell, eds., *The Scope of Our Art: The Vocation of the Theological Teacher* (Grand Rapids: Eerdmans, 2002), p. 119.

31. McLean, *Leading from the Center,* pp. 62-74.

The academic dean directs the decision-making process in many ways. First of all the dean, often in consultation with the president, determines who in the seminary community serves on key committees. Second, the academic dean helps set the tone, consultative or collegial, of how the committee reflections feed into the broader governance process and also makes a difference in the pace of the process. The cosmopolitan academic dean nurtures the stranger in the faculty and staff as well as in the student body. This may mean slowing down the process, which often uses cultural inertia to silence voices from the margin. "Conversation doesn't have to lead to consensus about anything, especially not values; it's enough that it helps people get used to one another."[32] A gifted leader and academic dean will be needed to keep this type of conversation alive.

Coalitions and Constituencies

The academic dean works with senior administrators, boards, and church leaders. The cosmopolitan perspective will have an impact on all these relationships. As part of the administrative team, the academic dean's effectiveness might be associated with "'the dean's fit' with the prevailing administrative culture."[33] The administrative culture is substantially more likely to operate with a positivist perspective. In that case, the dean will have to think strategically about how to provide an effective cosmopolitan perspective.

Sometimes the work with boards and church constituencies is easier to negotiate. The impulse toward expanding the table or framework of discourse finds a resonating core of persons in many contexts. The dean shares information and embodies a transparent practice. The board that represents church leaders provides allies for a growing cosmopolitan perspective in the seminary. However, the debate with positivists on the board and among church leaders on these matters should be anticipated.

Coda

Cosmopolitanism speaks to the academic dean who experiences one's own faculty as a stranger. It invites such a dean to think theologically and philo-

---

32. Appiah, *Cosmopolitanism*, p. 85.
33. McLean, *Leading from the Center*, p. 147.

sophically about the situation. The cosmopolitan academic dean works to enlarge the space for the stranger to speak and act in the seminary community. This requires the savvy dean to effectively subvert the positivist philosophical yearnings that sabotage the explicitly named and implicitly vetoed impulse to welcome the stranger.

Locating Multiple Immigrant Identities and Belonging in Relatedness: Insights for Intercultural Leadership

Faustino M. Cruz

Locating Oneself in Relatedness

While waiting for a connecting flight to Manila at Tokyo's Narita airport, I overheard a very familiar pattern of communication between two Filipino U.S. immigrants meeting at the departure lounge. "Where are you from?" a retired accountant asked a young male professional from the Silicon Valley. "I am from Baguio, pô [an expression of respect toward one's elder]," he replied. "Oh, I know a family, the Astorgas, who are from Baguio. Do you know them?" The need to discover and claim common identities and belonging, both local and translocal, describes a Filipino way of locating "oneself in relatedness."

I am serving a second three-year term as academic dean and executive vice president of the Franciscan School of Theology (FST), one of the member schools of an ecumenical partnership called the Graduate Theological Union (GTU). I concurrently serve as convener of the Council of Deans of the GTU, facilitating monthly gatherings of chief academic officers representing each of the ten partner institutions and participating in the collective leadership of the consortium. In addition, there is another "council of deans" to which I am accountable.

Among eight surviving siblings, four of us are administrators in higher education. Currently my sister, Victoria, a former dean of the College of Medicine, is vice president for health and allied services at the West Visayas

State University in the Philippines. My oldest brother, Jose, a Jesuit priest, is dean of the School of Social Sciences at the Ateneo de Manila University. My youngest brother, Isidoro, a nationally awarded poet, is dean of the College of Arts and Sciences at the University of San Agustin in Iloilo City. Where does the "dean gene" come from?

I grew up in a family that has valued formal education over several generations. There were several educators in my extended family. My maternal grandfather was a regional superintendent of schools, while my grandmother was a high school teacher. Both my parents earned college degrees, my mother graduating from a national teachers' college. All their children attended college; eight of them pursued post-graduate or professional degrees.

Excelling in school has effectively been a routinized task; it has felt as spontaneous as singing in the school choir or going camping with friends. Across the lifespan, I have been socialized to make meaning "in relatedness," achieving creativity only by collaborating with diverse communities of teaching-learning. As an immigrant educator, I have reflected on these multiple identities and belonging, particularly through the frames of race and ethnicity, social class, language, gender, and liminality, focusing on how each location has informed, formed, and transformed my vocation as chief academic officer.

Race and Ethnicity

What does it mean to be a person of color in a predominantly white academic community? Educators argue that while people of color examine the essence of "being culturally different," most white people still lack critical awareness of their whiteness.[1]

As a newly hired professor, I was destined to be a "poster child" who regularly appeared on promotional videos, posters, and brochures, giving the impression that theological schools are no longer predominantly "lily white." At a faculty meeting, a senior colleague publicly delivered these instructions: "Tito, I want you to look Filipino when they take your photo for the Web site." My somatic response (my whole body leaning forward in a posture of disbelief) underscored my challenging words: "When you look at me, what do you see?"

---

1. Alice McIntyre, *Making Meaning of Whiteness: Exploring Racial Identity with White Teachers* (Albany: SUNY Press, 1997).

A few months after I was appointed academic dean, two members of FST's administrative team approached me with a race-related question: "Tito, do you know that someone in leadership believes that you should not have been appointed because you are Asian?" One of them, possibly in an attempt to mitigate the insult, remarked, "I hope you don't take this personally."[2]

The following day, there was a workshop on the Critical Engagement of Theological Education in Asia and North America, sponsored by the GTU, at which I was a presenter. On my way to the event, I felt the urgency to confront first my colleague who allegedly believed that Asians did not have a place in the dean's office. If I were not committed to making racism public, anything I would have articulated at the workshop on the importance of theological education would have been both irrelevant and irreverent. In "speaking my truth," I chose to proclaim the prophetic telos of critical engagement: transformative action.

Being Asian (specifically Filipino) is deeply grounded in my positive feelings of belonging to my family and cultural group; therefore, it is personal. In fact, it is intrinsically communal. To develop a greater sense of belonging and historical continuity with Filipino communities — in the Philippines and the diaspora — is a basic psychological need that evokes very deep unconscious feelings. Therefore, to ignore, alter, or denounce my ethnic identity by changing my name or rejecting my familial roots and communities of origin would seriously jeopardize my well-being.[3] My only choice is "to speak my truth."

So, when you look at me, what do you see? From a position of whiteness, I have been perceived by some as an "abnormality," a disruption to their "business-as-usual" ways of knowing and habits of being, an "otherness" equated with ineffectiveness or failure that endangers the school's normative system of decision making, stewardship, and collaboration. Ironically, whiteness has established that "I do exist." Otherwise, why will anyone view my race and ethnicity as potential threats to leadership? Being a person of color has made me more visible — though vulnerable — to the academic community.

2. Prior to my appointment as dean in 2005, I had served the faculty for five years. I was convinced that the hiring of a professor of color was in pursuit of the school's inclusive, multicultural vision and strategic plan. In fact, it could have been construed positively as an intentional attempt to comply with ATS accreditation standards that advance diversity.

3. Faustino M. Cruz, "Ministry for a Multicultural Church and Society," *Reflective Practice: Formation and Supervision in Ministry* 27 (2007): 46.

Peggy McIntosh writes about white privilege and describes the literary silence that protects "a pattern of assumptions that were passed on to [her] as a white person."[4] White privilege, she says, is "an invisible package of unearned assets that I can count on cashing in each day, but about which I was 'meant' to remain oblivious."[5] It perpetuates the myth that people of color "either don't exist or must be trying, not very successfully, to be like the people of my race."[6] This privilege offers a "cultural permission not to hear voices of people of other races or a tepid cultural tolerance for hearing or acting on such voices."[7] McIntosh challenges the role of education in socializing whites "to think of their lives as morally neutral, normative, and average."[8]

Similarly, Alice McIntyre, a white educator, urges other practitioners to "go public" with the forms of racism they encounter at work as well as the "racism that some of us perpetuate."[9] She appeals to "critical friends," white people and people of color, who journey with whites to become "more self-reflective about our understandings of racism, and who join us in our individual and collective determination to challenge racial injustice."[10]

Whiteness has been canonized in dominant curricula of schools and colleges.[11] Consequently, some of our graduate students come with grave misconceptions about ethnic groups of color and a white bias.[12] Therefore, we must make whiteness and color public.[13] Second, we must design and implement an anti-racist curriculum that enables teacher-learners to identify white allies with whom they can critique and challenge issues of whiteness

4. Peggy McIntosh, "White Privilege and Male Privilege: A Personal Account of Coming to See Correspondences Through Work in Women's Studies," in *Race, Class, and Gender: An Anthology* (New York: Wadsworth Publishing, 1992), p. 77.

5. McIntosh, "White Privilege and Male Privilege," p. 71.

6. McIntosh, "White Privilege and Male Privilege," p. 77.

7. McIntosh, "White Privilege and Male Privilege," p. 77.

8. McIntosh, "White Privilege and Male Privilege," p. 73.

9. McIntyre, *Making Meaning of Whiteness*, p. 41.

10. McIntyre, *Making Meaning of Whiteness*, pp. 41-42.

11. Beverly Gordon, "Knowledge Construction, Competing Critical Theories, and Education," in *Handbook on Research on Multicultural Education*, ed. James Banks and Cherry McGee Banks (New York: Macmillan Publishing, 1995), p. 184.

12. James Banks, "Multicultural Education: Development, Paradigms, and Goals," in *Multicultural Education in Western Societies*, ed. James A. Banks and James Lynch (New York: Praeger, 1986), p. 19.

13. David Mura, "Explaining Racism to My Daughter," in *The New Press Education Reader: Leading Educators Speak Out* (New York: The New Press, 2006), pp. 138-56.

and color as well as the resulting inequities in educational and ministerial op-portunities. Third, we must promote degree programs that intentionally teach perspectives from various U.S. ethno-cultural communities, as well as scholarship from Africa, Asia, Latin America, and other parts of the world. A critical reading of these global perspectives invites us to examine the relation-ships among race, ethnicity, and social class.

Social Class

How could I have learned, . . . if the only possible geography was the geog-raphy of my hunger? . . . In truth, we used to live a radical ambiguity: we were children prematurely forced to become adults. Our childhood was squeezed out between toys and work, between freedom and need.[14]

My family held education as the necessary solution to the daily life and struggle that Paulo Freire has described above. Teaching and learning has been such a vital part of the family psyche that, even as kids, my brother Sid and I used to play *teran* [a diminutive of *titser-titseran* or playing "teacher"] in the absence of "real toys" with which many of my more economically privileged classmates played. I depended on academic skills, leadership qual-ities, and emotional intelligence to acculturate into the values, attitudes, and behaviors of my middle-class Catholic school.

When I was in third grade, my oldest sister, Teresa, left for New York on a scholarship to pursue a Master of Science degree in physics at Rensselaer Polytechnic Institute. For decades, my grandmother's instructive voice in Ilocano resounded, urging the younger ones to apply ourselves as diligently as Teresa, who graduated summa cum laude: *"Tuladen yo met cuma ni Manang yo tapno macaadal kayo didyay America"* [I hope you all aspire to become like your sister so you can also study in America].

The symptoms of socio-economic deprivation and structural discrim-ination to which Freire refers are pervasive in U.S. education.[15] Many stu-dents resonate with him, from school children who depend on federally sponsored school lunches for basic nourishment to adults who cannot ac-

14. Paulo Freire, *Letters to Cristina: Reflections on My Life and Work,* trans. Donaldo Macedo with Quilda Macedo and Alexandre Oliveira (New York: Routledge, 1996), pp. 17-19.

15. Michael Knapp and Sara Woolverton, "Social Class and Schooling," in *Handbook on Research on Multicultural Education,* ed. Banks and Banks, p. 549.

cess education without a full scholarship or financial aid. When students attend schools that are inadequately funded, quality education becomes an unearned privilege derived from economic disparities. Ironically, U.S. society is perilously embedded in a myth that education is still "the great social equalizer" that transcends all sociopolitical boundaries including social class.[16] Yet "savage inequalities" stunt the growth and development of U.S. students.[17] Lamentably, such inequalities affect graduate theological education as well.

Those of us who work closely with our financial aid offices attest that students enroll despite rising costs and lack of funding. Consequently, students seek employment to cover room and board, books, health insurance, computer technology, travel, and other incidentals, while struggling to balance multiple affiliations and responsibilities. Despite the intentional measures we have taken to advance "self-care," many of our students suffer from neglect; they cannot afford what we teach. Absenteeism, inattentiveness, fatigue, and tardiness are some of the more common symptoms of academic anomie.

Faculty members are not immune to similar inequalities. One of my women colleagues often reminds me that, while there is no parity in pension benefits between lay and religious professors at FST, "we will all end up in the same nursing home," her point being that the cost of care is ultimately the same for all. The high cost of living in the San Francisco Bay Area makes it virtually prohibitive for some to find adequate housing or own cars without accepting weekend commitments to supplement their income, only to return to their full-time job site stressed out. Professors who depend on other financial resources (be it from a spouse or other professional consulting) find it less problematic.

Critics like bell hooks warn against traditional pedagogy that erases class differences, both in theory and practice, making academic discourse fundamentally incomplete.[18] The demographic composition of students in a given classroom, track, cluster, or school influences our perceptions of aptitude, expectations for success, teaching method, and manner of responding to diversity.

---

16. Knapp and Woolverton, "Social Class and Schooling," p. 548.

17. Jonathan Kozol, *Savage Inequalities: Children in American Schools* (New York: Harper Perennial, 1992).

18. bell hooks, "Confronting Class in the Classroom," in *Teaching to Transgress: Education as the Practice of Freedom* (New York: Routledge, 1994).

As educators, we tend to interact differently with students from different socio-cultural backgrounds. In general, we perform better when our social status effectively converges with our students' socioeconomic indicators. On the one hand, my inner-city upbringing in the Philippines, marked by a violent culture clash between the "haves" and the "have-nots," has undoubtedly boosted my empathy toward low-income students. On the other hand, I have acquired some resentment and intolerance toward those who demonstrate entitlement and privilege on the basis of their social class. However, this predicament challenges me to become more aware of how class differences inhibit educators from facilitating conversations that encourage teacher-learners to "feel more comfortable about being innovative and taking risk with their language," which may not necessarily fit the norm.[19]

Language Issues

In 1982 I realized at the orientation for new MDiv students that I wanted to get rid of my "foreign" accent. I was convinced that most of my peers struggled to understand me and simply dismissed me. Some showed some empathy; they patiently asked me to repeat or clarify.

Today, I teach in the very same classroom where I once felt muted. At the start of each semester, I poll my students to determine how many have had teachers who spoke with a "different" accent. The majority indicate that most of their teachers have been native English speakers. So, what do accents reveal?

My accent discloses my linguistic provenance (how I produce sounds to make intelligible words) as well as my system of knowledge construction (how I culturally make meaning). Howard Gardner's theory of multiple intelligences recognizes that academic institutions continue to privilege linguistic intelligence (I think therefore I am) as well as logical-mathematical intelligence over spatial, bodily-kinesthetic, musical, naturalist, interpersonal, and intrapersonal intelligences.[20] Consequently, we assess our students primarily based on how literate they are, that is, how well they read and write. This dilemma raises serious pedagogical and administrative issues for some immigrant teacher-learners like me who have culturally rooted, highly integrated interpersonal and intrapersonal intelligences that allow us

19. Knapp and Woolverton, "Social Class and Schooling," p. 565.
20. Howard Gardner, *Multiple Intelligences: New Horizons in Theory and Practice* (New York: Perseus Publishing, 2006).

to listen attentively and empathize deeply with persons we minister with, supervise, or mentor. Those of us with well-developed musical and bodily-kinesthetic intelligences facilitate meetings, preside at worship services, and emcee commencement exercises creatively and gracefully; these are clear marks of intelligence as well. As we support our institutions to maintain a "culture of evidence," measure outcomes, and close the loop toward achieving full accreditation, genuine respect and appreciation for "accented ways of knowing and habits of being" are imperative.

Generally, we are more comfortable engaging with students whose social locations resemble our own, which for the most part characterizes the profile of the dominant U.S. culture. Over the past two centuries, the United States has probably acculturated more bilingual persons than any other society in the world. Ironically, the U.S. experience is remarkable for the near mass extinction of non-English languages.[21] Whose language is official, privileged, or legitimate?

The issue of language in theological education must transcend any focus given to mere technical language proficiency. Some professors are more concerned about reducing foreign accents than advancing communicative competence, which is the ability of students to know when, where, and with whom to use grammatically correct sentences in a given situation.[22] Language theorists maintain that home environment (primary locus of socialization) and linguistic groups affect scholastic performance. Thus, the manner in which we "name" our students or validate their multiple identities and affiliation is crucial to their academic success.[23]

While attempts are made to diversify recruitment and enrollment, adequate measures have not been taken to address the linguistic needs of our students. To what extent do we provide remedial programs in reading and writing to help students excel? Do we challenge professors to apply various pedagogical methods so that they do not privilege those who are more profi-

21. Cruz, "Ministry for a Multicultural Church and Society," p. 51.

22. Misahiko Minami and Carlos Ovando, "Language Issues in Multicultural Contexts," in *Handbook on Research on Multicultural Education*, ed. Banks and Banks, p. 429.

23. I have documented how immigrant and international students at FST have developed more self-confidence when professors encourage them to construct meaning in English as well as in their native languages. The academic and personal growth of students diminishes with the collapse of student-professor communication. Immigrant LEP (limited English proficiency) students are particularly at-risk. Therefore, the discursive practices at school must complement those in the home to enhance their participation in all educational opportunities.

cient in English? For instance, it will be easier for some international students to learn course materials if professors enhance presentations by using visuals such as words on the board, video clips, or PowerPoint.

Some professors have gone as far as lowering assessment standards for students who speak with a "foreign" accent, equating limited English proficiency (LEP) to intellectual ability. Probably, that is why I even dread sending unedited emails especially to students, giving the impression that "the dean doesn't know English well," rather than "he was just in a hurry and his fingers did the thinking." Therefore, we must take serious steps to affirm our students' cultural and epistemological contexts, specifically by encouraging them to write final projects and theses in their native languages, such as Spanish, Mandarin, German, or French (languages in which many of us are trained to read).

Gender

Some educators admit that they have missed several opportunities to include female students in conversations by advancing androcentric language. They have called on white, middle class males more frequently than racial/ethnic working-class female students. They attribute such discriminatory behavior to the assumption that some women tend to remain relatively silent and powerless in society, and the classroom is no exception.[24] On the contrary, students self-identify and affiliate more fully with learning experiences that legitimize their gender-based ways of knowing and that promote equity and inclusion.

Being male offers me "an invisible package of unearned assets," borrowing McIntosh's expression.[25] In the Roman Catholic tradition, it affords me the opportunity to seek ordination. One way to understand how gender shapes my institutional culture is by examining stories, ceremonies, and rituals that depict the distinctive roles of the various actors and stakeholders: students, staff, faculty, benefactors, board members, administrators, former students, and friends — as if it were theater.[26] If you were one of the spectators, what impressions would you make of the various roles men and women play?

24. Banks, "Multicultural Education: Development, Paradigms, and Goals," p. 19.

25. McIntosh, "White Privilege and Male Privilege," p. 71.

26. Lee Bolman and Terrence Deal, *Reframing Organizations: Artistry, Choice, and Leadership* (San Francisco: Jossey-Bass, 2003).

We can gauge the extent to which women are invited to key leadership positions by simply locating where they sit or stand at commencement. Do they get to speak, read, hand out diplomas, or hood students? As the chief academic officer, to what degree do I encourage women on the faculty to support women students by (1) advancing courses that are grounded in women studies and spiritualities; (2) offering scholarships that recognize the particular needs and contributions of women in ministry; and (3) maintaining a sound ratio of male and female students, faculty, and staff. When decisions are made that affect the lives of all, who do we include or exclude? The role my gender plays reveals the various insider and outsider positionalities that I either claim or are bestowed upon me, marking the multiple liminal locations in which I reside.

Integrated Liminality

As a seminarian, I could not visit the Philippines often. In fact, I waited four years from the time I entered my religious congregation to see my family again. One of the most poignant memories of that first visit was an argument I had with my father. He rendered a verdict by saying, "You talk too much now, like an American." His words indicated that I had acted like an "outsider." Ironically, I had gone back to be home with him again.

When I return to the United States after visits to the Philippines, a similar feeling of being an "outsider from within" persists, perpetuating a dissonant sense that "this is not my home, either." Becoming a naturalized citizen, a decision I made after fourteen years of continued residence, has not guaranteed me an "insider" identity and belonging that echoes what Latinos refer to as *lo nuestro* [one of our own].

Korean American theologian Jung Young Lee contextualizes marginality in describing his predicament in the United States:

> I am situated ambivalently between two worlds — America and Asia — and I absorb the repulsion and attractions or the rejection and acceptance of each. [I have] to live in these two worlds, which are not only different but (also) often antagonistic to each other. . . . I am unwanted by both worlds.[27]

27. Jung Young Lee, *Marginality: The Key to Multicultural Theology* (Minneapolis: Fortress Press, 1995), p. 43.

Lee laments that to be *in-between* two (or more) worlds means existentially to be fully in neither.[28] Marginality coerces a person's "existential nothingness," mutes one's symbolic system of meaning-making, and subsequently forms a *culture of silence*.[29] As the U.S. society becomes more acutely aware of pluralism and regains an interest in ethnic roots, a new definition of marginality has emerged that enables "marginal persons" to reject the demeaning definition of a central group more aggressively.[30]

In-both is a self-affirming definition of contemporary ethnic minorities in a genuinely pluralistic society. Marginal groups functionally remain *in-both* rather than *in-between* by challenging, denying, and resisting the power of centrality.[31] Essentially, "every [person in the United States] brings to the whole, whether from the majority or minority perspective, his or her ethnicity. . . . [T]his alone is the norm of real America."[32] Potentially, everyone is liminal, living within in-both or multiple worlds, by simply being part of a pluralistic society.[33] Therefore, a self-affirming concept of liminality imposes a transformed and integrated reality that transcends marginalization — to be fully *in-both* or *in-all* worlds. We can understand our journey to integrated liminality *(in-between* to *in-both)* more concretely by exploring Robert Kegan's theory of human development.

In *Evolving Self: Problem and Process in Human Development,* Kegan presents human maturity as a meaning-making activity.[34] This activity, he asserts, is a unifying and generating context for both thought and feeling as well as for self and other (subject and object). At each phase, a person negotiates and renegotiates the social context of the meaning of self and others.[35]

For Conn, human development constitutes the motion of defending (confirmation), surrendering (contradiction), and reconstructing (continu-

---

28. Lee, *Marginality.* According to a study of social interaction between white and yellow people, the more closely an Asian identifies with white friends, the more intense become the Asian's feelings of marginality and alienation. See Won Moo Hurh, *Comparative Study of Korean Immigrants in the United States: A Typology* (San Francisco: R. and E. Research Associates, 1977), p. 91.

29. Ira Shor and Paulo Freire, *A Pedagogy for Liberation: Dialogues on Transforming Education* (New York: Bergin and Garvey, 1987), pp. 122-23.

30. Lee, *Marginality,* p. 48.

31. Lee, *Marginality,* p. 52.

32. Lee, *Marginality,* p. 52.

33. Lee, *Marginality,* p. 52.

34. Robert Kegan, *The Evolving Self: Problem and Process in Human Development* (Cambridge, MA: Harvard University Press, 1982).

35. Kegan, *The Evolving Self.*

ity) a center of meaning. He examines the dialectic between a person's longing for independence and autonomy as well as for inclusion and distinctness.[36] He characterizes each developmental phase as a "relative triumph *of relationship to* rather than *embeddedness in* — a self that *has a relationship*, rather than a self that *is a relationship*."[37] A person-in-relationship has a profound sense of openness burgeoning from one's independent identity and self-ownership while recognizing their limits.

Thus, we do not lose others when the self emerges from our embeddedness in the interpersonal; on the contrary, we now truly find them. How do we find the other? In maturity, we gain new capacity for independence. We develop the ability to own *self* rather than our various relationships possessing its multiple aspects.[38] A maturing person freely lets go and risks a genuinely receptive relationship with others and with God, valuing the intimacy of mutual interdependence.[39]

The experience of transformed liminality is essentially the movement from "I am my culture" to "I have a culture." It bespeaks the transcendence from "my embeddedness in liminality" to "my relation with liminality." The integrated liminal person "has the capacity to join others not as fellow instrumentalists (stage two), nor as partners in fusion (stage three), nor as loyalists (stage four), but as individuals who are value-originating and history-making."[40]

Moreover, our *in-both* selves are brought to others [centrifugal] rather than derived from others [centripetal].[41] We surrender our rebellious independence for freely chosen interdependence with others and with God.[42] Integrated liminality denotes that we are no longer exclusively our race, ethnicity, language, gender, or social class. We challenge, deny, and resist the marginality-producing power of centrality and reflexively renew the converging, self-affirming definitions of liminality.

Thus, *in-both* persons transcend embeddedness by interrelating with multiple identities and affiliations, crossing borders and spaces, as well as engaging in public, empathic conversations that advance a more authentic

36. J. Wolski Conn, *Spirituality and Personal Maturity* (New York: Paulist Press, 1989), p. 50.

37. Conn, *Spirituality and Personal Maturity*, p. 51.

38. Conn, *Spirituality and Personal Maturity*, p. 51.

39. Conn, *Spirituality and Personal Maturity*, p. 57.

40. Conn, *Spirituality and Personal Maturity*, p. 57.

41. Conn, *Spirituality and Personal Maturity*, p. 57.

42. Conn, *Spirituality and Personal Maturity*, p. 57.

struggle for justice and the common good (right action-in-relationship). This vision must inform, form, and ever transform our vocation as intercultural leaders in theological education.

Today, as a theological educator, I strive to understand communities of teaching and learning with deep empathy, viewing them through a lens of particularity and suspicion. I work toward developing acute listening, keen observation, and relationships of trust while painting a thick description of my insider culture rather than apprehending daily realities as ordinary, typical, or routine. Moreover, I am determined to affirm, challenge, and transform the way we teach and learn, by examining how race and ethnicity, social class, language, gender, and liminality clarify and blur a transformative vision of educating in faith interculturally.[43]

In the Pursuit of a Community That Does Diversity Well

Sherwood G. Lingenfelter
(with Winston E. Gooden and Linda M. Wagener)

Fuller Theological Seminary is a multi-denominational and multiethnic school committed to the mission of preparing for ministry women and men who come from an increasingly global church. Fuller students come from more than one hundred denominations and from more than sixty nations of the world. President Richard Mouw speaks of the *missional diversity* of Fuller to describe the close link between our diversity mandate and the sem-

---

43. Cruz, "Ministry for a Multicultural Church and Society," p. 47. The prefix "inter" denotes positionality: between/among, within, or in the midst of. It also signifies mutuality and reciprocity. The term "intercultural" performs these functions by forging comparisons, exchanges, cooperation, and confrontation among ethnic affiliations. In a pastoral context, intercultural refers to a ministerial environment of mutual acculturation, collaboration, and communication. While the term "multicultural" typically stands for, in general usage, a relationship between majority and minority members of a community, "intercultural" defines a symbiotic relationship among all the different enclaves regardless of their position of power or privilege.

inary's purpose. The seminary's degree programs prepare students to function as pastors, therapists, scholars, and leaders in cross-cultural, international, and cross-ethnic contexts. My role as the provost and senior vice president is to serve as both the chief academic officer and the chief operations officer of the seminary.[1]

Fuller's leadership team has explored and sought to address five questions at the heart of our missional diversity. While I serve in the CAO/COO roles, I can do nothing apart from the team of people who serve as vice presidents, deans, faculty, managers, and staff of Fuller. Our teamwork centers on these five issues:

1. We have a diverse student body, but creating a community that does diversity well is hard work. How should we define and create a community that embraces diversity? And what work do we have to do to foster these values every year for each entering class of students?
2. How do we sustain our missional diversity and commitment to evangelical scholarship as well as increase our faculty diversity? What are some of the intentional actions we have taken, and have they made a difference?
3. How does Fuller keep its commitment to the authority of scripture while addressing the social questions of sexual orientation that are tearing apart the global church?
4. How do we make diversity a critical component of student learning, and how do we know that students will do and be what we hope they will?
5. How do we equip our staff of 400 people to serve people of more than sixty ethnic and national origins with sensitivity, care, and compassion?

Climate — Creating a Community That Does Diversity Well

Fuller has struggled for more than two decades to create a climate on campus that embraces diversity. In the 1980s faculty, administration, and students engaged the evangelical bias against women in ministry and made an institutional commitment to support women's concerns in the curriculum,

1. I am especially indebted to Winston Gooden and Linda Wagener, who have written reports from which much of this information comes, and to the members of the president's cabinet and provost's council and their management teams who have worked with me on these issues.

in the community, and in the church. In the 1990s the school launched similar initiatives for African American and Hispanic populations with less success. As with so many diversity initiatives, after hard-fought battles our fresh initiatives become routine, many of the gains won in the conflict are slowly lost in the processes of institutionalization.

When speaking to a large assembly of academic leaders in California a number of years ago, Paul Locatelli, president of Santa Clara University, challenged these leaders with a statement that I will paraphrase as follows: "The primary question is not, are your values eroding? Values are always eroding. The primary question is, what are you doing to renew your values?" The seminary's commitment to sustaining a climate where persons from all backgrounds feel welcomed, safe, and respected is a continuing struggle.

In its statement of community standards, Fuller has tried to define what it means to be a community that embraces diversity. These standards explicitly prohibit any disrespect of persons because of gender, ethnicity, or cultural background, and they provide for a process of filing and resolving grievances in this area. Further, in 2002 the joint faculty committee on multiethnic concerns led the joint faculty in developing a statement on diversity that expresses values that underlie a community of trust, respect, and tolerance. This statement, endorsed by faculty, students, and trustees, is now included in the student and faculty handbooks.

But these formal statements do not create a *climate!* To assess the degree to which students experience a climate that is accepting and tolerant of their varying cultural backgrounds, inside and outside the classroom, professors Cameron Lee and Juan Martinez recently conducted a study, supported by the Wabash Center for Teaching and Learning in Theology and Religion, that examined experiences of Fuller students related to diversity on campus. We were dismayed to learn that minority students found Fuller a difficult place, often unfriendly, and frequently less than hospitable to people of different cultural and ethnic backgrounds.

As we have reflected together as a community on these issues, we have realized that our values are always eroding and that we must be intentional about continually renewing those values throughout the community. Toward that end, we are framing ways to tell our stories, communicate our values, and begin conversations on diversity with each entering group of students, faculty, and staff. This requires intentional planning in our student, staff, and faculty orientations as well as follow-up throughout each academic year that includes teaching, mentoring, practice, and celebration of diversity.

We know that we must also continue to ask those who come to Fuller to tell us how they experience acceptance, significance, and validation in the community. An annual survey of students contains questions that ask about satisfaction with various aspects of campus life including diversity. Course evaluations that students fill out for each course ask about the teacher's respect for the experience of students from different backgrounds. While these surveys do not make up a systematic assessment of the climate of the Fuller community, they provide data that may be used, in conjunction with periodic reviews of complaints related to violation of community standards, to get a more systematic picture of this aspect of seminary life. The Wabash grant proved very helpful as a resource for assessing the climate of Fuller for our students, and we hope to conduct similar research every five to seven years.

Representation — Sustaining Missional Diversity and Increasing Faculty Diversity

The presence of people of diverse backgrounds among students, faculty, administration, trustees, and staff signals the intent of the seminary to create a community rich in diversity that supports learning within and outside the classroom. A profile of the gender and ethnic diversity among students, faculty, administration/staff, and the board of trustees graphically depicts the representation of diversity at Fuller (see table below). The student body is significantly diverse with students from sixty nations. Aside from Caucasians, the largest ethnic group is Asian, with large numbers of both first- and second-generations Korean students. There are smaller percentages of African American and Latino students.

2007-2008										
	Students		Faculty				Adm/Staff		Trustees	
			Male	Female	Total					
White	1408	46%	46	20	81%		261	63%	28	82%
Black	145	5%	3	4	9%		19	5%	2	6%
Asian	739	24%	5	1	7%		84	20%	3	9%
Hispanic	125	4%	1	1	2%		38	9%	1	3%
Unknown	627	21%					13	3%		
	3,044	100%	55	26	100%		415	100%	34	100%

In our strategic planning process in 2007-08, we examined the changing demographics in California, which show Latinos as the new dominant population in public schools across the state. While we have had a Spanish language program for nearly two decades, we have not made the recruitment of Latino students and faculty a high priority. In the current strategic plan, we have adopted new priorities to strengthen the Latino and African American programs and to increase the numbers of students and faculty in each program. These initiatives will require increases in financial aid and enhanced recruitment of students from these communities.

To recruit more diverse faculty members, we have taken a series of strategic steps. As provost, I stopped a New Testament search in 2003 when the only finalists for three open positions were white males. I asked the dean to work with the faculty to expand the search in 2004 to seek minority candidates, which resulted in three excellent candidates (Anglo, African American, and Hispanic). In 2006 I rejected a proposed white male candidate for the position of director of the MA in global leadership, asking the faculty to continue their search for women and minority candidates. In both of those searches, the second round produced top candidates who represented minorities and women. An African American woman was appointed in New Testament, and a Caucasian female mission leader/scholar was appointed to direct the global leadership program. In 2008 we added the following statement to our criteria for all faculty searches: "Preference will be given to applicants who have experience teaching and serving in multicultural settings and/or among the principal ethnic groups represented among the student body. The ability to teach at a Masters level in at least two languages is highly desirable (FTS teaches courses in English, Korean, and Spanish.)"

While we have made progress in developing a diverse faculty in Fuller's three schools, the profile shows that more needs to be done in recruiting and retaining a diverse faculty. However, between 2000 and 2009 significant strides were made to diversify this generation of new faculty. By 2009 the School of Theology had four African Americans, two Koreans, and two Hispanics among its forty-four faculty members; the School of Intercultural Studies had increased the diversity of its twenty faculty by recruiting and hiring African, Lebanese, Korean, and French scholars; the School of Psychology contained two African Americans, four Asian Americans, and one Latina among its eighteen core faculty members.

While we are encouraged by the progress we have made in developing a diverse faculty, we have not agreed on a benchmark that would help us to evaluate our progress or to identify important goals in this area. These are essential steps for both maintaining and furthering a climate in which diversity thrives.

Authority of Scripture and Social Issues of Sexual Orientation

In 2004-05 President Mouw appointed a faculty study group on sexual orientation to explore several issues regarding intimate same-sex relationships. The study group, comprised of seven faculty members from the Schools of Theology, Psychology, and Intercultural Studies, employed a combination of information-gathering strategies. Key articles representing a range of positions advocated by Christian and secular scholars were identified and shared. Representatives from various constituencies within the Fuller community were invited for either individual or small group conversations with the committee. These included faculty with homosexual family members, international students, homosexual alumni, and alumni who are actively involved in reparative therapy. Faculty from across the three schools were also asked to describe how they address issues of same-sex intimate relationships in their courses. A search was conducted to survey the relevant standards and policies of comparable evangelical Christian institutions. The study group began with an understanding of the following:

> At the core of Fuller's community teachings and standards is consensus that God's intention for humankind is heterosexual union within the bonds of marriage. We consider that homosexuality is evidence of the fall and the sinfulness of humankind. We also believe that homosexuality does not exist in a special category of sinfulness. We all are fallen; heterosexual and homosexual alike. We are encouraged to respond pastorally to brothers and sisters in Christ who are struggling with all forms of sin and we confess that as a community we have often fallen short.[2]

The study group found that Fuller lacked resources to support members of the Fuller community who are gay, lesbian, bisexual, or transgendered or to address any other sexual issue. While therapy offered through the Fuller Psychological and Family Services clinic has been helpful to some students, homosexual individuals and their families reported high levels of emotional and psychological distress. Many expressed fear to the study

---

2. Report of the Faculty Study Group on Sexual Orientation, 8/17/05.

group that they will be excluded from the community if their orientation is discovered under the current seminary behavioral standards. Some have been open to a particular faculty member who felt "safe," while others made their way into therapy. Some sought out sympathetic or like-minded students, although many clearly struggle in isolation and silence.

Among faculty, students, and staff, the study found a range of attitudes and behaviors regarding sexuality generally. Some, particularly Asian and international students, fear that Fuller is or will become too liberal with regard to sexual standards. Their critique is that we have not sufficiently maintained a biblical perspective on homosexuality and other "high profile" issues or that we fail to adequately enforce our existing policies. The study observed that we have students, heterosexual and homosexual, who are not abiding by our sexual standards. For many, our culture might be interpreted as a "don't ask, don't tell" community, and they are forced to live a "split" existence that is likely to be harmful to their faith and spirituality.

Examining curricular offerings on the topic of sexual diversity across the seminary, the study found that only one course examined these issues in depth. Other faculty members may provide a lecture on the topic in scattered courses across the three schools, but the curriculum was extremely thin. The faculty concluded, "it may be that the 'thinness' of curricular and extracurricular offering . . . is in part a result of a fearfulness of engaging in true discussion. If members of the community are fearful of being identified as not agreeing with or abiding by community standards and subsequent discipline, it makes it difficult to engage in true exploratory dialogue."

In October 2005 the faculty study group gave its report to the joint faculty of the seminary and made four recommendations for action:

1. Expand curricular and extracurricular offerings so that students have the opportunity to witness experts discuss the sexuality issues that are currently dividing the church and challenging our community
2. Make scholarship in sexual issues a value in future faculty searches
3. Create support groups for the development of healthy masculinity and femininity that cultivate a climate of openness and vulnerability addressing the full array of twenty-first-century challenges — including sexual identity
4. Provide specific support services for students who are struggling in diverse areas of sexuality including infidelity, promiscuity, pornography, and sexual orientation

As follow-up, the deans of Theology, Psychology, and Intercultural Studies faculties made this report a focus of a future school faculty meeting. Out of these discussions faculty developed new courses and created opportunities for discussion of these issues in existing courses. The faculties of Psychology and Intercultural Studies created opportunities for students to participate in mentor groups in which conversations about sexuality may and do occur.

In addition to these faculty discussions, the study group recommended that I appoint two committees to study further Fuller's curricular and co-curricular needs related to sexuality. The report of the co-curricular research group indicated that, while Fuller students struggle most with pornography and heterosexual celibacy, they face a variety of struggles related to sexuality. The committee proposed three alternative funding plans to support co-curricular discussions and support services about sexuality, none of which survived the cuts to balance the FY09 budget. The faculty committee reviewing the theology curriculum found that faculty spent very limited time discussing issues of sexuality in classes. However, they did express a desire to learn from one another about how to approach, discuss, and teach about issues of human sexuality and committed themselves to a two-hour faculty workshop.

Diversity and Student Learning

As CAO one of my biggest challenges has been to help faculty understand the importance of gathering evidence on student learning and reflect on that data before making decisions on revision of courses or the curricula of various academic programs. Because issues of diversity are so important to many members of our faculty, the deans and I agreed that we would focus our initial efforts for assessment on diversity. The joint faculty of Theology, Psychology, and Intercultural Studies approved the following seminary-wide, diversity-related learning outcome: "Graduates will demonstrate the ability to identify critical issues of diversity and make appropriate responses." Each school's faculty then discussed and framed learning outcomes related to diversity for their degree programs.

To share faculty experiences and stimulate discussion, we asked the dean of Psychology to lead the joint faculty in a workshop designed to allow faculty to share examples and approaches to diversity in their courses. Faculty members from all three schools worked in groups and shared examples of how each member addressed diversity in particular courses, describing the resources used and the ways in which learning was assessed. The faculties were surprised by and welcomed the many creative approaches to teaching and learning about diversity shared by their colleagues. In keeping with the commitment made by the joint faculty, some members of the faculty reported that they routinely include work authored by diverse persons in required reading assignments and use illustrations from the experiences of varied communities in classes. Others commented on the lack of good resources for addressing diversity in certain courses.

Though most faculty members indicated that diversity was important and addressed some issues in their courses, we concluded that the ways faculty addressed diversity were not synchronized among courses in a program and were not part of a considered plan to develop knowledge and competence. Out of the workshop, we encouraged faculty to think more deeply about how to engage students on issues of diversity and ministry for each degree and to provide a coherent set of expectations about what students should know and be able to do when they graduate. Once they have clearly articulated those expectations, they must then review how these goals are achieved in the required course and practicum work for the degree.

A second joint faculty workshop, held ten months later, focused on the knowledge, skills, and attitudes needed if graduates are to function effectively in a diverse world. Faculty presenters shared how they sought to teach students attitudes of openness, humility, a capacity for self-critique, and a learning posture. Other faculty members focused on helping students acquire knowledge of cultural differences and knowledge of one's ethnic background and the backgrounds of others. The faculty concluded that two of the most important skills that should be emphasized and practiced throughout the curriculum include (1) the ability to listen with sensitivity to stories different from one's own cultural narrative, and (2) the ability to apply those listening skills to framing constructive pathways for resolving conflict.

While all three schools have established learning outcomes at the program or degree level, there are enough differences in the approaches taken in each to justify a brief discussion of the differences. The School of Psychology requires students in both of its degree programs (clinical psychology and marriage and family therapy) to take a required course in diversity. The competencies gained in this course are supplemented in several other courses, especially courses that address strategies of intervention with specific populations such as psychotherapy with ethnic minority children.

Because of the cross-cultural nature of its work, the School of

Intercultural Studies offers many courses that address cultural differences and the practice of ministry. To enable students to acquire skills as learners and to be compassionate servants in other cultures, faculty members have framed diversity learning outcomes for multiple courses that are linked to their degree learning outcomes. In addition, the dean and the Intercultural Studies faculty have designed a capstone course in which student attitudes, knowledge, and skills for serving in diverse and multicultural contexts will be assessed.

The School of Theology has specialized degree programs for Hispanic ministries, African American church studies, and Korean studies. While the three specialized degree programs provide a rich array of options for students interested in working with these specific cultural groups, because of language and other requirements, those courses may not be readily available to the general student population. However, the African American church studies program has streamlined and strengthened its curricular offerings so that these courses are now attractive to and drawing a significant diversity of students.

For the English Master of Arts and Master of Divinity students, the faculty seeks to prepare graduates through the general curriculum to serve in ministry settings that are multicultural. The School of Theology developed its learning outcomes in 2005 through the classical Bible, theology, and ministry divisions of the Master of Divinity degree. Faculty members in each of these divisions have sought to reframe these classical studies to incorporate diversity of literature and research resources, diversity of perspective on text and context, and diversity of application and practice for ministry to people in urban multicultural congregations. As a result of the 2006 Master of Arts program review, the faculty task force has revised the core requirements for the masters programs to include cultural literacy requirements that prepare graduates for ministry in multicultural settings. The theology faculties continue to discuss their diversity objectives for the very different students who enroll in Fuller's Master of Divinity program. They also have struggled with the issues of aligning their course work to assure the diversity outcomes they seek for graduates. Many of the faculty members in the School of Theology completed a course portfolio in 2007 and 2008 to assess student learning in that course on diversity and other learning outcomes.

What do we know? At this point in time, we know that faculty across the seminary are thinking intentionally about how to prepare students for ministry in a diverse world. We know that students are taking courses that have been redesigned to assume engagement with literature from Western and non-Western sources. We know that faculty members work to bring students from different backgrounds together in the classroom and have created team assignments that require students from diverse backgrounds to do research, thinking, and writing together. We know that students are being challenged across the curriculum to question their own cultural assumptions and to consider the values and practices of others. And we know that faculty members have begun to reflect on their assignments and the work that students do on those assignments to see if these students are in fact getting it!

We have made a good start, and we are now looking for ways to document when we have been successful and when we have not. The faculties of all three schools are experimenting with ways to assess student learning and to use that data to improve our curriculum, co-curriculum, and student learning so that our graduates will be ready and able to learn how to be effective ministers in our diverse and changing world.

Equipping Staff to Serve People of Sixty Ethnic and National Origins

Fuller employs nearly 300 middle managers and staff to serve its population of more than 4,000 students. These people work in the admissions, financial aid, housing, academic advising, finance, library, bookstore, and other service departments of the seminary. Most students at Fuller encounter someone in each of these service areas at critical junctures in their study programs. These people are often the face of Fuller, and the experience the student has in those encounters communicates the values and climate for diversity in our community.

In a proactive step to enhance the diversity climate of the campus, I asked the director of human resources and her staff to develop programs of training for the seminary community that addressed issues of diversity and encouraged a customer service orientation for seminary staff. Thirteen staff, administrators, and students received training in 2006-07 on how to train others to develop a workplace hospitable for persons of all cultures. The team, now informally called the diversity team, began a multi-year training program for administrators, faculty, and staff to make people aware of their "default" attitudes and relationships in a diverse world and then to assist them in taking steps toward meeting, accepting, and serving those who are different. The first group to begin this training was the senior administrators. The team then shared their knowledge with the seminary community through workshops designed for faculty, students, staff, and administrators. By June 2008 we had completed a full year of "awareness" seminars that touched nearly every person who serves students. This was only the first step in what will be continuing engagement of the seminary community in encounters that identify our biases, affirm our values, tell our stories, and provide skills and mentoring for all who serve our diverse students.

In addition to our service departments, we have a network of programs and committees that support various groups of students, affirm their cultural identity, and provide services that help retain students who may be at risk of leaving the program prematurely. These programs and committees have provided safe space for diverse groups of students while supporting their pursuit of degrees at Fuller. The School of Theology's African American, Hispanic, and Korean studies programs provide both curriculum and support for the identity and social life of their students. Denominational groups and chapels for students also provide similar support for students from specific denominations. The international students office provides support and advice to international students who must navigate the new and complex culture in which they now reside.

Finally, student leaders on the all seminary council and those in the student government of each school support and serve on the multicultural concerns and women concerns committees that plan programs to support the development of positive relationships and deeper understanding on campus. Various ethnic groups meet informally to share experiences and garner support in times of stress.

Worth the Work

My professional training is in social anthropology, and I have taught students in State University of New York, Biola, and Fuller the skills for learning and understanding culture and doing practical work and ministries in those settings. In my provost's role at Fuller, I have learned that creating a culture that embraces diversity, as well as equipping and mentoring people to live with appreciation, compassion, and care in a multicultural community, is far more difficult than teaching about it. One of the most challenging issues is the normal movement of people into and out of the community. Every quarter new students come with cultures and assumptions that may or may not embrace others. While we hope that faculty and staff will remain longer than students, many staff are in fact student employees, and others move to better-paying jobs elsewhere. The work of renewing values, creating awareness of others, teaching the skills of listening, and conflict resolution is never-ending.

Recognizing the hard work, sometimes painful self-examination, and long-haul dedication needed to address the challenges and opportunities of diversity, the preparation of students for ministry in a global context is the most rewarding experience for all of us and greatly worth the effort. In a community where persons from varying backgrounds learn together in a climate of tolerance and respect for differences, we are all changed. When we value the practices, contributions, and experiences of students from around the world, our curriculum and conversations become rich, and our graduates leave with experiences and skills that enable them to work with competence, empathy, and wisdom among groups of persons who differ from themselves. That is why we continue to work conscientiously to ensure representation on campus of persons of varied cultural and ethnic background among faculty, staff, administrators, students, and trustees. That is why we affirm the heritages and backgrounds of these diverse people and work to help those who find their first exposure to Fuller different and sometimes painful. We have learned that we will never *be* a community that does diversity well, but we can commit to and engage in the unceasing work of *becoming* a community that does diversity well.

ADDITIONAL RESOURCES

Depree, Max. *Leading without Power: Finding Hope in Serving Community.* San Francisco: Jossey-Bass, 1997.

Heifetz, Ronald L., and Marty Linsky. *Leadership on the Line: Staying Alive through the Dangers of Leading.* Cambridge, MA: Harvard Business School Press, 2002.

Hofstede, Geert, and Gert Jan Hofstede. *Cultures and Organizations: Software of the Mind.* New York: McGraw-Hill, 2005.

Reflections about Gender and Administration in Theological Education

Barbara Brown Zikmund

I spent ten years as a faculty member, ten years as an academic dean (CAO), and ten years as a president (CEO). When people ask me which of these roles I like the best, I always answer, "Being a dean (CAO)!" Why do I respond this way?

It is hard to explain. Being a CAO is being in the middle of a school's multiple constituencies and circumstances. The dean lives betwixt and between. Sometimes one's energy has to focus on the internal tasks, cultivating people and policies that make for quality theological education. Sometimes one's energy has to focus on wider institutional challenges and resources. Even with fantastic faculty and an outstanding CEO, I have come to believe that the difference between a good and a truly outstanding institution depends on the CAO. Back in the 1980s I gave a presentation at an informal breakfast for CAOs at the 1984 ATS Biennial Meeting,[1] which concluded with a quote from a popular 1970s book by Harlan Cleveland on academic administration entitled *Seven Everyday Collisions in American Higher Education.* He highlights some of the important attributes of the effective CAO:

> there is a set of attitudes which are indispensable to the management of complexity: the notion that crises are normal, tensions are promising, and complexity is fun; the understanding that paranoia and self-pity are reserved for non-executives; and the conviction that there must be some more upbeat outcome than would result from the sum of available expert advice; and a sense of personal responsibility for the whole.[2]

Another way for me to express my enthusiasm for the role of the CAO is to use the images of "hedgehog" and "fox." These images are rooted in the ancient Greek writings of Archilochus, who said, "The fox knows many

---

1. "The Role of the Chief Academic Officer in Theological Education," *Resources in Theological Education,* Issue 8 (October 1984): 8 pps.

2. Harlan Cleveland, *Seven Everyday Collisions in American Higher Education* (New York: International Council for Educational Development, 1974), p. 31.

things, but the hedgehog knows one big thing." In the twentieth century, philosopher Isaiah Berlin used these images to divide the world into two types of thinkers . . . hedgehogs and foxes. The fox is complex, open to change, on the move, and resistant to a single unifying theory. The hedgehog is the opposite, always looking for a single unifying concept. Isaiah Berlin writes, "There exists a great chasm between those, on one side, who relate everything to a single central vision . . . and, on the other side, those who pursue many ends, often unrelated and even contradictory. . . . The first kind of intellectual and artistic personality belongs to the hedgehogs, the second to the foxes." Hedgehogs set goals, and they have systems by which they accomplish things. Foxes tend to go off in all directions, without a methodology, goals, or systems.[3]

In the academy, where the majority of CAOs grow up, the most valued citizen is the intellectual — the faculty member, the one with deep knowledge — the "hedgehog." Producing and protecting hedgehogs is what educational institutions are all about. Therefore, because most chief academic officers come to their positions from the faculty, they often live with a certain amount of ambivalence about being called to embrace the work of a fox, even when they may find they are well suited to such work.

When I think about the role of the CAO, as much as I value "deep knowledge," I want to celebrate the importance of the fox. Being a fox is not easy, involving risk and misunderstanding. As I look at the role of the chief academic officer in theological education I see that person as a fox — someone who is balancing many things; who is smart, shrewd, and sly. As with many images, calling someone "foxy" has both positive and negative connotations. I realize that "foxy" can be used to describe a person as devious, sexy, or frivolous. But it also can mean that a person is energetic, flexible, and creative, and these are the qualities I am lifting up in this reflection on gender and academic leadership. Over the years I have come to believe that foxes are at the heart of all healthy educational ecosystems. I have also come to the conclusion that, as more women take on administrative roles as chief academic officers, the tension between being a hedgehog and being a fox becomes even more complex. A fox may be devalued because she or he is spread thin, but a fox is a leader who takes risks, deals with change, makes and corrects mistakes, and helps institutions claim new futures. A fox is not just doing his or her duty until allowed to go back to "deeper things."

3. A brief summary of these images may be found at http://www.internetmarketing secrets.com/news/126/126/hedgehog-fox.html (retrieved 12/31/09).

There are many ways to explore women's journeys as academic administrators of theological schools. First, what are the *facts and statistics* about women who have become CEOs and CAOs during the past two decades (1991-2009) in ATS schools? What do they reveal? For many years CEO and CAO work was folded together into one job description. As institutions became more complex and responsibilities were divided between two people, in some settings having women as CAOs became "normal" — a glorified extension of an administrative assistant to the head of the school. In other contexts, female CAOs remain a rarity. Reflections about gender and administration in theological education are changing. Women and men serving as CAOs need accurate data about the history of academic administration in theological schools.

Second, alongside greater information about the numbers and patterns of academic administration, we can learn from the individual voices of women serving as CAOs. When women gather, the interaction of various expectations and perspectives about women's roles and the actual experiences of women sometimes collide. This is especially the case when the generic assumptions about Anglo women ignore the realities of women of color. Among women there is tremendous diversity with regard to race, ethnicity, denominational heritage, theological assumptions, and many other factors. As women move into positions of power and authority, it is important to honor their differences.

Efforts to hold these dynamics in creative tension are necessarily complex and often messy. The ATS Women in Leadership Research Project interviewed fifty-nine of the sixty-three women serving as CEOs and CAOs as of November 2007 (it attempted conversations with 100 percent of women serving in these roles and was animated by a passion to include every voice in every circumstance). The honest, diverse, "real" voices of individual women serving as academic leaders (CAOs) offer new insights into how women think about the complexities of the CAO role in relation to gender.

Third, what are we saying when we use the fox and hedgehog imagery? Suggesting that a CAO is like a fox can be a constructive metaphor. As more women take on administrative roles as chief academic officers, the tension between being a hedgehog and being a fox can be a helpful framework for exploring effective academic administration and can illuminate what it means to cultivate the art of "thinking institutionally."

BARBARA BROWN ZIKMUND

Women and Theological Education

The place of women in theological education has changed over the past century. Early in the twentieth century small numbers of Protestant women began enrolling in theological schools to earn degrees in religious education and to prepare for mission service. Roman Catholic women flocked to religious orders, benefiting from and enriching education. New congregations founded after World War II did not have enough pastors; that situation encouraged young men (and young women) to enroll in theological schools. By the 1970s and 1980s female enrollments began rising dramatically. Over the past twenty years, the overall percentage of female students in ATS schools has hovered between 30 and 35 percent. In some mainline Protestant theological schools, women make up between 70 and 90 percent of the students. During this same time period, the percentage of female faculty in ATS schools increased slowly, rising to about 25 percent. Faculty turnover is always slow, and hiring criteria are often weighed down by biblical and denominational limitations related to women. Furthermore, in the 1970s there were fewer women with the academic credentials who were eligible for faculty appointments in theological schools.

Nonetheless, in response to the rising presence of female students and faculty, theological schools began hiring more female administrators. By 2001 women represented more than 23 percent of chief development officers, 34 percent of chief student personnel officers, and almost 33 percent of chief financial officers in ATS schools.[4]

Yet in spite of the dramatic increases in female students and steady increases among female faculty and some administrators, top female administrative leadership has remained low. A look at the numbers for 1991 through 2009 illustrates this lag. While the number of female CEOs and CAOs increased over that period by 300 percent, by 2009 only 9.5 percent of CEOs and only 20 percent of CAOs in ATS schools were women (see the table on p. 237). Put another way, women CAOs are found in only one of every five ATS member schools. When we compare these statistics to a recent general survey of CAOs in higher education, the number of female CAOs in theological education is lower, but not dramatically so.[5]

4. The relevant ATS Annual Data Table (ADT 3.6) aggregates the statistics for all female administrators, tracking CEOs, CAOs, chief financial officers, chief development officers, head librarians, and staff overseeing student personnel, field education, and continuing education offices together.

5. In 2009 the American Council on Education released its first comprehensive cen-

Women in Leadership in Theological Education 1991-2009

Year	Schools	Female CEOs	% of all CEOs	Female CAOs	% of all CAOs
1991	210	6	2.8%	15	7.1%
1996	225	7	3.1%	20	8.8%
2001	244	11	4.5%	29	11.8%
2007	252	21	8.3%	42	16.6%
2009	251	24	9.5%	50	20%

How are these women doing? What happens when theological education becomes intentional about supporting women in the top leadership positions in theological schools? In 1995 Sharon Ringe, a New Testament profes-

---

sus of chief academic officers in American higher education. For many years, the ACE has been doing a long-term survey of CEOs in higher education, *The ACE American College President Study,* but this is the first comparable census of CAOs. It is based on information from more than 1,700 individuals at regionally accredited, degree-granting colleges and universities nationwide. In the news release marking the publication of *The CAO Census: A National Profile of Chief Academic Officers,* dated February 9, 2009, the president of ACE stated, "The core functions of any campus — teaching, research, service — fall under the purview of the institution's chief academic officer. Yet, surprisingly little is known about who these people are, how complex their jobs are, and how they got to this position."

For our purposes it is interesting to note that in this national *Census* 40 percent of all CAOs are women. They are 50 percent of the CAOs at associate degree granting institutions; 38 percent at master's institutions; 37 percent at baccalaureate institutions; 33 percent at special focus institutions; and 32 percent at doctorate-granting institutions. These percentages are considerably higher than ATS percentages.

ATS and Auburn research on theological education shows that CAOs in theological education are on average younger than CEOs. There are more female CAOs than female CEOs. As with male CAOs, most female CAOs reach their positions from within their institutions, whereas CEOs (male and female) are more commonly hired from outside their institution. Even though ACE data show the most common path to becoming a CEO is moving from a CAO position, only 30 percent of all CAOs nationwide say that they intend to seek a presidency. With female CAOs only 25 percent say that they have presidential ambitions. Although ATS research does not ask about "aspirations," we do know that almost 80 percent (79.4%) of the female CAOs presently serving in ATS schools came to their positions from inside their school.

"ACE Releases First National Census of Chief Academic Officers," http://www.acenet .edu/AM/Template.cfm?Section=Search&template=/CM/HTMLDisplay.cfm&ContentID =31096 (retrieved 12/31/09).

sor at Wesley Theological Seminary in Washington, DC, wrote an essay about women and theological education for the World Council of Churches journal *Ministerial Formation.* In that article Ringe spells out various ways that increasing numbers of women challenge institutional habits. Schools start scrambling to adapt schedules and policies in order to survive. More importantly, however, Ringe argues that when women are taken seriously, "we are talking about a new method of going about the theological task — a panoramic array of views reflective of the diversity of women's stories and realities, which destabilizes the theological task." In chaos theory, she continues, destabilization is not necessarily bad. In fact many writers insist that destabilization is good, because chaos is the basis and prerequisite for all life.[6]

I like Ringe's analysis because I think it is important to realize that the increasing numbers of women in leadership in ATS schools is "destabilizing." Women in theological education are shaping a new future as educational and ecclesiastical institutions and programs that have been male for centuries are changing. And students, faculty, administrators, trustees, and donors are all being shaped by these trends. I rejoice that the increasing numbers of female CEOs and CAOs are producing "chaos."

In order to support women's growth as academic leaders, it is important to celebrate and support both the institutions and the individuals navigating change. Rates of change vary dramatically, but in many settings the women serving as CAOs are serving as the "first woman" in that role. How do these women find sustenance for the journey? The ATS Women in Leadership Research Project provides some answers to that question. When women responded to a particular set of questions, their voices reflected some of the energy, flexibility, and creativity that characterize "foxy" leadership.

Personal Reflections of Female CAOs

For the past fifteen years the ATS Advisory Committee on Women in Leadership has planned and sponsored programs to provide various forms of support for women in leadership in ATS schools, holding seminars and retreats and pressing schools to become more intentional about meeting the needs of women. The Auburn Center for the Study of Theological Education has gathered important survey data. In 2005 the ATS Advisory Committee

6. Sharon Ringe, "Women and the Viability of Theological Education," *Ministerial Formation* #70 (July 1995): 19-21.

for Women in Leadership (WiL) decided to seek funding for a new research project focused on women. The committee was eager to learn more about the experiences and the needs of women in top leadership positions. Who are these women? How do they get into these leadership settings? What do they do when they encounter resistance to their leadership? What are their most difficult and satisfying relationships? What do they do to survive?

Assisted by funding from the Carpenter Foundation, the WiL Committee decided to do in-depth interviews with all sixty-three women serving as top administrators in ATS schools. The goal of the research was to guide the future work of the Association to (1) support the professional development of women in theological education, (2) enhance the capacity of theological schools to utilize the gifts and abilities of women faculty and administrators, and (3) inform educational programs for women students.[7]

When the research sample was selected in November 2007, it consisted of twenty-one CEOs and forty-two CAOs. In many research projects it is impossible to sample a complete population; however given these numbers, it was feasible. Although getting 100 percent participation is almost impossible, the project came close. It completed interviews with fifty-nine of the sixty-three women (twenty CEOs and thirty-nine CAOs). The quotations in this essay are gleaned from confidential telephone conversations with thirty-nine of the forty-two female CAOs, almost 93 percent of the female CAOs in ATS schools at that time. These women were eager to share their stories and to reflect about the challenges facing women in leadership in theological education. Excerpts that follow are organized around four themes: (1) how women come to seek or accept the role of CAO and whether they experience taking the position as a "call"; (2) how they encounter and respond to resistance; (3) how they relate to the CEO; and (4) what theological images, narratives, or convictions shape their leadership. They are presented as transcriptions of spontaneous oral responses to questions posed in an informal setting.

Seeking and Accepting the Job

We asked ATS female CAOs how they were hired. Very few women (or men for that matter) formally apply for administrative positions. When individu-

---

7. A full report of insights gleaned from the interviews with both CEOs and CAOs is published in *Theological Education* 45, no. 2 (2010).

als are approached to consider a CAO job, they are filled with questions. Men and women both wonder "Why me?" But women have additional questions. Do they really want me, or do they need a woman? Am I being asked because of who I am, or because diversity is required and the search process needs candidates who are not white men? One woman said that she resented the fact that she might be asked to consider the job simply because she is female and not because of her qualifications. Yet, she admitted that this situation helped her clarify her awareness of herself "as a woman, and as a younger faculty person." The more she thought about it she realized that if she accepted the position she would be able "to represent different constituencies" [because she was a woman], and that was a worthy goal. Many female CAOs reported that the recruiting and hiring process they went through was not very professional and even patronizing. Their experiences suggest that schools need to be more balanced and clear when they seek out female leadership.

We asked ATS female CAOs if they felt "called by God" to their positions. Their answers were honest and varied:

> I'm never real confident about saying I am called by God to do something, because I'm aware of my capacity to delude myself, so I'm really hesitant to blame this on God. If what you're asking is "are there questions of soul-searching and spiritual discernments?" certainly. I was part of that; I just don't want to blame things on God, that God led me to take responsibility for.

> It's more this kind of nagging. . . . What should I be paying attention to, points of clarity? Intuitively I have known for a long time that some kind of academic administration, whether it was exactly dean, I didn't know, but some kind of academic administration [was in my future]. I ended up hearing this kind of odd refrain from the book of Esther . . . maybe it's you "for such a time as this" — "for such a time as this."

> Yes, absolutely. I mean, no spooky voices in the night, but absolutely I felt a call, because everything rational in me, and I'm a very rational woman, said, "Why would you work twelve months a year, instead of nine, and get very little additional salary? Why would you do this, and take the flack, and take the heat? That makes no rational sense to me. I had the perfect job, thinking, teaching and writing, so the only reason to accept a position that runs against your rational choices, is that you feel called by God to do the work.

Female administrators in theological education wrestle with gender issues in numerous ways. They do not want to stereotype. They want to celebrate the collegial and caring gifts of women *and men.* They know that biology is not destiny. Yet, they find that their experiences as women are different and that those experiences shape their work more than they sometimes want to admit. One woman put it this way,

There are all kinds of non-hierarchical men, of course, and various sorts of women. I went through an era where I thought, oh, these traits are evenly distributed in the population, but it is not true. I'm a mother, and of course men can have the early years at home, but in caring for an infant who cannot speak, one is constantly trying to discern the needs, and wants, and feelings, and comforts and discomforts of the infant. It requires a constant practice in discerning what's happening. Turning your glance for ten seconds from the needs of an infant can sometimes mean life and death. In this situation one doesn't have the luxury of not attending to the other. In parenting certain patterns develop, whereby I hold my own needs and wants in abeyance, and I am conscious, all day long, of the well-being of this other human being in my life. I learn that to ignore them, even momentarily, can be disastrous.

She went on to say that women's experiences make women in leadership more attentive. Women are not born that way; it is a learned skill often related to the common life experiences of women as they raise children or care for elders. Another woman told us,

I was socialized among a lot of men. I mean, I'm very comfortable with men. I just know that I'm different and I have to work the more masculine side of my personality. I have to banter with them in a male kind of way that I don't have to do with other women and because I was socialized among a lot of boys, I can do that. It's just very clear to me how different it feels.

Dealing with Resistance

Inasmuch as the legitimacy of women in leadership is still an issue in some ATS schools we asked the women we interviewed to talk candidly about situations where they experienced resistance and how they deal with resistance to their leadership:

> I am a licensed minister and my church does not ordain women. I went through all the processes that an ordained man does. I was for the most part well respected. There were times when I was a little uncomfortable when I was labeled a feminist, because I've never considered myself in that camp. But, just by virtue of being who I am, called to ministry, exercising my gifts, and being high profile, I am here. I have learned to be very careful.

> How I do it is by just not going away, and continuing to consistently raise questions, like after a year of being on that council all I'd have to do is raise my hand when they were appointing members to this committee or that and making decisions and just thinking of the good old boys. People knew what I was going to ask. I don't create a scene, but I don't go away, and I'm consistent. That's what I do.

One of the most troubling sources of resistance for many women in leadership is the resistance of other women. One woman lamented this discovery:

> It has been such a surprise, because my whole life I've always had such a sense of solidarity and support from women. I have always, and still have, a wonderful web of women colleagues and friends, of pastors and other administrators, especially through the ATS program, and community organizer friends who are women. Yet the greatest challenges have been from some of the other women on the faculty. And that's been painful. I don't want to overstate it. But when things go bad with a woman colleague, they tend to go really bad. I don't know what that's about. I want to think more deeply about what is going on, and I haven't, just haven't, figured it out yet.

Relationships with the CEO

Over and over, interviewees highlighted the importance of relationships between male and female CEOs and CAOs. Many of the women indicated that the relationship they have with their CEO is the single most important professional relationship they have. Yet, there is no standard recipe for success. One woman mused, "Our relationship is very open and direct, probably not as structured as I would like, but it kind of works for both of us. I can say anything to him. He can say anything to me. We work very well together. We understand each other's patterns of work."

Another described her relationship to the president of her school:

> I do a lot of sounding board things. We're not friends in a palsy-walsy way, in fact, I think I avoid that simply because you can't be seen as in the pocket of the president. I think women have to watch out for that. I'm really accountable to a variety of constituencies, but certainly our relationship is amiable and certainly it's constructive and it's professional. He'll say what do you think about this? What would happen? What do you think the faculty would do if this happened? . . . Sometimes it's more directional. [Yet] I can count on my one hand the times now in three years that I've said to him "you absolutely need to do this."

There are times, however, when the CAO-CEO relationship is difficult. We asked for examples. One CAO reported that her president (male) is always "micromanaging."

> I worked with him for years. I was the smiling, smooth, efficient, cheerful co-worker for years waiting to, you know, make some head-way with him on this, waiting to earn his trust or whatever it took. After a few years, when nothing had changed, when if anything he was getting to be a much worse micromanager, I just started to push back . . . but, he could not deal with that. . . . We have not been able to reach an agreement on how we should work together. Anything that works for him feels like he is down my throat and on my back and in my face to me. Anything that works for me feels to him like he's not involved enough.

Another woman talked about the patronizing habits of her CEO.

> While he is very respectful of me, there's a patronizing edge in it. . . . He's the big daddy, uncle type, and he'll call me "kiddo," "hey love." He says that to all the women, "Hey love" or "Hey kiddo," and there's something about his view of me and others under him in that way of speaking to people, of which he is not entirely aware.

Several women reflected that "men often see women who are part of their staff or their administrative council as either mother, or sister, or daughter." Therefore, one CAO said that she is very explicit, with her CEO, telling him, "I don't play those family roles, and I know that we all get tracked into them. You need to know that as soon as I see myself being pulled in that direction, I will pull back, because I will not be your sister, and I will not be your mother, and I will not be your daughter."

Female leaders also need to learn how to push back. One CAO said,

> I have been a good Christian girl, and so, my tendency is to say, "Well, yes, I see where you're coming from," and I try to put myself in the other person's shoes. It has been hard for me to learn to say, "No, you're simply wrong," and to fight back. Yet, sometimes I need to.

Theological Reflections about Leadership

As the WiL Committee discussed the interview questions for the research project, there was a desire to craft questions that would allow us to explore the arena of ideas. Do ATS women in leadership have a theology of leadership? What nourishes that theology? How does their theology challenge the historic male system, if indeed it does? We wondered if the presence of women in top leadership in theological education might suggest different patterns of thought about leadership, so we asked them to share metaphors, images, and symbols that inform their understandings of leadership. Specifically, we asked, "Are there theological or biblical images of leadership that guide you in your work? If so, what are they?"

The answers to these questions were revealing. One CAO said, "I really resist, at this point in time, notions of servants. But pastoral, or in the sense of equipping the saints. Those are the images that work for me."

Other women did not talk about servanthood but told us about biblical characters and stories that inspire them:

> I am inspired by the story of Shiphrah and Puah [Ex. 1]. They're my heroines, because I love that there's a little bit of the oppressed and a little of the oppressor in each of us. We're always kind of on these boundaries of underestimating the power and authority that we have or overestimating. I think sometime leadership really is subversive, which is another thing I like about that story. I love it that they go to the Pharaoh and they're going to stay alive if they can so they're not going to tell him, "We

disobeyed you." They're going to say, "You know those women — they're just so tough they have their babies before we get there."

I was thinking about Lazarus's sisters Martha and Mary, because I think I identify with both. . . . Being more the Martha I always say I'm a "do for," I'll do for you. I'll do for, I'll work, I'll do something, but Mary's the one who is the person of presence. . . . So I try and get a combination of not just being the work horse and doing the work, but being the person of presence and listening.

Anybody can have a vision. The ones who are wise are the ones who can find the resources to support . . . and carry out their vision. So that story of the wise and foolish virgins reminds me that it's not quite having an idea about theological education or about the church; it's trying to find what's necessary and making it real. I like that story both in terms of my fundraising role here, but also in terms of trying to save us from foolish notions of what the vision is. Anybody can make an ideal out there, but trying to make it happen in these circumstances with these limitations, that's a lot harder.

I like to think of women who are called to something special, not necessarily with the power of a prophet. I think of Mary being called to give birth to this Christ child as a prophetic role, but not necessarily one that would be identified as powerful. I tend to like the underdog. I like people in the Bible who were the ones no one expected to do what they did.

Of course many of our interviewees talked about Jesus and his ministry as a model for their leadership. For example,

I think about Jesus' leadership and the way he really heard and responded, and sometimes even changed. I think of the story of the woman who said, "Even the dogs eat the crumbs." And he said, "Oh, yeah okay." So that kind of listening and engaging people is of critical importance for me as I think about leadership. I think of his attentiveness to prayer, as well as attentiveness to the people around him. I look at Jesus' example of leadership in a lot of different ways.

I envision Jesus . . . as a teacher and leader who looked people squarely in the eyes and so deeply that he didn't see any of the rest of them. He didn't see what color, he didn't see what gender, he didn't see what background, he didn't see what class, and if you look folks in the eyes and try to see who they are, then you can work with them as creature of God to creature of God, and that's what I try to do.

Yet not all of our interviewees found biblical stories, images, and texts helpful. One said,

> . . . there aren't a lot of women to look for in the Bible. I could talk about Esther, I suppose. But, the Bible does not offer me very much. I can say that the idea of a servant leader is built into me as a Christian, but . . . I've lived in this world (a man's world) the whole time I've been a professional, and it's always been a struggle to find a model. So I don't know. I tend to look more to fictional models or fantasy, like "Wonder Woman." The Bible has not been friendly to me.

Other women heard our question about "biblical and theological images" more broadly and did not focus upon texts, stories, or people, but used more general phrases and classic theological concepts to describe key ideas that shape their leadership.

> In the dean's office you do a lot of atonement. You absorb anxieties and you absorb hurts and suffering, deep suffering of people. Some way or another you need to take all those feelings and transform them into positive energy. I think that's what atonement is.

> I have an image of the dean standing at the tomb and pushing away the boulders. It's not only the women at the tomb identifying the empty tomb, it's more the angels and the guardians pushing the boulder aside so that you can see that the tomb is empty and you can act on that image.

> I think about theological and biblical images of hope. I like Romans 15:13, "God of hope." That's a name for God that's not in those traditional lists of names for God. We are practitioners of hope, and every time I walk into a meeting, that's what I want to be, an agent of hope, a practitioner of hope, because that's what we're trying to be in this world.

Thinking Institutionally

A recent book by Hugh Heclo entitled *On Thinking Institutionally*[8] suggests that there is a difference between "thinking about institutions" and "thinking institutionally." Drawing analogies from sports and business, Heclo says that many people are very skilled managers of institutional success. They are sports stars and successful educational and corporate CEOs; they make smart moves and build winning organizations and careers. But they are mostly thinking *about* institutions and not "thinking institutionally." They are like hedgehogs. They have deep insights about the way things work, and they know how to use specialized knowledge to get things done.

"Thinking institutionally," Heclo says, "is different. . . . It is not a purely intellectual exercise. It is a mixture of cognition and emotional attachment yielding habits of action. . . . It happens when people do what they are supposed to do to uphold the values of their profession and their organizations' larger purposes." "People," continues Heclo, "recognize the dysfunctional, unsatisfactory quality of an anti-institutional way of living."[9]

I know that good faculty members think a lot about institutions. Professors want to be part of a strong school. They want their research and teaching to produce excellence. However, when a faculty member becomes a CAO (or a CEO for that matter), something more is needed. Top institutional leaders need to do more than think *about* institutions; they need to "think institutionally."

Most of the women interviewed in the Women in Leadership project recognized the difference between the faculty and the administration. They also said that sometimes women "think" differently about leadership. The differences are subtle. No sweeping generalizations can be used because there is a great deal of variety among women. Yet, because many women are newcomers to institutional leadership, their experiences are not the same as men's. Because the settings in which they serve are complex and old gender habits do not work, female CAOs are able to challenge theological education to think in new ways (institutionally and theologically) about leadership. Women can remind us of our common biblical loyalties, even as texts are read differently. They can insist that theological schools are not secular institutions promoting gender equality as a human rights issue. They can note

---

8. Hugh Heclo, *On Thinking Institutionally* (Boulder, CO, and London: Paradigm Publishers, 2008).

9. Heclo, *On Thinking Institutionally*, pp. 6-9.

that most Christians believe that in Christ Jesus there is neither slave nor free, Jew nor Greek, male nor female (Gal. 3:28). And even when we interpret that text differently, the presence of women in leadership suggests to all of us that female leaders are a gift and not a problem.

Most women who are chief academic officers in ATS schools are new-comers to administrative power, yet they understand what Heclo means. They care deeply about their schools. They are foxes — open to change, on the move, and resistant to simplistic unifying theories. Their horizons are stretched. They believe in the enterprise of theological education, not just in their respective institutions and not merely in their personal skills. They have learned to "think institutionally." Furthermore, they are willing to take personal and institutional risks to strengthen theological education and help all of us think more deeply about our values. May their tribe increase.

ADDITIONAL RESOURCES

Zikmund, Barbara Brown. "'Three Coins in a Fountain': Female Leadership in Theological Education," *Theological Education* 45, no. 2 (2010).

DEVELOPING COMPETENCIES

10. Orchestrating People and Processes

The Dean as Administrator: "It's All a Matter of Relationships"

Gary Riebe-Estrella

Just as there is no theology that is not contextual, there is no reflection on the work of deans that is not in so many ways determined by the specific characteristics of their schools. What is said about the work of a dean in one school may be able to be said of deans in other schools, but emphases and styles of leadership will differ.

Mine is a Roman Catholic, freestanding graduate school of theology and ministry, founded in the wake of the Second Vatican Council and the result of the coming together of a number of religious orders (some twenty-five at present). Originally focused on the training of seminarians for ordination, the school now has among its 450-plus students a mix of seminarians and lay women and men preparing for ministry in the church. In the first years the faculty was composed entirely of priests; now there are priests, women religious, lay women and men, and even an occasional Protestant pastor or rabbi on the faculty. The student body was once almost exclusively white; now at least a third of the students come from Asia, Africa, and Latin America.

What defines the school is this coming together of diverse people to serve a common mission, the preparation of Roman Catholic ministers for the church and the world. The success of that mission depends on the quality of collaboration in the midst of this diversity. In this context, the work of the dean is primarily in facilitating that collaboration, which is dependent on the level of trust and confidence among the players. It's all a matter of relationships!

Relating to Constituencies: "Standing in the Middle"

Jeanne McLean in her very helpful book on the work of an academic dean uses the image of "leading from the center."[1] My preferred image for the dean is "standing in the middle." I fear the "leading" metaphor, not only because of the now-famous saying about "herding cats" (a good dean never looks back; there may be nobody following!), but because the dean's job is less about being out front and more about "directing traffic," a task best done by standing in the middle of the intersection where the divergent interests of the school's constituencies meet (sometimes crash, sometimes converge, sometimes pass by one another like ships in the night!). The dean's role should not be construed as academic, narrowly understood. There is nothing in the life of the institution that does not affect the learning environment and, therefore, the accomplishment of the school's mission. As a result, the dean needs to relate to all the dimensions and constituencies of the institution.

The dean's role is most often thought of as entailing work with the faculty. The word *administer* has its Latin root in the word *ministrare*, which means first and foremost to "serve" or "wait on" and secondarily to "supply, provide."[2] A dean can best serve the faculty by helping them to articulate an "enlightened self-interest," that is, what is of significance to them, but within the context of the larger reality of the school's mission, in which there needs to be a balance among competing priorities. Providing a voice for the faculty in the inner workings of the school can have its place in the work of a dean. But a prior step is inviting the faculty into the academic tasks confronting the institution. Assessment, curriculum review and development, the use of technology in teaching and learning, accreditation, all present ongoing opportunities for members of the faculty to grapple with the complexity of fulfilling the school's mission. However, this entails clear articulation by the

1. Jeanne P. McLean, *Leading from the Center: The Emerging Role of the Chief Academic Officer in Theological Schools* (Atlanta: Scholars Press, 1999).

2. D. P. Simpson, *Cassell's New Latin Dictionary* (New York: Funk & Wagnalls Company, 1959).

dean of the factors at play, including finances, the priorities of the other major administrators, and educational trends. Transparency is critical here. Faculty ownership of possible solutions to complex and difficult issues is born out of their collective understanding of the institution's limitations as much as out of their convictions and preferences. The dean must paint the broad connections among the interests of the diverse constituencies that make up the institution, directing traffic so that those interests converge rather than collide.

Inviting faculty into the complexity of the institution's life entails discerning which faculty members appear to be best suited for which tasks. Not all colleagues have the same gifts and capabilities. Some have the necessary flexibility and astuteness to tackle the truly complex issues where competing agendas collide, such as curriculum review and issues of faculty load. Others do better in the more tranquil waters of ongoing program review. Some have a particular shrewdness in dealing with personnel issues, promotions, and faculty reviews. Some are better at companioning other colleagues as mentors than in dealing with the often contentious issues brought forth by students. The dean's wise choices about where to assign faculty members can help build dean-faculty relationships, particularly as faculty colleagues find that the assigned tasks offer them opportunities to use and to be recognized for their gifts. The ability to identify the varying gifts of members of the faculty, to empower the use of those gifts, and to facilitate their employment in tasks where different constituencies with different priorities converge allows the faculty to own its work and yet to view it in the larger context of the overall effective functioning of the school.

If a dean wants to sleep at night, it is necessary to identify and accept the role of the chief academic officer. The dean is not the president, and it is the president who makes the final decisions. A good relationship with the president depends on a non-begrudging acceptance of this distinction of roles. While the president's vision for the school and involvement with the larger church and secular community context is only one of the avenues of traffic in the institution, it is the one with the motorcade! Vis-a-vis the president's role as chief executive officer, the dean's task is primarily one of facilitation rather than representation.

The dean's office is not the headquarters for a courier service that delivers messages from the president to the faculty or from the faculty to the president. Rather, the dean's service to the president is in helping get inside the faculty's corporate mind, allowing the president an inside sense of their motivations and morale. Equally, the dean needs to help the faculty under-

stand the variety of pressures the president faces, what's driving this particular solution, what underlies the president's preoccupation with that particular issue. By directing the traffic and interpreting its flows to the parties
involved, the dean is able to grease the wheels of collaboration. But again,
that calls for relationships of integrity and trust with both president and
faculty.

The same might be said of the dean's role with the other major administrators in the school. The deeper the dean's professional relationship with
the president, the more seriously the dean will be taken by the other officers.
Each of them also has a particular agenda and private vision of the school's
future. While needing to respect those agendas and visions, the dean also has
to ensure that they rise to the surface and gain articulation in conversations
across departmental lines. The dean can't be very effective in directing
school traffic if he or she only sees the surface avenues and is blind to the
subway lines running underneath.

Professional and clerical staff are the backbone of any institution.
While the majority do not work directly for the dean, they often look to the
dean. Most staff in the ATS schools I have visited (and faculty as well) have
not taken on their positions because of the high salaries. Most are in our institutions because they are committed to the mission, that is, educating
women and men for ministry. They see the institution first and foremost as a
school, and it is the dean who most clearly wears the "school" name badge.
The dean, in fact, is the one who most visibly represents the loyalty they all
share to the institution and its mission. A dean has an unparalleled opportunity to bring cohesion to a school, even if only on the level of morale, by taking an interest in staff colleagues, recognizing the value of their contributions to students and faculty, and talking openly about the institutional
traffic jams that affect their work and, therefore, their lives. Building relationships with members of the staff goes a long way in keeping the dean's
finger on the pulse of the school, something which other major administrators have fewer opportunities to do because of what is oftentimes the more
narrow focus of their work.

In my experience the dean's relationship with students is generally a
mediated one. Certainly this varies with the size of the student body and the
amount of teaching a dean does. But except for disciplinary situations,
grievances, and mediations between professors and students, the dean is
more often a figure working in the background. Within the institution, the
students' primary relationships are with the faculty and each other. The institutional traffic (of administrators, faculty, and staff) that the dean directs

deeply affects the effectiveness of the school in providing theological and ministerial formation to the students. But direct intervention in the lives of students by the dean is a rare occurrence.

The dean's relationship with the members of the board of trustees is an equally mediated one, but this time through the president. The board members are primarily the president's people. The dean needs to be supportive and accessible to the board, but those relationships need to be transparent to the president.

All of these relationships need to be conducted with good humor. A dean should not allow difficult interactions to become personalized. Engaging the challenges inherent in delivering quality formation for ministry demands that the dean always remember that "the enemy is not us." My point here is that the dean needs to see not just the bright side of things but also *all* sides of things. To do that the dean has to be able to step back, and it is the distancing that provides the space for both humor and equilibrium.

Relating to Tasks: "Towers Aren't Always So Bad"

Directing traffic can be a dizzying experience. A dean needs a control tower from which to see the traffic patterns, the points at which interests are bunching up and restricting the flow, or the unhelpful detour a fellow administrator has taken to move a particular agenda ahead. Obviously, the control tower is not a physical space. It is a breadth of perspective to which the dean needs to continually return.

In the frequent frenzy of directing institutional traffic, the dean's vision can narrow and even become myopic. Oddly enough, it is a thoughtful committee structure that can keep the dean's vision broad. In my school there are four major faculty committees where institutional traffic can converge. One deals with curriculum and faculty development, one with the directions and policies of degree programs, one with faculty hiring and evaluation, and one with assessment. While the four committees together map the academic landscape fairly well, each has a particular focus that needs to be addressed on a regular basis to keep the school healthy. Participation in each of these committees forces me to hold in tension each of these foci and to help them shed light on one another. While committee members bring their own interests and commitments to the focus of their particular committees (for instance, department chairpersons to curriculum development), I bring the agenda and priorities of the other major committees. In that sense, my role as dean is to direct the interests and concerns of one group so they converge with the interests and concerns of the others.

While the primary foci of these four basic faculty committees might define the academic landscape, it is the strengths and weakness of the school that usually determine to which area the dean needs to commit the most personal and the faculty attention. A helpful lens for discerning the strengths and weaknesses of the school are the ATS Commission Standards of accreditation. While it may be true that in the mind of many a dean the standards are very closely associated with the "dreaded" decennial visit, all of us have experienced that the greatest benefit of the standards is not in their use by the visiting team to make judgments about the school, but rather in the school's use of them in its work of preparing for the visit, especially in the work of producing the self-study. Perhaps in some institutions the work of self-study is a two-year process in immediate preparation for the accreditation visit. However, "study of self" might better be thought of as the daily focus of the work of the dean. The standards can act as a helpful guide, a kind of examination of institutional conscience that guides the dean's work with faculty, administration, and staff.

The institution's life does have a certain rhythm to it; that is, some critical tasks, while not continuous, recur at particular intervals, such as curriculum revision or reaccreditation. Since the institutional traffic that the dean directs doesn't cease when one of these critical tasks needs attention, the dean really can't afford to leave the intersection to address it. At the same time, the dean usually can't simply load another major project onto an already abundant workload. Critical here is the dean's knowledge of and relationship with the members of the faculty. A few years ago, when it became clear that my institution would need to do curriculum revision because we were moving from quarters to semesters, I spent many a sleepless night trying to figure out how I was going to manage one more project, especially one of the size and critical importance of curriculum revision. Luckily I paid attention to the fact that, in the midst of the tossing and turning, conversations with different members of the faculty came to mind — about curriculum, about the changing face of ministry, and about new pedagogical styles. My luck was that I paid more attention to the faculty with whom I had had these conversations than to their content. In my mind's eye, I started to build a team of creative and thoughtful folk for whom the issues most critical to curriculum revision were issues they had already considered. Then it was a matter principally of exercising the relationships I had cultivated with them to invite them into the work ahead, particularly by letting them know what strengths I perceived they brought to the task at hand.

Relating to Self: "Don't Fear Your 'Behind'"

A perennial question for every dean is how to manage the workload. In smaller institutions such as mine, there often is no associate dean. As a result the work piles up. In my first year as dean I thought that a clean and ordered desk was a sign that I was on top of things. By the third year I had surrendered "clean" and felt that ordering the piles of files was enough. By year five my desk looked like a pile of rubble! I had to come to terms with the fact that there were no more hours in the day, that I wanted to have a life of some kind, and that I had interests other than "deaning." I had to come to terms with the fact that I would always be behind and that the best I could do was to establish workable priorities; but I could no longer fear my "behind." As I became more settled with what I could and could not accomplish, I also began to overcome my reticence to let the faculty know the time challenges I faced and the very real limitations I would have in addressing some issues that were of critical importance to some of them. Inviting them into the traffic control tower to get an inside picture of what I was dealing with sometimes helped faculty members see how they could be part of the solution; other times, while not relieving their dissatisfaction with my limitations, it led at least to an improved level of understanding.

Learning to live with the tension of always being behind allows a dean to become involved, at least on a limited basis, in other interests that provide distance from the daily. For most of us it is important to get out of the house with some regularity and immerse ourselves in different tasks and a different environment. Sometimes that may be ATS activities, which can give the dean a space for thinking and visioning. Being with other deans can also help put into perspective the concerns and tasks that seem so gargantuan when faced alone. Other times it may be activities that have nothing directly to do with the dean's school or with theological education but offer new energy through experiences of immediate satisfaction. Self-care is more important than we may sometimes think. The quality of my relationships with others depends in large measure upon my relationship with myself. The ability to direct institutional traffic is not unconnected to the dean's ability to direct the traffic of competing personal needs and interests.

JOHN T. CARROLL

A Wild World of Relationships

A dean's world is a wild one! Calming competing demands, visioning the future, smoothing feathers, discerning gifts, appreciating staff, helping the faculty articulate institutional vision and interests, holding up the broader picture of the school's life and mission, explaining folks to each other, this is the daily diet of every academic dean. There certainly are other images of a dean's work than the one I have used, "directing institutional traffic." But whichever one is most helpful to you, it will need to take into account the peculiar place where the dean stands in the life of the institution. To be an administrator is to serve, more than to provide services. And effective service employs relationships to accomplish its work: relating to constituencies, relating to tasks, relating to self. In the end it really is all a matter of relationships!

Focusing a Complex, Multidimensional Role: Observations from a Protestant Seminary Dean

John T. Carroll

The administrative portfolio of the chief academic officer is complex and multidimensional. Effective administrative leadership demands energy, patience, humor, capacity for attentive listening, and the talent of managing myriad details while also keeping eye and ear on the big picture — the

I am grateful to my dean colleague at Austin Presbyterian Theological Seminary, Michael Jinkins, as well as my dean predecessor at Union-PSCE, Sib Towner, each of whom generously shared his wisdom on the subject of this chapter. Their profound insights served as the catalyst for my own experientially based reflection on the administrative role of the theological school dean. Among the publications I have found useful in my own thinking about the challenges of the work are Jeanne P. McLean, *Leading from the Center: The Emerging Role of the Chief Academic Officer in Theological Schools* (Atlanta: Scholars Press, 1999); and Ronald A. Heifetz, *Leadership Without Easy Answers* (Cambridge, MA: Belknap, 1994).

school as system and its strategic visioning in relation to multiple environments and constituencies. The job requires strong interpersonal skills and an ability to "get it" quickly, to read people and situations, and to retain and control a vast amount of information. Effectiveness in the role demands the ability to communicate clearly and a commitment to do it promptly and regularly, even and especially when dealing with contested matters and conflicts. The competent dean is adept at multitasking and, in the face of relentless demands on attention, time, and energy, must be able to prioritize so as to be sure to attend to the most important, and most pressing, concerns. Without strong skills in organization and prioritizing, time management will always be an enemy.

Among the major duties that claimed my attention during the three-month period while I was writing this essay were the following: assisting a first-year president in crisis management of two governance and interinstitutional challenges; serving as *ex officio* member and staff support for a faculty search committee; preparing for, conducting (with the president), and writing official reports for nine faculty performance reviews; coordinating and managing information flow in course planning for the next two years; preparing academic catalog copy for academic programs and faculty; reviewing budget requests in areas supervised by the dean and submitting budget documents; participating in a two-day retreat and another two-day business meeting of the board of trustees, as well as two all-day (off-site) meetings of the strategic planning committee; drafting plans for the annual (two- or three-day) faculty retreat; evaluating the recently implemented portfolio-based student assessment process; and assisting faculty committees in the design of a process for major curriculum revisioning. All of this came in addition to ongoing duties as teacher in a required spring-term course in New Testament, as member of my faculty department, as primary advisor for two PhD students completing work on their dissertations, and as participant in the president's executive cabinet. Which of these tasks might I have deferred, delegated, or avoided? In my school system: none. These are all high priority tasks — no "administrivia" here, and the dean has primary responsibility to execute them. If the school is to flourish, the dean must also do them well. With this formidable array of duties — perhaps typical of the CAO's portfolio — as backdrop, the dean's role may be outlined in relation to four particular areas: (1) the governance of the theological school; (2) assessment and revisioning of curricula; (3) hiring, nurture, and evaluation of faculty; and (4) communication.

Issues of Governance

The dean is by definition a "middle child" in the academic system, playing the role of mediator or broker — a Janus, facing toward administration and (with the president or CEO) the board of trustees (directors) on the one hand and toward faculty on the other. While representing, speaking, and advocating on behalf of the faculty to administration and board, the dean also speaks and advocates on behalf of the administration and board to the faculty. In this liminal space, it is crucial that the dean be comfortable with tension and conflict and be willing to acknowledge, name, and honor — as well as encourage open discussion of — competing interests, values, and commitments. The primary concern of the dean is to keep the educational mission of the school before all these groups as well as other important stakeholders and constituents.

Though typically much smaller than colleges and universities, and with fewer faculty to share in the work of governance, theological schools are complex enough to require many standing and *ad hoc* committees. Which committees in the school's governance system are priority concerns of the dean? Especially important are the committees that: (1) address faculty issues (including evaluation, work load, professional development and nurture, and promotion and tenure); (2) provide oversight of academic programs and curricula; (3) manage student recruitment and admissions; and (4) superintend the school's processes of strategic planning and assessment. Many deans, myself included, serve on additional committees, but attention given to these four areas will be well repaid in enhanced functioning and overall coherence of the school system.

However the dean comes to possess information about the work, challenges, initiatives, and creative dreaming occurring at various places in the school's governance system (whether by direct information, by reports from committee chairs, associate deans, or other administrative officers, or by reading committee reports and minutes), the dean has an invaluable gift to offer the school. Given the complexity of the theological school and the inertia of both the institution and the faculty as a collective body, considerable energy must be expended to keep the big picture — the educational mission and effective administrative systems to foster it — before these various committees and *ad hoc* groups if the school is to flourish, adapt, perhaps even survive. If the dean, collaborating closely with the president, does not bring significant energy and big-picture awareness, no one else may take up the slack. No one in the school likely has a comparable vantage point from which to see at play so much of the working of the whole institutional system.

Assessment and Revisioning of Curricula

The dean has a vital role to play in both healthy functioning of existing curricular systems and assessment of their effectiveness with a view to curricular change and revision. The dean must wear multiple hats here, supervising the faculty as it engages its teaching vocation and also leading the faculty in deep and thorough evaluation of a program's educational effectiveness — overseeing the ongoing operation of the academic program but also, at the same time, serving as change agent, pressing for reimagining of teaching practices and revisioning of curricular patterns in the light of the theological school's unfolding educational mission. Among the formidable challenges confronting any dean are institutional inertia and silo-mentality of faculty who specialize in separate disciplines, both of which may generate faculty resistance to substantive curricular change even when it is widely recognized that such change is needed. Academic deans, though usually located in one or another academic field themselves, must lead the faculty in creating processes for curricular shaping, evaluation, and reshaping that aim at integration of learning in its multiple dimensions, both vertical (as students advance through a curriculum) and horizontal (e.g., interdisciplinary and theory-praxis connections), both diachronic and synchronic.

It is not unusual for faculty to embrace the formal task of assessment of learning outcomes with reluctance, perhaps not yet connecting the dots, not clearly recognizing the extent to which they are already regularly engaged in processes of assessment, both in the individual courses they teach and in their work as active researchers and scholars. It may prove helpful to recruit faculty to the task of program assessment, initially, by encouraging them to identify all the assessment practices in the school to which they already contribute and to begin to do so more self-reflectively and explicitly than before. In my school, the recent implementation of a portfolio-based student assessment process has provided yet another lure to engage faculty in thoughtful and intentional processes of learning-outcome and curricular assessment in their role as academic advisors.

The previous strategic plan of my school over-ambitiously committed the faculty to a regular four-year cycle of curricular review for each of our nine degree programs. After some trial and error, the pattern at which we

have arrived (at least for now) involves a fifteen-year cycle of curricular review and revisioning (for each cluster of degree programs — the basic or
master's-level degree programs and the advanced degree programs) comprised of three five-year sub-cycles, with one deep and comprehensive assessment and two more limited reviews in the course of the fifteen years. For
comprehensive curricular revisioning, it is helpful — if not indeed necessary
— to entrust leadership of the process to a dedicated task force or committee, interdisciplinary in composition and having a high level of credibility
and thus authority for its work because its members enjoy the trust and respect of the wider faculty. The dean should be integrally involved in the
work of the task force or committee, guiding the faculty in its formation,
providing direction as the group is mobilized (e.g., recommending timeline,
structure, and process), making available needed materials (e.g., data, assessment tools, and resources), and continually pressing the participating faculty to think holistically and not (just) from their own particular turf. Moreover, the dean should ensure that students are an integral part of the group's
work and that voices within the school (whether faculty or student) are not
the only voices to which the group is attending but rather are augmented by
voices outside the day-to-day school context (alumni/ae, congregations,
community, and the wider church). Outside eyes and ears can help focus for
a faculty the actual learning outcomes their students and graduates embody,
outcomes that may differ materially from stated (or assumed) degree program goals and, even more, from the churches' needs for leadership and expectations of readiness for service. How well is the school equipping students for the vocations to which they are called? It is part of the portfolio of
the dean to keep this question before a faculty and to counter the understandable impulse of a busy faculty to dodge the question or answer it hastily
or superficially.

From Hiring to Retiring: Nurture and Evaluation of Faculty

In large measure, the faculty *is* the curriculum of the school, not only in the
courses professors teach and the methods they use to teach them but also in
the ways they model the life of faith and learning in community, the ways
they nurture students' emerging vocational identity and spiritual formation,
and the ways they engage the world outside the school's (at least relatively)
safe space.

Hiring of Faculty

In my school, the academic dean formerly chaired all faculty search committees, an approach that lent considerable efficiency and intentionality to the search process but also created unnecessarily complicated, multiple roles for the dean in interactions with prospective and future colleagues. We have shifted to a process in which the dean serves as an *ex officio* member and resource for the committee. It would be difficult to exaggerate the importance of the conversations that occur between dean and prospective colleague in the course of a faculty search. From the beginning, the dean has the opportunity to establish with the candidate a mutually respectful relationship marked by transparency (e.g., about the search process and the mission, needs, strengths, and challenges of the school); attentive listening; hospitable welcome and affirmation balanced by appreciative, honest critique; encouragement to interdisciplinary and full-program thinking beyond narrow disciplinary specialization; and clear communication of expectations for the position and for faculty performance. The groundwork for healthy participation in the work of the faculty and school is laid already in the search process.

Evaluation and Nurture of Faculty

Clear communication to faculty (especially new and pre-tenure colleagues) of the school's expectations for faculty performance and consistent application of expectations and evaluation criteria are equally important institutional practices. New and pre-tenure faculty members stand to benefit greatly when other colleagues participate actively, though non-obtrusively, as mentors and experienced guides with regard to the school's culture, expectations (both written and unwritten) to be met by faculty, strategies for professional development, and processes of performance evaluation. This should not be left to chance, but intentional structures of collegial support and mentoring should be developed and monitored; often enough, newly hired faculty members will encounter high levels of dysfunction in an immediate, primary colleague or in the department where they are lodged. Proactive, intentional mentoring and nurture are formative and especially critical for entry-level faculty and for colleagues from under-represented groups and from other cultures.

JOHN T. CARROLL

Retirement and Transitions

Sooner or later, every dean supervises the work of one or more faculty members who underperform or who fail to meet institutional expectations. At precisely this point, the dean's role as more than simply advocate for faculty and faculty interests looms large. The work of the faculty as a whole and the theological school's educational effectiveness demand that the dean, working through collegial structures, hold faculty members accountable for the work they do. Naturally, this delicate task grows even more complicated and difficult when the faculty member holds tenure. It is crucial to follow the book, to deal with such challenges according to approved institutional policies. The dean's mastery of the faculty manual must be impeccable and precise. (Moreover, whenever implementation of existing policies exposes problems, the dean should lead the faculty, through established procedures, to amend the manual promptly in support of more effective institutional practices.) Regular, substantive performance reviews provide the mechanism whereby the dean, president, and board can fairly and responsibly address performance concerns, whether in a remedial fashion leading to improvement or with a view to eventual termination of employment. In all cases, the dean as administrator is also a human being and person of faith who seeks to treat colleagues pastorally and justly.

More commonly, it is simply advancing age or the opportunity to accept another employment offer that leads to a faculty member's departure. The dean will ensure that appropriate recognition of the colleague's accomplishments and contributions — ideally an extension of the school's *ongoing* practices — accompanies this transition. However, the dean's job within such moments of transition is to lead the institution in planning for the future shape of a faculty that will carry forward the theological school's educational mission. An especially helpful resource is a faculty- and board-approved statement of policy and practices for faculty retirement, including protocols and incentives for early retirement and a description of the rights and benefits that retired faculty enjoy (e.g., access to email, office space, library privileges, and occasional teaching opportunities). Such a document should balance (1) a clarity and consistency of approach that guard against (both the perception and the reality of) capricious, *ad hoc* treatment of faculty members and (2) flexibility for the dean and president that is responsive to the particular circumstances and needs of faculty members, departments, academic programs, and the theological school as a whole.

The Dean as Communicator

Whatever other skills deans may possess, "if they have not communication, they are but a noisy gong or a clanging cymbal." The best counsel is to listen well, and listen often, carefully attending to implicit messages. To be effective, and to last in the job, deans will quickly acquire thick skin, realizing that they should not take personally the inevitable expressions of frustration and anger that arise in the high-stakes, high-stress arena of theological education. The healthy dean is secure enough to listen supportively but, at the same time, to push back as needed, balancing the needs of the one with the needs of the school as a whole.

When safe space exists within a theological school and faculty for open and candid communication about important matters, conflicts will surface rather than remain hidden (only to erupt later). In such a setting, one of the interpersonal challenges (and opportunities) of the dean is dealing effectively with the "faculty curmudgeon." (Every faculty on which I have served has at any given time included at least one such colleague.) Encouragement and restraint of that faculty member are both needed. Such colleagues deserve affirmation insofar as they bear significant institutional memory and remind the faculty of significant lessons, values, and commitments from the school's past, thus serving as a sometimes helpful check on too-quick and enthusiastic embrace of the latest passing fad. However, resistance to change and curricular and institutional inertia are such potent and fierce forces that the curmudgeon must not be allowed to become an obstruction to needed change for which the rest of the faculty and institution are ready.

Transparency about the dean's own work, values, and commitments and about the rationale that has informed decisions will help build and sustain trust and the confidence of faculty colleagues as well as other staff members. No less important, though, are discretion and trustworthiness in maintaining confidences. At this point, the supporting work of the dean's chief executive assistant and any associate deans is worth highlighting. Of necessity, the dean will often be away from the office, and an efficient, graceful, and reliable administrative support team will contribute to the healthy functioning of faculty, academic system, and school in ways whose importance would be difficult to exaggerate. The dean should insist on clear and regular communication with and among the various offices that provide administrative support for the academic program. Confusion stemming from failure to communicate or from incomplete communication, from inconsistent practices (e.g., in the information provided and in policy enforcement), and the like, will multiply quickly and exponentially. Communication is the dean's ally; ineffectual communication will prove a potent and tenacious enemy.

The dean is in a position to help a school craft and employ efficient processes of communication and dissemination of information, seeing that needed documents and resources are accessible in support of the work of teaching, evaluation, and governance. Employing the software platform of Blackboard, the faculty of my school and the board (with somewhat more mixed success) migrated from primarily paper distribution of materials for committees and faculty (and board) meetings to almost exclusive reliance upon Web access. I can only imagine that schools making heavy use of distance modes of education and governance (e.g., multiple campuses) discovered long before we did the ways in which such information technologies can increase efficiency of operation and enhance communication throughout the theological school system. Not surprisingly, this transformation in governance and communication patterns has added more layers to the dean's task list.

Keys to Effective Academic Administration

The seminary dean occupies a position and role of special importance in the work of the institution, exercising a particular kind of leadership that relies on several key qualities.

First, it is crucial to balance attentiveness to the details and big-picture, whole-system, future-visioning thinking. Academic deans bear a heavy share of the burden for program maintenance and nurture, but at the same time, their access to so many layers of information about the whole system also enables them to aid the faculty, executive arm, and board of the school in thinking and acting strategically. Perhaps no one else in the theological school, with the possible exception of the president, has a comparable vantage point from which to make such a strategic contribution.

Attention to details, of course, only succeeds when good ideas on paper actually get implemented — and effectively interpreted and evaluated. Follow-through on plans and projects, whether directly or by delegating to others (and then monitoring task accomplishment), is a *sine qua non* of the dean's work. Here, too, the dean will benefit from the contributions made by an academic administrative support team. In this connection, committee chairs need to be kept accountable for their organizational leadership and also provided sufficient staff support and resources to serve effectively in an administrative role (not one that, for many faculty colleagues, comes easily or naturally).

From my first day as dean to the present, the image that best captures the role of the academic dean as administrator is that of a juggler straining to keep dozens of balls in the air. The role requires discipline, energy, and efficient organization — but also a cultivated capacity to improvise. As Michael Jinkins observed (in private correspondence), "a good dean actually values good administration. Not all deans value administration, and in those cases it shows." I would add: and the mission and operation of the school are very likely to suffer as a result.

It does not take many weeks on the job for the academic dean to discover that the dean-as-administrator needs, above all, the intangible qualities of wisdom, sharp discernment, and keen, intuitive judgment. *What is most important and most needs close attention? When should I press for more and when should I back off and extend grace and care?* The competent dean remembers nearly everything, yet wise deans forgive and leave behind much of what they cannot forget (including, one may hope, their own mistakes, for which the job affords such ample opportunity). No manual can teach deans how to earn and maintain trust, but unless they are perceived by colleagues (as well as students, staff, and board) as trustworthy and reliable, they will not lead a theological school well. They will be wise, therefore, to place a premium on actions that express consistency and fairness and to listen patiently and closely. Trust, once damaged, is not easily or quickly repaired. In this dimension of a dean's relationships with faculty, other administrative officers, students, and board, there will be no excess capital from which to draw.

This is even more crucial in the dean's relationship with the theological school's CEO. No other working relationship in the school is more critical to its health than that of dean and president. When they share a common vision of the mission and future of the school, when they talk with each other regularly and honestly, when their complementary strengths align with the complementary demands placed upon them, and when they model mutual, collegial respect, the basis has been established for strong administrative functioning in the whole school system.

Finally, the dean, full as the portfolio already is with administrative duties, is most effective when engaged, as a colleague among colleagues, in the work of teaching and scholarship. To be sure, like the uncommonly gifted athlete who makes everyone else play better on the court, academic deans help the faculty and other administrative officers do their jobs more effectively, and this service — for some deans, it is a matter of genuine vocation — inevitably calls for sacrifice of much of what would otherwise have constituted a vital research and teaching program. The coffee shop, the classroom, and the library are all important extensions of my ministry as theological school dean. The easiest thing to jettison, simply to survive the relentless flow of work — with dozens of concrete tasks each week, each with its own deadline — is regular teaching and research. To step back from these aspects of the faculty role, however, comes at great cost. For credibility with faculty and students alike — and to gain the knowledge and perspective that are requisite to speak with authority to the board and other constituencies of the school — the academic dean needs to stay connected to the students, to the dynamic processes of teaching and learning in the company of remarkably diverse contemporary students, and to the energizing, renewing disciplines of research and creative dissemination of one's discoveries that drew one into this work in the first place.

Building Consensus and Negotiating Conflict

Jack L. Seymour

The last curriculum revision was so painful that I don't want to face that again.

There is a group — a powerful group — in the trustees who do not understand what we are doing. They want to totally redirect our mission.

Professor King silences students. In his classes, they lose confidence. And he intimidates many of us, too.

The decisions they made about my promotion were not based on evidence; they were based on our differences. How will I ever be treated as a colleague?

Here are four obvious instances of typical conflicts that emerge in theological schools, reflecting core activities of theological education: developing curriculum, serving the church, teaching students, and building a faculty.

268

Academic deans are regularly faced with conflict and called to help colleagues and institutions fulfill their commitments to scholarship, to ministry, to the church, and to the public.

Difference is a significant dimension of most, if not all, seminaries — difference of age, theological positions, ethnicity, and perspectives on ministry. Even those seminaries that have a more uniform theological identity are filled with differences in ethnicity, church background, age, and vision. We celebrate those differences because they enrich the life of the seminary. Diversity is the character of the world. Yet conflict is inevitable as persons with differing experiences, opinions, convictions, heritages, and religious commitments seek to engage, shape, and heal a broken world — which is precisely what we are called to do!

Moreover, conflicts within denominations and among religious groups inevitably spill over into theological seminaries. Faculty members, trustees, administrators, students, and church stakeholders passionately care about their work, the church, and the faith. Those passions reflect our commitments and our willingness to work for them. In an imperfect world, where we seek for ways to honor God's creation, educate ministers who participate in the healing of creation, and empower others to know and do the faith, conflict is inevitable.

Nevertheless, we too often fear conflict. Many evaluations of seminary education ring with concerns by church leaders and laity alike that pastors do not know how to address and engage in conflict. I wonder: Is the fear of conflict or its avoidance within the seminary causing a truncation of our students' education? Instead of instilling fear, conflict can lead us to consider seriously and focus our curricular goals, evaluate our educational programs, and engage in learning-centered teaching. Frankly, conflict can be a sign of passion and renewal as the seminary seeks to effectively prepare leaders for churches that make differences in the world.

The academic dean is therefore involved in that conflict because the dean is at the center of decisions that affect faculty, curriculum, students, and in turn, the churches graduates serve. In accepting and working with the inescapable clashes of the job, the dean must consider the following:

- In a world that is divided, where hope and healing are unclear, where diverse commitments and experiences are held deeply, how do we creatively recognize, engage, and move in the midst of conflict?
- What does consensus mean when passions are held deeply, when experiences differ, and when directions are unclear?

- How do we work together to direct faithfully the work of theological education — work that indeed does matter?

Conflict — Learning from Difference

Conflict is inevitable. Both theologically and practically, conflict is evidence that we are trying to be faithful to our calling to be a seminary in a broken world. Yet conflict raises fears and anxieties. Those anxieties sometimes cause people to imagine frightening scenarios and fear that their taken-for-granted realities will be shattered. Fear generates rumors. Moreover, we all have encountered persons (including faculty members and administrators) who fight unfairly, who subvert decision making, or who raise their voices to control.[1] Too often we have seen persons hurt and divided by conflict.

Decisions can be avoided, controlled, or engaged by the ways conflict is addressed. Frankly, conflict cannot be "managed"; it must be respected and engaged. How we learn to avoid the damage of conflict and mine its depth is an art — an art of ministry. Experience in that art suggests several principles for engaging conflict and some structures through which we can engage it to fulfill our ministries.

Conflict is inevitable, but incivility and lack of respect are not.

Considering the climate of the seminary and its institutional culture is crucial. Faculties develop "rules" — sometimes spoken, often unspoken — about how they relate to each other and to decision making. The dean, with other administrators, needs to deal specifically with the institutional culture. If wholesome patterns of engagement are not present, the culture itself must be addressed. A long-time faculty colleague reminded me that the characteristics of respect are passion, openness, a sense of humor, collaboration, vulnerability, and maturity. I think he is correct.

If a culture of respect and engagement is not present, the first agenda is to address that institutional culture. We often cannot do this by ourselves, because the culture is itself broken. Consultants trained in church or organizational dynamics can help. For example, one seminary has worked hard for the last five years to begin to address deep-seated issues of institutional rac-

---

1. For an excellent and sometimes frightening discussion of faculty incivility and intimidation, see Darla J. Twale and Barbara M. De Luca, *Faculty Incivility: The Rise of the Academic Bully Culture and What to Do About It* (San Francisco: Jossey-Bass, 2008).

ism and privilege in its culture. The effort has required several meetings, consultants, and truth-telling in a hope-filled environment. It has also required vigilance to continue advances.

Second, faculties can explicitly define procedures and expectations of how they engage each other with respect. Majority votes and "Robert's Rules" are not enough. In fact, these traditional processes can exaggerate divisions. Church bodies, drawing on their theological heritages, offer procedures for engaging the difficult issues about which we care and that matter for our futures and identities. They have not always been successful but provide illustrations for faculty members to consider. For example, as United Methodists prepared for the 2008 General Conference where conflict was expected, guidelines for "holy conferencing" were offered.[2] Similar proposals are used in other church bodies. "Agreeing and Disagreeing in Love: Commitments in Times of Disagreement" was designed for the Mennonite Church General Assembly in Wichita, Kansas, in July 1995. Earlham College publicly lists on its website its "Principles and Practices" for "Consensus Governance."[3]

Expected practices outline how people should relate to and work with each other and to engage in decision making on campus. Indeed, faculties need to clarify the procedures by which they engage together in their important and difficult work. The dean oversees this work.

Finally, we cannot be afraid of directly confronting interpersonal patterns that tear at the fabric of seminary life. Practices that silence and intimidate are as present in individuals on faculties and administrations as they are present in daily life. These practices need to be courageously and directly challenged by the dean — first informally and then, if necessary, using the formal processes of grievance and review that are part of faculty life. The failure to do so results in divided and broken seminaries.

Clarify and enhance decision-making structures.

Who is to make a specific decision? Who is affected by the decision? Often we seem to be confused about which seminary governing group has responsibility for which issues. Because of the small size of many seminaries and because of our good efforts to work at mutuality among faculty, administrators, and trustees, sometimes we lose clarity about who is to make a decision. We violate boundaries and confuse roles. Conflict ensues.

2. See "'Holy Conferencing': Speaking to One Another as Christians despite Differing Views," http://gbgm-umc.org/global_news/full_article.cfm?articleid=4684.

3. www.earlham.edu. Check section "About Earlham" and "Community Principles and Practices."

For example, seminary faculties are usually given, by faculty handbooks and often by seminary bylaws, the responsibility for curriculum and the primary responsibility for review and hiring of faculty colleagues. While trustees, administrators, students, and church judicatory bodies need to be consulted, the decisions are those of the faculty.

Trustees have a right to raise questions about the effectiveness of a curricular practice. That is why we take assessment seriously and make it a mutual process. But in most seminaries, trustees do not have a right to demand particular curricular requirements. In turn, faculty should have input into financial aid policies, institutional renovations, and auxiliary enterprises, but faculties usually are not responsible for these decisions.

A lack of clarity about decision-making processes causes much conflict in seminaries. The dean is in a key position to help clarify the decision-making processes and must be responsible to see that procedures are followed or revised.

Encourage sufficient time for reflection about crucial issues and decisions.
Consultation, however, is a key to constructive decision making. Stakeholders and participants have a right to be heard, and decisions are better when they have a wide hearing. In contrast, proposals are too often brought to faculties or trustees with insufficient input or before full development.

Here the work of the dean is critical. For example, part of every faculty meeting can be focused on simply discussing the dimensions of important issues facing the school. Such time should include intentional theological reflection about implications for teaching and ministry. Taking this time to air and consider concerns generates options that may provide a foundation for fully-formed proposals.

Participants affected by decisions need to know their concerns and commitments have been heard. Many a faculty meeting has deteriorated into confusion, anxiety, and conflict because a proposal is only partially developed. Conflict fills the void. Confusion and anxiety themselves become sources of conflict. Feelings are generated that expand into everyday relationships.

Provide administrative support for faculty committee work and communication.
Much of the time, the dean's role is one of service. Because of interconnections with a variety of stakeholders, deans can appreciate and respond to the complexity of the seminary's commitments and effects.

One servant role of the dean is to supervise or support colleagues so that concerns receive sufficient hearing from appropriate sources in a timely fashion. One dean meets regularly with every committee chair to plan directions and to recognize interconnections. Faculty committees then can be given the direction and support to hear appropriate concerns of stakeholders and fully frame proposals. The dean needs to assist faculty colleagues in these governance functions because the faculty vocation is to teach and to research, not to govern. Leadership means keeping schedules, encouraging conversation, making connections, providing support, and fulfilling promises.

Moreover, another servant role is to help trustees and faculties communicate with each other. For example, misunderstanding can arise when individuals from the academy and the corporate world — two very different cultures — encounter one another. The role of a chief executive officer in a corporation, a role some trustees may play, is very different from that of a university dean or seminary president. Differences of roles and backgrounds affect the ways we understand each other's perspectives.

The academic dean is at a unique place to assist each to understand the culture of the other and to see that the faculty has sufficient input about the decisions they must make and that the concerns of the trustees are adequately heard. A president or dean who seeks to "protect" faculty colleagues is in fact doing a disservice by hiding real conflicts of commitment and style that must be addressed.

Don't take it personally, even when it is personal.

Without a doubt the dean is a "role" as well as a person. Concerns or anger that faculty members have about the church, the trustees, etc., can be projected onto the dean. Very difficult and hurtful things may be said as anxieties are shared and decisions made. A dean must have integrity — following procedures, seeking appropriately to serve the seminary constituencies, building patterns of communication, addressing abuse and interpersonal hurts, and clarifying boundaries.

Deans who become defensive and spend their time answering rumors divert the school from its mission. Of course, when directly questioned, the dean must be clear about how a decision was made — what parties were included in the decision-making process and what procedures were followed. Also, a dean asks for forgiveness and seeks reconciliation when procedures have been broken or when practices were not fair or faithful. Yet the dean's work is for the common good and common mission of the seminary. The work of the dean is not about the dean; it is about the school and its mission for the church, its students, and the world.

Conflict is inevitable because conflict reveals our passions and our commitments. As we work together in love and respect, seeking to fulfill our mission in the world, conflict is present. Some conflicts cannot be resolved. We must find ways to continue to hear each other and "seek more light." Others conflicts indeed enhance our consideration as we seek to build communities and fulfill missions. By assisting stakeholders to hear each other, by clarifying procedures, by addressing abuse and inappropriate actions, and by providing support, a dean can assist a faculty to hear conflicts, engage them, and build common projects for their common ministry.

Consensus — Engaging in a Common Project and Vocation

Consensus does not mean seeing alike and moving in the same direction. Rather, consensus has a much more dynamic meaning of engaging together around a common project or a common mission. To help us understand consensus, a parallel image is that of a community organization working on a neighborhood project. The people may be very different and may hold very different commitments, yet for the good of the neighborhood develop a coalition to engage in a common project. Difference remains, as do conflicting commitments, but consensus is the common work — the decision to seek together to fulfill the common purpose of theological education. The dean will help to build consensus by assisting colleagues to pursue three major strategies:

Develop ways to reflect on, clarify, and empower the seminary's core purpose and long-range plan.
Our theological seminaries serve diverse constituencies and have differing commitments that shape their curricula.[4] Some are focused on particular denominations; others are ecumenical. Some do a better job preparing persons for urban ministries; others are more effective for emerging ministries. Some reach out more to provide education for people of God in congregations; some are more focused on preparing scholars for the church. The

---

4. See Jack L. Seymour, "Curriculum Metaphors and Practices: Understanding the Master of Divinity Curriculum," in *ATS Folio: Master of Divinity Curriculum Revision,* ed. William Myers (Pittsburgh: Association of Theological Schools, 2006), pp. 45-54.

standards of the Association of Theological Schools encourage seminaries to be clear about their various missions and work to assess how faithfully they fulfill those missions.

When moving from one seminary to another, common activities of teaching, research, and service are recognized. Nevertheless, the differences are apparent — the constituencies are different, students reflect different contexts, and faculty time is used differently. These differences are due to the location of each seminary, its stated mission, and its institutional culture.

While the mission statement of a seminary is set by its board of trustees, that statement is set in consultation with the stakeholders of the seminary and its faculty. The mission statement and long-range plan are theological statements about the nature of ministry, the church, and the seminary's identity and vocation. They are often discussed in and guide the work of the administration.

Yet the faculty is in a unique place to assist the trustees, administration, and church to reflect theologically on the nature of the seminary and its mission. Therefore, a primary task of the academic dean is assisting the faculty to reflect on and empower the seminary's core mission and assess its faithfulness to that mission.

Faculties can assist their churches and the wider culture to understand the dynamics affecting religion; how theological traditions and emphases are being expressed, understood, and embodied; and how the church, its ministry, and the seminary can be faithful to the call of God in today's context. Too often today, church judicatories do not have adequate resources or structures for research and theological reflection. A vocation of the seminary is to speak directly to the church, to denominational affiliations, and to the culture. This is mutual work — work across seminaries; with churches, trustees, and clergy; and with the people of God in other faith communities. A task of the dean is to encourage research for the purpose of the church, to seek to build mutuality among faculty interests, and to enable this research to affect the seminary itself.

What is the core purpose of the seminary? How does it provide a focus for the work of the seminary? Is it dynamic, reflecting faithfully the vocation of the seminary? These are the questions that the faculty needs to regularly address, that are shared in major conferences sponsored by the seminary, and that fuel conversations among faculty, administration, and trustees. The dean stimulates conversation about these questions. As faculty members consider the mission and explore the results of student learning assessment, they are building a common project and vocation.

Support faculty to connect their work and commitments to the agenda of the seminary.

Faculty workload is often defined by number of courses each faculty member teaches. Yet while teaching is at the center of faculty vocation, faculty work consists of far more: of advising and mentoring, of serving the church and the community, of academic guild responsibilities, of research and writing, and of seminary service. Often we simply list all of these tasks without adequately reflecting on or empowering them and without adequately understanding a faculty member's full contribution to the expansive life of the seminary.

A dean's task in both support and evaluation is to assist colleagues in defining how their workloads indeed live out both their own commitments and those of the institution. Recent studies of higher education and of clergy education focus on the importance of education as empowering practical reasoning or "shaping the life of the mind for practice."[5] In clergy education, this activity is called pastoral imagination. Yet how does the dean, through the processes of evaluation, help faculty members think critically about the tasks they engage in their vocations and identify their individual contributions — to embody practical wisdom?

I am convinced that it is necessary to move beyond conceiving faculty workload in terms of courses taught in a given year and to look more comprehensively at all of what faculty are expected to contribute as theological educators. It may be more helpful to explore ways of looking at faculty workload that span two to three years in order to better clarify and balance the activities of teaching, research, service to the seminary, and service to the church that individual faculty colleagues strive to fulfill — with some activities taking greater time than others in any given year. In such a way, the commitments of faculty members are supported and the common work of the faculty is encouraged.

A new study of doctoral education has argued that "creating intellectual *community*" is the best way of educating new scholars for the university.[6] The old patterns of individual work and apprenticeships seem not the

---

5. William M. Sullivan and Matthew S. Rosin, *A New Agenda for Higher Education: Shaping a Life of the Mind for Practice* (San Francisco: Jossey-Bass, 2008). Charles Foster, Lisa Dahill, Larry Golemon, and Barbara Wang Tolentino, *Educating Clergy: Teaching Practices and Pastoral Imagination* (San Francisco: Jossey-Bass, 2005).

6. Italics are the author's. George Walker, Chris M. Golde, Laura Jones, Andrea Conklin Bueschel, and Pat Hutchings, *The Formation of Scholars: Rethinking Doctoral Education for the Twenty-First Century* (San Francisco: Jossey-Bass, 2008).

best means of generating ideas, taking risks, and serving the common good. Most faculty members were trained in the lone scholar or lone teacher mold, yet find themselves on faculties that function as communities. A key task of the dean (and it is a key practice of consensus) is to work at the agenda of sharing the workload across the intellectual community of the faculty.

Work for processes of promotion, review, teaching, and community that nurture faculty development.

Surprisingly, a few years ago, a university provost told me that he was delighted that his university tenure review committee was focused on excellence; only 40 percent of those recommended by departmental action for tenure were in fact tenured. Why was he so proud? Do his comments reflect a commitment to excellence or rather a "fraternity hazing practice"? Of course, my rhetoric reveals my answer. I do believe that Darla Twale and Barbara De Luca are correct when they analyze *faculty incivility* and locate it in the culture of the academy.

Several deans have decried the fact that some faculty members seem to operate for their own interest — focusing more on what will get them the next job instead of how to fulfill the present one. Why? I am afraid that some of the key practices of the academy build distrust instead of community. If persons are not clear that support for their contributions and development is present, they will indeed be focused on the next job. Faculty members have as much need as anyone else for security and community.

Support focuses on the faculty vocation. The appropriate question, in a ministerial vocation such as seminary teaching, is how we together are serving God to the best of our abilities and how we are growing together in faithfulness.

Consensus is built as we serve together and find support and community in our common work. This will not happen in an environment of suspicion and division. Of course, faculty members who engage in inappropriate activities and/or intimidation or incivility must be directly challenged. There is no excuse for permitting behaviors that tear down and destroy colleagues and students. Fortunately, this kind of abusive behavior is not the norm. Faculty members do care for the students they teach, promote the ministry of the church, contribute to seminary life, and share in a common and enriching community of scholars. They are responsible, mutual, and faithful. Their faculty vocations need to be nurtured in an atmosphere of trust and purpose.

Therefore, it is the responsibility of the dean to help administrators and trustees understand what it means to nurture and support colleagues for excellence and community. We respond much better to nurture rather than suspicion. Financial support for attendance at conferences and for research is an example. Such support can encourage intellectual interests and the communities of academic discourse. And this support should be offered openly, rather than with the suspicious you-can-attend-only-if-you-present-a-paper-attitude that results in make-up scholarship. To support the teaching of faculty colleagues, excellent programs like those run by the Wabash Center for Teaching and Learning in Theology and Religion are available. Furthermore, regular faculty conversations — about syllabi, about scholarship, about teaching, and about the commitments of the seminary — will help to build community.

An apparent paradox many of us have seen is that faculty members in institutions struggling with financial crisis are often more committed to the institution and its mission than are faculty members at stronger and wealthier schools. The fact is that those who share in a crisis together often work together to address it. In such a way, they clarify the vocation of the seminary and their work in its midst. They are willing to endure hardship for the good of the community. Institutions do not need such crises to build community; instead, processes of support, nurture, and growth can be built into the very fabric of a school.

Characteristics of the Dean

The dean can enhance the structures of the seminary to negotiate conflict and build consensus. Nevertheless, the character and practices of the dean profoundly affect how conflict is addressed and consensus nurtured through several key commitments and practices:

- As a colleague and as a leader, the dean understands and appreciates the mission of the seminary, communicates the deep values at the heart of the institution, and models working to seek its growing faithfulness.
- The dean cares for and interprets the constituencies of the seminary and is motivated by a desire to serve them and enhance their education.
- The dean works with colleagues to assess the contributions and effectiveness of the seminary and seeks to enhance its faithfulness.

- The dean is truthful about the realities facing the seminary, is open, and is willing to say no when necessary.
- The dean has the courage to challenge those who would intimidate colleagues.
- The dean is proud of the contributions of the school community of scholars, teachers, and ministers, communicating their contributions and seeking support for their nurture.

Conflict is an inevitable part of seminary life, yet it can lead to open discussion of a variety of perspectives that affect the seminary's mission and faithfulness. Conflict engaged in mutual and respectful ways can build consensus as persons come together to work on the common — and worthwhile — enterprise of theological education.

11. Building the Academic Budget

The Budget as a Mission Tool:
Vision, Principles, and Strategies

Robin J. Steinke

A Guiding Vision and Principles

There may be few issues in the life of the chief academic officer that create more anxiety than the work of putting together a budget. This work, undertaken alongside the CEO, CFO, and other senior colleagues, can be onerous and complicated, particularly in the early years of an academic dean's tenure. The budget process includes concepts, terms, and practices that are foreign for some. With the steep learning curve surrounding so much in the work of a CAO, the budget process can be one more daunting task for which a PhD in a theological discipline is inadequate preparation.

A frame of reference I have found helpful is to think first of how the resources available in the instruction budget can support the *total* mission of the school, to participate in budget building with a vision of the whole rather than looking solely at the part of the budget for which I have primary responsibility. This requires a broader context for budgeting than simply replicating the budget from the previous year and arguing for modest increases or viewing the budget as a cluster of silos, of which the instructional budget is the part the dean oversees. This holistic approach can mitigate the tendency for the CAO to be viewed as either Santa Claus, with the power to fund key faculty initiatives, or Scrooge, with the power to deny even the most basic instructional requests.

In the economic environment of the last couple of years, where at almost every turn our institutions are being called upon to "do more with less," trying to figure out where the "soft" places are in the budget, places where there may be some flexibility, is challenging. If the CAO, along with others in senior leadership, can work together to bring wisdom, discipline, creativity, and perhaps even some joy to the task, guided by a sense of the privilege and opportunity of creating a budget that reflects institutional mission, the institution is well served. (Yes, I used the words *joy* and *budget* in the same sentence!)

I came to this task of building the budget with a sense that both the budget process itself and its implementation are ways to enact the mission and outcomes the institution has identified and prioritized. Perhaps my previous vocation as a financial planner helped me to see the interrelatedness of all aspects of institutional mission and the spending plan or budget, and instilled the sense that the process of preparing a budget can be almost as important as the budget itself.

Understanding one's role as CAO in the budget-building process can help avoid the pitfall of simply "negotiating" for specific items like faculty salaries, sabbatical funding, and other instructional funds over against staff salaries, maintenance needs, or new projects. If one understands the work of the CAO as being "positioned at the center" of institutional life,[1] then the set of questions that are informative for budget-building asks how accurately the budget reflects the mission and goals of the whole institution rather than seeking a way to garner a bigger piece of a finite pie for "my area."

The time required initially for becoming conversant with the particular nomenclature and processes at any given school around building the budget can be significant. In a recent survey of CAOs by the American Council on Education, participants were asked how much time is spent on budget-related matters. Twenty-four percent of CAOs said budgeting and financial management were among their three most time-consuming activities.[2] Later in this same essay the data shows that 48 percent of all those sur-

---

1. Jeanne P. McLean, *Leading from the Center: The Emerging Role of the Chief Academic Officer in Theological Schools* (Atlanta: Scholars Press, 1999), p. 38.

2. Peter D. Eckel, Bryan J. Cook, and Jacqueline E. King, "Duties and Responsibilities of CAO'S," *The CAO Census: A National Profile of Chief Academic Officers* (Washington: American Council on Education, 2009), p. 7.

veyed reported that the top frustration was "never enough money."[3] It is clear that matters of budget loom large for CAOs.

It is difficult to quantify how much time it takes, particularly if mission issues and questions are at the center of budget preparation. When mission is at the center, the CAO is always thinking about budget, priorities, trade-offs, implications, and creative possibilities for achieving the school's mission together with faculty, staff, students, the president, senior colleagues, the board, and other constituencies.

Time invested early on in the CAO's tenure can save countless hours of frustration, uncertainty, and downright fear about a process that is complex. Investing the time to demonstrate to faculty that you will be fair and transparent, to the president and other senior staff that you will be a colleague and partner in this difficult work, to student leaders that their concerns will be given a fair hearing and weighed alongside many other institutional issues, and to the board committee with which you work that "deanly wisdom" can help inform other larger institutional budget and mission issues, is time well spent.

Some principles that I hope guide my work include keeping the school's mission at the center, being mindful of the multiple and at times competing claims for diminishing resources, being both collaborative in spirit as well as clear about the role of the CAO in this process, and — not the least of these — recognizing my own finitude. At the end of the day I cannot eliminate tuition so our students can graduate debt free. I cannot raise faculty salaries so they could have time to do more research rather than needing to teach weekends to put their own kids through college. I cannot significantly raise staff salaries so that the pressure of issues around low wages is removed, and I cannot infuse the endowment with large amounts of fresh capital so that board members can spend their time thinking of creative ways to spend money in support of our mission. However, there are many things I *can* do to engage in a faithful budget process "at the center" of institutional life. These strategies pertain to learning and using the lingo, attending to longer-term budget issues, and leading colleagues to do their best work through the budget process.

Learning and Using the Lingo

Be a student of your CFO.
A pattern in some institutions is that the CAO simply receives the draft budget from the CFO and pleads for increases in some areas or reluctantly

---

3. Eckel, Cook, and King, "Duties and Responsibilities of CAO's," p. 12.

agrees to decreases in other areas. It can be helpful to become a student of your CFO early in your tenure as dean, requesting regular meetings to review detailed parts of the budget well before it is time to begin budget drafts. Deans can do a lot to honor the vocation of CFOs by respecting their expertise and by demonstrating a posture of readiness to learn from them so that informed decisions about the budget can be shared.

It had been the practice prior to my arrival for the dean to keep a one-page sheet of the expected expenditures for the next budget year that would be submitted to the CFO, who would work out where in the budget these expenses should go. The full budget draft was not readily transparent to anyone but the CFO because there was not any way to tell where those costs had been allocated and consequently no way to sort out where there was genuine flexibility in the budget. If the CFO can serve as your tutor so that you become adept at Excel spread sheets and clearly understand the way the budget is structured, you really can work as a team to think through competing claims for resources. Being a student of the CFO is one side of the coin. The other side is to serve as a teacher of the CFO and perhaps even the president.

Serve as a teacher of your CFO.

CFOs must be partners in understanding the academic missions of the schools they serve. They have likely been educated and credentialed as CPAs or controllers and bring wisdom concerning the sound operational matters of the school. CFOs may not have many insights regarding the disciplined work of the faculty and may sometimes even begrudge this group of "employees" who don't keep very regular hours, are away for long periods of time in the summer, and only have a few hours a week actually in front of a class. Taking some regular time to help the CFO catch a vision for the complex work of faculty, including being transparent in reports to the board concerning the integral link between supporting faculty and institutional flourishing, may help your CFO catch a glimpse of this critical aspect of the school's mission.

Study the operational budget.

Once the CAO has a clear sense of the broad categories and related costs, it can be helpful to review the key mission strategies of the school to verify alignment of costs with mission priorities. This requires consultation with key administrative and faculty work groups. This process may identify areas where the budget allocation or institutional policies are not in alignment with mission priorities. For example, several years ago at my school there was a desire to increase the capacity of our faculty to teach online courses.

However, we had a longstanding practice of requiring a "co-pay" for faculty development funds, and these funds could not be used for anything but attending a professional meeting. This meant that a faculty member who wanted to attend a workshop needed to pay for 20 percent of the cost personally. If that faculty member wanted to use funds for the purchase of some digital resources, there wasn't a basis in the policy to provide for this. Not only was the "co-pay" a sore spot for the faculty, but also the narrow vision of how these funds could be used mitigated against the seminary's support of key faculty leaders who could be early adopters of new learning technology. With the support of the president and CFO and with full faculty and board consultation, we changed the policy, eliminated the co-pay, and established that these funds could also be used for other creative purposes that enhanced faculty development and supported the school's mission.

Find sustainable ways to further faculty development.

Budgeting an adequate amount for regular faculty development and sabbatical time is an area that is difficult to maintain. The institutional pressures work against regular funds for activities that appear to be not directly related to immediate instructional needs. It is not possible for the CAO alone to hold the line on maintaining these budget items. Working with trustees over time to understand the relationship between faculty flourishing and the educational enterprise is critical to cultivating wisdom with the trustees.

At my school, for example, "use it or lose it" was a counterproductive practice related to the operational budget. Perhaps many readers are familiar with the practice that, when nearing the end of the fiscal year, CAOs find ways to spend the entire budgeted amount so that in the next round of budget negotiations they can argue for modest increases on the basis that it had all been spent the year before. This can result in some very odd and, some would argue, perhaps wholly unnecessary expenses at the end of the fiscal year. It may be due to my own very frugal upbringing or perhaps my knowledge of some of our donors who give joyfully and are living on very limited resources that I sometimes imagine sitting with benefactors describing how the seminary has been a faithful steward of their benevolence. I imagine talking with our students, some of whom are taking on enormous debt to be at our school, and describing how the seminary has used their resources. I have not found the practice of spending out at fiscal year-end to be a helpful practice. In this time of fiscal restraint and reworking of institutional mission, I am even less inclined to engage in this kind of spending. Thus, finding ways to sustain faculty development amid challenging fiscal times in my context meant advocating for policies that allow for carryover (e.g., by establishing restricted funds for faculty development) as a way of stewarding resources that eliminates any need for a year-end "spend or lose it" mentality and assists faculty to achieve professional goals that in turn benefit the seminary.

Understand what depreciation is and why it is important.

Depreciation is an accounting tool that takes the cost of a major expense and spreads it out over a specified period of years. The expense is allocated each year so that an institution takes into account the total funds needed to operate the school, assuming that major assets will need to be repaired and/or replaced over time. During a short-term financial crunch, many institutions do not fully fund depreciation and get into difficulty with deferred maintenance. To fully fund depreciation means that unless the budget is balanced *including* depreciation, which means that the *total cost* of running the school is included, there may be major unfunded capital expenses down the road.

Some CFOs may talk about review of the operational budget and claim that there is a balanced budget before depreciation is taken into account. The usual reason is that depreciation is a non-cash expense but the expense is being stretched out over time. The CAO needs to be fully aware that the *total* budget needs to be balanced; otherwise it could adversely affect the instructional budget and consequently impair the flourishing of the mission of the school.

In the instructional budget, this surfaces in critical areas like instructional technology. Many schools have funded upgrades in computer hardware and software with grants. When those computers wear out, if depreciation has not been fully funded, there can quickly be an urgent need for major cash outlays just to maintain the vitality of the instructional program. Integrating learning technology costs into both the operational and capital budget can be critical for long-term sustainability.

It is possible to stretch the budget from time to time by not factoring in depreciation, and many schools have done that during times of economic crisis, but it is not a sustainable strategy. The CAO plays a critical role in asking these kinds of questions of the CFO and the president, because if depreciation is left untended, there may be significant negative consequences for the educational enterprise.

Take into account the capital budget.

The capital budget is an additional budget prepared alongside the operational budget. This is the budget that deals with major lump sum expenses, for which many institutions establish a threshold amount, e.g., $10,000. The CAO may want to keep in mind any needed upgrades in faculty office furniture, classrooms, or common space that facilitates better teaching and learning. These expenses can easily be overlooked because these costs typically do not appear in the operational budget yet can have a significant impact on teaching and learning.

Learning technology, including faculty development resources to fund ever-expanding mission expectations from a wider range of constituencies, is a costly reality in today's academic environment. Some learning technology will appear in the capital budget, e.g., major upgrades in equipment or some software upgrades. Other aspects of learning technology may appear in the operational budget, such as expense for an instructional technologist.

A significant capital expense is the library acquisition budget, normally books and periodicals. In a time of economic uncertainty, this is a very vulnerable capital item. Some may argue that since there are so many online resources now, we may not really need to have a big building with all those books and periodicals. This is where integrating the mission of the school with capital and operational expense is critical. The CAO is called upon to make a sensible case that strengthening the library enhances the lifeblood of a school; that case must be rooted in the school's own mission. It is insufficient to simply assert that we need to keep buying books and periodicals; this argument must demonstrate that the school's mission is integrally tied to the strength of its library.

Be conversant about the endowment draw rate.

It can be easy to think of the endowment like the handful of meal in a jar and a little bit of oil in a jug of the widow of Zarephath in 1 Kings 17:8ff. It never runs out and is available every time the cupboard is opened. Economic crisis, however, can remind us that endowment draw rates *do* matter and less is better. Most of our schools do not have an endless supply of donors who fill the coffers and make up for overextending the draw rate.

I have found it invaluable to be aware of and able to enter into conversations about the draw rates and the financial vitality of the institution. It helps me in my work with the board committee responsible for academic oversight. It helps me lay important groundwork in anticipation of future needs. It helps all of the senior staff be accountable to one another and keep our collective focus on the mission. It also stands an institution in good stead vis-à-vis standards and guidelines established by our accreditation bodies relative to endowment utilization.

Exercise leadership with restricted accounts.

Restricted accounts are those funds that have some kind of donor limits on how they can be used. Not all restricted accounts are created equal. Some are replenished, and others are simply spent, then disappear. I serve an institution that has been around for 184 years, so a multitude of accounts are restricted for use around specific purposes, some that are part of the endowment and some that are one-time gifts. It is worth the time to sort out with your CFO which of those accounts are related to areas over which you have direct oversight. Collaboration with the advancement staff can help in coaching the faculty or other staff who relate to areas that have some donor-restricted funds. Honoring the wishes of the donor is paramount. Sometimes the original purpose is not entirely clear. The CAO may help interpret how those funds can best honor the explicit and implicit wishes of the donor and serve the mission of the school, particularly when dealing with a fund that directly relates to faculty, students, or curriculum.

Through the hard work of our advancement staff and many conversations with me and other key faculty, we were able to get a much better handle on funds that had not been used for many years and then to employ them strategically. One of the examples of this process occurred with the seminary's special events and lifelong learning faculty committee. It had been the practice that "special requests" for use of restricted funds were made directly to the CFO. The first step was to move those decisions to my office so I could help the faculty colleagues responsible for those areas use the funds creatively and still be consistent with the donor's intent. Following a couple years of this, once I became very comfortable with the diversity and scope of these funds, the CFO and I, along with some key staff, worked with faculty members responsible for oversight on this committee to understand these funds and use them appropriately for specific annual budgeted events. This allowed us to move money from restricted accounts to offset current expenses.

The additional benefit of this process is that it brought new life to the special events and lifelong learning committee because now committee members actually had some control over how best to use these funds in support of the outcomes for continuing education. It has also been a significant benefit to me because now there are some faculty colleagues who can join in the discernment about how this part of our mission can be funded. And it has led to some time saving because now, instead of all of these decisions coming through my office, faculty members share in this discernment. They have been creative in thinking about combining some of these funds in order to bring in a high profile speaker for a major event. Finally, it has led to greater commitment on the part of faculty members to take seriously their responsibility in thinking with me on the best use of these funds.

Attending to Longer-Term Budget Issues

The work of building a budget that reflects the core values of a school's institutional mission is demanding. We often breathe a collective sigh of relief and enjoy the few months break when we finish one round of budget discussions before gearing up for the next. Yet there is another aspect of building the budget that requires a more long-term approach and invites the CAO to anticipate longer-term consequences of short-term budget priorities.

For example, several years ago we received notice that the outside grantor who had funded our faculty sabbaticals for many years would stop that funding in the near future. The president immediately intervened, which resulted in a delay of the change for one academic year. This delay bought me some time to work with the faculty and board to begin laying the groundwork for fuller direct support of sabbaticals.

I sensed the devastating impact that losing sabbatical funding could have on both the kind of research faculty could undertake on their sabbaticals and their ability to travel during this period of extended research. It was also clear that this loss of funding would work at cross-purposes with our institutional commitment to global issues. In close collaboration with the president, we worked with the faculty in their pre- and post-sabbatical reports to the board to include specific references to how their research was strengthened by being able to travel to specific areas around the globe and work in archives of distant places, as well as how the funding directly resulted in a stronger publication. In essence we built a case over time so that when the funding finally ended, the board included a new line item in the budget to replace it. This process served two purposes: it educated the board on how this money was used and it helped the faculty demonstrate accountability by quantifying exactly how this money supported their work with clear evidence of outcomes.

Leading Colleagues to Do Their Best Work

Lead faculty in thoughtful participation around the budget.
It can be a challenge to invite faculty colleagues to think with you about budget issues. A key indicator is when you put "budget matters" as a faculty

agenda item and then observe the glazed eyes and other "multitasking" activities that occur during faculty meetings at moments of disinterest. When the time comes for making budget cuts, then the lobbying will begin. A challenge for the CAO is to find the creative space for conversation that does not degrade into mind-numbing talk about budget details but rather promotes thoughtful faculty engagement with these issues central to the flourishing of institutional life.

I remember at a faculty meeting distributing a forty-plus page of detailed budget information and inviting any suggestions or ideas for reductions in expenses. This approach only led to frustration on the part of faculty members because they had not been given the information in a way that could be thoughtfully discussed. The faculty had not been part of a process that allowed them to do their best work. Ironically, senior administrative colleagues felt good about being transparent, while the faculty adjourned thinking there were things hidden in this detailed document that they were left to sort out without the tools to do so. The silence of the faculty was received by senior administrators as implied affirmation of the budget as well as the process, when in fact it reflected frustration that the faculty as a deliberative body did not have a constructive way to enter the process that invited them to do their best thinking *as a faculty*.

The next year we adopted an alternative approach, which has helped enormously in setting the stage so that the faculty can do its best work as a deliberative body with responsibilities in shared governance. The president and I, along with senior faculty leaders, try to raise issues around the mission and budget projections, selecting a few major issues that get at the heart of key budget decisions. We invite conversation in structured faculty meeting time to think about the current reality, what we think it should be in the future, and the major issues getting in the way of the desired future.[4] For example, as we approached a recent retirement of a long-serving faculty member, we spent considerable time thinking about the role of contextual education in our curriculum. That was a very different kind of conversation from that which would have ensued if we had distributed the budget forecasts and asked, "Where do we cut?" The result was a careful, two-year plan

4. This is a process introduced to our school by a board member and the president. The process identifies the current reality and the future imagined state and then teases out the dominant tensions or things that are blocking us now that need to be addressed in order to get to the future imagined state. It is based loosely on the work of Jim Collins, *Good to Great: Why Some Companies Make the Leap . . . and Others Don't* (New York: HarperCollins, 2001).

for covering the areas taught by the retiring colleague, which gave the faculty time to think creatively about long-term possibilities.

The strategy of framing budget questions around mission and thinking about that mission in terms that provide the faculty the deliberative time to think creatively can be helpful in sharing the wisdom of the faculty in difficult budget issues. With our faculty, as well as trustees, we have also found it helpful to accompany pages full of numbers with a "budget narrative" that highlights key assumptions and identifies areas where decisions can and must be made.

Work with the advancement staff.

There is another group of colleagues with whom the CAO needs to be in creative conversation on a regular basis. The advancement or development staff plays a large role in helping to sustain the future of the school. If the CAO is in close conversation with advancement colleagues, then many creative possibilities may emerge that can further strengthen the mission of the school. If regular conversation does not happen, then it is possible that two critical parts of the institution will be working at cross-purposes.

On one occasion, I discovered just how difficult things become when regular conversation does not happen. I left for an eight-month sabbatical near the end of my first term as dean and returned to discover that our very hard-working advancement staff had cultivated a generous and well-meaning donor to provide a significant cash gift to fund a specific course that happened to be offered as an elective about every fourth year. By the time I got involved, I learned that one of the donor's provisions was that all students would need to be required to take this course in order for us to receive the major gift. I learned that my task was to get the faculty to put this course in the curriculum so the gift could be received. My initial reaction was to begin counting the days until my next sabbatical. Because of my long absence I was unavailable to be part of the early conversations with the advancement team. This is a classic example of how easy it is for advancement work to get ahead of the academic mission of the school. It is far more difficult to redirect a donor once things get to this stage than it would have been if conversation had occurred early on with colleagues in advancement about this kind of possibility.

Endowed chairs offer another opportunity for collegial work with the advancement staff. The process for establishing, raising money, selecting, and inducting a faculty member into an endowed chair can also play a critical role in the life of the faculty and the mission of the school. Many of us have "chairs" that were never fully funded yet carry with them the expectation that a full-time faculty member will serve in that field of study in perpetuity. Some institutions have also had to field initiatives from well-meaning donors whose passions simply do not align with institutional mission and curricular emphases.

Finally, the advancement staff can be invaluable in helping CAOs to assist students and faculty to resource mission needs which require grants. There are, thankfully, a number of organizations that support theological education. Some are geared for students, such as the Fund for Theological Education; others aim to strengthen teaching and learning, such as the Wabash Center for Teaching and Learning; others support faculty research, such as the grants programs of the Association of Theological Schools and the Louisville Institute; and still others are geared to major institutional initiatives, such as Lilly Endowment Inc. and the Teagle Foundation. For major institutional grants it is important to think about how projects might be continued after the grant money is gone. This is a mission question, not simply a budget question. It may be that some "request for proposals" (RFPs) should simply be ignored because they do not cohere with the mission of the school or with the range of priorities currently facing a school. If the decision is that the RFP is consistent with the mission, then careful attention to the application, oversight of the grant, implementation, staffing, and follow-up reports can be strengthened with the wisdom of the advancement colleagues.

Work with the president and board to lay the groundwork so that budget priorities reflect mission priorities.

It may be easy for CAOs to disengage from the difficult budget issues that face theological schools, but such disengagement will not spare them from having to face the consequences of institutional cuts that may appear to be "painless" but in fact have long-term institutional consequences. There are areas of the budget, particularly in times of fiscal uncertainty, that are very vulnerable to so-called "painless" cuts. The library is first on the list, quickly followed by cutting faculty research funds, globalization funds, and faculty sabbatical funds; leaving faculty positions vacant; and increasing student fees and tuition. CAOs who are positioned "at the center" can bring perspectives and wisdom, as well as convening other key groups to share the wisdom, so that the best thinking of all involved will have both the opportunity and capacity to re-imagine this project we call theological education. In the current economic environment, sadly, some schools' leaders must wrestle with the bottom-line budget related question, "Can we go on?"

Exercise budget accountability as a team: from a discouraging problem, a renewed possibility.

What happens when the wheels fall off of a school's best and thoughtful planning around the budget? What happens when an endowment-driven school suffers a dramatic drop in the value of the endowment resulting in a dramatic income drop? What happens when a tuition-driven school has a sudden drop in admissions? What are the institutional mechanisms in place to deal with these exigencies? In some schools the president and the CFO decree across-the-board cuts in all areas. Another option that has been used is to cancel all non-essential institutional travel. Yet another possibility is to cut faculty development funds. These are all viable and often successful measures.

Given what we all have experienced in the financial markets, it might be time for us all to have clear institutional mechanisms for making urgent cuts in current spending that attempt to draw together wisdom from key constituencies. Often it is up to the CFO along with president to make such decisions. In our school we are implementing a board-led committee that includes key senior administrators and faculty who will think together about creative ways to live within our means when exigencies arise. Since we use a three-year rolling average on our endowment draw, we are in the process of adjusting to the full consequences of the economic meltdown that surfaced in 2008. I hope that, by cultivating the wisdom of more of our key constituents, we may find solutions to these perennial issues of finding a long-term sustainable path forward for theological education that deepens our collective creativity and opens new possibilities for imagining our common future.

Budget Building as a Practice of Community

Building the budget can be a demanding yet creative and even joyful way to enact the mission of the school. I have argued for fuller faculty involvement and greater collaboration with senior administration, including the advancement team as well as the president and the board. This approach may be resisted in some places. Faculty colleagues may feel that the reason they elected you dean was so that they did not have to deal with such matters. The CFO and president may feel that it is their responsibility within the school to handle these matters.

The current economic realities of our schools do not afford us the luxury of keeping these deliberations and decisions to ourselves. Perhaps it is a hidden gift in this time of economic uncertainty that we find creative ways to draw upon the best thinking of our faculty, staff, students, and board members, coming together in order to do the hard work ahead in re-imagining our institutional mission and the structures that enliven that mission.

ADDITIONAL RESOURCES

Ford, David F. *The Shape of Living: Spiritual Directions for Everyday Life.* Grand Rapids: Baker, 1997.

Entering Unfamiliar Territory: Budget Basics for the Dean of a University Theological School

Tite Tiénou

The chief academic officer of a theological school is an academic leader who has leadership responsibilities that include setting a vision and implementing it as well as managing a variety of resources. Academic leaders can foster hope and confidence through the prudent and careful management of resources. Since money is a key element of the resources necessary for institutional life — both in theological education and in higher education in general — dealing with budgets becomes a significant aspect of academic administration. In her study of deanship in theological schools, *Leading from the Center: The Emerging Role of the Chief Academic Officer in Theological Schools,* Jeanne P. McLean notes the findings of a 1993 survey of deans of theological schools in which 82 percent of the deans interviewed stated that they have "primary administrative responsibility for academic budgets."[1] In light of this, building the academic budget and managing it are very important elements of the competencies required in a successful deanship. Yet the nature of theological schools and the path to deanship in them seem to indi-

---

1. Jeanne P. McLean, *Leading from the Center: The Emerging Role of the Chief Academic Officer in Theological Schools* (Atlanta: Scholars Press, 1999), p. 28.

cate that matters related to money and budgets may be challenges for many deans, especially those appointed to their positions from faculty ranks.

William G. Enright has observed that "[m]ost clergy" and "[m]ost faculty appear to see [the] topics [of money] as beyond their interest or beneath them."[2] Consequently, for deans who may be clergy or faculty, or both, the idea of being in charge of the academic budget can be daunting or frightening.[3] While this discussion includes attention to budget issues that arise for most deans, it is particularly focused on the role of the dean in a university theological or divinity school located within a university system. Deans in this context sit at the budgeting table with the deans of other schools within the university and, in that position, must learn not only the budget considerations that their own schools face, but also how to manage their own schools' budgets within a larger educational enterprise.

Beginning with Budget Basics

Whether new or experienced, a dean will often find it helpful to start with budget basics. This review of budget basics will focus on two in particular: the purpose of a budget and the types of budget.

A budget is, of course, a financial document that expresses an institution's life in terms of dollars and cents. But it is much more than that. In the words of David F. Bright and Mary P. Richards, "a budget is a planning document,"[4] and as Margaret F. Barr notes, it is "the primary means for the institutional administration to convey to the governing board the real priorities of the institution."[5] As such, the budget plays a crucial role in all dimensions of institutional life and, because of that, merits the careful attention of all academic administrators, especially the chief academic officer. Taking seriously the words of these three authors can help deans invest significant intel-

---

2. William G. Enright, "The altered landscape of religious giving," *Colloquy,* vol. 16, no. 2 (Spring 2008): 21-22. This publication of the Association of Theological Schools in the United States and Canada is also available at the ATS website: www.ats.edu.

3. Given the nature of theological schools, it is reasonable to think that most deans of ATS accredited schools would be clergy or faculty, or both. I did not engage in an investigation of this matter for this essay.

4. David F. Bright and Mary P. Richards, *The Academic Deanship* (San Francisco: Jossey-Bass, 2001), p. 136.

5. Margaret J. Barr, *The Jossey-Bass Academic Administrator's Guide to Budgets and Financial Management* (San Francisco: Jossey-Bass, 2002), p. 34.

lectual energy in the processes required for oversight of the academic budget in the wider context of the leadership of the theological school.

As deans attend to the academic budget, they do well to remember that an "institutional budget reflects the plans, priorities, goals, and aspirations that drive the institution. The budget is a blueprint of what is important."[6] Remembering this will help the dean frame the questions to be asked in budget meetings and is essential for building and managing the academic budget because it should undergird all conversations relative to budget review and requests as well as negotiations with other senior administrators.

In addition to the purpose of a budget in the institutional life, deans must keep in mind the relationship of the academic budget to the various types of budgets in their schools. These are the three types of budget commonly used in schools: the operating budget, the capital budget, and the auxiliary budget.

The operating budget is the total amount of income and expenses for all areas of a given institution for a fiscal year. In a theological school, as in other academic institutions, most of the expenses incurred are related to personnel. Since a theological school's primary mission is education, expenses associated with faculty compensation (salaries and benefits) and other instructional costs represent a significant percentage of the operating budget. The capital budget has to do with the school's plan for expenditures for fixed assets such as equipment and facilities. The auxiliary budget has to do with a school's non-instructional support services, such as dining, bookstore, and parking facilities.

The academic budget is normally part of the operating budget, and it has to be proposed by the dean and managed in that context. Chief academic officers do not usually have oversight of capital or auxiliary budgets, though they normally have a voice in determining capital and auxiliary budgets in consultation with other members of the school's executive leadership. Deans therefore need good general familiarity with capital and auxiliary budgets, but it is essential to have a thorough understanding of the operating budget.

As they attend to their responsibility of providing oversight to the academic budget, deans will find budget basics, such as the two reviewed here briefly, useful. They will also find that consulting the best practices contained in good budget books or online resources constitutes a strategic investment of their professional development energy, time, and money. It should be kept in mind that all generalities about budgets, even the best

6. Barr, *Jossey-Bass Academic Administrator's Guide*, p. 30.

ones, need to be tested in specific institutional contexts. Ultimately, contextual history and factors determine, to a large extent, the nature, methods, and processes involved in building the academic budget and its management. Every individual with responsibility for an aspect of an institution's budget should demonstrate thorough familiarity with contextual reality.

Institutional Context of the Academic Budget

Understanding the institutional context of the academic budget can help deans acquire competence in the oversight responsibilities required of them. This is an especially critical task for deans of theological or divinity schools located in a university context, where understanding the institutional context of the academic budget is rendered more complex because the theological school is a school among schools within the larger university. The university dean must understand not only the culture of the theological school, but the web of interests and histories that other schools, as well as the university president and CFO, are bringing to the budgeting table.

The quest for understanding begins with the recognition that budget realities in all institutions of higher education are influenced by particular factors and histories. The budget model used in the institution, as well as the decision-making process employed for budget approval and monitoring, is representative of realities rooted in institutional history. Deans should therefore make every effort to know that history and remain constantly attuned to how the current leadership of the institution understands it, thus ensuring that all their thinking and decisions regarding the academic budget are informed by a realistic understanding of context.

While all deans need constant awareness to their institution's context for success in fiscal management, new deans should resolve to acquire the understanding of context rather quickly. During the first one hundred days in office, deans who are new to the school or to the role of budget manager in the school should devote considerable energy to understanding the institutional culture relative to budget matters. Knowing the school's budget culture, or what Barr calls "understanding what you inherited," requires "that new budget managers understand what mores regarding the budget and financial management were formerly part of the organization."[7] This understanding will be achieved through reading numerous files and documents;

7. Barr, *Jossey-Bass Academic Administrator's Guide,* pp. 80, 78-79.

asking countless questions of various persons familiar with the financial situation of the institution; and formal and informal conversations with the president, chief financial officer, the development officer (if the school has one), and other senior administrators. In the course of time, deans will realize the value of the time and effort spent on this matter as institutional budgetary and financial policies and procedures become less nebulous as they gain the respect of the other senior administrators of the school. They will find that the respect of these other senior administrative colleagues is essential for credibility and success in building and managing the academic budget.

The budget cycle is an example of how understanding a school's budgetary culture is essential. According to Margaret J. Barr, "[e]ach fiscal year budget has eight distinct phases,"[8] though they may not be so clearly delineated in a given school or institution. A theological school may not have published documents for all aspects of budget work, but it does have a tradition, culture, and practices pertaining to budget. The school's tradition, culture, and practices determine the articulation of the budget phases and their implementation. Consequently, developing a budget cannot be done by simply recycling the previous year's budget or applying sound guidelines secured through careful research and study. Rather, budget work is accomplished through the skillful combination of technical expertise and patient negotiation with full awareness of contextual factors. This skillful combination is the essence of the art of budget work; it rests on principles that deans can use for guidance in building and managing the academic budget.

Principles for Building and Managing the Academic Budget

The Necessity of Technical Expertise

Since technical expertise is necessary for success in budget work, deans of theological schools in a university context must acquire it either personally or by appointing a budget director. Unless the dean has come to the deanship already trained in budget and fiscal management or wants to spend ex-

---

8. Barr, *Jossey-Bass Academic Administrator's Guide*, p. 49. Here are the eight phases: "setting institutional and unit budget guidelines, developing the unit budget request, identifying the budget implications beyond the fiscal year in question, approving the budget, monitoring the budget performance, adjusting the current operating budget, closing the fiscal year and analyzing the results" (pp. 49-50).

traordinary time and energy to develop these skills personally, appointing an appropriate person for this task seems the most reasonable and prudent way to acquire technical expertise. This person, regardless of title, should have proven ability in budget work and should be respected by the various constituencies of the school, especially the faculty.

How technical expertise is acquired will be different, depending on the situation. At Trinity, there were two associate dean positions that were already budgeted, making it possible to use one of those positions to appoint someone to serve as an administrative officer with the budgeting expertise needed to position the divinity school as a strong partner in budgeting processes. In fact, the divinity school has been praised by the Trinity International University's CFO for exhibiting the best budget management in the university.

Budget management need not be a person's only responsibility in the school. In fact it helps if the budget director has other responsibilities which require the kind of close collaboration with the dean where "a relationship of mutual support and confidence" is fostered.[9] Deans who are able to call a colleague to such a position should seek the following personal qualities: "reliability and a keen eye for detail," "creativity in solving puzzles," "openness," and "a disposition to share rather than hoard information and ideas."[10] A budget director who is respected in the school and who has the full confidence of the dean as well as the foregoing personal qualities, is one of the greatest assets a dean can have in matters related to budget work. Such a director, as many deans have found, becomes a key ally of the dean in strategic conversations, another principle for building and managing the academic budget.

The Need for Strategic Conversations

It has been noted that all aspects of budget work require patient listening and the ability to negotiate, essential qualities for entering into strategic conversations with other senior administrators of the school, especially the chief financial officer. Strategic conversations are the basis for seeking the help of other administrators when budget problems arise in the institution. Here, as in other areas of academic administration, "[t]he ability of senior adminis-

9. Bright and Richards, *The Academic Deanship,* pp. 130-131.
10. Bright and Richards, *The Academic Deanship,* p. 131.

trators to work together effectively is critical to the cohesiveness and well-being of their institutions."[11] In order to facilitate the kind of strategic conversations that will become useful in budget work, deans should take the initiative to get to know their senior administrative colleagues through office visits or other occasions for personal interaction. It is imperative for deans to know the other academic administrators personally, not just professionally. Deans should make sure that information relative to all strategic conversations is shared with their budget directors. Ultimately, the dean's relationships and conversations with individuals in the wider institution are essential to the tasks of solving the complex problems inherent in institutional budget work.

The Necessity of Remembering the Mission

Relating budget decisions to institutional mission is one area that requires ongoing negotiation. The dean, as chief academic officer, should ensure that the school's budget processes remember the mission. This principle is particularly important in the budget approval phase.

Deans, like other administrators, must defend "their" budgets against others. In the university setting, theological/divinity school deans sit at the budgeting table with the CAOs or other deans of the university's various schools, all championing their own academic programs. Deans will strengthen their positions if they are able to appeal to the mission of the institution as a whole when they make their case, stressing the fact that institutional success is about serving the mission and not about making or keeping jobs. Appeal to the mission, for example, is useful in requesting additional funding for the academic budget. But it is also the focus on the mission that helps the dean make recommendations about institutional academic programs. In general, the proliferation of programs should be avoided. Additional programs can divert attention away from the school's mission and tend to increase costs more than revenue. So, rather than proliferate programs, deans should seek ways to maximize flexibility as they prepare the academic budget for review and approval. Deans can use comparative data to help them establish the basis for their budget recommendations.

11. McLean, *Leading from the Center*, p. 145.

The Recourse to Comparative Data

The use of comparative data in budget work can provide external validation for a dean's budget choices. For example, the president and other senior administrators may have questions about the percentage of the budget being allocated for instructional expenditures. The dean's personal desires or opinions on this matter are less convincing than an argument grounded in comparisons to what takes place in peer institutions. For theological schools there is considerable comparative data available through the Association of Theological Schools. The Institutional Peer Profile Report (IPPR) and the Strategic Information Report (SIR) are especially useful. These and other helpful resources are available to ATS member schools at the ATS website.[12]

The Value of Setting Priorities

Many deans of theological schools know that "there are never enough resources to cover all or even most needs and there is much less flexibility in [academic] budgets than any outsider could imagine."[13] Indeed, except for a few well-funded schools, many deans have to deal with situations of scarcity in their institutions. Since faculty members do not usually have this knowledge, they may present funding requests that increase the dean's frustration in budget work. Other institutional realities, such as required budget adjustments, can add to the frustration. Deans will decrease their frustration if they employ the strategy of setting priorities consistently. In a given year it is prudent, for instance, to tackle one project, maybe two, as a priority for funding. Once the project is determined in consultation with the budget director, the dean should communicate it to the various constituencies of the school. The project need not be a big one. Since the improvement of the physical surroundings and the material culture of the school enhances morale, a dean may want to update the furniture in faculty offices. The financial

12. See www.ats.edu/Resources/Pages/InstitutionalDatabase. In addition, deans can make judicious use of the materials provided in the Auburn Studies published by the Auburn Center for the Study of Theological Education and available at the Auburn website: www.auburnsem.org as well as the annual *Almanac Issue of The Chronicle of Higher Education*. Comparative data, such as provided by the Auburn Center, the Association of Theological Schools, or the *Chronicle of Higher Education,* are valuable resources for ongoing yearly budget work and for strategic planning.

13. Bright and Richards, *The Academic Deanship*, p. 130.

situation of the school may be such that there is no institutional source for funding this project. The dean can still embark on this project by making it a priority, funding it through the careful management of the academic budget, and doing it over a few years.

Investing in faculty and staff must be one of the priorities in building the academic budget. This is done by making sure that funding is provided for professional development and equipment. In addition, it is a good idea to "budget for fun" so that occasional recognition dinners or other forms of appreciation can be provided for faculty and staff. The money spent on these and other tangible ways of saying "thank you" to the people crucial to the mission of the school will generate good will and boost morale. In a particular theological school, for example, coffee was available to faculty in the faculty lounge with the understanding that faculty members should make donations for the coffee enjoyed. A new dean decided to change this by providing free gourmet coffee to all academic personnel. This decision was greatly appreciated. In the course of conversations about the dean's decision, it became clear that the tradition of contributing to the coffee fund was an annoyance for many faculty members. In this case, the savings made by the school were not worth the aggravation. Good budget management must avoid the pitfall of attempting to balance the budget through multiple small savings because the "annoyance of small economies eats away at the soul of professors" in theological schools, as Mac Warford states so well.[14] Consequently, deans do well to resist the temptation of small savings.

Inasmuch as deans can use the academic budget to care for the souls of faculty colleagues and enhance the quality of the workplace, their work as budget managers is central to their calling as chief academic officers. The current situation of many theological schools in the United States and Canada is one that demands much from academic leaders. As these schools face scarcity and threats to their well-being and future, deans are increasingly required to help instill hope and confidence by managing resources well. Implementing sound principles and practices — those discussed in this chapter as well as others to be learned from other colleagues — will contribute to sound budget management and to fostering institutional morale. Money is a key resource that must be managed by deans because there cannot be success in academic leadership without success in building and managing the academic budget; the rewards of exercising this leadership well are worth the effort.

14. This statement was made by Mac Warford on June 17, 2008, during his final comments to the participants of The Lexington Seminar held at Northeast Harbor, Maine.

12. Balancing Formation, Academic Learning, and Ecclesiastical Goals

Developing a Curriculum for Academic, Spiritual, and Vocational Formation

Bruce P. Powers

Background

In 1996, following an extensive review of accrediting standards, ATS adopted standards that included personal and vocational formation (Standard 4, sections 4.1.1 and 4.1.2) and required that degree programs focused on ministerial leadership include personal and spiritual formation components (e.g., MDiv Degree Standard A, section A.3.1). The intent was that member schools would provide a curriculum that would integrate the various facets of formal and informal learning experiences:

> In both the more comprehensive and the more narrow sense, the entire curriculum should be seen as a set of practices with a formative aim — the development of intellectual, spiritual, moral, and vocational or professional capacities — and careful attention must be given to the coherence and mutual enhancement of its various elements. (Standard 4, section 4.1.2)

The curriculum of a school is based on assumptions that inform the content, methods, and learning outcomes ascribed to various degree programs by the faculty and governing body. The curriculum is the structure that enables the institution to do its work. From an accrediting perspective, this process begins with the institution's purpose or reason for being.

The decision to include formation as a distinct expectation in the curriculum was influenced significantly by the changing environment since the original standards were adopted in 1936. Due to a shift from the original "audit" list of essential resources to less-defined guidelines and an ever-increasing diversity among member schools, the characteristics and practices of good theological education became increasingly difficult to interpret.[1]

Perceived gaps in theological education and the problems cited were not related so much to what graduates know, but to how they work with people, perform the skills expected in parish ministry, and respond to the spiritual and personal issues in their lives and among congregants. While the problem was framed initially as concerning an *academic* orientation vs. a *praxis* orientation, there has been a gradual refocusing that addresses (1) institutional purpose; (2) goals that, in addition to academic matters, incorporate affective and performance expectations; and (3) a coherent, integrated curriculum with a *formative* aim. These issues have been documented through the ATS study process that led to the adoption of the 1996 standards.[2]

The Role of the CAO in Balancing Formation and Academic Learning

In most schools, the CAO is the person who manages the various facets of the curriculum and the person to whom all parties look for administering the assessment process. From the faculty's perspective, it is the content, for-credit courses that deserve attention; for students, their ability to do well in courses, their sense of community, and their need for nurture/understanding of their call to ministry are most important; for student services personnel, happy students and high quality support services are primary objectives; for admissions people, finding large numbers of gifted, motivated, and academically qualified applicants is primary; and for the president/chief executive officer, affirming words from the governing body, strong financial support, few inter-

---

1. Michael Gilligan, "The 1996 Accrediting Standards: Reflections a Decade Later," *Colloquy* 14, no. 6 (2006): 5.

2. A summary of this process was presented by Michael Gilligan in a plenary address at the 2006 ATS Biennial Meeting. The address was published in *Colloquy* 14, no. 6 (2006): 4-9.

nal problems, and alumni who perform well in their professions and support their alma mater are the key factors.

So how does the CAO approach balancing formation and academic learning? What do we need to understand? How do we guide in reframing the definition of curriculum? When and how do we administer the process in the institutions in which we serve?[3]

Understanding the Changing Landscape

Theological education is changing. Formation has become an issue because of a changing landscape. As academic officers, it is our duty to reflect on the type of education our schools offer and also on the needs in our society and among the constituencies on which we depend for students, support, and placement.

We must ask questions like: Do our graduates perform well in their professions? What is the student retention rate in our school? What is the retention rate of our graduates in ministry? What is the spiritual climate in our school? Do our students strive for excellence as scholars and as ministers? How do prospective students rate us? Or, said another way: How compelling are our visitation days, promotional materials, and recruitment strategies? Or, as an assessment question: When prospective students are accepted for admission, what percentage actually enroll and how many graduate?

Two words illustrate many of the changes in our society: *vetting* and *transformational*. *Vetting* is the process of checking everything. People want to know the real truth about any person, product, organization, or belief system in which they have an interest or by which they may be affected. Prospective students, faculty members, and donors want to know the truth about our schools, so they can decide whether to commit. Accrediting agencies want to know if what we publish in our catalogs and in promotional materials about our schools is the truth. And search committees ask, "Can we trust their recommendations for our vacant ministry position?"

The other word is *transformational*. No longer can we simply put on a

---

3. Two excellent resources provide background for these issues: *Master of Divinity Curriculum Revision Folio* (Pittsburgh: ATS, 2006); and Barbara G. Wheeler, Sharon L. Miller, and Daniel O. Aleshire, *How Are We Doing? The Effectiveness of Theological Schools as Measured by the Vocations and Views of Graduates* (NY: Auburn Studies, 2007).

new facade (start a new program, get a fresh paint job, tweak the schedule, renovate a few classrooms, add an additional faculty or staff member, or design an impressive Web site) nor can we send out graduates who demonstrate a lack of spiritual passion or do not give adequate attention to pastoral care and related duties. Are we, and our graduates, the same outside and inside? Is who we are, what we believe, and how we teach, preach, and care for people consistent with the beliefs we profess and the traditions we represent? Does the education in our institutions change (transform) our students and prepare them for a responsible life in faith?

> In a theological school, the overarching goal is the development of theological understanding, that is, aptitude for theological reflection and wisdom pertaining to responsible life in faith . . . (Standard 4, section 4.1.1).

In reflecting on the nature of theological education during most of the last century, it is apparent that we have experienced a dramatic shift from a content-driven and other-directed education to one that is informed by community and interpreted through personal experience. Consider the differences in theological education outlined in figure 1 on page 306.

Implications for Curriculum

There is a formal statement of purpose for each accredited school. That purpose exists only in documents until it is translated into the lives of those in the seminary community and among the school's constituencies. Further, there are elements of knowledge, attitudes, and skills that comprise the curriculum and, when appropriated, will lead toward personal and professional competence. In looking at curriculum, three issues arise:

1. A significant portion of learning takes place in the classroom, through the formal instruction provided by the faculty. Traditional classroom instruction primarily is conceptual, focusing on knowledge and understanding.
2. Praxis learning is assigned to field education, or ministry under supervision, and courses focused on practical theology.
3. Personal, spiritual, and vocational formation experiences are relatively new in the theological education curriculum.

Figure 1. Changes in Theological Education

My theological education:	*Today, my students expect:*
Individual Research	Individual *and* Collaborative Research
Intelligence = I.Q.	Attention to Multiple Intelligences
Primarily Lecture	Presentation *and* Interactive Methods
Extrinsic Motivation	Extrinsic *and* Intrinsic Motivation
Overall Performance = Grade Point Average	Comprehensive Evaluation
Parish Ministry	Parish, Institutional, *and* Lay Ministries
Theology of Great Thinkers	Great Thinkers *and* Personal Theology
Scholarly *vs.* Professional	Scholarly *and* Professional
Library	Library *and* Field-based/Context Sensitive
Centralized	Centralized *and* Dispersed
Reflexive/Reactive	Considered/Reflective
Incremental Change	Systemic Change
Curriculum = Courses	Curriculum = Courses + Context
Student Services = food/lodging, records, and student activities consistent with faculty policies	Student Services = student life + academic support services + formation/assimilation curriculum + collaboration with faculty and administrative leaders

We are at our best when delivering #1. Faculty members are prepared and schools are designed to deliver classroom instruction. We are struggling to respond to #2 and #3, however, because the context of ministry and the community in which students live and/or serve often are disconnected from the classroom. Students gain knowledge in the classroom but craft their values in community, and develop their skills in a ministry setting. We cannot control all factors in a graduate professional education, but we can shift to a more inclusive model, a *formation curriculum,* that blends the strengths of formal and informal educational methods.

We must acknowledge that theological education happens in the classroom *and* in the hallways, in the chapel *and* in the offices, in the library *and* in the parking lot, at school *and* in each student's ministry setting. Students spend more time in learning experiences outside the classroom than they do listening to lectures and writing papers. If the process outside does not complement what is taught in the classroom, students experience a disconnect. They may learn the material and pass the course but sometimes don't have a clue about the relevance of what they have been taught to life and ministry in various contexts.

Historically, much of the discussion has focused on formal vs. informal curriculum, with strong proponents for each perspective. A formation curriculum, however, builds on strengths of both. It becomes transformational, causing changes in all dimensions of a student's life.

In many schools, the faculty manages the formal curriculum and student personnel officers manage the informal. We don't usually say that, however, because the faculty is responsible for the curriculum. But, without learning outcomes that include the formal *and* informal elements of curriculum, formation will continue to be disconnected for many students. We need the cooperation of faculty, staff, and students. We need the integration of academic programs, academic support services, and student life. Without change, we will increasingly struggle for relevance in a world that is vetting and with students who are seeking theological education that is transformational.

Finding a Balance

The two models of education shown in Figure 2 — the classic model and the formation model — include the same elements but prioritize them differently. The answer is not to choose the classic model or the formation model but rather to understand the strengths and limitations of each, then blend and balance the content and experiences of each into a unified curriculum.

The primary experiences of students in a classic form of theological education are derived from the traditional, content-oriented courses, primarily in the biblical, historical, and theological fields.

The formation model, in contrast, begins with assumptions about primary values and the educational experiences that will instill and construct related knowledge, skills, and convictions. The core courses, then, are chosen and designed by the faculty based on the contributions each will make when biblical, historical, and theological content is blended with the school's ethos and the personal calling and spiritual journey of students forming a theological frame of reference.

Questions to consider include: What is the dominant model of theological education in our school's tradition? What are the strengths and weaknesses? How is the school adjusting to changes in the culture and in theological education in relation to its peers? What are the issues raised in ATS meetings, leadership groups, and publications that need to be discussed with faculty and administrative leaders?

Figure 2. Classic and Formation Models of Education

Classic Model of Education	*Formation Model of Education*
Core Curriculum	Core Values
Core Experiences	Core Experiences
Core Values	Core Curriculum

Core Values = vision and mission ideals that drive the curriculum
Core Experiences = signature courses and events that link all experiences
Core Curriculum = required conceptual, spiritual, and vocational studies

The CAO as Shepherd

Early in their tenure, many CAOs search for identity. Faculty member or administrator? Manager or facilitator? Second fiddle to the CEO or chair of the faculty? Gatekeeper or bookkeeper? The model that has developed out of the formation tradition, however, does not focus on a single function but on multiple, and contrasting, roles. Perhaps, in our best moments, we can be identified as shepherds. We lead and follow; we proclaim and listen; we control and enable; we are authorities and servants. It is from the role and theological image of shepherd that the following suggestions for curriculum revision are presented.

Consider the following expectations and commitments, for they are the starting points:

1. The published vision/purpose of a school defines the curriculum.
2. The curriculum reflects the best practices for a school's context and constituencies.
3. The curriculum includes all the intentional experiences provided by a school from the recruitment of students through support for alumni.

4. A school's curriculum is most effective when all intentional experiences are integrated and correlated with clearly stated outcomes.

5. The administration, faculty, staff, students, alumni, and representatives of the school's constituencies will understand and be involved in interpreting, supporting, and evaluating the curriculum.

6. An integrated formation curriculum will increase student retention, satisfaction with one's theological education, effectiveness in ministry, and retention in the profession.

7. The process of change holds potential for institutional and personal renewal.

Such renewal of purpose calls for an intentional assessment and reconsideration of program. In a recent catalog, Bethel Seminary in St. Paul, Minnesota, acknowledged its commitment to such an intentional process:

> When we assessed Bethel Seminary in light of these findings, we discovered that Bethel, like most seminaries, effectively educated to meet the first of these goals (biblical grounding), but too often fell short in the others (character formation and leadership skills). We set out to change how we did seminary in order to address what was missing in seminary education.
>
> What has happened during this process of self-examination and change has refocused the energies of Bethel's faculty and administration. We have renewed our purpose to educate students in a holistic way for transformative leadership in God's church.[4]

Guiding the Process

> *No dean wants to instigate a turf war among faculty members and their guilds, but curricular revisioning almost always leads to such a moment unless a rapprochement can be reached via a faculty's shared vision and understanding of a common mission.*[5]

The need for curriculum revision often becomes apparent during a self-study or when significant change occurs, such as the need to add or delete

4. Bethel Seminary, St. Paul, MN, *2007-2008 Catalog*, p. 9.
5. William R. Myers, "Academic Program Assessment and the Academic Dean," *Master of Divinity Curriculum Revision Folio*, p. 35.

degree programs, a significant turnover or restructuring within the school's faculty or administration, or substantial shifts in the needs and expectations among the school's constituencies. Although the CAO usually initiates curriculum revision, it is the responsibility of the faculty to plan, design, and monitor the effectiveness of the curriculum (Standard 6, section 6.1.4). Thus, the following procedures are guidelines the CAO can use in working with the faculty and other administrative officers during a curriculum revision process. An excellent resource to review prior to initiating the formal process is the *Master of Divinity Curriculum Revision Folio,* available from ATS.[6]

Consult with your CEO and key faculty members/committees. When consensus is reached regarding curriculum revision and the timing is right, begin the process.

1. Define the Context: Purpose and Curriculum

What is the school's theological frame of reference? The first step requires clarity concerning the relationship between the school's purpose and the curriculum. This statement is the foundation on which a curriculum is built and is the binding covenant among all parties. In an older school or in a transitional environment, the existing statement and anecdotal principles that guide teaching and assessment must be reviewed and updated to reflect current context and governance. In a new school, such a document must be prepared and adopted as the framework by which decisions will be made in areas such as courses and related academic activities, personnel, facilities, and admission practices.

Preparing or reviewing a statement regarding the school's purpose and the curriculum is usually assigned to a faculty committee or to an ad hoc team of respected faculty members and representatives from other constituencies, such as staff, students, alumni, and trustees, as is the practice during a self-study. Either way will work, but the draft statement must be widely discussed and gain consensus before it is presented for formal adoption as one of the school's primary documents.

At Campbell University Divinity School, for example, a document titled "Reflections on the School's Purpose and Curriculum" sets forth a phi-

---

6. The *Master of Divinity Curriculum Revision Folio,* cited earlier, is a collection of resource materials useful for faculty discussion and as background information for committees charged with the responsibility for curriculum revision.

losophy of ministry that is "Christ-centered, Bible-based, and ministry-focused." It then goes on to explain the implications of that theological frame of reference on the school's curriculum, which is designed to "balance these theological understandings with practical skills for serving in a local church or church-related organization." See Appendix A for the full statement.[7]

2. Determine Curriculum Objectives

A complementing process during curriculum design/revision is to prepare or revise learning objectives. These are the outcomes designed to help students develop "intellectual, spiritual, moral, and vocational or professional capacities" (Standard 4, section 4.1.2) for effective life and ministry; this, in turn, will contribute toward fulfilling the purpose for which the school exists.

The process of developing curriculum objectives may be handled by the same work group that prepared the statement of purpose; however, the entire faculty must be involved in research, review, and approval of the objectives. See Appendix B for a sample of curriculum objectives.

3. Develop the Formation in Ministry Sequence

Drawing from the curriculum objectives identified in the previous step, determine the vocational and spiritual formation courses/experiences that will complement the school's content-oriented courses. Place courses and experiences in a sequence from awareness of call and church-related experience, through graduation and service in ministry or other related profession. Make notes about the topics and experiences that will be important during each phase. See Appendix C for a sample formation in ministry sequence.

Although a committee may be assigned to do the preliminary work, the entire faculty must be involved in developing and approving the sequence and content of formation courses and experiences. Student services personnel should also be included in the discussion and, following faculty approval, assist in the design and interpretation of the courses and activities.

---

7. This appendix and further appendices offered were developed by the author in consultation with Dean Michael Cogdill and colleagues at Campbell University Divinity School, Buies Creek, NC.

This phase of curriculum revisioning often is the major agenda item during a retreat or a workshop for the faculty and administrative staff. Reports from work and study groups should be discussed. In addition, if desired, consultants can interpret the needs and guide the process, or speakers from schools that have developed a blended curriculum can share their experiences. Books and research reports, such as those referenced in this chapter, can be studied in advance and provide background for discussion and the decisions that will be made. For example, a review of one study by the Auburn Center for the Study of Theological Education — *How Are We Doing? The Effectiveness of Theological Schools as Measured by the Vocations and Views of Graduates* — would provide background information and recommendations for curriculum revision as well as data that could help frame changes in related areas, such as admissions, recruitment, retention in ministry professions, and alumni relations.[8]

4. Develop Formation Courses and Experiences

Once the formation courses and experiences have been determined, make decisions about credit hours for courses and requirements for non-credit activities through the normal approval process in your school. This information will be important for the next step, which will begin concurrently with this process.

Make assignments for developing the courses and related activities. Persons responsible should be encouraged to review programs at other schools, discuss resources and course designs with peers, evaluate textbooks and related materials such as workbooks and online resources and, when possible, visit a colleague involved in similar work or attend a professional conference related to the assignment.

5. Revise Courses and Degree Programs

The final phase of curriculum revision requires a review of existing courses and restructuring of the curriculum to reflect revised learning objectives and the integration of formation courses and experiences.

Course content, teaching-learning methods, and assessment procedures need to be examined and adjusted as necessary. Normally, this is done

8. Wheeler, Miller, and Aleshire, *How Are We Doing?*

by the professors who teach the courses, with peer review by colleagues in the same discipline and/or complementing fields of study.

Adjustments in the core of required courses, sequence of study/prerequisites, degree requirements, and performance standards must then be determined for all degree programs. Admission requirements, if affected, will need to be revised. A record of the final review and formal approval by the faculty should be documented in faculty meeting minutes.

Outcomes for the Curriculum Revision

In addition to a revised curriculum, a renewed sense of purpose, and a new vision for effectiveness, there are several other indispensable outcomes that ultimately will determine the success of the new curriculum. These outcomes create the ethos and provide the foundation for the overall attainment of excellence in theological education, and they depend on the diligence of all members of the faculty and staff. Thus, the CAO must ask, "What are the outcomes needed from our people?" The answer is, we need for our people to:

1. Understand the purpose, design, and systemic nature of the curriculum.
2. Understand their functional responsibilities: all jobs are important and part of the curriculum.
3. Affirm interdependency and complementing roles among all partners on the educational team.
4. Align their professional goals with curriculum and school goals.
5. Learn and implement the best practices for their respective positions and professions.

Planning for the Future

Develop a Time Line for Implementation

In consultation with faculty and staff, determine necessary decisions and deadlines for implementing the revised curriculum. For example, what changes will be needed in promotional and admission materials, such as the catalog and the Web site? What orientation and training will be provided for faculty, staff, and student leaders? What changes will be required in the budget, allocation of faculty teaching duties, assignment of facilities, and procedures related to planning and assessment?

Commit to Excellence

A commitment to excellence requires that we study the needs and develop models for effectiveness and best practices appropriate for the particular context and purpose of the school and the constituencies we serve. We must develop appropriate assessment models and devote ourselves to achieving the benefits that accrue from a curriculum design that integrates formal and informal educational experiences. In addition to collecting data regarding academic performance, enrollment, financial stability, graduation rates, and fund raising, we must use research concerning student retention, student satisfaction, effectiveness in ministry, and retention in the profession to inform our decisions about best practices and the standards for success in our schools.

Serving as shepherd and guide, we must invite members of our community (students, faculty, staff, administration, and related constituencies) into a conversation and process that will continue as we consider curriculum outcomes, areas of assessment, performance of students and graduates, and ultimately, achievement of the purpose for which the school exists.

Finally, we must develop an environment — a culture — that enables and expects excellence. This requires deliberate and strategic changes in the ways in which we work together and in which we plan, organize, and deliver theological education. This requires an understanding of and commitment to achieving (1) clarity of vision/purpose and desired learning outcomes; (2) shared responsibility among faculty, staff, and students for teaching and learning; (3) a structured curriculum that blends academic excellence and personal/spiritual/vocational formation; (4) teamwork among faculty members, student services personnel, and administrative staff; (5) methods of evaluation that are consistent with specified outcomes; and (6) institutional affirmation (blessings and benefits) for developing a culture that balances academic achievement and formation.

ADDITIONAL RESOURCES

The Association of Theological Schools, www.ats.edu: The section under *resources* on the ATS web site provides access to a variety of indispensable information related to the topics discussed in this chapter.

Auburn Studies: Auburn Theological Seminary, through its Center for the Study of Theological Education, is the source of high quality research and insightful reports on major issues in theological education and in the practice of ministry (often referred to as the Auburn Studies series). To be placed on the mailing list of the Center for the Study of Theological Education or to order copies of Center publications, write to CSTE at Auburn Theological Seminary, 3041 Broadway, New York, NY 10027, or go to the web site: www .auburnsem.org.

Master of Divinity Curriculum Revision Folio, Pittsburgh: ATS, 2006: Materials related to curriculum revision are provided in this ATS folio as background information for faculty discussion and for leaders/committees charged with the responsibility for curriculum review. It is available from ATS or may be downloaded from the web site: www.ats.edu.

APPENDIX A   Reflections on the School's
                Purpose and Curriculum

Our desire is to guide students into a commitment to the mission of the Church in every facet of life. We believe this is at the heart of a philosophy of ministry that is *Christ-centered, Bible-based,* and *ministry-focused.*

The focus of a student's philosophy of ministry must be on the Church — the People of God and the Body of Christ. As such, the Church must be understood as people who have chosen to participate in a unique way with each other and with their God. In a paradoxical way, students must come to see themselves in a servant-worship relationship to, as well as partners with, God in the God-purpose: to bring all persons and creation into a saving, redemptive, and productive relationship with the Creator.

This is a theological frame-of-reference that students must embrace in order to gain clarity of vision regarding (1) Christian calling and vocational identity, (2) job duties, (3) leadership style, and (4) spiritual growth. Clarity about these issues and their relationship to the nature and mission of the Church gives students a perspective for interfacing the work of vocational ministry with the life and work of a local church or church-related ministry.

The role of vocational ministers, then, would be not only to proclaim and teach the gospel but also to assist believers in being and doing Church.

The objective is for Christians to be actively involved, within the purposes of God, in all dimensions of creation. On a theological level, each person would be engaged in seeking to understand and practice how best to bring all persons and creation into a saving and productive relationship with *Jesus Christ* as Redeemer and Lord, with *God* as Creator and Sustainer, and with the *Church* as the Fellowship of Believers.

On a practical level, this means each person would be engaged *generally* in the life of a congregation, and *specifically* in discovering, developing, and using in Christian service the gifts he or she has been given by God.

This theological focus on the Church enables a student to develop a rationale and principles for leadership that will inform all actions in his or her ministry. It is the intent of this school, moreover, to balance these theological understandings with practical skills for serving in a local church or church-related organization.

The areas of practical theology include skills in guiding and administering the functions of worship, proclamation, education, and ministry — both with and on behalf of the Christian community. The focus of these functions, based on the theological foundations described above, is both inward and outward: *inward* as Christians relate to God and to each other, and *outward* as they relate to the world.

Actions of Christians, therefore, must be viewed as related potentially to every part of creation and, certainly, to every social context related to humankind. Wherever there is discrepancy in terms of the God-purpose, Christians must be willing to act. Similarly, vocational ministers must be willing and able to equip and provide leadership for their congregations in dealing with ethical issues and ministry needs within and beyond the local parish.

This school is committed to education that will prepare students to function effectively in both the theological and the practical dimensions of ministry. The desired outcome is that graduates and those with whom they serve will actively be involved in the world as the *People of God* and the *Body of Christ*.

APPENDIX B   Curriculum Objectives

The curriculum will encourage and prepare students to demonstrate knowledge, skills, and values in four key areas. In each of the four areas, the outcomes listed for students will guide the faculty in developing and teaching appropriate courses and in designing complementing extra-curricular activities.

Biblical, Theological, and Historical Studies
1. Understand, interpret, and teach the Bible.
2. Relate biblical teachings to doctrinal, ethical, philosophical, and practical issues.
3. Interpret historical and contemporary applications related to the Christian life and to the nature and mission of the church, particularly the practices of worship, missions, evangelism, church leadership, and Christian education.
4. Understand, interpret, and teach church/denominational distinctives, polity, and heritage.

Spiritual Formation Studies
1. Demonstrate commitment to Jesus Christ as Lord and Savior.
2. Demonstrate commitment to the Bible as the source of faith and practice, and to Bible study, prayer, meditation, and congregational worship as personal means for spiritual growth.
3. Demonstrate commitment to the local church and to vocational, bivocational, or volunteer Christian service in a church or church-related position.
4. Demonstrate commitment to and involvement in church-related service and mission projects.

Leadership Development Studies
1. Understand, explain, and practice a philosophy and style of leadership compatible with the teachings of Jesus Christ.
2. Demonstrate skills in working with people in a team relationship, with the ability to follow as well as to lead.
3. Demonstrate diagnostic ability and motivational skills to develop strategy and guide people in achieving common objectives.
4. Appreciate the value of and demonstrate skills in establishing, devel-

oping, and nurturing relationships that will result in personal and professional support for ministry.

Ministry Skills Studies

1. Understand, appreciate, and be able to perform effectively the appropriate ministry tasks and duties required for the context of ministry in which one serves. This will include but not be limited to proclamation, teaching, worship, evangelism, missions, counseling, care-giving, and administration.
2. Exegete, interpret, and communicate the Bible in a variety of formal and informal contexts.
3. Establish, develop, and nurture relationships that will result in conversions, spiritual growth, and/or establishment of Christian groups and local churches.
4. Integrate biblical, theological, and historical studies; spiritual formation studies; and leadership development studies in the practice of ministry.

APPENDIX C Sample Formation in Ministry Sequence

1. **Readiness for Theological Education**
   Review of each student's call to ministry, experience in the church, educational preparation, and references; interview and evaluation

2. **Foundational Formation Studies**

   Introduction to Theological Education
   The journey from God's call to the classroom
   The nature, mission, and purpose of theological education and of this school
   Commissioning service

   Worship and Spiritual Formation
   Developing narratives: My story, God's story, and our story
   Significant markers in each student's spiritual journey
   Finding acceptance in the community of faith
   Precept groups

3. **Vocational Formation Studies**

   Life and Work of the Minister
   Functions, objectives, approach to life and ministry

   Supervised Ministry
   Experience in a ministry setting, theological reflection, application of
     vocational studies to ministry issues

4. **Integration Studies**

   Formation Course or Activity (at least one each semester)

   Senior Synthesis
   Integration portfolio and ministry management plan
   Vocational and personality instruments, readiness for ministry review
   Presentation and review with faculty panel
   Senior chapel, covenant and hooding service

5. **In-service Studies**

   *Continuing Education Opportunities for Personal and Professional
   Development*

   Peer Group Support for Personal, Spiritual, and Professional Nurture
   Focus on personal and professional growth,
   contextual awareness, and theological reflection

Balancing Formation and Academic Learning

Ronald A. Mercier

Occasionally the way a question is posed reveals a certain challenge at the
outset; from the perspective of theological ethics, the framing of the "case"
dictates much of the outcome. The title of this essay, one felicitously proposed to me, reveals exactly such an invitation to a broader dialogue, one

which touches on the very heart of the ministry of a chief academic officer of a school dedicated to preparing candidates for service in the church. Indeed, the "balance" proposed here asks us to consider not just one particular aspect of our programs but rather the entire project of our enterprise.

A cursory review of *Theological Education,* beginning with the first volume of the journal published in 1964, reveals that the topic of "formation" has become an ever more important subject for reflection. As the question has developed, however, what becomes clear is that we move from asking how formation constitutes a particular dimension of a program to the deeper issue of the location of schools of ministry within our culture and within the communities of faith that we serve. The emergence of formation as a critical issue ultimately reveals that we live in a different world, one markedly removed from what would have been normal even a generation ago. *Formation* itself may be a problematic word today because the idea of "being formed" for too many people represents a challenge to a sense of personal autonomy.[1]

Edward Farley articulated the challenge succinctly in an interview about ten years ago, roughly the time of the move toward the "good theological school" model within the Association of Theological Schools.

> One of the features of the postmodern epoch is that certain deep cultural values that used to be taken for granted have eroded. Values such as tradition, reality, obligation, beauty, nature, transcendence, nature [sic], mystery, hope — the things whose power makes a society work — are not operational in typical postmodern institutions, the workplace, the government, the media, the entertainment industry. This erosion of deep values seems to be culture-wide and thus applies to congregations and their members. If this is so, the preaching and education that take place in congregations cannot pretend that business is as usual.[2]

His point is well taken. Most of our traditional models for theological education have presumed that a theological school could rely upon a "feeder culture" that would have formed both students and faculty members before

---

1. While *formation* is meant to apply to all students within a school of ministry, the emphasis here will be on candidates preparing for ecclesial ministry, ordained or lay; the formation of students preparing to be professors is a separate issue that lies beyond the scope of this discussion.

2. Edward Farley, "Toward Theological Understanding: An Interview with Edward Farley," *Christian Century* (February 4-11, 1998): 113.

they arrived. This assumption, one which Farley and many others rightly note to be dangerous, allowed schools to focus on the distinctive elements needed for ministry, mostly academic learning and skill acquisition. These continue, for the most part, to be the heart of theological curricula and programs of study. If one takes seriously, though, the challenge of our age, then the question is not so much how one balances formation and academic learning as discrete elements within some program of study, but rather how schools re-vision themselves to accommodate a decidedly different world. As Farley asserts, ". . . the first aim of theological education is not to teach pastoral skills or to mold scholars but to convey 'wisdom' about 'the believer's existence and action in the world.'"[3]

To frame the question in this way may seem much more daunting, but it speaks to the reality that every CAO recognizes today. The challenge before us is not simply to find better ways of being about some element called *formation,* usually spiritual in nature. Rather we must ask what it means for us to be about the task of "sapiential" education, recognizing the changed locus that the school of ministry occupies within a context that can no longer rely upon the "cultural formation" of either faculty or students. We do not merely encounter students who do not know the basics of Christian faith, but more often students — and faculty — who are unsure of their place within the Christian community and of the relevance of the Christian faith for our culture. We too often forget this radical change of environment, and so at times place the "burden" of formation upon some particular person or team within the school, creating the preconditions for the kinds of turf battles that can bedevil theological education. This division can too easily reinforce the dichotomy, let alone distinction, between "the spiritual" and "the religious," undermining the ways in which formation places us within a tradition and a faith community. We too often miss the broader question of the ecclesial vocation of the theological school with all that this intends, a vocation that includes all the faculty and staff.[4]

In that light, three different sets of questions emerge, each of them of real importance. First, how does a school envision its character as sapiential, seeking to facilitate the dialogue between faith and the world the

3. Farley, "Toward Theological Understanding," p. 113.

4. Cf. Gordon T. Smith, "Spiritual Formation in the Academy: A Unifying Model," *Theological Education* 33, no. 1 (1996): 83-91. His concern that a "false premise or assumption" of the disconnect between the academic process and the formation of character shapes much of our discourse is very apt and leads to an excellent perspective on an integrated model of theological education.

school, its faculty, and its alumni/ae will serve? Second, given the critical role of faculty within the broader frame of a more sapiential understanding of theological education, how does the CAO help shape a faculty that can engage formation as an integral whole? Third, in what way does a pattern of spiritual, personal, academic, and professional formation shape the life of the students as a community within the school? Generally we equate the formative with the spiritual, however that may be construed within a particular tradition. As Mary Margaret Pazdan points out, however, what is proposed is the development of "wisdom communities," a model that seems profoundly strange in an academic context, yet very much at the heart of the Christian tradition.[5]

If Farley, Louis Dupré, and others are right, however, the separation of the spiritual within the curriculum can lead to its marginalization and perhaps irrelevance. We can, and at times do, create the space wherein there is a choice of the spiritual *or* the academic, a problematic choice at the best of times, even as within much of the Catholic tradition, the "ascetical" was kept deliberately at arm's length from the systematic or the ethical. This can accentuate a private/ public split; Richard Foster notes that while all Christian traditions in the last thirty years have made great progress on "the formation of the soul," we have not attended to the ways in which we need to "incarnate this reality into the daily experience of individual, congregational, and cultural life."[6] While my reflections will focus on the spiritual element within the broader program, it is important to continually foster a more integrated and integrating vision of formation, recognizing that this may well be more common within Roman Catholic discourse.[7]

Articulating the Vision and Character of the School

In an excellent article published in 1994, Donald Senior and Timothy Weber note that the relationship between the curriculum and spiritual formation has to be driven by the mission of the school.[8] They hit at the core of a foun-

5. Mary Margaret Pazdan, "Wisdom Communities: Models for Christian Formation and Pedagogy," *Theological Education* 34, no. 2 (1998): 25.

6. Richard Foster, "Spiritual Formation Agenda," *Christianity Today* (January 2009): 30.

7. United States Conference of Catholic Bishops, *Program for Priestly Formation* (Washington, D.C.: USCCB, 2006), p. 28.

8. Donald Senior and Timothy Weber, "What Is the Character of Curriculum, For-

dational good within theological education. If the mission of a school is the formation of ministers for the sake of the church and of society, then the school must have at least an implicit sense of the character of a "good minister," a successful alumna/us. Daniel Aleshire has often spoken of the affective response of joy — or dread — a faculty experiences as it witnesses graduation and views the graduates it is sending into the world to be about the work of ministry in all of its forms. Viscerally we know what we are about as members of a faculty and staff. The personal quality of the "norm" which we set for ourselves in our common work becomes evident in and through our response to those who have been formed by us. Nor is it simply helping people to fit a ministerial role, as if it could be captured and defined. Lisa Hess summarizes it nicely: the "improbable quest for a pastoral identity amidst the observable reality of multiple identities, chosen and imposed."[9]

This "norm" is, however, not merely programmatic; it is not achieved through the compilation of more experiences or more class or workshop time. The visceral quality of the response of which Daniel Aleshire speaks invites us into the seemingly intangible but important world of "discernment." While this is a term admittedly often associated with Jesuits, it points to the richer reality of theological education in which we encounter persons as existential realities, whether they are students who seek to become ministers, members of a faculty, or CAOs. Academic leaders must navigate not in the realm of categorical realities they can easily adjudicate, but in a space that is more relational and far richer in its terms of reference. It is very much the realm of "wisdom" that Farley sketches, recognizing and celebrating gifts and asking how one fosters such gifts for the sake of the church.

In its search for balance, a school must ask itself how it understands the sapiential nature of its educational ministry, especially in the context of the faith tradition within which it stands. How does this particular tradition reply to the question of how it will shape people for the challenge Farley poses, existentially bringing the riches of the tradition to one's world in a way that engages with and integrates the various dimensions of a person's life, not merely their faith life? In a sense, how does one's tradition help one bridge the spiritual/material divide that permeates so much of our culture?

This seemingly intangible question invites us into an important issue

---

mation, and Cultivation of Ministerial Leadership in the Good Theological School?" *Theological Education* 30, no. 2 (1994): 24.

9. Lisa M. Hess, "Formation in the Worlds in Theological Education: Moving from 'What' to 'How,'" *Teaching Theology and Religion* 11 (2008): 1.

that we rarely explore, namely the corporate culture of our schools as they stand within a tradition.[10] We often view formation, especially spiritual formation, as something a school *does,* a function, rather than a foundational element of its very *nature.* We are accustomed to thinking of the intellectual and professional formation of individuals, but as communities of faith, theological schools — like any school — embody and transmit critical values and visions that, one hopes, are rooted in an implicit sense of the school's identity. The ATS General Institutional Standards call for clarity within a school about its own character or culture. This character, which can be recognized but not defined, sets the school in relationship with its faith tradition, the world it serves, and the members of its community. As such, this character provides an important point of departure for any discernment of the balance between — or rather the integration of — academics and formation. It also roots one in the broader foundation of the resources for faith formation already present within a tradition.

Exploring my own tradition offers a case in point, revealing both the challenge and the possibility implicit in this call to "character." The school of which I was dean identifies itself clearly as standing within the Jesuit tradition within Roman Catholicism, heir to a rich spiritual lore. Therefore many made the assumption that the school had the formation element well in hand. Yet the quest to understand how formation forms the program is a more difficult one. The Society of Jesus itself had in many ways separated the spiritual element from the intellectual; for centuries *The Spiritual Exercises,* which lies at the core of Jesuit spirituality, was experienced through preaching rather than as the personal journey of discerning prayer envisioned by Ignatius Loyola.[11] As the cultural context changed and as the external structures upon which formation relied began to collapse, a gradual process of retrieving *The Exercises* began in the late 1960s, with an emphasis on the na-

---

10. Terrence E. Deal and Allan A. Kennedy, *Corporate Cultures: The Rites and Rituals of Corporate Life* (Reading, MA: Addison-Wesley, 1982). This early account of the ways in which institutions have not only "organization" but "corporate" cultures, systems of values that shape and provide continuity, provides a helpful framework for discerning the particular culture and hence mission of a theological school.

11. While the move to the personal was important for the development of Ignatian spirituality, Louis Dupré notes the ways in which in our contemporary era the "integrating synthesis of values" has become an individual and isolated affair, one which has left faith vulnerable within the context of a "functional atheism" in modern culture. Louis Dupré, "Spiritual Life in a Secular Age," in George Schner, ed., *Ignatian Spirituality in a Secular Age* (Waterloo, Ontario: Wilfrid Laurier University Press, 1984), p. 16.

ture of discernment, both personal and communal, as a mode of integrating life and faith. That process of retrieval and renewal is still underway, and the formation programs within the Society of Jesus are themselves in flux. The role of the study of philosophy and theology itself began to change, evolving from simply a necessary means of preparation toward ministry to a mission already accepted and into which one was growing. It became a way of engaging and enriching the spiritual and ministerial life and growing in one's sense of being part of the Catholic community.[12]

The challenge to theological schools within the Jesuit tradition in the United States and Canada, however, was twofold. First, whereas previously "spiritual formation" occurred within the private sphere between a student and his "spiritual father," parallel to the broader academic program and within the well-ordered life of the seminary, now the task was one of asking how theological studies — and the seminary — played a role within Jesuit formation itself. Second, felicitously this occurred within the context of the rise of lay ministry within the Catholic community and the call to ask what a formation in the light of the Jesuit tradition would mean; this could no longer remain an in-house discussion. While we could easily make the transition into allowing lay women and men into classes, what would it mean to be a forming *community*?[13] What had always been an easy assumption, "being Jesuit," now asked for an intentional focus on the distinctive elements of this character and on the practices that would foster it, including the spiritual, the personal, the intellectual, and the vocational.

This led to the retrieval of important aspects of the Jesuit/Ignatian tradition, like spiritual direction, for lay leaders and Jesuits alike, as well as a response to the call of the Society of Jesus for more explicit understandings of the relationship between faith and justice in a multifaith and culturally complex world. The relationship of the academic to the formative raised the broader question of the nature of the school itself and the need to re-appropriate its own tradition. As Mary Kay Oosdyke points out, such clarity about one's tradition, its formative and transformative resources and the vision it provides, represents a critical aspect in knowing what one seeks to

12. George P. Schner, *Education for Ministry: Reform and Renewal in Theological Education* (Kansas City, MO: Sheed & Ward, 1993), pp. 1-22.

13. An excellent account of a similar development within a Dominican school, Aquinas School of Theology, can be found in Mary Kay Oosdyke, "Vocation in a New Key: Spiritual Formation and the Assessment of Learning," *Theological Education* 41, no. 2 (2006): 1-10.

achieve as well as a foundational way of framing the role of formation within the curriculum.

Admittedly this question goes beyond the role of the CAO, yet insofar as it implies the shaping of the programs of the school, the role of its faculty, and the assessment of its impact on the church, the CAO is uniquely positioned to pose these issues and foster the discussion. For me, a providential confluence of two realities was most helpful in framing the question of formation. A self-evaluation process in preparation for our accrediting visit provided two critical tools: information and the need to reflect. Ironically, of course, we were all aware on an inferential level of the kinds of changes that had occurred within our student body and our faculty. The dramatic shift to an overwhelmingly lay student body and a concurrent movement toward more lay faculty members came into sharp focus when the raw data and the results of student questionnaires on formation became part of the materials for common reflection. The parallel process inherent in the "good theological schools" model, relying on a sense of our own identity and mission, asked us as a faculty the kinds of questions that enabled us to recognize the strengths and the needs of each degree program as well as of the character of our overall educational ministry during this kairos moment. However much we already knew through working with and observing the student body, the juncture of crucial data and a clear, external set of questions and criteria gave the college and the faculty a framework for further deliberations and decisions. Such moments of critical mass are the CAO's friend, since for those immersed in the nitty-gritty of academic life, formation questions can seem too ephemeral.

Such discussion may very well touch upon the very nature of the school; it will certainly reveal those elements of the school's tradition that are in need of complementary resources. The discourse ultimately situates those who enter it not merely within their own ecclesial traditions but also within the broader Christian tradition with all its richness, especially when such discourse includes considering the needs of the communities seminary graduates will serve and how they are constantly evolving. Moreover, if as Hess suggests this is less a matter of training and more a question of empowering people to form a sense of self within those relationships that give their lives meaning, then a clearer sense of context becomes a prerequisite for being able to pose the issue of "balance." This is a discourse that, while it can achieve a certain clarity at any given time, requires openness to ongoing reflection, a formative element in its own right. H. Frederick Reisz Jr. frames the question nicely for all interested in this area: "[d]oes spiritual formation at this place have a defining core and sufficiently broad intentionality and actuality to be a 'communal' enterprise?"[14]

Shaping an Integrative Faculty

The mediation between the vision of the school and the formation of the student occurs through the creation of an integrative faculty. Arguably there is probably no more important task for a CAO than the choice of faculty members and the shaping of a common identity among them. The faculty not only teaches courses and provides advising, but it embodies perhaps in the most direct way the character of the school to the students. Moreover, it is the members of faculty who together shape the curriculum and weigh its various elements.

George Schner poses the question of the integration of formation into the life of a theological school as he notes the four dimensions that need to be considered:

> Four general areas concerning the establishment of a profile of a theological faculty can be set in conversation with the preceding chapter's remarks on pedagogy. The first two issues shape a faculty's identity because of its students: reflective appropriation of what notion a faculty has as an overarching designation of their relationship with students (mentoring, parenting, modeling among other possibilities); and the harmony produced out of the plurality and diversity necessary within a faculty's membership if it is to carry out its corporate task. The second two issues shape a faculty's identity because of its accountability to academy, Church, and society at large: the conception of the nature and aims of theological inquiry operative within a faculty, particularly as it relates to the current state of the Church and the academy; and the sense the faculty has of the relation of its work to the contemporary issues of society and culture.[15]

This is a particularly helpful phrasing of the question at hand as it poses two very different kinds of issues. One set of issues necessitates that a

---

14. H. Frederick Reisz, Jr., "Assessing Spiritual Formation in Christian Seminary Communities," *Theological Education* 39, no. 2 (2003): 33.

15. Schner, *Education for Ministry*, p. 152.

faculty do what it is usually loath to do, namely give itself a definitive character, and in two ways. It must name the relationship between students and faculty in a deliberate way, which gives shape and meaning to the formative nature of the task of theological education in the given school. To do this the faculty must name and embody a dominant metaphor, an image of its own ministry to students, rather than accepting the mere fact that a plurality of academic areas of expertise fulfills the profile of a theological faculty. This implies that the faculty as a whole own its formative role, rather than delegating it functionally to some person or persons within the school. Such an identity, however, becomes a clear point of self-reflection, a way of assessing the mission of the faculty beyond academic expertise. It also requires of the faculty the kind of sapiential frame of reference that Farley delineates, and it requires that the faculty own the vision of the school so that it becomes more than a mantra. Shaping such a corporate culture, however, one that can sustain a corporate mission, is perhaps one of the hardest challenges of a modern, functional culture. Moreover, such a vision and mission will necessarily have to be adapted to meet changing cultural/ecclesial contexts and an ever-changing student body. Such a reflection must be an ongoing aspect of a faculty's self-understanding and vision.

At the same time, however, an articulation of vision and mission leads to a criterion of selectivity for the creation or re-creation of a faculty. Schner's second point, namely, how vital it is to guarantee diversity within the faculty sufficient to fulfill its mandate, requires that a school, and in particular a CAO, be willing to embrace the character of the faculty and its formative role. It is not difficult to ascertain the academic credentials of a candidate for a position; with these we are quite at home within the academy. More difficult, however, are the dual tasks of assessing aptness for the formative role of the faculty and creating the diversity necessary to meet this formative role in its fullness. This is not simply diversity for its own sake, but diversity for the task of formation, one that perceives not only the needs of the students but the needs of the contemporary world. It requires of the CAO the gift of imagination in fostering the growth of a formative faculty.

Schner is right, of course, in noting that this will necessarily be in dialogue with the school's relationships *ad extra*. There can be no more thorny issue than how a faculty positions itself with respect to both the academy and the church. Such a question can easily — and problematically — be resolved by simply ignoring it or opting for one over the other. Taking seriously the accountability of members of the faculty and of the faculty as a whole to both church and academy can help crystallize the discussion on formation as it highlights the tension between the academic, ministerial, and faith dimensions of theological formation for ministry. It will also emphasize, however, the challenge of the ongoing formation of the faculty in its own corporate mission.[16] Similarly, this will ask that the faculty question how it stands before the suffering and needs of the world at large, a way, perhaps of living out Barth's call to reflection holding together Scripture and the newspaper (or its modern analog).

In a sense, using Schner's typology, the three final criteria he suggests are ways in which the faculty itself lives out the wisdom role of theology, asking its own way of being. As such it already models what theological reflection is for its students. The balance of academic study and formation, therefore, is already cast in the way the faculty embodies this balancing act; if formation is marginal to the faculty (and the faculty status of those involved in formation speaks volumes about this), a lesson has been communicated to the students about what really matters at a school. There may be no more difficult issue facing schools of theology today, and perhaps no question in which the future of theological education is more clearly cast, than the shape of theological faculties as formative.[17] I am not suggesting that all members of a faculty have to act as spiritual directors or be those who teach the skills of theological reflection; rather, it is in the way in which they teach and engage students and broader publics that they already provide icons, as it were, of what the school proclaims theological education to be. At the same time, existentially they validate the importance and place of the wisdom tradition within the school, though in a way that flows directly from the charism or identity of the particular school and tradition.

Fostering Formation in the Lives of Students

Finally, we come to the question of how one engages formation as part of theological education for students. As should be clear by now, my concern

16. Cf. Shelly Cunningham, "Who's Mentoring the Mentors? The Discipling Dimension of Faculty Development in Christian Higher Education," *Theological Education* 34, no. 2 (1998): 31-49. Her emphasis on the value of integration of faith into academic study on pp. 40-41 is particularly important.

17. Katarina Schuth, *Seminaries, Theologates, and the Future of Christian Ministry: An Analysis of Trends and Transitions* (Collegeville, MN: Michael Glazier/The Liturgical Press, 1999), p. 116. Schuth notes how such an intentional focus on the multiple roles of faculty has been mandated within the Catholic community by a variety of episcopal/Vatican documents.

remains that often such reflections begin from a "remedial" perspective, focusing on how to provide for a perceived lack within the students who come largely unformed, perhaps as "seekers." Of course, that is very often the case among incoming ministerial candidates. Yet to place the focus there frequently reinforces, as I noted earlier, exactly the kind of privatized role of spirituality that too often bedevils contemporary Christianity.

I would follow Oosdyke's suggestion in the model developed at Aquinas Institute of Theology. She notes the following steps, all of which spoke of a model that

> would call for a complete revision of the admission to candidacy procedure and further work on assessment strategies. Before this occurred, the faculty needed to complete the curricular revision it had planned. Other institution-wide projects occurring simultaneously resulted in the new articulation of the mission statement. While many structural elements of the plan remain, the curricular revision and the integration of a new mission statement have made significant changes that are being incorporated into the Aquinas assessment plan.[18]

This process led to a clear delineation of particular skills that needed to be included within the curriculum as a whole, including "social analysis skills, knowledge of the Catholic tradition, a holistic yet focused spiritual formation . . . , and the skills for ministerial leadership. . . ."[19] The recognition of the skills required for fully embodying a faith able to engage the world flowed from the broader sense of identity and mission of the school, rooted in a Dominican preaching charism, and a curricular model that fostered students who could live out such a vision in practice. The entire school became involved in such a process since it embodies the charism into which the students are invited.

Within this perspective, however, the usually described "spiritual elements" (liturgy, spiritual direction, counseling, confession, retreats, spiritual conversation, devotions) do not stand apart from the broader reality of the life of the theological community.[20] On the contrary, they are ordered to-

---

18. Oosdyke, "Vocation in a New Key," p. 4.

19. Oosdyke, "Vocation in a New Key," p. 5.

20. Reisz, "Assessing Spiritual Formation," p. 34, raises important questions regarding the integration of spiritual formation (which can touch on the most intimate parts of a person's life) into more general questions of competency. Questions of confidentiality are criti-

ward and enriched by the broader sense of the community's wisdom function in the world. The foundational question is whether the spiritual disciplines, as well as theological reflection, help foster the integrity and vitality of the whole curriculum, creating ministers who can act sapientially and who can see the dialectical relationship among spirituality, the academic study of theology, ministerial engagement, socio-cultural awareness, and personal growth. The test is not just whether the spiritual disciplines make a student more spiritual and human, but rather whether they make the entire curriculum more "sapiential," in Farley's sense. Those persons charged with "spiritual formation" become not peripheral adjuncts in a school, but rather important colleagues in the process of a theological education for ministry shaped by a school's identity and mission.

I was fortunate during my tenure as CAO to see members of the spiritual formation faculty move from the periphery to the center of all our programs. This occurred largely as a result of the teaching these spiritual formation colleagues did in a two-year MA in Ministry and Spirituality program that emphasized spiritual and practical formation, which clearly had had a deep impact on the students. In reflecting on the impact of this program, we recognized that this model responded to the kinds of needs emerging from MDiv students as well. As we began to re-imagine the curriculum following the ATS accrediting process, these colleagues' foundational work with MA students became the template for the initial process in other programs, notably in specific coursework (a revised "Introduction to Ministry" course) and informed continual reflection on the place of formation in the curriculum. This "reaping of the fruit" helped the faculty as a whole come to appreciate the work and the role of these "peripheral" faculty colleagues who became much more deeply embedded in the faculty. This also initiated a discussion of the value and meaning of the DMin degree within faculty ranks, since two of the professors held this degree.

As Pazdan proposes, a sapiential model of education suggests the kind of reintegration of learning, discipleship, and ministry that marked early Christian communities. As Farley submits, it is a model proposed for adults. In some ways, it is closer to the mystagogy[21] that marked early Christian for-

---

cally important in this regard. Yet he worries about too rigid a boundary as it "seems again to draw walls between the personal and communal, the inner and the outer, the soul and the mind." He calls for "clear principles articulated for any model of spiritual formation" with respect to its relationship to broader questions of assessment.

21. Rowena Roppelt, "Baptism — and Then What? A Catechumenate for the Already Baptized," *Worship* 82 (2008): 214-42. She develops a model for children of what a mysta-

mation, but always in dialogue with the world and with a keen eye to questions of justice. As Reisz notes, such programs "need to be world-encompassing . . . not be just exercises of interiority."[22] In a sense, then, we are not so much balancing two goods, spiritual formation and academic study, as asking Farley's basic question: How we shall be about the work of theological wisdom for our age?

ADDITIONAL RESOURCES

Klimoski, Victor J., Kevin O'Neil, and Katarina M. Schuth. *Educating Leaders for Ministry: Issues and Responses.* Collegeville, MN: Liturgical Press, 2005.

Wheeler, Barbara, Sharon Miller, and Daniel Aleshire. *How Are We Doing? The Effectiveness of Theological Schools as Measured by the Vocations and Views of Graduates.* Auburn Studies 13. New York: Auburn Center for the Study of Theological Education, 2007.

Living Fruitfully in the Tensions between Academy and Church

Ervin R. Stutzman

If the church — all of it — were to rise up and say to the seminaries: "we don't want you or your graduates," most ATS schools would be like cursed fig trees; they would wither and die. By contrast, if the seminary were to say to the church: "we are tired of your intrusion and would like to chart our own future," the church would likely walk away, shaking our academic dust from its feet.

Daniel Aleshire[1]

gogical education could look like. The question she raises, namely of an integration of faith into learning and life in a communal and prayerful/liturgical model, raises interesting parallel questions for theological education.

22. Reisz, "Assessing Spiritual Formation," p. 38.

1. Citation from a speech entitled "What Is the Future of the Relationship of Theo-

ATS president Daniel Aleshire is a learned man not given to hyperbole or sensational speech. So when he voiced the preceding assertion to a CAOS conference in 2007, I took particular notice. He went on to claim that "the future of a meaningful and viable relationship is more crucial for the organizational future of theological schools than it is for the church."[2] I wondered what might prompt him to speak in such ominous tones.

The Changing Face of Religion

In his addresses to a variety of ATS groups, Aleshire has voiced skepticism about the ability of traditional means of higher education to prepare transformative religious leaders. He wonders aloud about the value of a theological education. I sense that he is rightly worried about the ability of theological schools to make necessary adaptations to new social and spiritual realities. Trained as a sociologist, Aleshire observes vast changes on the religious front in North America. Recent sociological research paints a gloomy picture of the state of religion and, more particularly, its leaders. Although Alban Institute researchers admit in a 2001 report to a paucity of "thorough, high-quality, empirically based research" on the topic, they conclude that American congregations are in turmoil and crisis.[3] They cite three key indicators of trouble: (1) shortage of clergy, (2) quality of pastoral leadership, and (3) retention of women in ministry. Further, they aver that many entering seminary students are less equipped and less eager to serve as leaders in established congregations.

Many lay at least partial blame for the depressing state of church leadership at the door of seminaries. After all, many if not most of the pastors of the church bodies in trouble were trained in seminaries. Perhaps theological schools are producing leaders with "trained incapacities" to lead their congregations in adapting to new social realities. Edward White writes, "Another dimension of the [leadership] problem relates to the process used to prepare and credential candidates for the ministry. Seminaries are engulfed in the academic model and they do a fine job of teaching Bible, theology,

---

logical Schools and the Church?" presented at the Chief Academic Officers Society Conference, March 2007, p. 3.

2. Aleshire, "What Is the Future?" p. 3.

3. James P. Wind and Gilbert R. Rendle, *The Leadership Situation Facing American Congregations*, Alban Institute Special Report, 2001.

church history, polity, and ethics. They don't, however, teach much about *leadership!*[4] He laments that smart students who can preach good sermons may lack the "competencies (emotional intelligence) to be fruitful leaders."[5]

At the same time, giving patterns in religious bodies are changing. Statistics from across the spectrum of ATS schools show that financial support for seminaries from official church bodies is steadily declining. Schools must increasingly depend on donations from individuals to balance their budgets.

In the midst of the gloom on the larger religious scene, Alban Institute researchers have found some cause for hope. Observing a stirring of revitalization movements in some sectors of society, the authors assert that "the congregations of America — and the people who lead them — are simultaneously encountering great new spiritual vitality and a crisis of legitimacy of their established patterns and practices."[6] Yet they have determined that much of the new growth is happening in emerging churches who do not look to established seminaries for training.

Although theological schools were birthed by the church and were nurtured for years in its cradle, they now share rooms in the academy with distant cousins who claim no relationship with the church. In the first centuries of its life, the church prepared its leaders through apprenticeship in apostolic teams or local churches. This apprenticeship involved a complex interaction among knowledge, skill, and a normative ethos that served as distinctives in particular communities of faith. With the rise of higher education, such apprenticeships gave way to formal education in classrooms. Edward Farley has helpfully traced the history of theological education, explaining the ways that theological schools have either adopted or adapted the conventions of higher education as the primary means by which to pursue the goal of preparing professional clergy for the church.[7]

For a variety of reasons, but at least partly because of the difficulties discussed above, some church communities are creating alternative structures for ministerial education. At a time when emerging church movements and the influx of immigrants from other faith traditions are changing the face of religious life in North America, established seminaries will do well to re-examine the ecclesial mandates given by their sponsoring church bodies.

4. Edward White, "The Shortage of Capable Clergy: Root Causes," *Congregations* (Fall 2006): 52.

5. White, "The Shortage of Capable Clergy," p. 52.

6. Wind and Rendle, *The Leadership Situation*, p. 17.

7. Edward Farley, *Theologia: The Fragmentation and Unity of Theological Education* (Minneapolis: Fortress Press, 1983).

Striving for Academic and Ecclesiastical Balance

Maintaining balance between academic and ecclesiastical goals is a good thing — yet difficult to achieve. Theological schools inhabit a space at the intersection of two communities or spheres, each with a vastly different ethos or culture. The specific amount of overlap or relationship between them may vary considerably, depending on the school. Both of these communities are influenced by social changes in the context of the broader culture, and both have goals that must be balanced. The ultimate goals of each sphere reflect broad trajectories, not easily quantifiable goals that might appear in a strategic plan. To speak of balance between such broad goals requires an understanding of the interrelationship between these broad spheres or trajectories.

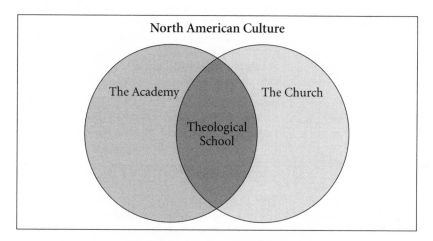

A full-fledged description of any culture must include many elements, from the surface level of artifacts and practices all the way down to the core of its worldview. The table on page 336 lists a few of the salient components of culture in both the academy and the church. The characteristics listed in the left column will be found in any regionally accredited institution of higher education, most notably in a large research institution. The characteristics listed in the right column will likely be found in many of the churches represented by ATS member schools. The middle column lists a few of the ways that theological schools have sought to balance the aims in these two other worlds.

The main point of this table is to show that the ethos of the seminary is

Academy	Seminary	Church
Artifacts: school catalogs, lecture halls, diplomas, transcripts, gowns, research libraries	*Artifacts:* All of those in the academy plus most of those in the church	*Artifacts:* sanctuaries, pulpits, pews, vestments, worship bulletins, confessions or creeds
Practices and procedures: registration, tuition and fees, assigning/grading student work, degree programs, matriculation, course loading, faculty promotion or tenure, academic disciplines	*Practices and procedures:* All of those in the academy plus worship liturgy from the church	*Practices and procedures:* worship liturgy, baptism, confirmation, church membership, ordination, weddings, funerals, pastoral counseling, pledges or free will offerings, voluntary church attendance, communal gathering
Worldview/values: positivist or postmodern assumptions, academic freedom, theoretical rigor, ideological critique	*Worldview/values:* knowledge may yet be discovered, but must be informed by the assumptions of Christian faith and worldview	*Worldview/values:* authority of scriptural revelation, Christian tradition, and personal faith in triune God
Affiliation: Regional accrediting association(s), professional guilds	*Affiliation:* Denominational or other religious association, regional accrediting association and/or ATS, professional guilds	*Affiliation:* congregation/parish, district, conference, denomination, interfaith association, etc.
Aim: Quest for knowledge through scholarly research (critical inquiry)	*Aim:* To draw on knowledge in academic guilds to produce theologically-trained professional leaders for the church — *theologia,*[8] *paideia, Wissenschaft,*[9] missional training[10]	*Aim:* To call persons of all ages to holistic Christian faith — discipleship, peace and justice, service to the poor and marginalized, membership growth, interfaith dialogue, civic responsibility

8. See Farley, *Theologia,* for an in-depth treatment of the term *theologia.*

9. For an in-depth analysis of the aims of *paideia* and *Wissenschaft,* see David H. Kelsey, *Between Athens and Berlin: The Theological Debate* (Grand Rapids: Wm. B. Eerdmans, 1993).

10. For an explanation of a missional approach, see Robert Banks, *Reenvisioning Theological Education: Exploring a Missional Alternative to Current Models* (Grand Rapids: Wm. B. Eerdmans, 1999).

inevitably shaped through some form of adaptation (a balancing act, so to speak) between academy and church, regardless of the specific terms employed in any of the columns. With Aleshire, I believe schools will do well to consider how the balance in their particular institutions may affect their ability to produce effective leaders for the church.

Considering Curriculum

Some of the ecclesial bodies represented by ATS schools prescribe a large percentage of their curriculum; other schools have no such connection. Some church constituencies require a professional theological degree for ordination to ministry, while others look with suspicion at institutions of higher education. Whatever their connection with the church, the faculties of theological schools have difficult determinations to make. How then is the curriculum of a theological school (particularly for professional ministry programs) best connected to the contexts faced by their graduates?

Consider first the following assumptions:

- Seminaries exist for the sake of particular church constituencies, not the other way around.
- Seminaries aim to prepare students to minister effectively in those contexts.
- Seminary curricula commonly reflect the inherent tensions between the differing ethos of the academy and the church.
- Ecclesial contexts are currently in considerable flux, making it difficult for seminaries to meet the changing needs.
- A significant change in the ecclesial context may prompt a need to change the educational preparation process.
- To best meet the changing needs of any ecclesial context, the seminary must cultivate a dynamic relationship of trust and interaction with decision leaders in that context.

Chief academic officers can have a vital influence in determining a proper balance of academic and ecclesiastical goals. The majority of this influence will be exercised in the development of a theological curriculum that best prepares students for ministry in their chosen contexts. Perhaps the most important role for a CAO is to pose the right questions for the faculty to engage. Five questions in particular may serve as a guide in the process of discerning a proper balance between academic and ecclesiastical goals.[11] If these questions are explored in adequate scope and depth, they will likely uncover most of the issues that require careful discernment in the balance between the academic and ecclesial context.

What is our educational mission as a school?

ATS underscores the importance of this question by addressing it in the first of ten standards by which member schools are assessed. "Each member school shall have a formally adopted statement of institutional purpose. The statement of institutional purpose should articulate the mission to which the school believes it is called and define its particular identity and values."[12] Further, the first of the General Institutional Standards lists "ecclesiastical bodies" as one of the constituencies that the school should engage in the process of developing such a statement.

When schools take seriously the mandate to engage "the religious constituencies served,"[13] they can more readily move toward the balance of goals in tension with one another. Representatives of the church constituency will most likely press for goals that reflect an ecclesial mission, bringing balance to the academic goals more likely to be birthed in the school.

The stated educational mission of the school should accurately reflect its identity and vocation. The more closely a school is aligned with a particular ecclesial constituency, the more the school's ethos should reflect the values, practices, and theological convictions of that ecclesial tradition.

The figure on page 339 expresses the importance of purpose in a graphic way. Although one could argue about the use of these specific terms, the chart is meant to convey a sense of movement from the top down. One's purpose comes to bear on one's philosophy, which in turn shapes one's principles and procedures, which finally produce practices that are consistent with the preceding steps. Some refer to it as "laser thinking," the ability to focus the power of one's purpose intensely onto the specific expressions of that purpose. Particularly in the process of curriculum revision, it is important to spend adequate time in the upper levels of the diagram — looking at the

---

11. These questions are adapted and abridged from a list of ten that appear in a folio prepared by ATS for schools contemplating MDiv curriculum revision.

12. "General Institutional Standards," Standard 1, section 1.1.1., ATS *Bulletin* 48, part 1 (2008), p. 134.

13. "General Institutional Standards," Standard 1, preamble, ATS *Bulletin* 48, part 1 (2008), p. 134.

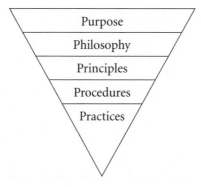

big picture — before moving too quickly toward the arrangement of specific pieces of the curriculum.

How well is our curriculum working as the delivery system for our educational mission?

In its etymological origins, *curriculum* referred to a racecourse. In this vein, an academic curriculum may be considered a "course of study" or a way to "put students through their paces." It conveys the notion that we know what it means to have "finished the race," with markers to demonstrate one's progress along the way. Broadly considered, curriculum is much more than the courses offered for credit. Elliot Eisner argues that every school has three curricula.[14] There is first of all the *explicit* curriculum "articulated in mission statements, courses of study and syllabi." But perhaps of equal importance is the hidden or *implicit* curriculum "found in the rituals and organizational structures, values and assumptions, and patterns of relationship and authority that make up the culture" or ethos of a school. The explanatory power of this concept was illustrated in a sociological study[15] that observed widely differing formative effects on students who attended two different ATS member schools. The authors argue that the *ethos* of each school indelibly shaped its students' educational experience. Finally, there is the *null* curriculum that encompasses all that students are *not* taught.

Faculty discernment about the adequacy of the curriculum should include a discussion of the role that all three curricula play in the delivery of the school's mission. Deep ironies may rise to the surface as faculties struggle

14. Cited in Foster et al., *Educating Clergy: Teaching Practices and Pastoral Imagination* (San Francisco: Jossey-Bass, 2006), p. 49.

15. Jackson W. Carroll et al., *Being There: Culture and Formation in Two Theological Schools* (New York: Oxford University Press, 1997).

honestly with the ethos of their schools. For example, the majority of the curriculum may be designed to teach students the long tradition of the church, with the hope that students will serve as visionary, transformative change agents in the world.

The adequacy of any educational delivery system must be measured by specified criteria. This process is spoken of in the first of the ATS General Institutional Standards: "A comprehensive evaluation process is the primary resource an institution uses to determine the extent to which it is accomplishing its purpose."[16] In an address to the 2006 biennial meeting, Daniel Aleshire observed that the paradigms for evaluation of schools are shifting. The old paradigm focused on the quality of teaching and the accountability of *learners*. It assumed that good teaching would create the context for good learning, and students were accountable to learn. The idea was that if you developed good inputs, you were assured of good results. Some ecclesiastical bodies specify the inputs that a theological school must provide, likely in terms of courses that a student must have successfully completed in order to be ordained.

A new wind, however, is blowing in North America. Departments of education, supported by legislature, are voicing a concern for *outcomes*. While quality inputs may be essential to yield quality outcomes, the emphasis has shifted toward measuring the latter. The emerging paradigm focuses on the quality of learning and the accountability of *teachers*. This shift, which arises from the surrounding culture, assumes that failure of students to learn is a failure of the institution. This change requires a larger focus of assessment, a prospect that is very difficult for faculty to undertake. It is far easier to measure input than it is to measure outcome.

Accreditation agencies are pressing hard to engage schools in assessment processes. ATS aims to assist schools in the move toward assessment-based changes in curriculum. To this end, it publishes a *Handbook of Accreditation: A Guide for Evaluating Theological Learning.*

What are the missionally informed capacities we hope our students will have when they graduate from seminary?

The language of "missionally informed capacities" reflects the concept of outcomes. Capacities are skills, abilities, or competencies that can in some degree be measured as outcomes of the educational process. Again, some ecclesiastical bodies specify a list of competencies or capacities they hope that

16. "General Institutional Standards," Standard 1, section 1.12.3., ATS *Bulletin* 48, part 1 (2008), p. 135.

graduates will be able to demonstrate before taking up a role in a congregation or other ministry.

Several years ago, our small denomination — Mennonite Church USA — sponsored a forum that brought together all of the various programs that offer some aspect of pastoral training. We were amazed to find that there were fifty such programs in addition to our two seminaries. We hoped for some way to coordinate these efforts into a more efficient pattern, an endeavor about as likely to succeed as herding fifty cats into a small kennel. An ad hoc group was appointed to specify certain educational inputs that all ordained pastors should have. By the time they finished with their task, they had moved instead to write a paper that focused on competencies. Further, they specified that it made little difference to them how potential pastors obtained these specified capacities. The paper put our two seminaries on notice that outputs were more important to them than inputs.

How might our faculty build a curriculum that serves to produce the desired capacities in our graduates?

In this arena, perhaps more than in any other, one can sense the tension between academic and ecclesiastical goals. There are four areas where faculty members may feel the tension most keenly.[17]

Academic disciplines vs. professional practice.

The majority of theological schools hire their faculty and design their curriculum with an eye to specialization and compartmentalization into discrete fields of knowledge. Even a small faculty may categorize its courses under broad rubrics such as biblical studies, theological studies, practical theology, etc. The larger the school, the more possible it is to offer courses in increasingly esoteric spheres of knowledge. Faculty who wish to make their mark in the academic environment will naturally press toward the goals of greater specialization. Yet in a small school, faculty may rarely have the opportunity to teach on the growing edge of their discipline. They must settle instead for teaching more basic courses.

In contrast to academic specialization, the ecclesial mandate begs for educational aims that equip students with general skills and integrated thinking. The divisions represented by academic disciplines have little meaning in the parish.

---

17. I owe some of the ideas in the discussion of these four areas to Daniel Aleshire, who touched on them in a speech to new faculty members of ATS schools.

Critical thinking vs. character.

Another tension arises when faculty consider the broadest aims of their teaching. Is it to create critical thinkers or committed Christians? Most seminaries will attempt to teach for both ends, but there is an inherent tension between the two. Critical thinking requires a conscious distancing, a stepping back from churchly or devotional commitments to examine beliefs in a rational, dispassionate manner. The commitment to read biblical texts through a historical-critical lens was forged in the academy, not the church. The church longs for reflective, mature practitioners who cultivate the *habitus* of Christian character.

To deal with the tension in these two modes of instruction, theological schools may offer some courses that emphasize the academic goals and others to achieve the churchly goal. But some students may find it difficult to live with the inherent tension between the two or to make good transitions into parish ministry.

Good scholars vs. good practitioners.

Many competent teachers would love, in their heart of hearts, to see other gifted students pursue the same field of inquiry. Yet they are hired to teach students to do and love a different kind of work — the work of parish ministry. Faculty in a professional school, then, live with a tension. Unlike masters in days of yore who taught their apprentices to imitate them and to pursue the same roles, today's professors hope to equip students for a different vocation.

Exacerbating the tension between a critical distancing and a full-embraced owning is the commonplace academic paradigm that bifurcates theory and application. In this way of thinking, you begin with theory and proceed to application as a sort of secondary concern. Cognition is given pride of place, and application is forced to take a back seat. When such is the case in a theological school, the entry of graduates into the pastorate may require a process of decompression, a period of time to integrate or re-integrate theoretical concepts taught in the classroom into the everyday life of a parish. Clergy who are unable to achieve such integration may well become the strongest antagonists of theological schools. They may well leave behind the theological insights that could best inform and shape their parish ministry.[18] Perhaps the best way to balance this tension is to aim for a greater

---

18. Malcolm Warford, director of the Lexington Seminar, personal correspondence. See also Malcolm Warford, *Practical Wisdom: On Theological Teaching and Learning* (New York: Peter Lang Publishing, 2004).

dialectic between theory and practice in theological studies, with the aim of producing "practical theorists" and "reflective practitioners."

Individual work vs. corporate work.

For the most part, teaching is an individual enterprise, both in the theological school and in other academies of higher learning. Scholars are taught to do individual work in the long climb to the climax of a terminal degree. It would be rare to award PhDs to a group of individuals who collaborated on a dissertation project. Faculty status and tenure are rarely dependent on one's ability to collaborate and work for the common good. Promotions are awarded to individuals, not groups.

The individual nature of scholarly work easily leads to territorialism, which readily leads to protectionism. Indeed, one of the greatest fears bedeviling the curriculum-building process in theological schools is that of "turf wars." Consequently, it is nearly impossible to lead the faculty in a dispassionate discussion of the common curriculum — that which is owned by everyone for the good of all.

In sum, then, a typical faculty with PhDs from schools of higher learning will lean naturally toward the achievement of academic goals. The church community, in contrast, will value different goals. Resolving this tension through some sort of negotiated balance is essential for the health of the church.

How might we test the adequacy of our curriculum as demonstrated by the effectiveness of our graduates in their chosen contexts of ministry?

Theological schools need a variety of strategies in order to maintain a relationship of trust with constituents in the church. There are the standard means of interaction with constituents, sometimes represented in departments or staff roles such as alumni relations, church relations, development, and marketing. These interactions can at times lead to changes in school policy or curriculum. Too often, however, these efforts may appear to be self-serving for the sake of building the institution.

In recent years, Lilly Endowment Inc. has offered generous grants as an invitation to seminaries to propose creative new ways to meet the needs of their constituencies. Partly as a response to such an invitation, Eastern Mennonite Seminary has engaged our constituency in a new way through an emphasis we call Church Partnerships. This approach is an attempt to develop programs of study with particular relevance for the church. Although we have maintained ultimate governance of the programs in every case, we have worked closely with church groups to develop "ownership" by them.

These programs include such partnerships as: (1) a preaching institute, (2) a youth program shared with several church entities, and (3) a collegial arrangement with an undergraduate department in the university to provide basic instruction for bi-vocational pastors who do not have a college degree. Each program is unique in its partnership arrangements, but all have the following in common: (1) they were designed to meet the training needs of a group that would not normally attend seminary, (2) they were shaped through sustained interaction with highly qualified personnel who represented the church on a regional level, (3) they function with advisory committees who represent the church on a regional level, and (4) they involve the church in the recruitment of participants, either through a nomination process or through recommendations. All four of these practices were developed with ecclesial goals in view.

At EMS, we have determined that in order to fulfill our mandate to the church, we must step "outside the walls" of the seminary. This determination has led us to develop online courses to be offered to students who cannot readily move to the seminary, most of whom are from our denominational constituency. We have also launched a satellite campus, a strategy often used by ATS schools to increase their accessibility. Finally, we have determined to develop a curriculum that provides adequate resources for leadership development.

It takes extraordinary wisdom and courage on the part of a CAO in a traditional seminary to address the needed balance between academic and ecclesiastical goals. As theological educators, we aim to equip mature practitioners with the knowledge and skills they need to lead in both the church and the public sphere. This goal requires a level of integration that cannot be achieved solely through a classic schooling paradigm.

13. Understanding and Using Assessment and Accreditation

Understanding and Fostering a Culture of Assessment: A Primer for Academic Deans

John F. VerBerkmoes

The work of the academic dean is diverse and complex, as this volume illustrates. One of the most important aspects of the role is that of steward, steward of the organizational culture and mission. On behalf of the governing board, president, faculty, students, constituent churches, and other institutional stakeholders, the academic dean is responsible to foster "big picture" interdisciplinary thinking and mission-focused conversation within the institution. It is the academic dean who is in the best position to foster this kind of critical engagement and collaborative learning in relation to the organizational mission. The hard questions must be asked, and the dean is the one to do it:

- How successful are we in achieving our organizational mission?
- What are our core values, and is there a gap between espoused values and enacted values?
- How well are our students achieving the outcomes we intend within our courses and degree programs?
- How well prepared are our graduates for vocational ministry and/or advanced study?
- How open are we to learning, innovating, and changing as individuals and as an organization?

These important questions, and the desire to answer them with credibility and integrity, inevitably drive the academic dean and the faculty to the work of assessment and evaluation. Offering wise leadership to assessment and evaluation processes requires, first, that the dean articulate and help colleagues to embrace a right understanding of what assessment is. Second, it is helpful to understand the multiple facets of assessment and evaluation as well as the processes and methods employed. Finally, fostering a culture of assessment is vital.

Fostering Right Understanding

A Theological Task

In attempting to engage the faculty and other administrators in the work of assessment, assessment and evaluation should be framed, and in some cases re-framed, as a theological task inherent to the work of theological educators. Faculty resistance to assessment is well documented.[1] This resistance is often rooted, however, in the fact that assessment has been presented as an external imposition brought on by governmental bodies and accrediting agencies.

Despite the unique heritage of faith within theological schools, few theological faculties have been invited to consider this work from a theological perspective. Academic deans will find greater success in their efforts to engage faculty members in the work of assessment by inviting them to consider how the work of assessment can be an act of stewardship and a tool for institutional transformation. Theological schools from the Reformed tradition might consider how assessment provides institutional engagement in the notion of "reformed and always reforming," while schools from the Wesleyan and Methodist traditions might think about assessment as a means for the institution to "move on to perfection." Continuous quality improvement can be understood from a theological perspective, and the academic dean should foster such thinking within the unique theological framework of the school.[2]

---

1. B. E. Walvoord, *Assessment Clear and Simple: A Practical Guide for Institutions, Departments, and General Education* (San Francisco: Jossey-Bass, 2004), and P. T. Ewell, "An Emerging Scholarship: A Brief History of Assessment," in T. W. Banta, ed., *Building a Scholarship of Assessment* (San Francisco: Jossey-Bass, 2002), pp. 3-25.

2. John F. VerBerkmoes, "Student Outcomes Assessment: A Study of the Organizational Factors that Foster or Inhibit Progress in Establishing a Culture of Assessment within Graduate Theological Schools," Diss., Michigan State University, 2006.

A Process of Organizational Learning

In addition to considering assessment from a theological perspective, the academic dean should frame the work of assessment and evaluation as a process of organizational learning. In *The Fifth Discipline*, Peter Senge describes the learning organization as a place "where people continually expand their capacity to create the results they truly desire, where new and expansive patterns of thinking are nurtured, where collective aspiration is set free, and where people are continually learning how to learn together."[3] Continuous learning and collaboration with peers are core values within the academy. The academic dean will secure greater ownership of the work of assessment when it is described and enacted as a learning process and in collaboration with peers.

A Matter of Accountability

While assessment should be framed and engaged based on shared theological commitments and the desire for organizational learning, it must also be understood as a legitimate form of accountability. Theological schools are stewards of the theological heritages they represent, and we should not be surprised that stakeholders wish to evaluate how well our schools are doing in representing these interests. If our graduates are not performing particularly well in ministerial assignments, individual churches and denominational bodies have a right to ask the difficult questions. The outcome of these conversations may result in greater clarity concerning the limitations of theological schools and the need for greater collaboration with churches in the education of future ministerial leaders. However, some substantive curricular changes may be in order, and the academic dean must skillfully facilitate these conversations and processes. The point here is that key stakeholders have a right to ask the institution to demonstrate that it is achieving its stated mission, and the academic dean must foster an understanding of assessment among faculty and administrators that welcomes this kind of scrutiny and accountability.

---

3. Peter M. Senge, *The Fifth Discipline: The Art and Practice of the Learning Organization* (New York: Currency Doubleday, 1990), p. 3.

An Ongoing Cyclical Process

Assessment should not be understood as an occasional frenzied effort to demonstrate competency in the achievement of a school's mission before an accrediting agency. Rather, it is more rightly understood as an ongoing cyclical process intended to yield ongoing improvement in performance and the achievement of intended outcomes. This cyclical process is relevant to all forms of assessment and evaluation within an academic environment: assessment of student learning, program review, evaluation of faculty work, evaluation of administrative performance, and assessment of institutional effectiveness. In describing the assessment of student learning as a cyclical process, Palomba and Banta suggest that "assessment is the systematic collection, review, and use of information about educational programs undertaken for the purpose of improving student learning and development."[4] Sustaining the cyclical processes related to all forms of assessment described above is central to the work of the academic dean, providing the unique opportunity to effect the professional development of individuals and the overall health of the organization.

A Foundation for Integrity and Data-Based Decision Making

In addition to the concepts outlined above, credible systems of assessment and evaluation enable the institution to function with greater levels of integrity by expanding the institution's self-knowledge and building an objective basis for quality improvement decisions. Without credible data derived from assessment, administrators will be hesitant to address and assist underdeveloped and/or underperforming personnel. They will know a problem exists, even have anecdotal information about the problem, but not possess sufficient data to address it with clarity and conviction.

Similarly, without credible systems of assessment, faculty promotion and tenure processes will become a "rubber stamp" experience largely based on longevity and good citizenship within the institution. Without credible systems of assessment, the strategies and curricula employed to foster student learning and ministerial formation will go unchanged. They will tend to reflect faculty research interests and academy values more than

4. C. A. Palomba and T. A. Banta, *Assessment Essentials: Planning, Implementing, and Improving Assessment in Higher Education* (San Francisco: Jossey-Bass, 1999), p. 4

the needs of students and the requirements of ministerial leadership roles. Such situations reflect unintended compromises in systems and institutional integrity. In contrast, well-crafted systems of assessment enable the institution to function with greater integrity in regard to the fulfillment of its promises and mission, since the process of assessment fosters a more objective view of the strengths and growth edges of personnel and programs. This objective view then provides a basis for decision making about quality improvement.

Once a foundation has been laid for a right understanding of assessment, deans are better able to help colleagues undertake the multiple dimensions of assessment and evaluation common in educational environments.

Fostering Multiple Dimensions of Assessment and Evaluation

Assessment of Student Learning

Assessment of student learning is often distinguished in the literature from other forms of assessment by such phrases as outcomes assessment, value-added assessment, and more recently learner-centered assessment.[5] Traditionally, the term *assessment* was used by practitioners synonymously with testing and measurement. More recently, scholars are defining assessment as a process with a focus upon improvement in student learning. For example, Walvoord defines assessment as "the systematic collection of information about student learning, using the time, knowledge, expertise, and resources available, in order to inform decisions about how to improve learning."[6] Huba and Freed describe assessment in similar terms:

> Assessment is the process of gathering and discussing information from multiple and diverse sources in order to develop a deeper understanding of what students know, understand, and can do with their knowledge as

5. T. W. Banta, ed., *Implementing Outcomes Assessment: Promises and Perils,* New Directions for Institutional Research, no. 59 (San Francisco: Jossey-Bass, 1988). D. F. Halpern, ed., *Student Outcomes Assessment: What Institutions Stand to Gain,* New Directions for Institutional Research, no. 60 (San Francisco: Jossey-Bass, 1987). M. E. Huba and J. E. Freed, *Learner-Centered Assessment on College Campuses: Shifting the Focus from Teaching to Learning* (Boston: Allyn and Bacon, 2000).

6. Walvoord, *Assessment Clear and Simple,* p. 2.

a result of their educational experiences; the process culminates when assessment results are used to improve subsequent learning.[7]

Another key aspect of assessment of student learning relates to the focus of assessment. In other words, what should be assessed? The most basic answer to this question is that intended student learning outcomes should be assessed. These intended student learning outcomes need to be crafted by faculty to establish the basis for future evaluation of course and program effectiveness. But what should be the character of those outcomes? As institutions largely focused on preparing persons for vocational ministry, seminaries are generally interested in the holistic formation of students. With this in mind, academic deans should foster the development of student learning outcomes that reflect diverse forms of knowledge and competency. Cognitive formation is extremely important, but it is not the only aspect of emphasis in learning and should not be the only emphasis in the assessment process. Affective and behavioral competencies should also be fostered by the curriculum and routinely assessed.

There are three primary units of measure that represent different levels of assessment. One unit of measure is the student. If the goal is to aid an individual student in learning and growth during the course or program of study, then the unit of measure would be the individual student. Thus, a system should be developed to assess individual student learning. Increasingly, this is done by use of a student learning portfolio with routine points of progress review and the formation of developmental growth plans as needed. A considerable body of literature has emerged on the use of student learning portfolios in the assessment of individual students.[8]

A second unit of measure is assessment focused upon a particular course. A course-level focus in assessment can be used for mid-course corrections (formative assessment) and to facilitate changes to improve the course at its completion (summative assessment). Program-level assessment is a third unit of measure and can also serve formative and summative purposes. With course-level and program-level assessment, structures and systems must also be developed and routinely enacted to engage faculty in the processes of formative and summative assessment. This requires significant

7. Huba and Freed, *Learner-Centered Assessment*, p. 8.

8. R. L. Larson, "Using Portfolio Assessment to Assess the Impact of a Curriculum," in T. W. Banta, *Portfolio Assessment: Uses, Cases, Scoring, and Impact* (San Francisco: Jossey-Bass, 2003), pp. 7-10. Huba and Freed, *Learner-Centered Assessment*.

institutional focus and discipline, and the academic dean should provide the necessary leadership.

As noted above, assessment is more a process than an event. A number of models exist to aid the academic dean in managing the process. Banta provides a four-step process that demonstrates the meaning of assessment in operational terms: (1) setting objectives for student learning, (2) ensuring that these objectives are taught and/or fostered within the curriculum, (3) assessing student learning, (4) using findings to improve instruction.[9] Similarly, Walvoord provides a three-step model in relation to assessing student learning: (1) articulate your goals for student learning, (2) gather evidence about how well students are meeting the goals, and (3) use the information for improvement.[10] Regardless of what model is employed, the academic dean will need to foster sufficient organizational attention and discipline to sustain the cycle and to do so on an ongoing basis.

For example, consider the program level summative assessment work of the Old Testament division of Grand Rapids Theological Seminary, the school for which I serve as academic dean. In conjunction with faculty colleagues, the division developed intended student learning outcomes for the Master of Divinity degree program. One of the intended core student learning outcomes was that the student would be able to "conduct disciplined biblical interpretation and application with reference to the Greek and Hebrew texts" (fulfilling step one of the Walvoord model).

Subsequently, the division identified the crucial documents for inclusion in the student learning portfolio. One of these documents was the exegetical paper for our Old Testament III course, the last in the sequence of exegetical courses in Old Testament. Students were required to submit copies to their student learning portfolios, thus providing a data pool in relation to the intended outcome noted above (fulfilling step two of the Walvoord model).

Next, the division engaged in an assessment project to evaluate how well the students were doing in achieving the intended outcome noted above. To do this, they developed a grading rubric which consisted of a set of six sub-outcomes related to the central intended outcome. The sub-outcomes included the following:

---

9. T. W. Banta, ed., *Hallmarks of Effective Outcomes Assessment* (San Francisco: Jossey-Bass, 2004).

10. Walvoord, *Assessment Clear and Simple.*

1. Demonstrates knowledge and skill in relation to biblical genre
2. Demonstrates awareness and respect for historical context
3. Demonstrates proficiency in research using exegetical tools and secondary sources
4. Demonstrates competency with the original languages in exegesis
5. Demonstrates proficiency in drawing theological conclusions from exegetical work
6. Demonstrates proficiency in linking exegetical work to ministry and life application

The division used this rubric as an assessment tool to read across a sample of Old Testament III papers, papers collected within the student learning portfolios over the previous two years. Each paper was scored on a 1-5 scale (1-weak and 5-outstanding), and each paper was read by both Old Testament professors. After all the documents in the sample were read and scored, they were totaled and averaged across the six sub-outcomes. The resulting dataset provided the division the basis to make informed judgments about how well they were doing in fostering student learning in relation to the intended student learning outcome. It also provided the basis to propose changes in the teaching and learning process and assessment structure (fulfilling step three in the Walvoord model) to foster increased levels of student learning.

A number of methods for assessing student learning have emerged within higher education. Many of these same methods are routinely employed by graduate theological schools. Lopez identifies a valuable distinction between direct measures of student learning and indirect measures of student learning. Direct measures provide evidence of actual growth and development of a student in relation to the educational experiences at the institution. Direct measures prominent in the current literature include capstone projects and experiences (e.g., thesis, practicum, internship, etc.), portfolio assessment, standardized tests, and locally developed tests.[11]

The second type of measure is an indirect measure. Indirect measures of student learning "enrich and illuminate aspects of what the direct measures tell us about a student's academic achievement."[12] Indirect measures include alumni surveys, employer surveys, student surveys, exit interviews

11. C. L. Lopez, *Opportunities for Improvement: Advice from Consultant-Evaluators on Programs to Assess Student Learning* (Chicago: The Higher Learning Commission, 1997).

12. Lopez, *Opportunities for Improvement*, p. 14.

and student focus groups, job placement data, and graduation rates. It should be clearly understood that accrediting agencies view direct measures of student learning as crucial for credible systems of assessment. Direct measures should be viewed as the core data of assessment, while indirect measures should be viewed as quite important, but supplemental data. The academic dean of the theological school will need to foster conversations and processes to aid the faculty in determining which methods of assessing student learning are most appropriate to the intended outcomes of the particular degree programs.

Evaluation of Faculty Work

Evaluation of faculty performance is another dimension of assessment that typically falls within the responsibilities of the academic dean. While this task is generally the academic dean's to initiate and monitor, it is enacted as a shared process with faculty colleagues. While institutions vary in the methods and processes employed, generally a well developed system of faculty evaluation includes at least three types of data collection and four systems of formational evaluation and judgment. The three types of data collection include (1) student evaluations, (2) peer review of classroom instruction, and (3) curricular vitae or faculty load report (tracking annual contributions in teaching, research, and service). Normative patterns of data collection should be established for each type, both in frequency and methodology. Standardized templates for the evaluations should be used, whether these are purchased or developed internally. Generally, standardized student evaluations are purchased, while the other assessment processes are internally developed and rightly take on the distinctives of the particular institution.

As noted above, there are generally four systems of formational evaluation and judgment: (1) annual self-evaluation with growth plan, (2) annual evaluative meeting with the academic dean or division chair, (3) promotion review, and (4) tenure review. Literature exists to nuance these evaluative processes. Institutional discipline in data collection in the forms outlined above yields significant fruit for the formational evaluation and judgment systems. If the institution is disciplined in the various forms of data collection, the strengths of the faculty member will be clear and the growth edges will be identifiable. This will enable the academic dean or division chair, or the promotion and tenure committee, to enact sound judgments and provide substantive guidance in the professional development of the individual.

Neglect of the data collection systems results in crisis data collection and/or thinly founded personnel-related judgments. Such a situation creates great problems for the institution, both in its treatment of persons and in its aspirations of quality improvement.

Evaluation of Administrative Work

In addition to fostering systems for the evaluation of faculty work, the academic dean must invest in developing and sustaining credible systems for evaluating the work of staff and administration. A number of standardized evaluative systems can be purchased that include both self-assessment and supervisor assessment. Consideration should also be given to a 360-degree approach to personnel evaluation. This approach solicits evaluative feedback from individuals above, beside, and below in the organizational chart. Such an approach carries some inherent risks but models commitment to collaboration and learning. If, as academic dean, you aspire to foster a culture of learning and improvement, what better opportunity to show you are serious than by giving faculty and staff an opportunity to evaluate your own performance? By offering them an invitation to contribute to your professional growth and development, you build trust and respect as you model the core value of being open to new learning and growth.

Program Evaluation

Using the data and findings of the work associated with assessing student learning, the academic dean and faculty should engage in iterative and patterned program evaluation. Program evaluation should be engaged as a process that includes all of the central stakeholders associated with the particular theological school. This should extend beyond the walls of the theological school and include alumni, clergy, congregational leaders, and denominational leaders. While employing this perspective, program evaluation should consider whether the current student learning outcomes of the particular degree program were adequately achieved by students. They should also consider the sufficiency of the program outcomes, given the changing face of ministry within the given cultural context. Changes to student learning outcomes generally lead to changes in courses or elements of courses and often require consideration of changes in teaching methodology. A number of comprehensive sources are available to guide the academic dean in this work.[13]

Good Practice and Compliance with ATS Standards of Accreditation

Standards of accreditation, including the ATS General Institutional Standards, are intended to guide institutions into habits of "good practice" and organizational well-being. Like the work of assessment, the academic dean is wise to frame this work as an opportunity for learning and organizational growth. Assessment and accreditation are intimately related, reinforcing one another. Organizational discipline in the work of assessment fosters continuous quality improvement and puts the institution in a healthy position to engage in self-study and accreditation-related site visits. If the institution has attended to the work of assessment in the various domains described, data and data-based decisions will abound, making the self-study process quite manageable. Neglecting assessment will create a crisis management approach to the self-study and the re-accreditation process.

In combination, these various forms of assessment and evaluation provide a roadmap for the academic dean to foster learning and growth. It remains to consider how the dean helps an institution sustain these commitments over time and fosters a culture of assessment.

Fostering a Culture of Assessment

For the work of assessment to yield its full potential and be sustainable, it must be more than a task to be achieved. Rather, it must become a core value of the institution, a core value for both faculty and administration. This means it must become a part of the cultural fabric and institutional rhythm. But how can this ideal be accomplished? It is hard enough to simply get institutional participants to do the work of assessment, much less embrace it as a core value. What can the academic dean do to foster a sustainable culture of assessment within a theological school?

Robert Duncan developed a model for diagnosing organizational de-

13. J. S. Stark and L. R. Latucca, *Shaping the College Curriculum: Academic Plans in Action* (Boston: Allyn and Bacon, 1997).

sign and fostering change to organizational culture. According to Duncan, the elements of the model serve as levers to organizational change. Each lever (i.e., mission/vision, structure, strategy, reward systems, decision support systems, human resource systems, and leadership behavior) must be aligned with the other levers to support the desired organizational culture. Thus, if a culture of assessment is a desired attribute for a theological school, the levers must be aligned to support such a culture.[14] Duncan's model offers a way to explore how the academic dean in a theological school might approach the work of assessment from a holistic perspective, creating a more favorable environment for the work of assessment to take root and thrive into the future.

Figure A: Fostering a Culture of Assessment

Vision and Mission

According to Duncan, vision is the "aspired future state of the organization."[15] While mission has to do with what we do and what we are about in

14. Robert B. Duncan, *Leading Strategic Change Process Toolkit* (East Lansing, MI: Broad College of Business, Michigan State University, 2003).

15. Duncan, *Leading Strategic Change Process Toolkit*, p. 52.

the present, vision speaks to what we want to become in the future. In regard to assessment, the academic dean should consider how the organizational vision, that future desired state of the organization, can be enhanced and achieved by the work of assessment and the processes associated with it (i.e., setting objectives and outcomes, data collection, evaluative judgment, and organizational learning). Consider the following questions for collaborative discussion among key institutional stakeholders:

- How might the work of assessment enhance the achievement of the institutional mission?
- How might the work of assessment aid in refining and achieving the institutional vision?

Strategy

Strategy is described in relation to customer groups served, customer needs satisfied, products and services sold, value added to the market, and anticipated changes to markets and customers. For theological schools, strategy should be understood in relation to educational markets, educational services, educational outcomes, and the key stakeholders of graduate theological education. Strategy has to do with how a theological school intends to fulfill its vocation and mission. Consideration should be given to the potential synergies that exist between institutional strategy formulation and the work of assessment. If a theological school seeks to foster a sustainable culture of assessment, steps must be taken to align the work of strategy formation with the work of assessment. Questions worthy of consideration include the following:

- How might strategy formation better support the work of assessment?
- How might the work of assessment better support strategy formation?

Structure

Structure has to do with how the institution is organized. It has to do with the reporting lines of institutional participants and patterns of workflow. Structure is expressed in the organizational chart and helps to define the lines of responsibility, authority, and accountability. In relation to assessment, the academic dean should consider whether the current structures are appropriate and sufficiently clear to foster broad-based ownership and engagement in the work of assessment. Institutions most successful at the work of assessment tend to have substantive structures to support assessment (e.g., assessment director and/or an assessment and planning committee) and normative patterns to the process of assessment (e.g., predictable patterns of data collection, annual assessment projects by divisions, routine assessments of faculty and administrative work). The following questions should be considered by the academic dean in relation to structure:

- How well does the existing structure support the achievement of the work of assessment?
- Are there any structural boundaries or barriers inhibiting the work of assessment?
- What adjustments to structure are needed to better support the work of assessment and to create broad-based engagement?

Decision Support Systems

Decision support systems relate to the adequacy of information, the effectiveness of decision making, and the effectiveness of resource allocation and budgeting. If a culture of assessment is desired within a theological school, then the decision support systems must be aligned to support such a culture. Specifically, this means that the institution must work at securing credible and meaningful data, make data available in a timely manner for strategic decisions, make use of the data in decision making and communicate this to institutional stakeholders, and support these decisions with financial resources. The academic dean should foster conversations and system analysis by asking some key questions:

- How timely and accurate is the information used for decisions?
- Is the information necessary for decisions available to the people making decisions?
- Is the data derived from the work of assessment being used in strategic decision making, and do institutional participants know that it is being used?
- How effective are the resource allocation systems and budgeting systems in supporting decisions informed by assessment data?

Reward Systems

Organizations use reward systems to motivate organizational members toward higher levels of excellence and achievement. Rewards can include financial compensation, but they can also include recognition in various other forms. In relation to assessment, the academic dean needs to consider how the existing reward systems of the organization foster or inhibit the work of assessment. If a culture of assessment is desired within the theological school, the reward systems must support this desired culture. Questions for consideration include the following:

- Does confusion exist concerning assessment as an organizational priority (i.e., desired performance objectives compared to criteria by which reward decisions are made)?
- Do the institutional reward system encourage engagement in the work of assessment?

Human Resource Systems

Human resource systems concern the recruitment, training, evaluation, and developmental efforts enacted in relation to the people of the organization. For theological schools desirous of a sustainable culture of assessment, consideration must be given to how its systems and practices of human resource support or inhibit the work of assessment. Specifically, the academic dean should consider knowledge of and appreciation for assessment as important criteria in faculty and administrator recruitment and hiring. Personnel evaluations, both faculty and administration, should include consideration of engagement and productivity in the work of assessment within the institution. Assessment should also become a more significant aspect of faculty and staff professional development efforts. The academic dean should consider the following human resource–related questions:

- How might faculty with social science backgrounds provide leadership to the work of assessment?
- What recruitment practices need to change to develop new desired competencies for the organization in the area of assessment?
- Given the commitment to foster a culture of assessment, what

assessment-related knowledge and skill should be considered in future faculty and administrative hiring?

• Given the commitment to foster a culture of assessment, what changes need to be made to faculty and administrative training and development?

Leadership Behavior

Leadership behavior confirms what is most valued within the organization. The attention, speech, and actions of organizational leaders foster or inhibit the desired organizational culture. If a sustainable culture of assessment is the goal of a theological school, the behavior of its leaders must align with this espoused value. Two simple questions for consideration are as follows:

• How closely does the communication and action of the organizational leaders align with the work of assessment?
• How might the attention, speech, and actions of organizational leaders need to change to better support the work of assessment?

A Wise Investment

The work of the academic dean requires a number of competencies and significant administrative discipline. In the midst of the pressures of the role, assessment and accreditation can be viewed as burdensome and tasks that simply need to be achieved to fulfill institutional obligations. On the other hand, assessment and accreditation can be understood and advanced as related opportunities to foster institutional stewardship, collaborative learning, and quality improvement. The wise academic dean will choose this later path, and in so doing engage in a process that fosters increasing levels of institutional well-being and integrity.

ADDITIONAL RESOURCES

Aleshire, Daniel O. "The Character and Assessment of Learning for Religious Vocation: Master of Divinity Education and Numbering the Levites." *Theological Education* 39, no. 1 (2003): 1-17.

Braskamp, L. A., and J. C. Ory. *Assessing Faculty Work: Enhancing Individual and Institutional Performance.* San Francisco: Jossey-Bass, 1994.

Jurkowitz, C. M. "What Is the Literature Saying about Learning and Assessment in Higher Education? *Theological Education* 39, no. 1 (2003): 53-92.

Klimoski, V. J. "Getting to the questions: Assessment and the professional character of ministry." *Theological Education* 39, no. 1 (2003): 35-52.

Myers, W. R. *Ten steps towards implementing an institutional culture of assessment in a theological school.* Paper presented at the annual meeting of the Evangelical Deans, Phoenix, AZ, 2004.

Shifting Models of Assessment of Student Learning Outcomes: A Key to Renewal, Improvement, and Effectiveness

Leland V. Eliason

A Paradigm Shift in U.S. Education

"Paradigm shift" describes the change in benchmarks used by accreditation agencies to define good theological education. The shift has moved the focus of assessment from institutional attributes to student learning outcomes. The primary question in the latter model asks, Are students learning what we say they are within a given institution?

At the 2006 ATS Biennial Meeting, John Harris highlighted the inadequacy of assessing institutional outcomes when he stated that "the correlation is zero or so small that it is negligible" between the faculty, facilities, finances, and library of an institution and the learning outcomes of its students. At the same meeting, Daniel Aleshire stated,

> In the emerging paradigm, the failure of students to learn is perceived as an institutional failure. This shift makes teachers accountable to good learning instead of students accountable to good teaching. Students need to study, of course, and do their part, but if learning fails to occur, an institution can no longer think of itself as a 'good' school. The definition of educational integrity is shifting.

One way to understand the paradigmatic impact of the new criteria for what constitutes good theological education is to envision the pervasive impact of assessing student learning outcomes:

- Presidents will have new data to inform decisions regarding institutional priorities and the direction of institutional growth.
- The faculty will reevaluate their teaching methods in light of new data being provided in answering the question, "How do students learn?" Course syllabi will likely be in a process of continual improvement based on learning outcomes data.
- Students will be more motivated and take greater responsibility for their learning within an educational environment that seeks to give them every advantage to learn at their maximum capacities.
- Faculty members and deans will examine curriculum design so that both the design and the kinds of courses offered are aligned with stated goals.
- The educational ethos of the school will be characterized by new energy derived from "data-driven incentives" tailored to institutional mission and establishing realistic benchmarks by which to measure development, growth, and quality of learning.
- CAOs, whether provosts or deans, will discover that they must constantly design better methods of gaining insightful data. Clear data can be used to leverage unprecedented changes to achieve the goals that define what comprises good theological education. A new platform will have been built for the leadership roles and responsibilities of CAOs.

If this portrayal of the anticipated outcomes of the new paradigm for assessment is accurate, the challenges before us will be well worth the effort. The impact of assessing student learning outcomes effectively could be a key factor in the continual renewal and improvement of the effectiveness of theological education. But it takes considerable effort both to establish a framework for thinking about assessment and to create effective assessment processes.

One of the most challenging aspects of living through a paradigm shift is discovering what parts of a previous way of doing things will survive. It is dangerous to assume that because something has not been assessed well that it is therefore not worth doing; or that because a learning outcome is difficult to assess it should be minimized or eliminated; or that the burden of proof lies entirely with the current way of doing theological education. In fact, not all assessment tools are helpful; some new ones need to be invented, and there are inappropriate ways of doing assessment. Nevertheless, a major shift is taking place, and we must seek to understand what belongs to the new and what belongs to the old. We need to ask, What do we need to let go of because holding on will impede progress? and What is peripheral to the new paradigm, and what will be lasting and worth so much that no effort should be spared in finding a way to do it?

Answering those questions goes beyond the scope of this discussion. What does seem clear is that CAOs must understand the art and science of assessing student learning outcomes. The questions we must ask are significant, e.g.: Are the goals of a class or of a degree program the right goals? What learning outcomes do we want to assess? What are the best assessment instruments? How do we analyze the gaps between the goals for a class (or a degree program or a seminary) and wisely use data from assessment to narrow those gaps, to improve outcomes, and to further the likelihood that the goals will be accomplished? How do we offer faculty members the kinds of professional development that will enable them to embrace assessment as something worth doing?

Perhaps it is wise to manage expectations as we enter the world of assessment and ask what "good enough" assessment looks like. When I used to lead seminars on developing parenting skills, the phrase "good enough parenting" both reduced the expectation of doing this enormously important job perfectly and elevated the importance of intentional efforts. Similarly, good assessment recognizes that it is not possible to assess all areas of theological education perfectly and at the same time it is crucial to lift up the value of persistent, intentional assessment.

"Good enough" assessment identifies student learning outcome goals that are stated within courses, degree programs, and institutional commitments that together constitute the vision and core values of the school. Good enough assessment is ongoing rather than sporadic; is done systemically rather than in silos; is selective rather than compulsive about doing everything; is patient rather than seeking for quick fixes; is invitational rather than coercive; and learns as much from failed attempts to help students learn as it does from successes.

This discussion seeks to (1) provide pointers to developing and nurturing a culture of assessment; (2) identify domains of assessment and select examples of different assessment tools that are appropriate for the diverse kinds of student learning outcomes that need to be evaluated; and (3) ask how the assessment process can embrace institutional goals and objectives and help in effective institutional planning.

Many examples are drawn from my own school, Bethel Seminary of Bethel University, not because we do assessment perfectly, but rather because concrete examples may be more helpful than a list of "shoulds" and "oughts" wrapped in theory. Bethel is on a journey of learning the art and practice of assessment with other seminaries and schools of theology. Hopefully we can be helpful to one another in the process of becoming more effective in achieving the student learning outcomes that matter so much for the effectiveness of our respective graduates.

Developing and Nurturing a Culture That Values Assessment

The mandate to assess learning outcomes was part of the report by the U.S. Secretary of Education Margaret Spelling, and this mandate is now embodied in the ATS standards of accreditation as well as in the benchmarks of the various branches of the Higher Learning Commission.

The fact that assessment is now required tempts leaders to use unhelpful approaches. A *coercive approach* declares to the primary stakeholders, "We must do it because accreditation requires it." While there is a truth to this declaration, it lacks the encouragement of an invitation and an appeal to the highest motives of faculty and staff. We might be tempted to *scold*: "Seminary faculty have earned a reputation for being the most resistant of all faculties to using assessment tools." And the appeal of the *expedient approach* is constantly with us: "Our self-study is coming in two years, and we must find some data to demonstrate our effectiveness."

There is a better way to move into the arena of assessment with effectiveness. Ronald Heifetz encourages leaders to step back and take a view from the balcony.[1] From this vantage point one may gain greater clarity about the big picture and discernment regarding the most important actions that can be encouraged by each of the key players. The following two strategies are particularly helpful in gaining a perspective from the "balcony."

1. Cultivate curiosity that leads to the exploration of core issues.
Curiosity may be one of the most underrated human traits within seminary education. A consultant friend who visited sixty schools during the past five years observes, "I find a culture of dynamic growth exists where deans take

---

1. Ronald A. Heifetz, *Leadership without Easy Answers* (Cambridge, MA: The Belknap Press of the Harvard University Press, 1994), pp. 252-54.

seriously their role to provide regular occasions for faculty to discuss their primary concerns about teaching." Such deans know that teaching is teleological and that faculty members want to achieve certain goals. Deans who follow their own curiosity about faculty interests will find doors through which the assessment process can move.

Curiosity permeates the story told by Richard Light at a 2007 Harvard Institute of Higher Education meeting on the theme, "Performance Assessment in Higher Education." Light was asked by four Harvard presidents — Derek Bok, Neil Rudenstine, Lawrence Summers, and Drew Faust — to lead an ongoing project to strengthen the college experience for students.[2] In his presentation Light described how his work on assessment began with a phone call from Bok, who asked, "Who around our wonderful university is systematically examining the effectiveness of what we do for our graduates?" When Light answered, "I can't think of anyone," Bok answered, "I can't either — come and see me so we can talk."

When it became clear that the president was concerned about such basic matters as teaching, advising, and the quality of students' lives, Light and Bok came up with a plan. They invited thirty faculty colleagues, thirty administrative colleagues, some students, and representatives from Boston University and the Massachusetts Institute of Technology to meet for one evening each month. The question put to the group was: "How do we ask students — the customers — how we are doing?" Twenty-five hundred face-to-face interviews later and with the benefit of the data that emerged, major changes have been implemented in advising, developing course offerings and student brochures, and assessing writing effectiveness. In this case, the story starts with a curious president who tapped the curiosity of a teacher. Together they listened intently to hundreds of students. When the findings suggested better ways of working with students, changes were implemented.

Most seminary interviews of potential new faculty colleagues employ curiosity. Interviewers request that candidates describe the most satisfying teaching experience they have had in recent months. In many cases, the answer to the first question yields stories about students "getting it," when "the lights went on," and how the teacher could sense that the class was growing to more deeply understand the implications of what they were discussing.

When assessment tools help to clarify what transpires in peak mo-

---

2. Richard J. Light has published several books. *Making the Most of College* (Cambridge, MA: Harvard University Press, 2002) won the Stone Award for the best book on education and society.

ments of growth and then a follow-up discussion provides helpful suggestions for increasing teaching effectiveness, assessment helps faculty members in their quest for greater effectiveness. Assessment is no longer a
burden to bear, an add-on that wastes valuable time, or a self-study hoop to
jump. Rather, assessment becomes a means of professional growth and development, a catalyst for refinements and clarifications of classroom assignments, and a key to improving the worth and quality of a course. Deans
and provosts will find that guiding assessment processes will be most effective within a culture of curiosity about what constitutes good theological
education.

2. Welcome assessment as an ally in the quest to achieve strategic outcomes.
In the fall of 2003 I was asked to address a faculty and staff workshop on the
theme, "Growing Edges at Bethel Seminary." Six different growing edges surfaced for the presentation:

- Improve teaching effectiveness
- Increase cross-cultural effectiveness
- Refine the seminary curriculum
- Attend to our own transformation
- Ensure the excellence of incoming students
- Create and implement a viable economic plan for the seminary

These six growing edges touched a responsive note for the faculty and staff,
and they adopted them as part of their own commitments. Eventually the six
initiatives became the backbone of a strategic planning document, now in its
fourth revision. Since 2003 each faculty retreat has been built around one of
the first four initiatives. Examples of classroom teaching have been shared,
including what worked and what did not. Results of research regarding formation goals and *outcomes have enriched discussions and clarified classroom
objectives.*

    In 2003 assessment of student learning outcomes had not been ele-
vated to center stage as it is today. But the goals of each initiative came about
as a result of an assessment; multiple kinds of data showed there was room
for improvement in each of these areas. The point is that every school is already doing assessment. Part of responding to the new mandate means developing ongoing records for something that we are already doing — not an
add-on to strategic planning but a vital part of the planning process. The
formal process of doing assessment and identifying gaps between goals and

performance, followed by revising goals and plans in light of the new data, can be harnessed to improve strategic planning initiatives.

Identifying the Domains and Tools of Assessment

Within a culture that values assessment, one must decide what to assess and how to assess. The following strategies have proven very helpful at my own seminary.

1. Create room for the learning outcomes from life's informal curriculum.
Graduate theological education offers a structured study environment for a short period of time in the life of students who may range in age from 22 to 62. Their lives already incorporate many learning outcomes that profoundly shape who they are. The learned outcomes from life that students bring to the seminary include a mixed bag of issues. Excitement to learn needs to be reinforced. Prejudices need to be deconstructed. Residues of doubt and cynicism need to be understood, perhaps modified, and used as fodder for additional growth and development.

The diagram below seeks to juxtapose key issues of life alongside a for-

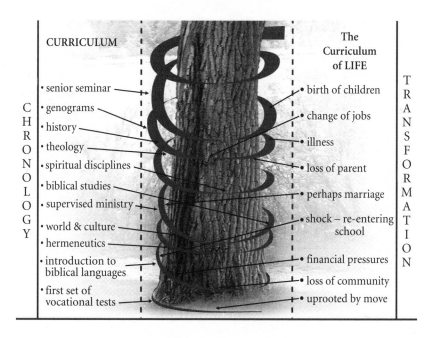

CURRICULUM — The Curriculum of LIFE

CHRONOLOGY

- senior seminar
- genograms
- history
- theology
- spiritual disciplines
- biblical studies
- supervised ministry
- world & culture
- hermeneutics
- introduction to biblical languages
- first set of vocational tests

- birth of children
- change of jobs
- illness
- loss of parent
- perhaps marriage
- shock – re-entering school
- financial pressures
- loss of community
- uprooted by move

TRANSFORMATION

mal curriculum. Often the urgency of "life's curriculum" takes precedence over the requirements of the "formal curriculum," and often the two curricula co-exist in uneasy tension. Whatever system of assessment is used to evaluate student learning outcomes in the formal curricula, needs to provide multiple points of cross referencing in order to ensure that the important issues of life are included in the learning experience.

A few years ago, two much-loved faculty members at Bethel Seminary died during the school year. One died from an extended battle with cancer, another from a sudden collapse (likely an aneurysm) after a workout at a gym. Life's curriculum within our community trumped the formal curriculum for many weeks. A significant number of faculty colleagues used the experience as grist for the formal curriculum requirements through class discussions and papers written. These focused upon a wide range of topics including death, grief, loss, depression, community, hope, resurrection, and heaven.

2. Identify the categories or domains of assessment within the formal curriculum.

In *Educating Clergy*,[3] the first in a series of studies for the Carnegie Foundation for the Advancement of Teaching, the authors examine how members of different professions are educated for their responsibilities within the communities they serve. The book begins with an overarching question: How do seminaries prepare students for their roles and responsibilities as clergy? The authors proceed by exploring how seminary educators foster among their students a pastoral, priestly, or rabbinic imagination that integrates knowledge and skill, moral integrity, and religious commitment in the roles, relationships, and responsibilities they will be assuming in clergy practice. They seek to identify what classroom and communal pedagogies seminary educators employ as they seek to foster such an imagination in their students. The results of their study center around four pedagogies:

- Pedagogies of interpretation
- Pedagogies of formation
- Pedagogies of contextualization
- Pedagogies of performance

---

3. Charles R. Foster, Lisa E. Dahill, Lawrence A. Golemon, and Barbara Wang Tolentino, *Educating Clergy* (San Francisco: Jossey-Bass, 2006).

While there may be other helpful ways of identifying and organizing the areas that need to be evaluated, for the purposes of this essay these four pedagogies will be used to identify the domains that a comprehensive assessment plan should address.

3. Select assessment tools appropriate for the goals within each domain.
Space does not permit identification of the many different assessment tools that might be employed in each of the four domains just identified for assessing student learning outcomes. Two of them, however, can be explored as illustrative: the domains of *pedagogies of interpretation* and *pedagogies of contextualization*.

Assessment tools appropriate for the goals surrounding pedagogies of interpretation. A rich variety of teaching methods are described in the Foster et al.'s chapter on "Pedagogies of Interpretation" and what emerges is a picture of robust and energized teaching. The summary section describes the central student learning outcome that is essential if the educational process is to be successful.

> Although pedagogies of interpretation vary significantly, clergy educators widely share the view that practices of interpretation require that students develop the ability to *think critically.* We saw this view in every aspect of our study: classroom observation, interviews, and the surveys.[4]

The teaching pedagogies described in the chapter on interpretation seek to introduce, develop, and cultivate critical thinking skills.

Assessing learning outcomes involves seeking answers to the following questions: How do you know that students have learned what you say they know? Is there a way to measure the levels at which these skills have been learned? Can you identify benchmarks of student learning vis-à-vis critical thinking skills so that when students fall short, there is a verifiable and consistent method of assessment that measures the gap? When the gap has been measured, what changes in teaching methods can be introduced to enhance student learning, and how have these new methods been implemented?"

Assessing critical thinking skills is not a new task of teaching and learning. Faculty members assess students on the basis of student papers, student class presentations, and quality of classroom interaction or the quality of contributions to an online threaded conversation if the class is taught by distance education.

4. Foster et al., *Educating Clergy,* p. 89.

In assessing critical thinking skills, faculty typically provide feedback that:

- calls attention to the lack of clear logic in written papers or gives high scores for clarity, coherence, and consistency;
- highlights failure to address key issues in presentations among peers or praises the capacity to discern and address substantive issues;
- shows the presence of apparent bias in the arguments or the capacity to provide arguments that are relatively uncluttered with ideologies;
- points out how students have failed to grasp (listen to) the content of original documents or underscores the capacity of students to grasp the context and message they have read;
- indicates inadequate analysis of contemporary issues or affirms the capacity to explicate forces that account for contemporary culture.

Many generations of students have developed and honed critical thinking skills through this kind of careful mentoring by faculty. What is more difficult in this individualistic interaction between professors and students is to establish patterns of student learning that can become markers for assessing the student learning outcomes in other classes. It is also difficult to create a cumulative record that identifies changes in course syllabi that a given professor incorporates as a result of the collage of experiences gleaned from grading students in a single class or a group of classes.

Is there a way to find benchmarks for patterns of student learning outcomes within a given class or series of classes within a degree program that create standards by which learning outcomes in subsequent classes can be measured? Promise for developing such assessment tools comes from research regarding the assessment of critical thinking skills being carried on in the pioneering work of Kurt Fischer and Theo Dawson. A member of the Harvard Department of Education, Fischer has studied the subject of mind, brain, and education. He described the significant challenges inherent in the task of helping students to learn critical thinking skills and introduced me to the work of Dawson, who has built upon some of Fischer's insights in understanding how people develop critical thinking skills. She created the Developmental Testing Service, LLC (DTS).[5]

5. Dawson's website includes the following description: "(DTS is) . . . dedicated to designing assessments that capture the transformations in thinking that occur up to 14 times over the course of the lifespan. Each of these transformations leads to a more complex, inte-

Because of the promise of the testing model that Dawson has developed, I explored with her how her methodology might be used within a seminary context. In the model she has developed, a key component to the assessment of critical thinking skills begins with a dilemma. Dawson provides examples of such dilemmas at her website. Faculty at Bethel Seminary wrote a dilemma that is suited to the tasks of theological graduate education. Dawson felt that the following dilemma provides what is needed to begin her assessment process.

All streams of Christianity affirm the Bible as a source of authority. The ancient story of creation in the Bible has parallels with other ancient Near Eastern accounts. In the Babylonian epic Enuma Elish, for example, the goddess Tiamat represents the primeval body of water, and her name is a cognate to the Hebrew word "tehom." Tehom appears in Gen. 1 as a description of the watery nature of the earth. In both Genesis and Enuma Elish there is a division of the matter from which God (Genesis) and the gods (Enuma Elish) create the heavens and the earth. In both creation accounts the first human beings, a man and a woman, are directly created at the initiative of God/the gods. In Genesis, Adam and Eve are created "in the image of God," and in the Enuma Elish, they are created from the blood of a slain God. Some Christians maintain that the presence of parallels to the Genesis creation account does not affect its authority. Others maintain that the existence of parallel creation accounts alters the authoritative nature of the biblical narrative.

The next step is to develop five probe questions (the minimum requirement for maintaining psychometric reliability). The dilemma regarding the authority of the Bible given above is an example of a reflective judg-

---

grated, and adequate way of thinking. Whereas traditional tests do a good job examining what people know, our tests examine *the way people think about what they know.* We are further dedicated to transforming testing by changing the way people think about assessment. Most tests provide information about how well an individual is performing relative to others. Our tests transcend comparison. They tell learners what they need to learn next in an empirically validated developmental sequence. *This turns testing into what it should be: part of the learning process.* To accomplish these goals, we design reliable small- and large-scale assessments of intellectual development in a range of knowledge domains. We also support the mass customization of learning by designing methods for matching individual learners with appropriate curricula." Further information can be found at http://www.devtestservice.com.

ment (critical thinking) dilemma. It has been crafted with two important qualities in mind. First, it poses an "ill-structured" problem, and second, this problem involves an important real-world issue. (Ill-structured questions are complex and abstract, without a single clear answer. In other words, rational persons can answer them differently.) Complex, ill-structured dilemmas and good probe questions push students to show off their best reasoning — how and what they are thinking about the issue.

Certified Lectical Analysts score student responses by examining their complexity and level of abstraction. The table on page 373 provides a brief, simplified description of the scoring criteria. Responses to each probe question are scored, and these are averaged to provide a single developmental phase score. DTS provides general descriptions of the kind of reasoning (reflective judgment/critical thinking) associated with each phase score. Students' essays are also delivered to their instructors (as they are completed by students), who use their own criteria to evaluate students' performances.

There appear to be many benefits to this method of measuring critical thinking skills. A baseline for all students in all classes can be established. Data becomes available regarding what is helpful and what is not helpful in teaching this important skill. Fischer says that teaching critical thinking skills is much more difficult than we imagine. In several classes assessed at the Harvard School of Education, only 50 percent of the students learned the skills listed in the stated goals of the class.

Dawson's approach illustrates creative efforts underway to develop more standardized ways to assess progress on one vital educational goal: assisting students to deepen their critical thinking skills.

Assessment tools appropriate for the goals surrounding contextualization. Because globalization defines the educational waters in which we all swim, the burden to become more effective in cross-cultural understanding keeps growing. Whether the key descriptors are ethnic diversity, cultural diversity, racial sensitivity, or globalization, every seminary wants to know whether or not progress is being made.

Prior to 2003 Bethel struggled with the task of implementing an education program that showed promise in achieving our mission to deliver the gospel in "culturally sensitive ways." Student evaluations indicated that substantial numbers of students were dissatisfied with an anti-racism emphasis and an anti-sexism approach to enhance sensitivity to ethnic and gender differences. Research indicated some students were demoralized while others were sympathetic at best. In 2003 the Developmental Model for Intercultural

	The Structural Criteria Employed in Lectical Analysis		
Level	**Hierarchical Structure**	**Phase**	**Horizontal Structure**
12	Logical structure: The logical structure is definitional. It identifies one aspect of a *principle* coordinating abstract systems.	12:4	Describes several principles, each of which coordinates highly complex systems. Does not make any attempt to coordinate principles.
		12:3	Describes at least two principles, each of which coordinates multiple systems.
	Order of abstraction: Concepts are 1st order *principles*. These integrate abstract systems into single principles.	12:2	Describes a single principle that coordinates multiple systems, resolving an apparent conflict between these systems.
		12:1	Describes multiple systems, many of which are nested, and describes the need to coordinate two or more systems in order to resolve an apparent conflict between systems.
11	Logical structure: The logical structure is the system. It coordinates multiple aspects of two or more abstractions.	11:4	Describes multiple complex systems, many of which are nested. Does not appear to notice conflicts or contradictions between systems.
		11:3	Describes multiple unrelated complex systems
	Order of abstraction: Concepts are 3rd order abstractions. These use or modify 2nd order abstractions.	11:2	Describes the elements of one or two moderately complex systems and some of the non-linear relations among these elements.
		11:1	Begins to organize what were long lists of variables into loosely connected systems; recognizes that variables are related to one another in ways that are non-linear.
10	Logical structure: The logical structure is linear or a mapping. It coordinates one aspect of two or more abstractions.	10:4	Produces long chains of logically linked variables and multiple lists of abstract qualities.
		10:3	Produces short chains of logically linked variables and/or long lists of abstract qualities.
	Order of abstraction: Concepts are 2nd order abstractions. These use or modify 1st order abstractions.	10:2	Produces multiple instances of two-variable causal statements and/or short lists of abstract qualities.
		10:1	Attempts to relate two abstract variables with one another in a causal statement.

Sensitivity (DMIS) was selected as a framework with the Intercultural Development Inventory (IDI) as a measure for effectiveness.[6]

The IDI focuses on human differences and how ethnocentrism can lead to intercultural conflicts that result in various forms of prejudice, racism, sexism, and other forms of institutional and personal ideologies that generate conflict and inter-group oppression. Faculty members who used this instrument found that the IDI helps students discuss the issues and reflect on their own experiences with differences. Moreover, faculty noted that the use of the instrument caused students to be more open to exploring specific cultural differences. In fact, the real challenges of avoiding the use of stereotypes and overcoming the temptation to develop defensiveness and prejudiced behaviors appeared to be better understood with the new approach.

In 2003 designated faculty members gave the IDI as a pre- and post-test measure with a comparison group to control for validity in testing the new approach. The comparison group class utilized a mixture of anti-racism, anti-sexism, and social justice approaches. There were no statistical differences between the comparison and the new approach group based on the pre-test results. All of the students were in need of intercultural development training for increased awareness and sensitivity. However, there were statistically significant post-test differences between the comparison group and the group provided with the approach based on the DMIS. In several instances, findings suggest that an intercultural development approach created a better in-class learning environment with open discussions and significant improvement in the capacity for intercultural awareness and sensitivity based on the IDI scores. As a result, Bethel has increased the number of faculty members trained to use the DMIS model and IDI instrument, and the goal is to improve effectiveness in and outside of the classroom.

The value of the IDI assessment tool is that it addresses desired student learning outcomes that include increased (1) awareness of students' own cultural identities, (2) ability for effective intercultural interaction (i.e. interpersonal communications), (3) ability to resolve intercultural conflict over differences, and (4) capacity for cross-cultural functioning.

The tool provides a way for those who take the instrument to measure awareness about (1) denial and defensive issues that inhibit one's ability for intercultural awareness and sensitivity, (2) sensitivity around issues of appreciation for cultural differences, (3) one's inability to empathize or take on

---

6. Further information can be obtained from: Mitchell R. Hammer, PhD, Founder of IDI, LLC, idi@idiinventory.com. IDI, LLC P.O. Box 1388, Berlin, Maryland, 21811 USA.

the perspective of others, and (4) one's ability to recognize one's own cultural orientation in operation.

In addition, there are many benefits for professors who teach the course. The results of the pre- and post-tests enable them to adjust and improve upon course content. Students are offered consultation as a part of their student assessment process and given developmental tasks. Students are required to incorporate their learning experience related to their Integration Project at the end of their degree program.

Since December 2003 six faculty members have become qualified administrators of the IDI. The costs include $1,000 per training session and $10 per student for the instruments. The results of qualifying six faculty members include (1) sufficient capacity for the seminary to administer the IDI across the seminary for staff and students; (2) increased capacity for intercultural awareness and sensitivity for growth opportunities and community building in the seminary; (3) improvement of the levels of intercultural awareness and sensitivity among faculty based upon the DMIS; (4) discussion of issues among faculty in a unified way using a common interdisciplinary language; (5) coordinated efforts for building capacity for intercultural awareness and sensitivity among faculty, staff, and students; (6) discussion of issues related to particular cases and approaches to instruction due to the framework and measured results; and (7) presentation of multiple perspectives during faculty professional development workshops using the DMIS and the IDI. Once the entire faculty was administered the IDI, many faculty colleagues communicated more openness to learn due to the nature of the intercultural development approach.

About 85-90 percent of entering students score in the ethnocentric range on intercultural development, which conflicts with our overall goal of advancing the gospel in culturally-sensitive ways. This also creates a stressful cultural environment for the small percentage of students of color, since their predominantly white peers are insensitive to cultural differences. On the positive side, the percentage of entering students in the most serious defensive range seems to be on the decline. Growth in intercultural development is associated with social justice activism and spiritual questing, yet students are not always clear how to integrate these commitments with evangelical traditions.

4. Choose assessment tools that help your school fulfill its educational mission.

No school can possibly incorporate all of the assessment tools available. What matters is that a school select the combination of assessment tools that address the learning outcomes that are central to fulfilling its mission and consistently incorporate these tools in a manner that is coherent with the values of the school. The example just presented of how a particular assessment tool helped achieve the seminary's goal of "advancing the gospel in culturally-sensitive ways" illustrates one of the ways we are exploring the relationship between mission and assessment of student learning outcomes at Bethel.

Many instruments that assess students' performance as ministers are imbedded in course work found in spiritual and personal formation, in transformational leadership courses, or in coursework attached to internship requirements. Some courses intentionally bridge between spiritual and personal formation and leadership. Others focus more on the leadership competencies. What is key to each of the courses is to have clearly stated outcomes that are measured by one or more of the assessment instruments available. For the sake of illustration, the following outcomes appear in course syllabi:

- Provide evidence of commitment to disciplines of Christian spiritual formation, personal maturation, and vocational skill development within the context of appropriate support and accountability relationships
- Provide evidence of spiritual, personal, and professional readiness for the Christian ministry to which the student believes she/he is called after graduation
- Identify and analyze, from biblical, theological, and theoretical perspectives, the dynamics of spiritual and personal formation
- Analyze the implications of the student's formation journeys for her/his ministry to and with persons on different formation trajectories — including persons of different gender, ethnicity, or socioeconomic level
- Demonstrate an ability to develop and monitor both individual and communal formation strategies for a lifelong relationship with God.

In this model, the results of psychometric tools are additive to the work of repetitive self-examination. Peer groups and faculty feedback are critically important. The questions, Who am I? and Who am I in community with others? are partially answered through interpretation and analysis of the assessments. These questions continue to be resolved through the entire seminary process.

5. Build in feedback loops.

Although space does not permit a thorough discussion of the assessment feedback loops that connect the four pedagogies of interpretation, formation, contextualization, and performance, the importance of connecting what is learned in each of these areas of assessment is vital.

For example, several feedback loops are provided for monitoring the elimination of gaps between identified student learning outcome goals and outcome achievement, but none is more critical (nor more subjective) than the establishment of a solid relationship between the student and someone in the Center for Spiritual and Personal Formation — usually the director of formation, supervised ministry, and placement or the associate director of personal and professional development. In certain cases where remedial or disciplinary development is required, a relationship between the director of student development assists in closing gaps. For the gaps identified specifically by the developmental assessments themselves, the feedback loop comes in several forms beyond the interpretive report:

- A thorough review of the assessment results and the interpretive report by the director of formation, supervised ministry, and placement
- Consultation between the student and director regarding the assessments as needed
- Additional testing by reusing the original instruments or the selection of alternatives (e.g., MMPI, CPI, NEO, TKI, etc.)
- Implementation of recommended action into the student's IDP or a developmental plan designed prior to commencement of the pre-internship process

The selection and use of instruments keeps evolving. Beginning in the fall of 2008 an integrative portfolio was instituted for all students in all masters level degree programs. The specific items included in the portfolio will be key to the materials that students will focus upon for their senior integrative seminars. While it is too early to give any concrete results, the IDP is designed to be the skeleton on which the flesh of assessments can be attached from the four pedagogical domains, two of which have been described in this essay.

Assessment and Institutional Planning

Student learning outcomes assessment is integrally related to institutional planning and how it aids the school with the following tasks:

1. Assessing overall institutional planning and priorities.

The four domains identified by the Carnegie study provide a grid of four domains that prompts the question, Are there "domain" omissions in our school's assessment of student learning outcomes? In each of the four domains, the results of assessment will call for faculty-wide discussions, not just the faculty member involved in the course being assessed. This may be true for findings regarding the development of critical thinking skills, formation issues, contextualization issues, or performance issues. Adequate assessment tools provide benchmarks regarding progress over a period of time. If the goal is continual improvement, and the assessment outcomes indicate that progress is being made, then a model of "good enough" assessment has been designed and implemented.

2. Extrapolating multiple levels of information from assessment data.

There is a "trickle up" effect in systemic approaches to assessment. If for example, when a school makes spiritual and personal formation a primary part of its vision and mission and discovers, as Bethel did, that there is an inverse relationship for some students between spiritual well-being and spiritual maturity, a faculty-wide discussion is in order.

Spiritual maturity includes the capacity to suffer with and/or empathize with people in great distress, for whom there is often no immediate solution. The experience of suffering with someone does not enhance a sense of "well-being," but may in fact lead to discouragement and depression. Thus, tests that indicate an increase in "spiritual well-being" may not capture what is most important. Naming expectations for what ministry in the real world requires calls for the engagement of the entire faculty.

3. Upgrading strategic initiatives and refining institutional plans.

Sometimes an area of great importance may not be funded adequately at all. In 1998, when the Lilly Endowment Inc. grant to "Increase Congregational Effectiveness" was received, Bethel's leadership was acutely aware of how little was being done in assessing matters pertaining to spiritual and personal formation. When the grant ended, the decision about whether or not to continue the funding was made in light of the benefits being received. Over a five-year period the total investment in spiritual and personal formation re-search has amounted to hundreds of thousands of dollars. Included in that amount are faculty positions, funding for continued research, and funding for an adequate support staff equipped to provide a relationship-rich environment in which the work of formation is being done.

Similarly, the findings from the IDI instrument directly bear upon one of Bethel's strategic initiatives to increase cross-cultural effectiveness. When it became apparent that Bethel was not achieving its goals in cross-cultural effectiveness, the decision was made to train many faculty and staff in the use of the IDI instrument. The $7000 invested in training faculty and staff to administer and interpret the IDI has turned out to be one of the best investments the seminary has made in order to increase cross-cultural effectiveness.

Summary

Our task as CAOs is to strategically use assessment data to advance the vision and to deepen the values of our respective schools. With regard to the enterprise called graduate theological education, we will be wise to commit ourselves to intentional, persistent, and carefully implemented assessment processes in order to gain deeper insight into the alignment between what we say students learn and what students actually learn. It is the hope of this writer that such assessment processes will contribute to a more robust educational ethos, will improve seminary effectiveness, and, as was stated at the outset of this chapter, become a key factor in the renewal of theological education.

14. Personal, Professional, and Spiritual Development

Finding Wholeness in the Role of the Dean

Bruce C. Birch

Most deans[1] come to the role of the chief academic officer from the ranks of the faculty. The process of selection varies widely. Some are invited to this role from a process of internal selection, while others are chosen as external candidates who have applied or been nominated for the role from outside the institution. Some serve for set terms; some inherit the role by an agreed institutional process of rotating the responsibility among senior faculty. But almost all deans have previously served as teaching faculty in one of the disciplines of the theological curriculum. As such they are trained and credentialed as scholar/teachers, and they seldom have any previous formal training in administration, management, or governance.

Some faculty members find a new and fulfilling vocation in the role of the dean, and most manage on-the-job training to become skilled and conscientious academic administrators. But even many of the best deans hope for an eventual return to the faculty role, and many regard the deanship as a temporary, though important, side trip from the course of their primary vo-

1. As stated in the introduction to this volume, the title for the chief academic officer in a theological school varies. A dean in a university seminary is the CEO while the CAO in that setting is often an associate dean for academic affairs. In some traditions the CAO is called a rector. For simplicity's sake in this chapter I use the title *dean* to indicate the CAO.

cational journey. The average tenure of an academic dean is currently less than five years.

It is, of course, not possible or desirable for deans to leave behind their previous identities as scholars and teachers in an academic discipline. But how this previous vocational path and the new calling of serving as dean are related and integrated can be crucial to the success of a dean's work. In particular, this chapter will focus on maintaining a sense of personal and vocational wholeness in the midst of what can be a dramatic change in role within a theological school.

I too became a dean from the ranks of the faculty. I spent thirty-eight years as a professor of Old Testament, serving the last eleven of those years as dean. Readers of this volume may have observed different ways that a dean's own field of scholarly inquiry shape the images and perspectives one brings to the deanship, beginning with dean/homiletician Jana Childers' use of communications theory to examine the skill of reading institutional context. Drawing from my own discipline, I have found an image from Psalm 137 helpful in shedding light on the transition to the deanship that many faculty members may experience.

Many deans, in the early months of their new role, find themselves considering variations of the psalmist's plaintive cry out of Babylonian exile, "How can I sing the Lord's song in a strange land?" (Ps. 137:4; author's own translation). Colleagues do not confide in them in the same way. Complaints now frequently end at their desk. Presidents, boards, financial officers, and external constituencies suddenly occupy major parts of their time and attention. They must deal with an entirely new rhythm to the days and weeks of their work. Exile is not a matter of geography. It is the time when centers of meaning and identity are changed and challenged. It is easy to fall into a pattern similar to the first exiles during the time of the prophet Jeremiah, hoping for the day of their return to the life they previously knew.

In this context Jeremiah's letter to those exiles may have some helpful advice for academic deans. His letter in Jer. 29 advised exiles to orient themselves to life in the place where they now lived and resume faithful life in the midst of those realities. His crucial advice comes in v. 7, "Seek the well-being *(shalom)* of the city where I have sent you into exile, and pray to the Lord on its behalf, for in its well-being *(shalom)* you will find your well-being *(shalom)*." The basic meaning of the Hebrew concept of *shalom* is wholeness. How do we seek wholeness in the new role of dean rather than thinking of our true wholeness, perhaps our primary identity, as something we left behind? How do we find wholeness in a new context and reality that will require new patterns and skills of vocational practice as theological educators and persons of faith?

The danger for those called to sing the Lord's song in a strange land is not the danger of perishing; it is the danger of settling for survival. Instead of seeing a new landscape as opportunity for new experiences of God's *shalom*, too many deans hope only to survive (albeit with integrity and competence) so they may return to the faculty role where they previously knew wholeness.

In Israel's exile, while some despaired of singing the Lord's song, others actually made this a time that brought forth wonderful singers of hope (Ezekiel, Deutero-Isaiah) and new institutional responses of creative community life (synagogue, Torah). Deans' attention to their own wholeness and that of the school they serve can bring great benefits and satisfactions in several areas.

The Dean as Scholar/Teacher

It is true that when a person accepts the role of dean it will not be possible to teach as many classes or to engage in research and publication to the same extent that it was possible as a faculty member. It is a matter of simple time constraints.

Many deans have found it life-giving, however, to continue to embrace the role of scholar/teacher in the new life of a dean. Too many have turned their back on these roles with a sense of a martyr's sacrifice, and it is not only unnecessary but also unhealthy to the full functioning of the deanship. The prophets urged the Israelites in exile to retain memory and identity rooted in their previous lives as an asset while becoming open to God's doing of a new thing in their midst.

For the dean to continue to engage in some teaching while serving as dean is to maintain contact with the realities of the classroom, the changing nature of modern pedagogy, and the constant shifting demographics of the student population. The dean serves a vital role in modeling how to value, in the press of obligations all faculty members face, the importance of constantly developing skills of pedagogy and vocational development, and this will be difficult to do without direct experience of the challenges to be faced. For the faculty to see the dean sharing the classroom realities builds bridges of trust and confidence that the dean has stayed in touch with faculty realities.

Of course, deans must be strategic and wise in choosing how to maintain their teaching roles. A self-study year in preparation for an ATS visit may not be the year to teach the eighty-student, yearlong intro course. But neither is it helpful to teach the same course every year simply because it is convenient. Deans should give themselves a growing edge as teachers alongside their colleagues. In one year this may be new subject matter and in another year it might be a new pedagogical practice. When particular administrative challenges make a fourteen-week semester course difficult, many schools have intensive teaching options available in January terms, summer sessions, or DMin courses.

Such teaching also keeps channels of communication open with students. One dean confided in me that, after choosing not to teach for two years, he suddenly realized that students no longer spoke to him readily in hallways and common areas as he encountered them.

Teachers on a seminary faculty are also expected to be productive scholars in their fields of study. (See Craig Nessan and Barbara Mutch's helpful insights in chapter 8 on the opportunities and complexities of this part of the dean's role.) Staying active in my own scholarly field as a publishing scholar has contributed to wholeness in my own life as a dean, even though I found it difficult to do this at the same level as before becoming dean. While serving as dean it will likely not be the opportune time to sign a contract for a monumental work that will be the capstone of your scholarly career. However, there are many opportunities to contribute articles to journals or collections, to stay active in professional societies, and/or to participate in panels or symposia. Faculty colleagues also struggle with finding time for these academic pursuits, and nothing encourages them more than to see their dean succeeding in maintaining some continuity of life as a scholar alongside them.

I found it empowering to set modest goals but adopt some discipline of time set aside to maintain the role of scholar even while meeting the new challenges of a dean's life. As Nessan notes in greater detail, the role of dean opens some new opportunities for scholarship and publication as one develops new expertise in understanding and commenting on the larger arena of theological education as a whole. I encourage deans not to hesitate to develop a new voice in new arenas of scholarship and publication. ATS publications, denominational publications, and theological education issues of major religious periodicals all provide possible venues for such publication.

In important ways a dean's success at maintaining some continuity with the previous identity as scholar/teacher helps preserve a sense of continuity with previous colleagues. There is no question that the role of dean has an effect on colleague relationships. You will not be privy to all the gossip and complaining around the coffee pot in the faculty lounge (which may be an advantage). In fact, you may not be welcome to go into the faculty lounge. But as you grow in the role of dean, maintain your faculty's confidence in you as a scholar/teacher who knows their realities, and cultivate a style of openness, you will find new dimensions of relationship to your colleagues opening. It is extremely rewarding to work with younger colleagues who view you as someone who can guide them through the insecurities and pitfalls of first publications. It is gratifying to be sought out for advice on vocational pathways or help in giving the right focus to a grant proposal. In addition, you may find opportunities to enjoy peer scholarly relationships and pursuits outside the school that are opened by your role as dean, and these may offer a place of respite where one may be a "peer among peers" and not "the dean."

The Dean as Person of Faith

Many faculty members at theological schools think of their teaching and scholarship in terms of ministry, whether they are lay or ordained. However, I have encountered more than a few deans who seem to think that their administrative work as dean is a distraction from ministry or a season away from ministry. Coupled with this is also an impression I have that the schedule and pressure of deaning can, for many, squeeze out the time needed to keep in touch with spiritual sources of renewal and strength.

It is extremely important for those who take up the role of dean to stay in touch with the spiritual and ministerial dimensions of the dean's work. This is not only renewing for deans as persons of faith; it is essential for the functioning of the deanship in the life of the community of the seminary.

For eleven years I worked with Mitchell Bond, registrar at Wesley Theological Seminary, and he was one of the very best at this important role. One of the reasons for this came out every time he participated in new student orientation. He always introduced himself by saying that he had been called to a ministry of papers and forms. It set a tone for his office that was unmistakable and made a difference in how people experienced the functioning of that office.

The call to be a dean is a vocational calling to a ministry. The handling of persons with care in the midst of problem situations must be pastoral in character. The writing of memos and reports and policies must reflect service to the seminary as a faith community and not just the efficient functioning of a bureaucracy. The words and actions of a dean are a form of proclamation given unusual visibility because of the nature of the office of dean.

It goes without saying that one who becomes a dean should make a strong effort to stay in touch with patterns of spiritual discipline that have proven renewing in the past. Prayer, Bible study, spiritual direction, participation in public worship, and time for theological reflection cannot be pushed to the margins by the press of responsibilities. Maintain practices that have been spiritually regenerative for you in life before the deanship. These, of course, take many different forms for particular individuals, but the pressures of deanship are not a good reason to abandon your own effective practices of spiritual well-being. Deans also need to be spiritually fed.

The focus of these practices may change. As I became a dean I realized that I would now be working more directly with members of our board of governors, a group I respected but only had shadowy contact with as a faculty member. Of course, I now had opportunity to work directly with many board members, but I also determined that I would pray for each of them individually over a period of time. This became wonderfully rewarding to me personally but I think affected the quality of my work with those board members. I then applied the same practice as a regular feature of my eleven years as dean. I would pray explicitly for persons I was working with in a given time — the faculty on a committee given a crucial piece of work, the students who came to me with issues to be addressed, the administrators working with me on joint concerns. I believe my own time for prayer and spiritual reflection actually became more disciplined and more centrally important over those years. Many seemingly intractable issues became, for me, more capable of resolution after I had spent time in prayer over the matter.

It is also extremely important for the community to see the dean as a person of faith. Only genuine emergencies should keep the dean from participation in the corporate worship life of the community. It speaks volumes when the dean is regularly absent from the worship life of the school. I believe it is symbolically helpful to take roles in worship other than that of featured preacher, such as scripture reader, celebrant, or liturgist.

The spiritual practice of *koinonia* should also not be neglected. Deans need to get outside of office walls to experience and demonstrate the importance of community in the life of a theological school. Meals in the dining room, appearances at coffee hour, willingness to stop for interactions in the hallway, participation in community mission projects, meetings held in other person's offices rather than one's own — all of these are not distractions from the work of the dean but part of the essence of that work. Of course, deans must be wise stewards of limited time, but they make their work easier and more effective by genuine and visible participation in the life and interactions of the school community.

In my experience, many an issue was helped to resolution or kept from becoming problematic by informal conversations outside of office time and committee work. Sometimes this was a simple matter of building human relationships with faculty, students, staff, and administrators outside of the formal role of dean. It is hard to spend an afternoon with others placing luminaries on our hillside to represent every life lost in Iraq and Afghanistan (for a prayer service each year at Veteran's Day) and then come into a committee meeting without some extra sense of common community and mission to aid us in common problem solving.

The Self Care of Deans

It is amazing how many in demanding roles of responsibility neglect their own self care. Adopt and/or maintain practices of good health. It is always important to eat a healthy diet, get plenty of exercise, see health care professionals regularly, and avoid unhealthy habits. We all know that these things are easier said than done, and we will all struggle with our own particular challenges at maintaining a healthy lifestyle. But face those challenges directly, and do not allow the urgency/importance of your role as dean to justify neglect.

Here are a few actual encounters I have had with colleague deans. One person told me he ate most of his noontime and evening meals during the week from the vending machine area near his office. Another colleague admitted that she had resumed smoking since becoming dean (at a level of a pack a day). Another told me he just could not afford the time for the running and exercise that was a previous part of his weekly routine. This same colleague was postponing his annual physical because he was afraid of what the doctor would tell him.

These must be named for what they are — self-destructive practices. They are false savings of time and ineffective ways of dealing with stress and pressure. Poor personal health practices take their toll in diminished energy, depression, and potential hospital stays. Failing to care for our own personal wholeness never proves to be a helpful strategy.

Tending to personal health needs must be matched by tending to healthy family and social relationships. Family and friends represent vital personal relationships, and these must be tended and nurtured in spite of the pressures of serving as dean. This is vitally important because of the constant evidence that clergy often fall into the practice of considering their calling so important that they neglect focused nurturing of their own family relationships. Deans should model, for their own faculty and students, lives that do not sacrifice family and friendships for the sake of the mission of their own vocational commitments.

Of course, this is not easy to do. The time demands are real and often compelling. Nevertheless, as with personal health, neglect of personal relationships for the sake of urgent tasks on the dean's agenda is a false economy. Those relationships, when tended lovingly, are supportive, renewing, and energizing. If neglected, these relationships become dysfunctional and demand even more time and energy.

Sources of professional support are also important in a dean's self care and finding wholeness. During my years as dean I think there were few things as valuable to me as time I spent with other deans and the support I gained from the friendship and colleagueship I experienced in gatherings with them. For me this included the annual meeting of CAOS (the Chief Academic Officers Society of ATS), the Council of Deans of the Washington Theological Consortium, and gatherings of deans from the theological schools of my denomination (United Methodist). It also included participation in the dean's listserv sponsored and maintained for CAOS by Rich Weis, dean at United Theological Seminary of the Twin Cities. The support, wisdom, encouragement, and friendship I received through these channels were among my most valued resources as a dean. More often than I can count, I have been saved from reinventing the wheel in some area of academic policy or practice by conversations with colleague deans in the forums mentioned above.

Completely apart from pragmatic concerns, the sense of community and support I have gained through contact with colleague deans has been invaluable. There is nothing quite as debilitating as the sense of isolation that can develop in the role of dean. There is no one else on your own campus who shares your job description or set of responsibilities, but there is a wide community of those who do in the other ATS member schools. I cannot emphasize enough how helpful that supportive fellowship can be. The impetus for this book has come from that community of colleagues and the desire that has pervaded our gatherings to be a source of support, encouragement, and wise counsel for one another.

When Things Go Badly

Finding wholeness in the role of the dean is a challenge under the best of circumstances, but when things go badly the plaintive cry of the psalmist with which we began this article becomes all too real. How can we sing the Lord's song in a strange land? This area could, of course, justify an entire article in its own right.

There are many ways in which theological schools in general and deans in particular can experience dysfunction. Personality clashes between key leaders, lack of agreement on the school's mission, tension with a sponsoring denomination, financial crisis, criticism from individuals or groups, erosion of self-confidence — all of these and more can create tension and stress beyond the normal day-to-day pressures of the dean's role.

I offer here not a detailed discussion of conflict management or crisis control. (Jack Seymour has provided that in his discussion of the dean as a conflict negotiator in chapter 10.) but simply some pragmatic considerations for *maintaining wholeness* in situations that are less than ideal.

- *Do not hesitate to admit when you have been wrong.* Deans are not superhuman, but some act as though they were. When I realized that I had not fully understood a matter or that I had made an error in judgment, I always found it best to admit my mistake as quickly and openly as possible. Presidents and faculties do not expect perfection in deans, and few mistakes cannot be rectified or mitigated by prompt and candid disclosure and reconsideration.
- *Communicate as openly as possible and as often as possible on all important matters.* Collaboration, transparency, and openness serve all institutions well and, particularly when practiced by the dean, build trust and mutuality in working relationships. Although there are some matters that must be held in confidence (personnel or disciplinary matters, for example), it is seldom that practices of secrecy serve the best interests of any theological school. What people imagine is usually more harmful than appropriate sharing of realities in all areas of the institution's life with those who share responsibility for the institution. The dean's office, in particular, cannot be labeled as a place where secrets are held and communication is spotty.
- *Seek out personal sources of advice and support that can be of help when problems arise or dysfunctions occur in the life of the school.* These, of course, should be put in place before a crisis occurs. In the case of

those newly coming to the role of dean I would advise finding a senior colleague in the community of deans who you could meet or call regularly in the early years of deaning. This was particularly helpful to me in my first two years in the dean's office. I talked with someone I respected and trusted once a month, sometimes for lunch and sometimes for an extended phone call. It was extremely helpful. But even experienced deans need mentors, colleagues, or spiritual directors who can listen, support, and provide perspective on the challenges that arise. Don't hesitate to use such personal supports. There is no virtue in going it alone.

- *Don't set unrealistic expectations for yourself, and express the need to adjust the expectations from others when necessary.* Everyone a dean works with wants particular concerns brought to the dean's attention and hopes these will be dealt with immediately. Deans must learn to set priorities and communicate them to others. I found I could avoid feeling overburdened with matters demanding immediate deadlines by simply communicating as realistically as possible when others could expect me to give attention to their issues. Some matters are urgent, but others can be placed on a longer timeline. Sometimes matters can be referred or delegated to others. I have found myself saying to the president of my school that I can't give him a report he wanted by next week because of other commitments but then try to offer an alternative. There are often others (registrar, admissions director, chairs of faculty committees, dean of students, etc.) who have worked on the issues and could give assistance. Or the president, or whoever is asking for a decision or product, might well be able to adjust the timeline. At all costs, do not accept from others expectations that you know you cannot meet.

- *Give yourself time away from the role of dean.* This is particularly important after a time of crisis or unusual pressure. Take the vacation time you are due. Observe your own personal patterns of renewal week to week even when crisis looms. Consider negotiating short sabbaticals from the office (one to four months) from time to time. Most deans end up missing sabbaticals they would otherwise have taken as faculty members, so asking for some shorter times is not out of the question. You are usually less indispensable than you think.

BRUCE C. BIRCH

Agents of Wholeness

Finding wholeness in the role of the dean can be a challenge, but it is deeply related to our efforts to be agents of wholeness to the schools we serve and the ministries of the church those schools equip. To paraphrase the letter of Jeremiah, we seek the *shalom* of the community we serve, for in its *shalom* we will find our own *shalom*. Deanship is not a term to be endured so that we can return to our faculty vocations. It is a rewarding ministry in its own right to which God has called us. It is a service filled with creative opportunities to sing the Lord's song even in a strange new vocational land.

ADDITIONAL RESOURCES

Bennett, John B. *Academic Life: Hospitality, Ethics, and Spirituality.* Bolton, MA: Anker Publishing Co., 2003.

Palmer, Parker. *Let Your Voice Speak: Listening for the Voice of Vocation.* San Francisco: Jossey Bass, 1999.

Zikmund, Barbara Brown. "The Role of the Chief Academic Officer in Theological Education." *Issues in Theological Education,* Issue 8 (1984), David Schuller, ed. Vandalia, Ohio: ATS.

AFTERWORD

The Scholarship of Academic Leadership:
A Postscript on the Work of Chief Academic Officers

Daniel O. Aleshire

The chapters in this volume tell a story that is lived out more than written about. The story is the complex, multilayered work of academic leadership in theological schools in North America.

The work is complex and multilayered for many reasons. Academic leadership in ATS schools involves a wide range of tasks, and deans cannot choose to specialize in some of them; the job requires deans to be good at all of them, and that is the beginning of the complexity. This work requires multiple intelligences — relational and academic, procedural and organizational — and very few people in theological schools routinely operate with the range of sophisticated intellectual effort that the deanship requires. This adds still another level of complexity. The work is also complex because the dean often does not have the final word on many issues. The final word comes from decisions that are the result of procedures that the dean superintends with faculty or administrative structures. The position is multilayered because the dean routinely relates to and interacts with the board and president, faculty and students, and prospective students and graduates. Few roles in a theological school require this range of relationships. Most deans want to continue their research in academic disciplines while gaining and exercising competence in their academic leadership; this desire further contributes to the multiple layers of work the job requires.

As I have read and reflected on this collection of thoughtful essays, three issues related to academic leadership have become more pronounced to me: the importance of a community of practice, the changing role of the deanship, and the critical importance of scholarship about the deanship. I would like to comment on each of these as a concluding postscript in this volume.

A Community of Practice

This book, and the ongoing meetings of chief academic officers that underlie the reflections in much of it, is an expression of what Etienne Wenger has termed *a community of practice*. He defines communities of practice as "groups of people who share a concern or a passion for something they do and learn how to do it better as they interact regularly." He goes on to explain that a community of practice consists of three primary elements: "a domain of interest" (in the case of the ATS-sponsored Chief Academic Officers Society, the work of academic leadership in theological schools), "a community" (in CAOS, the persons across schools who participate in the Society's meetings and discussions), and "practice" (in the case of CAOS, persons who are currently active practitioners of academic leadership in individual schools). In Wenger's words, "It is the combination of these three elements that constitutes a community of practice. And it is by developing these three elements in parallel that one cultivates such a community."[1]

The Chief Academic Officers Society has operated as a community of practice, and the essays in this volume bear witness to ways in which that community has provided a context for engaged learning — another insight that Wenger advances. The wisdom that good academic leadership requires is not contained in books or publications as much as it is in the community of persons who do the work. This is true for several reasons. Academic leadership is dynamic; its best practices change over time and are influenced by a wide range of variables and institutional idiosyncrasies. Sorting through these variables is done better in a community of conversation than seeking

1. Wenger's ideas about communities of practice are briefly explained in www.ewenger .com/theory/index.htm and written about more extensively in Etienne Wenger, *Communities of Practice: Learning, Meaning, and Identity* (Cambridge: Cambridge University Press, 1998).

to discern them from a more static, written text. Academic leadership always involves work with particular people in particular structures in particular situations, and it is best understood in the context of particular conversations with individuals who share the work and understand its particularity. The essays in this volume report a shared conversation of a shared experience. Their value is not so much as a definitive written text but as a guide to a sustained conversation that lies under and goes beyond the text.

This community of practice is particularly important for seminary deans. Few persons come to the deanship in an ATS school from another position in academic administration. Most come from the faculty, and most who come from the faculty come from the faculty of the school they serve as dean. They have backgrounds in their work as faculty members and expertise in their disciplines, but most do not have prior experience in academic leadership. The community of practice provides the setting in which they can learn to do their work and grow in competence as they exercise academic leadership. The average tenure of seminary deans has been increasing, but they do not serve in this role as long as chief academic officers in other higher education institutions. Most deanships have new occupants every six or seven years — many of the persons who prepared essays for this volume are no loner serving as deans — and the community of practice sustains an expertise about this work so that it can serve as a repository for learning that is available for subsequent generations of deans.

The Changing Role of the Deanship

The ongoing conversation of a community of practice is especially important because the role of the dean has been changing and continues to change. This change has been most noticeable in the dean's role as institutional officer and the increasing sophistication of academic administration needed in graduate professional theological education.

There was a time, or so it seems, when the pace of change in academic institutions was less rapid and the administrative structures more simple than is currently the case. It was possible for persons to serve as faculty members, rotate into the deanship for a short term, and then rotate back into the faculty. The dean was a kind of secretary of the faculty, facilitating the work of the faculty as an academic collegium that administered many crucial functions of the school. The dean's work was thus an extension of the faculty's work. Over time, as administrative structures grew, the faculty became less involved in the overall management of the school, and the dean became increasingly perceived as the faculty's voice in the administration that did manage the school. In many cases, the faculty elected the dean, which reflected this understanding of the role. The dean's job was to administer faculty academic decisions and advocate on behalf of the faculty with other powers in the institution's life. In most ATS schools, neither of these models is truly operative today, even though faculties often maintain expectations of deans in terms of either one or both of these models. Increasingly, the role of the dean is as institutional officer, as executive academic leader. The chief academic officer has emerged as a crucial member of the administration of the school responsible to the chief administrative officer (most typically the president) and, through the president, to the board, not to the faculty. In this role, the dean represents the academic programs of the school in its broader administration but is not a special representative of the faculty. The dean has become an officer of the institution, and while that includes advocacy on behalf of faculty concerns, it also means the dean advocates the president's and board's perspective to the faculty. The dean is an executive officer responsible at times for curtailing some faculty initiatives on behalf of the board and at others for advocating those initiatives on behalf of the faculty. The role is in transition, which means that it is conflicted in many schools. Some faculties assume the dean is primarily the faculty's advocate and are confused or frustrated when the dean exercises the role of institutional advocate. The shift from secretary of the faculty to executive administrative officer has complicated the job, but the trajectory of the role is increasingly in the direction of institutional officer for board-governed theological schools.

As with all other administrative officers in theological schools, the work of the chief academic officer requires a greater degree of sophistication than it has in the past. Student bodies have diversified significantly, the range of educational offerings has expanded, the financial pressure on theological schools is unrelenting, information technology has not only enhanced what can be done but is changing how almost everything is done — these and other factors require more sophisticated academic leadership. The deanship not only has changed from secretarial to executive in the overall governing structures of schools, but the work of the office also needs to be done in more systems-oriented and sophisticated ways than it was done in the not-so-distant past. The increasing sophistication required for the academic dean's work means that fewer people on the faculty have the administrative talent the office requires and that it takes longer for anyone who undertakes the office to learn the work well. While some schools are able to sustain a limited term and rotating cycle for their deans, an increasing number of schools cannot sustain that rotating structure and still have the level of technical and administrative expertise that the position requires.

The Scholarship of the Deanship

Upon accepting the job as dean, more than a few have been told, in one way or the other, that they have "gone over to the dark side" or that it is "a shame for a good scholar to waste talent in an administrative job." Academic communities tend to view scholarship as knowing a body of material with mastery, teaching that material with authority, and contributing to the advancement of that body of material through research and writing. While this is a traditional and highly accurate understanding of scholarship, it is limited. There are many forms of scholarship — highly intellectual effort that contributes to the teaching, learning, and research that occurs in a good graduate professional school — and schools need more than one kind of scholarship to do their jobs well. The essays in this volume bear testimony to advances in scholarship, not the loss of it. These essays reflect the research, integration, and fresh insight that are indeed markers of good scholarship, but the scholarly attention is focused on the practical and abstract issues of academic leadership. Faculty members who have become deans do not stop their scholarship; they bring scholarly habits and abilities to a new area of work. The temptation to view academic administrative work as something fundamentally different from scholarly work is a threat to good academic leadership, because good leadership utilizes exactly the same skills and critical ingenuity that scholarship requires in any other area. Persons trained as biblical scholars, theologians, historians, and pastoral theologians have used the very skills that made them effective in their disciplines to study the literature on academic leadership, listen to the perspectives of persons who have been engaged in this work, give critical attention to current practices and understandings, and advance new ways of thinking about and doing this work. Good academic leadership relies on a scholarship of the deanship.

While academic administration mandates scholarly abilities, it requires a broader range of skills than are necessary for the scholarship of an academic content area. It requires relational skills, systemic thinking, the ability to negotiate the interaction of abstract principles and concrete practices, and the capacity to handle multiple tasks in a sophisticated way. Deans are well advised to avoid devoting their intellectual energy to staying current in their academic discipline. The deanship needs their intellectual energy to be done well. The essays in this volume reflect the work of deans who have taken the deanship seriously as scholarly work and have contributed to the way that academic leadership is understood and how it can be exercised thoughtfully and effectively.

A Concluding Word of Gratitude

Two deans have contributed in unique ways to the scholarship of academic leadership, and I want to thank them. Bruce Birch and Kathleen Billman have done a wonderful job structuring, coordinating, administering, and editing this book of essays. By the publication date, one will have retired and the other will have completed a ten-year deanship and returned to the disciplinary work of pastoral theology. Both have served their institutions well, and both have served the scholarship of the deanship admirably in the work of this volume.

Academic leadership is complex and multilayered. It is crucial to the informed and effective work of the schools. It is enriched by the engaged learning that a community of practice provides, is undergoing transitions that make ongoing conversation and reflection more crucial than ever, and is served by a form of scholarship represented in the work of deans such as those who have contributed essays for this volume. In the end, it is a good form of work that makes it possible for schools to do their work well, and when their work is done well, students learn, the church and its ministry are served, and knowledge is renewed and advanced.

Contributors

Daniel O. Aleshire, Executive Director, Association of Theological Schools in the United States and Canada

Anne T. Anderson, President and Vice Chancellor, University of St. Michael's College

Richard Benson, Academic Dean and Chair of Moral Theology Department, St. John's Seminary

Kathleen D. Billman, formerly Dean and Vice President for Academic Affairs, and currently John H. Tietjen Professor of Pastoral Ministry, Lutheran School of Theology at Chicago

Bruce C. Birch, Dean Emeritus and Professor of Biblical Theology Emeritus, Wesley Theological Seminary

Linda W. Bryan, formerly Assistant Dean for Academic Affairs, and currently Associate Professor of Mission and Ministry, Shaw University Divinity School

John T. Carroll, formerly Academic Dean, Union Theological Seminary and Presbyterian School of Christian Education, and currently Harriet Robertson Fitts Memorial Professor of New Testament, Union Presbyterian Seminary

Jana Childers, formerly Dean of the Seminary and Vice President of Academic Affairs and Professor of Homiletics and Speech-Communication, and currently Professor of Homiletics and Speech-Communication, San Francisco Theological Seminary

Faustino M. Cruz, Executive Vice President and Academic Dean and Associate Professor of Theology and Education, Franciscan School of Theology at the Graduate Theological Union

Leland V. Eliason, Executive Director and Provost Emeritus, Bethel Seminary of Bethel University

Stephen R. Graham, formerly Dean of Faculty, North Park Theological Seminary, and currently Director, Faculty Development and Initiatives in Theological Education, Association of Theological Schools

Willie James Jennings, formerly Academic Dean and currently Associate Professor of Theology and Black Church Studies, Duke University Divinity School

Sherwood G. Lingenfelter, formerly Provost and Senior Vice President, and currently Professor of Anthropology, Fuller Theological Seminary

Randolph MacFarland, Provost and Dean, Denver Seminary

Jay Wade Marshall, Dean, Earlham School of Religion and Vice President of Earlham

Ronald A. Mercier, formerly Associate Professor of Christian Ethics, Regis College, and currently Associate Professor, Department of Theological Studies, St. Louis University

Ruth A. Meyers, formerly Academic Dean and Professor of Liturgics, Seabury-Western Theological Seminary, and currently Hodges-Haynes Professor of Liturgics at Church Divinity School of the Pacific

D. Cameron Murchison, Dean of Faculty and Executive Vice President Emeritus, Columbia Theological Seminary

Barbara H. Mutch, Charles Bentall Professor of Pastoral Studies and Vice President Academic, Carey Theological College

Craig L. Nessan, Academic Dean and Professor of Contextual Theology, Wartburg Theological Seminary

Gail R. O'Day, formerly Senior Associate Dean of Faculty and Academic Affairs, Candler School of Theology, Emory University, and currently Dean and Professor of New Testament and Preaching, Wake Forest University Divinity School

BRUCE P. POWERS, formerly Associate Dean, and currently Langston Professor of Christian Education, Campbell University Divinity School

STEPHEN BRECK REID, formerly Academic Dean and Professor of Old Testament, Bethany Theological Seminary, and currently Professor of Christian Scriptures, George W. Truett Seminary of Baylor University

GARY RIEBE-ESTRELLA, formerly Vice President and Academic Dean, and currently Dean Emeritus, Catholic Theological Union

RICHARD A. ROSENGARTEN, formerly Dean, and currently Associate Professor of Religion and Literature, University of Chicago Divinity School

JACK SEYMOUR, formerly Academic Dean and Vice President for Academic Affairs and Professor of Religious Education, and currently Professor of Religious Education and Director of the PhD Program, Garrett-Evangelical Theological Seminary

ROBIN J. STEINKE, Dean of the Seminary and Professor of Theological Ethics and Public Life, Gettysburg Theological Seminary

DALE R. STOFFER, Academic Dean and Professor of Historical Theology, Ashland Theological Seminary

ERVIN R. STUTZMAN, formerly Vice President and Seminary Dean, Eastern Mennonite University, and currently Executive Director, Mennonite Church USA

TITE TIÉNOU, Dean and Senior Vice President of Education and Professor of Theology of Mission, Trinity Evangelical Divinity School

JOHN V. VERBERKMOES, Vice President and Academic Dean, Grand Rapids Theological Seminary of Cornerstone University

ANNE B. YARDLEY, formerly Associate Academic Dean, Drew University Theological School, retired

BARBARA BROWN ZIKMUND, formerly Dean, Pacific School of Religion, formerly President, Hartford Theological Seminary, and most recently Director of ATS Women in Leadership Research Project